MW00640013

The Unknown God
Twenty-Five Selected Sermons on the Holy Spirit
by Charles Haddon Spurgeon

Edited by Kerry James Allen

Copyright © 2003 by Fox River Press

Published by
Fox River Press
P.O. Box 1094
Oswego, IL 60543
630-554-1847 Voice Mail
815-886-4144 Voice/FAX
kjallen@ix.netcom.com

Cover design by
Jeff Payne
Sable Visuals
815-462-3689

We welcome your contact, comments, suggestions, and constructive criticisms. Direct them to the address and numbers above. Quantity prices also available.

Many thanks to Bobette Shoger and Tim Zollers for proof reading and computer skills.

Publishers Note: These sermons have been selected from The New Park Street Pulpit series and the Metropolitan Tabernacle Pulpit series, originally printed by Passmore and Alabaster, and more recently reprinted by Pilgrim Publications, and are presented here in their entirety, without alteration of sermon titles, Bible texts or versions, or archaic English spelling. Fidelity to the original sermons has been meticulously sought with the exception of the use of a clearer and larger type font (11 point Century Schoolbook).

ISBN 0-9711434-2-0

The Unknown God

Twenty-five
selected sermons
on the subject of the
Holy Spirit

Charles Haddon Spurgeon

Fox River Press

Oswego, IL

Spurgeon Select Sermon Series

The Suffering of Man and the Sovereignty of God
(25 Selected Sermons from the Book of Job)

The Father' House
(25 Selected Sermons on Heaven)

The Unknown God
(25 Selected Sermons on the Holy Spirit)

Table of Contents

Foreword

The writings of Charles Haddon Spurgeon have been continuously in print for nearly one hundred and fifty years, as a testimony to their thoroughly Biblical content, fidelity to truth, and marvelous use of the English language. Spurgeon was one of God's choicest servants, filled with the Spirit of God, and a literary giant whose sermons and books spoke to the hearts of millions, and still do to this day.

His prodigious output is astounding for a man who lived a brief fifty-seven years, with much of that spent in illness. He wrote two to three books every year of his active ministry, and kept an entire printing firm busy with production of just his works. One luminary said that Spurgeon did the life work of fifty men, which may not have been an exaggeration. His largest printed contribution is the sixty-three volumes of sermons, begun when he was barely into his twenties and finalized twenty-five years after his death.

In this book, we present yet another offering of the sermons of the most enduring Baptist pastor of all time. What makes this volume of sermons on the Holy Spirit different from other topical selections of sermons by Spurgeon, and what is our motivation behind this series?

My first discovery was that even though small topical books of Spurgeon's sermons have been in print for over one hundred years, in reading many of these "Twelve sermons on..." books (and there are more than four dozen different topical volumes), I didn't feel that these were his best sermons on that given topic. Further investigation of each sermon in at least a dozen of the books that I examined yielded the fact that the selection of sermons had ended with volumes thirty-five to forty in most of them. The problem is

that the complete unabridged sermon set is sixty-three
volumes. Printers have evidently been reprinting these
small topical volumes without reading the last twenty-five
volumes from the original set, which of course contain over
one thousand more sermons, many of which never found
their way into the "Twelve" series. This "Spurgeon Select
Sermon Series" seeks to remedy that by including many of
the sermons that were missed.

Next, although they are not identical photographic repro-
ductions such as those offered by Pilgrim Publications, the
premier distributor of Spurgeon's books in the world today,
we have made every effort to retain the strictest adherence
to the original words and punctuation. Many archaic old
English words will drive the reader to their dictionary
(which is not such a bad thing). Only verified misspellings
(of which there were very few, amazingly, for the days of
setting type by hand) have been changed and corrected.
Many of the newer compilations of Spurgeon's sermons have
been heavily edited including updated language, and, in
addition to altering Spurgeon's own words to make him
"theologically correct," he is also softened so as not to be
portrayed as a foe of false doctrine and man-made religion,
which he was. This usually occurs without any admission of
these facts.

Thirdly, as alluded to earlier, the sermons have been
selected by meticulously combing the entire New Park Street
Pulpit and Metropolitan Tabernacle Pulpit sermon sets
(sixty-three volumes total) for every sermon on this topic,
and then reading and grading them by their quality. All of
Spurgeon is excellent, some of Spurgeon is superlative. This
is my admittedly biased selection of the twenty-five best
sermons on the subject of the Holy Spirit of God. My main
qualification for doing so is ownership of the sixty-three
volumes, as well as actually reading them. Very few people
will ever assemble and own this massive set, occupying nine
feet of shelf space (unless procured in a digital format), and
fewer still will ever read its nearly 45,000 pages. The reader
will benefit from the distillation of literally thousands of
hours of reading in the preparation of these volumes of carefully selected sermons.

Finally, they are set in a very readable eleven point

Century Schoolbook font. The first seven volumes of Spurgeon's sermons contain some of his finest material, yet the originals are set in a blindingly minute font size that makes reading them very difficult and tiring.

Thirty years ago, as a new Christian, someone pointed me to H.A. Ironside as one to read to help ground me in the basic doctrines of the Christian faith. Reading his entire New Testament commentary set did just that. In 1997, I procured and read a random volume of Spurgeon's sermons (Volume 35), and the effect on me was profound. It seemed the more I read, the more I wanted to read. The exaltation of Christ, overflowing use of Scripture, burning desire for the lost, and plain practical application to daily life have fed my soul like no other preacher I have ever heard or read. Thus began a six year excursion that rarely found a single day without Spurgeon. I have been everlastingly grateful for the man and his message, and have since read every sermon (3,561) in the set. My only regret is not having started sooner. Perhaps these books will make it easier for you.

Looking for that Blessed Hope,

Kerry James Allen

Introduction

I believe it was Dr. Walter Wilson who began calling the Holy Spirit "The Unknown God." God's Spirit is not as much unknown today as He is misrepresented, as people attempt to separate His offices and outworkings from the Word of God that He inspired. This, of course, is absurdity bordering blasphemy, to think that the infinitely wise Spirit would write one thing and do another. With so much "strange fire" burning today, many sincere Bible students have gone the other direction, and must very nearly say, "We have not so much as heard whether there be any Holy Ghost." Spurgeon was no such stranger to the Holy Spirit in his preaching and his personal life. Three of his sermons on the Holy Spirit in this book were preached by the time he was but twenty-one years of age.

Spurgeon made no claims to speaking in tongues, receiving visions, or dispensing revelation apart from the Scriptures as many do today, yet, who could dispute the fact that the man had the Bible proofs of being filled with the Spirit? Intense passion for the lost, a great harvest of converts, the Word of Christ dwelling in him richly, holiness of life; these and many other evidences would mark him out as a man filled with the Spirit of God. How we need the balance between power and a sound mind that Spurgeon had!

Hear Spurgeon's feelings about our ignorance: "Worship and adore Him specially and peculiarly. You say, 'Why specially and peculiarly?' I answer—because He is so much forgotten. Some people hardly know whether there be any Holy Ghost. Let the Father and the Son be equally adored; but be careful in reference to the Holy Spirit, for the failure of the church towards the Holy Trinity lies mainly in a

forgetfulness of the gracious work of the Holy Spirit. Therefore I press this upon you, and I beg you to laud and magnify
the Holy Ghost, and sedulously walk in all affectionate
gratitude towards Him all your days."

Should our ignorance not drive us to further knowledge of
the one who accompanied His Word with power to our
hearts, convicted us of our sins, presented the uplifted
Christ to us, regenerated us, now indwells us, is sanctifying
us, and will one day along with the other Members of the
Trinity resurrect us? Spirit of God, teach us about Thyself!

> "Holy Spirit, God's indwelling!
> All my being's pulses move;
> My unholiness dispelling,
> Teach me perfect love.
> Cleanse my human, harmful hating;
> Purge my passions and refine;
> All my nature re-creating,
> By Thy faith and mine.
>
> "Gentle, loving Holy Spirit,
> Quell the tumult and the strife;
> Sanctify by Jesus' merit;
> Grant me perfect life!
> Only by Thy wise selecting
> Can my words and deeds be true;
> Thy immaculate correcting
> Maketh me anew.
>
> "Holy Spirit! In Thy guiding,
> All my restlessness shall cease;
> In my heart, enthroned, abiding,
> Bring Thy perfect peace!
> Fashion me like Christ in pureness;
> Let my service praise His name;
> Nurtured by Divine matureness
> I shall be like Him.
>
> "Holy Spirit, my Refiner;
> Light and Comforter within;
> Joy of hope and prayer's Designer;
> Cleanser of my sin.
> Soul Instructor; Truth Revealer;
> Teacher of the Living Word;
> Heavenly Helper; Holy Healer;
> One with Christ the Lord."

1

A Fatal Deficiency

"...if any man have not the Spirit of Christ, he is none of his."
Romans 8:9

This is one of the most solemn texts in the whole Bible. It is so sweeping: it deals with us all. "If any man have not the Spirit of Christ, he is none of his." And it deals with the most important point about us, for to belong to Christ is the most essential thing for time and eternity. But we are not Christ's unless we have his Spirit. The text does not treat of external rites and ceremonies, it does not discuss a vexed question in doctrine, it does not speak of rare attainments and unusual virtues, but it lays its axe at the root of the tree, it points its sword at a vital part. The text probes to the quick; it pierces to the dividing asunder of the joints and marrow, dealing with the thoughts and intents of the heart. It speaks to the soul, and though it be the voice of the gospel, yet is its sound as terrible as the thunderclaps of Sinai. "If any man have not the Spirit of Christ, he is none of his."

Since the subject leads us to think upon the Spirit of Christ, let us entreat him to help us at this hour, so that our thoughts shall be honest, heart-searching, and therefore profitable to us. The preacher has prayed that he may be helped to discourse upon the text; let each hearer pray that what shall be rightly said may also rightly affect his heart and conscience. Do we not all earnestly desire to belong to Christ? Do we not tremble at the bare idea of its being said of us that we are "none of his"? With such desires and fears, I trust we shall come with the greater readiness under the influence of the heart-searching text before us.

I shall, at the outset, try to lead you to consider *the remarkable title which is here given to the Holy Spirit.* When we have considered that point, we will next observe *the absolute necessity of possessing the Spirit*; and, thirdly, meditate upon *the evidences which may help us to discover whether we have the Spirit*; and then close by weighing well *the consequences of being found without the Spirit of Christ*: "We are none of his."

I. First, then, let us consider well THE REMARKABLE TITLE WHICH IS HERE GIVEN TO THE HOLY SPIRIT,—for certainly it is the Holy Ghost who is here intended by "the Spirit of Christ." He is called, in the first part of the verse, "the Spirit of God," and then he is styled "the Spirit of Christ." Christ and God are essentially one. The Holy Ghost stands in intimate relationship both to the Father and to the Son, and is rightly called by either name.

Inasmuch as he is here called the Spirit of Christ, we may rest assured that a deep mystery is here dimly revealed. The Holy Ghost proceeds from the Son as well as from the Father. Upon this we will say but little, for we know but little. There was a great dispute, many centuries ago, between what are now called the Eastern and Western Churches, upon this question,—whether the Spirit of God proceeded from the Father only, as said the Greek Church; or proceeded from the Father and the Son, as said the Latin Church. I think, if we must have an opinion upon such a subject, that our text decides the point by declaring that the Holy Spirit is not only the Spirit of God but the Spirit of Christ, and proceedeth, doubtless, both from the Father and from the Son. But when we have said that, what do we mean? Does any theologian know what he means by these words? Will anybody ever know what is meant thereby? Can any of us by searching find out God or know the Almighty to perfection? Is not this a mystery into which our eyes will never be able to see? And, therefore, is it not better to leave it among the inscrutable things which belong to the blessed Trinity in unity, where understanding is swamped, but where faith finds waters to swim in?

Leaving that deep matter, we pass to notice that the title, "the Spirit of Christ," signifies, first, that *the Spirit peculiarly and especially rested upon Christ.* The Holy Ghost had much to do with the person of our blessed Redeemer. The manhood of Christ was begotten of the Spirit of God when the power of the Highest overshadowed the Virgin Mary. When our Lord first appeared in public to be recognised as the Son of God, when he went down into the waters of Jordan, and came up therefrom, the Spirit descended upon him like a dove, and rested upon him, while the divine voice proclaimed out of heaven, "This is my beloved Son." No sooner had the Son of God passed away from Jordan's brink, than he was "led of the Spirit into the wilderness to be tempted of the devil"—guided by the Spirit of God to undergo those processes of trial which were needful to make him perfect as the great High Priest, enabling him to sympathise with our infirmities, because he was "tempted in all points like as we are." We read that he returned into Galilee in the power of the Spirit. When he began to preach, the first chapter that he read in public was, "The Spirit of the Lord God is upon me, because he hath anointed me to preach the gospel to the poor." His ministry was not a dead ministry of the letter, but it stood in the power of the Spirit of God. He spake not according to the flesh, with the garnishings of human eloquence and winning flatteries, but with those forcible words of wisdom which the Holy Ghost teacheth; he taught the people as one having authority, and not as the scribes. All through the life of Christ you see that the Spirit of God rested upon him in fulness of power, for God "giveth not the Spirit by measure unto him." In him "dwelt the fulness of the Godhead bodily," and all the sacred gifts of the Holy Ghost were treasured up in his blessed person, that out of his fulness we also might receive grace for grace. Was it not so written of him in the Psalm, "Thou lovest righteousness and hatest wickedness: therefore God, thy God, hath anointed thee with the oil of gladness above thy fellows"? Because upon Christ, the Anointed One, the Holy Ghost rests in fulness, the term, "the Spirit of Christ," is most instructive.

A second explanation is equally to the point. *The Holy Ghost is called the "Spirit of Christ," because our Lord Jesus*

gives us the Holy Ghost. John the Baptist said concerning
him, "I indeed baptize you with water unto repentance, but
He that cometh after me is mightier than I, whose shoes I
am not worthy to bear; he shall baptize you with the Holy
Ghost and with fire." The baptism of the Holy Spirit is a
choice result of our Lord's work among men. Jesus spake of
giving to men living water, which should be in them as a
springing well, and this spake he of the Spirit, which was
given when Jesus was glorified. After his resurrection he
breathed on his disciples, and said, "Receive ye the Holy
Ghost," but indeed, the whole ministry of Jesus was a
revelation of the things of the Spirit. He did not preach upon
points of ritual and ceremonial observation, but he went into
inward matters, and with the fan in his hand thoroughly
purged his floor. His precepts concern not the washing of
hands, the straining out of gnats, the wearing of phylacteries, and the observance of holy days; but they deal with
the heart, the affections, the spiritual nature of man, and so
are far removed from the traditions of superstition and the
frivolities of false philosophy. Beyond all this, beloved, our
Lord Jesus Christ, at his ascension, procured for us the
descent of the Holy Spirit. "It is expedient for you that I go
away," said he, "for if I go not away, the Comforter will not
come unto you." He rose to his Father, and when the fulness
of time was come, the rushing, mighty wind was heard, and
the cloven tongues, as it were fire, were seen sitting upon
the disciples, and from that moment the Church of God was
baptized into the Holy Spirit. God grant that she may never
forget that day of days, but walk in the power bestowed upon
her at Pentecost. On that glorious day, the word of the Lord
by the prophet Joel was fulfilled: "I will pour out my Spirit
upon all flesh; and your sons and your daughters shall
prophesy, your old men shall dream dreams, your young
men shall see visions. And also upon the servants and upon
the handmaids in those days will I pour out my Spirit." This
being so gloriously fulfilled, we are waiting for that other
promise, "I will pour upon the house of David and the
inhabitants of Jerusalem the Spirit of grace and of supplications, and they shall look upon me whom they have
pierced, and shall mourn for their sins." Hence the Holy
Spirit is the Spirit of Christ, because he is the choice gift of

our ascended Lord.

Mark a third explanation of the passage: the Holy Ghost may be called "the Spirit of Christ," *because Christ lived peculiarly in the power of the Spirit*. Understand the "Spirit" as used in the text in opposition to the "flesh," and you will see my meaning. Never did the flesh rule Christ. Never in one solitary moment did bodily cravings and appetites master him; nay, he even forgot to eat bread, finding meat to eat which even his disciples knew not of. His love sought not its own, but made him lay down his life for his friends. The Spirit of God shone forth upon him in full lustre of unsullied light, revealing him as pure and spotless, a glorious person, in whom the prince of darkness could find nothing. Our Lord Jesus Christ was never moved by any passion of a sensual kind, or swayed by a motive of a fleshly tendency. It would be blasphemous to think of such a thing in connection with so divine a character. Some cry aloud and strive for mastery, but not he; some have high ambitions, and would thrust down others, but not he; some smite on the right hand and on the left, for their spirit is full of vengeance, but not he. The flesh that lusteth for vengeance, and that crieth after power, had no rule in him; he was meek and lowly of heart; but the Spirit of holiness and love was in him,—that Spirit which brings power and peace. Ever was the Holy Spirit to be seen in connection with the character and work of our blessed Lord. His life was a life in the Spirit. His teaching was a teaching of spiritual things. The objects that he aimed at in his teaching were all spiritual. There was nothing carnal, nothing gross, nothing earthy about him, but every thought, desire, and aim were of the highest, noblest, and most spiritual order; and therefore it is, I think, that the Holy Ghost is called the Spirit of Christ.

Mark, also, that the *Holy Spirit is he who quickens the entire mystical body of Jesus Christ*. All the saints are members of Christ's body, and all the members of that body are distinguished from other men by this,—that they are spiritual men, and seek after spiritual things. "There is one body and one Spirit, even as we are called in one hope of our calling." It is the Spirit that quickeneth the entire mystical body, and by one Spirit are we all baptized into one body, whether we be Jews or Gentiles, whether we be bond or free.

The true church of Christ, being in herself a spiritual body, acts in a spiritual manner, and strives after spiritual objects. Yonder church which is wrapped up in formalism, which cannot speak a word of prayer without her book, is she moved of the Spirit, or may it not be said of her sons, "Are ye so foolish; having begun in the Spirit, are ye now made perfect by the flesh?" Yonder church, which bows before images and pictures, and flaunts her banners and uplifts her crucifixes, burning her candles in the sunlight,— is she the spiritual church of Christ? I trow not. But ye shall find the church of Christ where faithful men worship God in the Spirit, and have no confidence in the flesh; men who, if they speak, seek to be moved by the Holy Ghost, or else had far rather keep silence,—who desire not the wisdom that cometh of man, nor the teaching which is the fabrication of human reason, but desire to wait upon the Scriptures for instruction, and upon the Spirit of God to show light upon the Scriptures. *This* is the church of God. O beloved, the times are just now very dangerous, and require of all Christians to bear their testimony as to the spirituality of true religion. True religion consists not in outward forms, peculiar garbs, or modes of speech, or anything that is ritualistic and external. "The kingdom of God is not meat and drink; but righteousness, and peace, and joy in the Holy Ghost." Again are men becoming subject to human ordinances after the commandments and doctrines of men, saying, "Touch not, taste not, handle not;" but the true faith standeth not in will-worship, nor in the inventions of the flesh. Neither is that acceptable worship which men's fancies have devised, that they may display the beauty of carvings in stone and wood, and the glory of gold and silver and copper, together with blue and scarlet and fine linen, and glass of many colours, and sweet odours of the merchants; but the true worshippers of God worship in spirit and in truth, for the Father seeketh such to worship him. Therefore is the Holy Ghost the Spirit of Christ, because, wherever the faith of Christ and the mystical body of Christ are found, there you will find spiritual worship, worship rendered by mind and heart, the worship of love, the worship of humility, and adoration, and obedience. The church of God brings not to him rivers of oil, or the blood of ten thousands of fat beasts; but she seeks to do justly, to love mercy, and to walk humbly with her God. Sacrifices and burnt-offerings are abolished; but broken and contrite hearts are still in the sight of the Lord of great price. Hence, then, the Spirit of God is rightly called the Spirit of Christ.

II. Now, secondly—and may the Lord help and guide us in our thoughts and utterances—LET US OBSERVE THE NECESSITY OF POSSESSING THE SPIRIT OF CHRIST.

Notice that, according to the text, *it is needful in every case*:—"If any man have not the Spirit of Christ, he is none of his." It does not say, "If any minister be destitute of the Holy Ghost he is unfit for his calling." That is quite true, but the text is not dealing with any supposed divisions of laity and clergy: it speaks not to a class, but utters its warning voice to men as men. "If *any man* have not the Spirit of Christ, he is none of his." It may be urged that some have an especially amiable nature and disposition; they were never known to speak an untruth, or to do an unkind action, from their youth up. They grow up in the garden of the family like lovely flowers, the admiration of all. Yes, I admit that it is even so; but I cannot help it, I must speak the truth as I have it in my text. "If any man," however amiable he may be, "have not the Spirit of Christ," I must say the same of him as of the drunkard and of the thief, "he is none of Christ's." The fairest flowers, as surely as the foulest weeds, are none of Christ's, if they are not of the Spirit's own planting. But we meet with instances in which, in addition to a natural amiability, the refinements of good society have exercised their best influence. The man has lived among Christian people; he has a title to birthright membership, if such a right can be; he has never mingled with the coarser sort of sinners, or learned the vulgarities of vice. The man is lovely to look upon. Ay, and as I repeat the words of my text, I say the truth and lie not, I feel a love to such an one, even as Jesus did to that young man who said, "All these things have I kept from my youth up. What lack I yet?" But we must not shirk the truth even in this case. This one lack, the lack of the Spirit of Christ, is fatal to the noblest character, and Christ disowns utterly every man who has not his Spirit in him. But can we not, by adding outward religiousness to moral excellencies somehow or other, rise by our own efforts

to be true Christians without the Holy Ghost? Can we not be
baptized, and kneel as God's people kneel, and sing as they
sing, and take the sacrament as they do? Yes, you can
readily do all these, but you will be none the forwarder, for
the text will still remain true, "If any man have not the
Spirit of Christ, he is none of his." And if it were possible
(which it is not) for you to produce the same virtues in
yourself which are produced by the Holy Spirit, yet even
those would not suffice, for the text is absolute, and it does
not say, "If any man have not the words of the Spirit," or,
"the influences of the Spirit," or, "the general results of
character which come of the indwelling of the Spirit;" but it
goes deeper, and declares, "If any man have not *the Spirit* of
Christ, he is none of his." The difference between the
regenerate and the unregenerate is not one of degree, but of
kind; a dead soul cannot develop into a living one, nor can
the carnal mind improve into a spiritual mind. Almighty
power is needed to bridge the separating gulf. This ought to
lead every rational man utterly to despair of saving himself
by any strength of his own. You must resort to divine
agency. You are driven to the Holy Spirit, because without
him whatever you may do or be, my text, like the cherubic
sword which kept the entrance to Eden, prevents your
hoping to obtain eternal life by your own power. "Except a
man be born of water and of the Spirit, he cannot enter into
the kingdom of God."

Note well that the text does not make any sort of exception, or so much as hint at any; for some might have said,
"But, surely, those who have long been members of the
Christian church, and those who are officers in her midst,
and those in high esteem, surely they are Christ's, and will
be saved in any case?" No, by no means, if they have not the
Spirit of Christ, even these are none of his. We are all on a
par here. The doorkeeper in our assemblies is, in this
respect, exactly on the same footing as the presiding elder of
the church. "If any man have not the Spirit of Christ, he is
none of his." I might even have said that the officers of the
church are in a worse position than other men for their
responsibility is so terribly great, and their temptation to
mere official religion so immense. Chrysostom said in his
day, "I wonder if any of the rulers of the church will be

saved?" and had he lived in these times he might with equal force have said the same. See ye not how the great ones of the church, who call themselves the bishops and shepherds of the flock, are suffering this nation to drift away to Rome, and into all the devilries of her idolatry and superstition, and yet they neither lift a finger nor speak a word to stay the evil. Hirelings as they are, what care they for the sheep? They sit in worldly state among the peers of the realm, and it frets them not though the whole land reeks and rots with superstition! God have mercy on them! Well didst thou say, O John of the golden mouth, "I wonder if any of the rulers of the church will be saved?" If in any other position men so shamefully neglected their master's business they would be discharged in disgrace. I speak thus in solemn soberness grieving that the charge is all too true. Nor is this all. What must be the lot of those of us who are ordinary ministers if we have not the Spirit of Christ? And is it clear that all of us have? How many there are who occupy the pulpit, the object of whose preaching is the display of their own eloquence or learning, by the giving out of well-turned periods and pretty essays upon philosophical subjects, instead of striking at men's consciences and dealing with their souls, in the name of God. The world is perishing, and the church is going to sleep over it. God have mercy upon all of us who are church officers, and make us faithful. Instead of needing less of the Spirit, we need a double portion; and if there are any men about whom it may be said, "If they have not the Spirit of Christ, they are none of his," it must be said with the greatest solemnity concerning the ministers, deacons, and elders of our churches. If they have not the Spirit of Christ they are worse than other men; their position puts them under extraordinary responsibility, and if they are false thereto it will bring them under terrible condemnation.

"If any man have not the Spirit of Christ, he is none of his." Now, observe that this is put in opposition to everything less than itself. For instance, there are some who glory in the *name* of Christians, as if the name were some great thing. We have a certain unbrotherly company who call themselves "brethren," and certain others who disapprove of sects, and therefore in the name of Christian unity set up a sect of their own, infinitely more exclusive than any before known. These

frequently claim to be especially denominated Christians, I
suppose because they would insinuate that they alone are
Christians. Brethren, in Paul's day, one said, "I am of Paul,"
another said, "I am of Apollos," a third said, "I am of Christ;"
now there was not a pin to choose between them, they were
all equally sectarian. It is not wearing the name of Christ,
but having the Spirit of Christ, which will prove us to be
accepted. Probably none were ever further off from Christ
than those who call themselves by his name, namely, the
Jesuits; little enough has Jesus to do with the Society of
Jesus. The Christian church has never been more pure or
more earnest than when it has been known by an
opprobrious name. There was far more power and life among
the despised "Quakers," than among the respected "Society
of Friends." I liked the "Ranters" better than the more quiet
"Primitive Methodists;" and the detested "Anabaptists" were
men of far more courage and principle than the modern
"Baptists." Give me the man who can render a reproachful
name illustrious; there is no shame in being traduced. The
reproach soon wears away; and if it did not, blessed are they
that are reproached for Christ's sake. But, beloved, you may
wear the literal name of Christ, and you may keep on
pushing yourself adrift from everybody into a state of
external peculiarity, if you like; but if you have not the Spirit
of Christ, you are none of his, for all that. You may take to
yourself very precise notions of how you should act, how you
should speak, what you should eat, what you should drink,
what you should wear—and you may become a very strait-
laced Puritan indeed; but recollect, after you have done all,
that "the kingdom of God is not meat or drink," and "if any
man have not the Spirit of Christ, he is none of his." Nothing
short of this will suffice, however commendable, however
much admired among men. We shall fare ill at the last great
day if the Spirit of God be not in us.

But the text is expressly in opposition to "*the flesh.*" There
is the point of its meaning. What does it mean, then, to have
the Spirit of Christ in opposition to being in the flesh?
Observe carefully, there are two states, in one or other of
which every man is found; there is no middle place. We are
either in the flesh or in the Spirit. Every man is born in the
flesh, and if let alone he will follow the desires and devices

of his fleshly nature, as every unregenerate man does. Some follow their fleshly nature coarsely, and run into vice; others follow it in a more refined manner, and live to gain wealth, to gratify taste, or to gain the approbation of their fellow men, all which is of the flesh. Now, there is another state, and that is called being in the Spirit; into this condition we are admitted by the new birth. When a man walks in the Spirit he recognises something higher than that which can be touched by the hand, and seen with the eye, and heard with the ear. He has entered into a new world, and is a citizen of a spiritual realm. He has come where God is real to him, where Christ is real to him, where truth is real, where sin is hateful, where holiness is lovely to him. Judge you, my brethren, whether you know anything concerning this. Many are in the flesh; they are as yet the mass of mankind: but there is a remnant who walk after the Spirit, because the Holy Ghost has renewed them. He who is in the flesh *is ruled by the flesh*; the animal in him is the master of the man; the mere sentient mind in him is dominant over the higher nature, the spirit. But the man who is in the Spirit tramples down the flesh, and labours to keep it under. When the flesh for awhile prevails, he laments his fault, and weeps concerning it, for he is not the willing servant of the flesh; but the Spirit in him strives for the mastery, and he greatly delights in its sway.

The man who is in the flesh *trusts to the flesh*. He looks to his own works for salvation. His prayers, his tears, his almsgivings—these are to save him; but the man who has the Spirit of Christ counts all his good works to be dross and dung, and trusts in the Lord through the Spirit. He trusts in the blood and righteousness of Jesus Christ, and builds his hope upon the mercy of God in his Redeemer. The man who is in the flesh *worships in the flesh*. His eye must be pleased with the peculiar dress of the minister, and the architectural beauty of the place of assembly, while his ear must be regaled, if not with sound of flute, harp, sackbut, and psaltery, yet with the swell of organs. His nose also must be gratified with sweet incense. He worships in the flesh, looking to crosses, and altars, and priests; while the man who has the Spirit utterly abhors these idols, and desires not to see but to believe, not to smell but to think. The sound of

truth is better to the spiritual man than tinkling bells, and
the noise of pipes and bellows. He wants something for his
soul to think upon, something to love, something to stir his
affections, something to strengthen him for goodness, and to
cast down the power of evil in his nature. Being a spiritual
man, he worships God in the Spirit. To him the hillside is as
holy as the meeting-house. He counts one place as sacred as
another. Neither in this mountain, nor yet at Jerusalem,
doth he worship the Father, but he worships God in spirit
and in truth. He will not yield to be judged by others in
meats and drinks, and new moons, and holy days. He scorns
to stoop to priests, but reckons himself and each believer to
be a priest unto God. He makes each garment a vestment,
and every meal is to him a sacrament. To him all things are
sanctified by the presence of the eternal God. He lives in the
Spirit, and, wherever he moves, he abides in fellowship with
the unseen Lord. He recognises spiritual things where
others see them not. He is swayed by spiritual motives; he
seeks after spiritual objects; and while the poor creatures of
the earth, like so many moles, toil to bury themselves under
its surface, and heap up gold and silver, and say, "These be
thy gods, O Israel;" this man is thankful for his food and
raiment, and the comforts of life, but feels that these are not
his God, nor is anything which can be seen worthy to be the
object of his pursuit. He derives his pleasure from springs
above, and drinks in draughts of life, not from this poor
dying world, but from the everliving and eternal God.
Blessed is the man who has come to this! We must all come
to it, or we are none of Christ's. Do not think I am setting up
some sublime standard; I am not. I am keeping to the level
of the text. "If any man have not the Spirit of Christ, he is
none of his."

III. And now I want you, for a few minutes only, to
meditate upon THE EVIDENCES OF HAVING THE SPIRIT; for
some will say, "Have I the Spirit?" yea, I trust all will make
the enquiry.

My hearers, you either have the Spirit or you have not. See
ye to it! If you have the Spirit, in the first place, as it is the
Spirit of Christ, *it has led you to Christ.* Have you, then,
been clean delivered from all confidence in yourselves? Have
you been brought to the cross foot, and made to see that

there hangs your only salvation? And are you trusting solely and entirely in the blood and righteousness of God's crucified Son? If you are, you have the Spirit of Christ, for the Spirit that leads a man to faith in Christ is the Spirit of Christ. You could not have come to Christ if you had not been drawn, and none will draw you but the heavenly Father by his Spirit. If you are resting wholly upon Jesus you have his Spirit.

I will ask you another question. *Do you feel in your soul a desire to honour the Lord Jesus*? Do you love to hear him extolled? Can you say that you hate everything which robs him of his glory? Do you love that sermon best which most exalts Jesus? Have you ever felt that you could die to crown our Lord's most blessed head? Do you now fall at his feet and adore him with your heart's truest love? Then you have the Spirit of Christ, for He delights to glorify Christ by taking of the things of Christ and showing them to us.

Again. If you have the Spirit of Christ *it will make you like Christ*. Like Christ, first, in relation to God. Christ lived for God. When he was but twelve years old he said, "Wist ye not that I must be about my Father's business?" and all his life long he could say that the zeal of God's house had eaten him up. His meat and his drink were to do the will of his Father who had sent him. Beloved, is that how you feel towards God? Then you have the Spirit of Christ.

The Spirit of Christ is a Spirit of prayer; it kept the Son in constant communion with the Father. You constantly find the Lord Jesus in converse with God. If you have the spirit of sonship as Christ had, you will be much in prayer too, and you will thus prove that you have the Spirit of Christ.

Christ's worship of God was always spiritual. You never find him worshipping otherwise than with his whole heart and soul. The traditions of men, their divers washings and observances were nothing to him; he walked with God and dwelt in him, and needed not these childish ordinances. His was a spiritual life. Is yours so?

Our Lord Jesus Christ towards God was always true. He was a faithful witness, you never find him flinching a word. He was full of love, but how he could thunder against false-hearted man. "Woe unto you Scribes and Pharisees, hypocrites!" Elijah was never more terrible against Baal than was the loving Saviour against Ritualistic Phariseeism; for towards his Father glowed a holy zeal and a sacred detestation of everything that would dishonour his beloved name. Have you the Spirit of Christ in you?

The Spirit of Christ was towards men a fulness of love. He was ready to do good to all. He fed the hungry; he healed the sick; he never considered himself, but spent his life for others, laying himself out for them. They would have made him a king in their momentary enthusiasm, but he wanted no kingdom. It was kingdom enough for him to help the miserable and succor the wretched. Do you feel in your soul a love to men for God's sake? Can you forgive them when they do you wrong? Can you pray for your enemies? Can you follow his command who said, "I say unto you, That ye resist not evil, but when they smite you on the one cheek, turn to them the other also"? Then I trust you have Christ's Spirit; but on the other hand, are you indignant when you are insulted? Are you pettish and ready to resent every little thing? You have not the Spirit of Christ if it be so. The Spirit of Christ is a gentle, forbearing, tender Spirit,—stern, as I have told you, for God and for his truth, but tender as a child towards the infirmities, and sorrows, and weaknesses of mankind; upright for that which is true and holy, but bending down towards that which is ready to die. Would you know the Spirit of Christ? Read his life, and you will see it there. Have you such a Spirit? Do you long to be perfectly like Jesus? For if you have not the Spirit of Christ, you are none of his.

My time will fail me if I continue much longer, and therefore I will close this head by saying that if we have the Spirit of Christ it will *show itself by its operations in your hearts*. We shall feel it moving within us. It will make us hate everything that is evil, false, unholy. It will move us to repentance of all that we have done amiss towards God or man. It will make us brave and courageous for God and for his truth. If the Spirit of God be in us it will move us to joy in God, to hope in God, to delight in God. Fellowship with God will become necessary to us. Prayer to God will be one of our most delightful exercises, and the praise of God will be our gladdest enjoyment. The indwelling Spirit within us will make us spiritual, move us in spiritual directions after spiritual things, and we shall thus be spiritual men to the praise of God; and if we are not this, we are none of Christ's.

IV. The last point is THE SAD CONSEQUENCES OF NOT HAVING THE SPIRIT. These are consequences for which nothing in this world can compensate. "If any man have not the Spirit of Christ, *he is none of his.*" Everything is gone if we are "none of his." Supposing it had said, "He is not a favoured disciple;" well one would have been sorry to miss the opportunity of the place nearest to the Master; but this is far worse, it says, "he is none of his." The Lord does not own him at all. "No disciple of mine," says Christ. "No, if he has not my Spirit he is none of mine." He is a lost sheep, but Jesus says he is "none of his." Whoever he may belong to, he does not belong to Christ. If he has not Christ's Spirit in him, he is "none of his." Whatever body he may be a member of, he is no member of Christ's body, for the Spirit dwells in all the members of that body, and he who has not that Spirit is none of his.

"None of his." The words wound my heart. They are like a dagger to my soul. "None of his!" "None of his!" Ah, if I am none of his because I have not the Spirit, whose am I? I beseech the man who has not the Spirit of Christ to look that question in the face. He who died upon the cross disowns me; he who is risen into his glory disowns me: what misery is this! When he comes in the glory of the Father, and calls his sheep to his right hand, that they may enjoy eternal blessedness in his company, he will say, "I never knew you." If you, dear hearer, are none of his, then whose are you? You are the devil's. Awful thought! Terrible words to use; but it must be so. There are two proprietors of men, two rulers whom they serve. "Ye are of God, little children," says the apostle; but of others he says they lie in the wicked one, and are heirs of wrath. There are two classes of men—the heirs of wrath and the heirs of God; if you are none of Christ's you are the prisoner of condemnation. My dear hearer, what are you if you are not Christ's? You are a waif, a stray, a wreck drifted out to sea, soon to sink for ever. And where are you if you are not Christ's? On the way to judgment, on the road to eternal condemnation. If you are not his, you are going as fast as time can carry you away, away, away to the gloomy land where ray of hope will never pierce the midnight dark-

ness; away, away, away, where despair lasts out eternity. O
God, it is a dreadful thing to live a moment in an unforgiven
state. "He that believeth not is condemned already, because
he hath not believed upon the Son of God." If you were set up
for an instant upon the top of St. Paul's Cathedral, poised in
the air upon the cross, with none to hold you up, how
dreadful would be your feelings as you looked beneath you
and knew that the next gust of wind would sweep you down
to sure destruction! Sinner, you are now in a similar
position. If you are none of his you are now in awful peril.
Thou standest over the mouth of hell upon a single plank,
and that plank is rotten. Thou hangest over the jaws of
perdition by a slender thread, and the angel of justice is
ready to cut that thread in sunder now. "None of his! None of
his!" Oh, how dreadful to live none of his, and to die none of
his, and to have this for your epitaph—"NONE OF HIS!" And
then to wake up on the resurrection morning and see the
King in his beauty on the throne, and to know that you are
none of his! To cry to the rocks to hide you, and to the hills to
cover you, for you are none of his! Then to be brought out
before the great white throne resplendent in its holiness,
and hear the fact announced so that all may hear, that there
is a Saviour, but you are none of his! Ah, what will it be to
see the pit open her mouth to devour you, and, descending
for ever, to understand that you are none of his!

> "Ye sinners, seek his face,
> Whose wrath ye cannot bear;
> Bow to the sceptre of his grace,
> And find salvation there."

If you look to Jesus by faith, the Spirit is with you as you
look; there is life in a look at the crucified Redeemer. Trust
him! trust him! trust him! And may the Lord constrain you
now to live as you have never lived before; may you now
begin the spiritual life, for if you have not the Spirit of God,
you are none of his!

2

Grieve Not The Holy Spirit

"And grieve not the Holy Spirit of God, whereby ye are sealed unto the day of redemption."   Ephesians 4:30

It is a very clear proof of the personality of the Holy Spirit that he can be grieved. Now, it would be very difficult to imagine an influence, or a mere spiritual emanation, being grieved. We can only grieve a person, and, inasmuch as the Holy Ghost may be grieved, we see that he is a distinct subsistence in the sacred Trinity. Rob him not of the glory which is due to him, but be ever mindful to do him homage. Our text, moreover, reveals to us the close connexion between the Holy Spirit and the believer; he must take a very tender and affectionate interest in us, since he is grieved by our shortcomings and our sins. He is not a God who reigns in solitary isolation, divided by a great gulf, but he, the blessed Spirit, comes into such near contact with us, takes such minute observations, feels such tender regards, that he can be grieved by our faults and follies. Although the word "grieve" is a painful one, yet there is honey in the rock; for it is an inexpressibly delightful thought, that he who rules heaven and earth, and is the creator of all things, and the infinite and ever blessed God, condescends to enter into such infinite relationships with his people that his divine mind may be affected by their actions. What a marvel that Deity should be said to grieve over the faults of beings so utterly insignificant as we are! We may not understand the expression literally, as though the sacred Spirit could be affected with sorrow like to human sorrow, but we must not forego the consolatory assurance that he takes the same deep interest in us as a fond parent takes in a beloved but wayward child; and is not this a marvel? Let those who cannot feel be unmoved, as for me, I shall not cease to wonder and adore.

I. The first point which we will consider this morning is THE ASTOUNDING FACT *that the Holy Spirit may be grieved.* That loving, tender Spirit who, of his own accord, has taken upon himself to quicken us from our death in sin, and to be the educator of the new life which he has implanted within us; that divine instructor, illuminator, comforter, remembrancer, whom Jesus has sent forth to be our abiding guide and teacher, may be grieved. He, whose divine energy is life to our souls, dew to our graces, light to our understandings, and comfort to our hearts, may be vexed by us. The heavenly dove may be disturbed; the celestial fire may be damped; the divine wind may be resisted; the blessed Paraclete may be treated with despite.

The loving grief of the Holy Ghost may be traced to *his holy character and perfect attributes.* It is the nature of a holy being to be vexed with unholiness. There can be no concord between God and Belial. A Spirit immaculately pure cannot but take umbrage at uncleanness, and especially must he be grieved by the presence of evil in the objects of his affections. Sin everywhere must be displeasing to the Spirit of holiness, but sin in his own people is grievous to him in the highest degree. He will not hate his people, but he does hate their sins, and hates them all the more because they nestle in his children's bosoms. The Spirit would not be the Spirit of truth if he could approve of that which is false in us: he would not be pure if that which is impure in us did not grieve him. We could not believe him to be holy if he could look with complacency upon our unholiness; nor should we think of him as being perfect if our imperfection could be regarded by him without displeasure. No, because he is what he is, the Holy Spirit and the Spirit of holiness, therefore everything in us which falls short of his own nature must be grievous to him: he helps our infirmities, but he grieves over our sins. He is grieved with us mainly *for our own sakes,* for he knows what misery sin will cost us; he reads our sorrows in our sins. "Ah! silly sheep," he seems to say, "I know the dark mountain upon which thou wilt stumble; I see the thorns which will rend thee, and the wounds which will pierce thee! I know, O wayward child, the rod which thou art making for thine own back by thy follies! I know, poor erring one, into what a sea of trouble thou wilt plunge thyself by that headstrong will, that quick temper, that love of self, that ardent pursuit of gain. He grieves over us because he sees how much chastisement we incur, and how much communion we lose. When we might have been upon the mountain of fellowship, we are sighing in the dungeon of despondency; and all because, from motives of fleshly ease, we preferred to go down By-path Meadow, and forsake the right way because it was rough. The Spirit is grieved that we should thus bring ourselves into the darkness of a loathsome dungeon, and subject ourselves to the blows of the crab-tree cudgel of giant Despair. He foresees how bitterly we shall rue the day in which we parted company with Jesus, and so pierced ourselves through with many sorrows. He foresees that the backslider in heart will be filled with his own ways, and grieves because he foresees the backslider's grief. A mother's grief for the wrong-doing of her prodigal son is not so much the pain which he has directly occasioned her, as the sorrow which she knows that he will bring upon himself. David did not so much lament his own loss of his child, as Absalom's death, with all its dread results, to Absalom himself. "O my son Absalom, my son, my son Absalom!" Here is deep sorrow; but the next sentence shows that it was by no means selfish, for he is willing to take a greater grief upon himself—"Would God I had died for thee, O Absalom, my son, my son!" Such is the holy grief of the Spirit of God for those in whom he dwells: it is for their sakes that he is troubled.

Moreover, it is doubtless *for Jesus Christ's sake* that the Spirit is grieved. We are the purchase of Jesus' death upon the tree—he has bought us dearly, and he should have us altogether for himself; and when he does not have us completely as his own, you can well conceive that the Spirit of God is grieved. We ought to glorify Christ in these mortal bodies; it should be the one end and object of our desire to

crown that head with gems which once was crowned with
thorns: it is lamentable that we should so frequently fail in
this reasonable service. Jesus deserves our best: every
wound of his claims us, and every pang he bore, and every
groan that escaped his lips, is a fresh reason for perfect
holiness and complete devotion to his cause; and, because
the Holy Ghost sees us so traitorous to the love of Christ, so
false to that redeeming blood, so forgetful of our solemn
obligations, he grieves over us because we dishonour our
Lord.

Shall I be wrong if I say that he grieves over us *for the
Church's sake?* How might some of you be useful if you did
but live up to your privileges! Ah! my brethren, how the
Comforter must surely grieve over those of us who are
ministers, when he sets us as watchmen, and we do not
watch, and the Church is invaded! when he commissions us
as sowers of the good seed, and our hands are only half
filled, or we scatter cockle and darnel instead of sowing the
good wheat! How must he grieve over us because we have
not that tenderness of heart, that melting of love, that
vehemence of zeal, that earnestness of soul which we ought
to exhibit! When the Church of God suffers damage through
us—the Spirit loves the Church, and cannot endure to see
her robbed and despoiled, her children left to wander, her
wounded sons unsuccoured, and her broken hearts un-
healed—because we are indifferent to our work, and careless
in our labour for the Church, the Holy Spirit is much
displeased. Thus is it not only with ministers, but with all of
you, for there is a niche that each of you should fill; and if
that be vacant the Church loses by you, the kingdom of
Christ suffers damage, the revenue which ought to come into
Zion is cut short, and the Holy Ghost is grieved. Your lack of
prayer, your want of love, your deficiency in generosity—all
these may be sad injuries to the Church of God, and
therefore is the loving Spirit of God much disquieted.

Remember, once more, that the Spirit of God mourns over
the shortcomings of Christians, *for sinners' sakes;* for it is
the Spirit's office to convince the world of sin, of righteousness, and of judgment; but the course of many believers is
directly counter to this work of the Spirit. Their lives do not
convince the world of sin, but rather tend to comfort trans-

gressors in their iniquity. We have heard the actions of
professors quoted by worldlings as an excuse for their sins.
Openly profane persons have said, "Look at those Christians! they do so and so, why may not we?" It is ill when
Jerusalem comforts Sodom, and when the crimes of the
heathens find precedents in the sins of Israel. It is the
Spirit's work to convince the world of righteousness; but
many a professor convinces the world of the opposite. "No,"
say the world, "there is no more righteousness to be had in
Christ than anywhere else, for, look at those who follow him,
or pretend to do so, and where is their righteousness? It does
not exceed that of the scribes and Pharisees." The Spirit of
truth convinces the world of judgment to come; but how few
of us help him in that great work! We live and act and talk
as if there were no judgment to come; toiling for wealth as if
this world were all; careless of souls, as though hell were a
dream. Unmoved by eternal realities, unstirred by the
terrors of the Lord, indifferent to the ruin of mankind, many
professors live like worldlings, and are as unchristian as
infidels. This is an indisputable fact, but one to be lamented
with tears of blood. Men and brethren, I dare not think how
much of the ruin of the world must be laid at the door of the
Church, but I will dare to say this, that although the divine
purposes will be fulfilled, and God will not miss of the
number of his chosen, yet the fact that this London of ours is
now rather a heathen than a Christian city, can be laid at no
one's door but that of the professing Church of God and her
ministers. Where else can it lie? Is the city wrapped in
darkness? It need not have been so. If we had been faithful
it would not have been so: if we be faithful in the future it
shall not long remain so. I cannot imagine an apostolical
Church, set down in the midst of London, and filled with the
ardour of the first disciples, remaining long without telling
sensibly upon the masses. I know the increase of our popu-
lation is immense—I know that we are adding every year a
fresh town to this overgrown city; but I will not—I dare
not—tolerate the idea that the zeal of God's Church, if at its
right pitch, is too feeble to meet the case. Nay, there is
wealth enough among us, if it were consecrated, to build as
many houses of prayer as shall be wanted. There is ability
enough among us, if it were but given to the ministry of the

Word, to yield a sufficiency of preachers of the Cross. We have all the pecuniary and mental strength that is wanted. The point in which we fail is this: we are straitened in spiritual power, poverty-stricken in grace, lukewarm in zeal, meagre in devotedness, staggering in faith. We are not straitened in our God, we are straitened in our own bowels. Brethren, I believe the Spirit of God is very greatly grieved with many Churches for the sake of the sinners in their congregations who are scarcely cared for, seldom prayed for, never wept for. Would that the thought of this might move us and our brethren to amend our ways!

II. Secondly, let us refer to DEPLORABLE CAUSES *which produce the grief of the Holy Spirit.*

The context is some assistance to us. We learn that *sins of the flesh, filthiness, and evil speaking* of every sort, are grievous to him. Note the preceding verse: "Let no corrupt communication proceed out of your mouth." Let a Christian fall into the habit of talking in a loose, unchaste style, let him delight in things that are indecorous, even if he shall not plunge into the commission of outward uncleanness, the Spirit of God will not be pleased with him. The Holy Ghost descended upon our Lord as a dove; and a dove delights in the pure rivers of water, but shuns all kinds of filthiness. In Noah's day, the dove found no place for the sole of its foot on all the carcasses floating in the waste; and even so the heavenly dove finds no repose in the dead and corrupt things of the flesh. If we live in the Spirit, we shall not obey the desires of the flesh; they who walk after the flesh know nothing of the Spirit. It appears, from the thirty-first verse, that the Holy Ghost is grieved by any approach to bitterness, wrath, anger, clamour, evil speaking, and malice. If in a Christian Church there shall be dissensions and divisions; if brother shall speak evil of brother, and sister of sister, love is absent, and the Spirit of love will not long be present. The dove is the emblem of peace. One of the early fruits of the Spirit is peace. My dear friends, I hope as a Church, if there be any secret ill feeling among us, any hidden root of bitterness, even though it may not yet have sprung up to trouble us, it may be removed and destroyed at once. I do not know of any such abominable thing, and am happy to be able to say so; I trust we walk together in holy unity and concord of heart; and if any of you be conscious of bitterness in ever so small a measure, purge it out, lest the Spirit of God be grieved with you, and grieved with the Church of God for your sake.

I have no doubt it greatly grieves the Spirit to see in believers any degree of *love of the world*. His holy jealousy is excited by such unholy love. If a mother should see her child fonder of some one else than of her; if she should know that it was more happy in the company of a stranger than when in the bosom of its own parent, she would feel it a very hard trial to bear. Now, the Spirit of God gives to believers celestial joys and abounding comforts; and if he sees us turn our back upon all these, to go into worldly company, to feed greedily upon the same empty joys which satisfy worldlings, he is a jealous God, and he takes it as a great slight put upon himself. What! does the Good Shepherd load the table with heaven's own dainties, and do we prefer to devour the husks which the swine do eat? When I think of a Christian man trying to find his enjoyment where the lowest of worldlings find theirs, I can scarcely imagine him to be a Christian, or, if he be, he must very greatly grieve the Spirit of God. Why, you set the world, which you profess to have found empty, and vain, and deceitful—you set that before the choice things of the kingdom of grace; and while you profess to be "raised up to sit together with Christ in heavenly places," you still grovel in the dust as others do. What does the world say? "Ah, ah!" say they, "here is one of those Christian people, coming after a little happiness! Poor soul! His religion gives him no joy, and, therefore, he is looking for a little elsewhere. Make room for him, poor fellow, he has a hard time of it on Sundays." Then the notion goes abroad that Christians have no joy in Christ; that we have to deny ourselves all true happiness, and only get a little delight by stealth, when we do as others do. What a libel is this! And yet how many professors are responsible for it! If we live in communion with Jesus, we shall not hanker after the world; we shall despise its mirth and trample on its treasures. Worldliness, in any shape, must be very grievous to the Spirit of God; not only the love of pleasure, but the love of gain. Worldliness in Christian men and women in imitating the world in dress—worldliness in luxury, or in conversa-

tion, must displease the Spirit of God, because he calls us a
peculiar people, and he tells us to "come out from among
them and be separated, and touch not the unclean thing;"
and then he promises, "I will be a Father unto you, and ye
shall be my sons and daughters;" but if we will not be
separate, how can we expect him to be otherwise than
grieved! Israel was constrained to quit Egypt for the wilderness, and God says, "I remember thee, the love of thine
espousals, when thou wentest after me in the wilderness."
He seems to doat upon Israel's early separation to himself;
and so I believe the Lord delights to see his people severing
fond connexions, giving up carnal pleasures, and going
without the camp, bearing the reproach of Christ. It
ravishes the heart of Jesus to see his Church forsake the
world. Here are his own words to his bride, "Hearken, O
daughter, and consider, and incline thine ear; forget also
thine own people, and thy father's house; so shall the king
greatly desire thy beauty." He loves to have his saints
entirely to himself. He is a jealous Saviour, and hence Paul
says, he laboured that he might present the Church as a
chaste virgin unto Christ. Jesus wants to have our chastity
to himself maintained beyond suspicion, that we may choose
him as our sole possession, and leave the base things of the
earth to those who love them. Beware, my brethren, of
grieving the Holy Spirit by worldliness.

Moreover, the Spirit of God is greatly grieved by *unbelief.*
What would grieve you more, dear friend, than to have your
child suspect your truthfulness? "Alas!" cries the father, "can
it have come to this, that my own child will not believe me?
Is my promise to be thrown in my teeth, and am I to be told
by my own son, 'My father, I cannot trust thee'?" It is not
come to that with any of us, as parents, yet, and shall it be
so with our God? Alas! it has been; we have done despite to
the Spirit of truth by doubting the promise and mistrusting
the faithfulness of God. Of all sins, surely this must be one
of the most provoking. If there be the virus of diabolical guilt
in anything, it must be in the unbelief, not of sinners, but of
God's own people; for sinners have never seen what saints
have seen—never felt what we have felt, never known what
we have known; and, therefore, if they should doubt, they do
not sin against such light, nor do despite to such invincible

arguments for confidence as we do. God forgive our unbelief, and may we never grieve his Spirit more.

Further, the Spirit is doubtless grieved by our *ingratitude.* When Jesus reveals his love to us, if we go away from the chamber of fellowship, to talk lightly, and forget that love; or if, when we have been raised up from a sick-bed, we are no more consecrated than before; or if, when our bread is given us, and our water is sure, our heart never thanks the bounteous giver; or if, when preserved under temptation, we fail to magnify the Lord; surely this in each case must be a God-provoking sin.

If we add pride to ingratitude we sorely grieve the blessed Spirit. When a saved sinner grows proud, he insults the wisdom of the Spirit of God by his folly; for what can there be in us to be proud of? Pride is a weed which will grow in any soil. Proud of the mercies of God! As well be proud of being in debt! Why, some of us are so foolish that God cannot exalt us, for if he did we should straightway grow dizzy in the brain, and should be sure to fall. If the Lord were to put so much as one gold piece of comfort into our pockets, we should think ourselves so rich that we should set up in business on our own account, and cease from dependence upon him. He cannot indulge us with a little joy: he has to keep us as the father in the parable did the elder brother, who complained, "Thou never gavest me a kid, that I might make merry with my friends." Oh! it is sad that we should be so foolish as to become proud of our graces. This is a great grief to the Spirit in a private person, and even more so when it becomes the fault of an entire Church. If you as a Church shall boast that you are numerous, or generous, or rich, it will be all over with you. God will abase those who exalt themselves. If your soul can make her boast in the Lord, you may boast as much as you will; but if you glory in anything else, God will hide his face, and you will be troubled, though your mountain once stood firm, so that you dreamed it could never be moved.

I cannot give you a full list of all the evils which grieve the Spirit of God, but let me mention here, particularly, one—*a want of prayer.* This is grievous, either in the Church or in an individual. Does not this touch some of you? How little do some of us pray! Let each conscience now be its own accuser.

My dear brother, how about the mercy-seat? How about the closet and secret communion with God? How about wrestling for your children? How about pleading for the pastor? Have you not been backward in interceding for the conversion of your neighbour? Could you read the story of Abraham's interceding for Sodom, and say that you have interceded for London like that? Can you read of Jacob at the brook Jabbok, and say that you ever spent an hour, much less a night, in wrestling with the angel? The prayerlessness of this age is one of its worst signs, and the prayerlessness of some of our Christian Churches, looks as if God were about to withdraw himself from the land; for in many Churches, as I am told, they have a difficulty in getting enough men to attend the prayer meetings to carry them on. I know of some—"Tell it not in Gath, publish it not in the streets of Askelon!"—I know of some Churches that have given up the prayer meetings because nobody comes. Ah! if this case were a solitary one, it ought to be daily mourned over, but there are scores of Churches in a like condition; the Lord have mercy upon them, and upon the land in which such Churches dwell.

To sum up many things which might be said, I think the Holy Spirit will be grieved with any one of us if we shall indulge *any known sin,* let it be what it may; and I will add to that, if any one of us shall neglect any known duty, let it be what it may. I cannot imagine the Spirit of God being pleased with a brother who knows his Master's will, and does it not: I know the Word says that he shall be beaten with many stripes. Surely, beating with stripes must be the result of grief on the part of the hand that administers such stripes. Let any person or any Church know good and do it not, and to him or to it, it shall be sin; and that which might not be sin in the ignorant, will become sin to those blessed with light. As soon as your conscience is enlightened, and you know the path of duty, you need not say, "Others ought to do it" (so they should, but to their own Master they must stand or fall). If your judgment be enlightened, make haste and delay not to keep the commandments of God. John Owen, in his treatise upon the Holy Spirit, makes a remark that he believes the Spirit of God was greatly grieved in England by the public affirmation in the articles of the doctrine that the Church of God has power to decree rites and ceremonies for herself. God's Word is the only rule of God's Church: inasmuch as the Church of England, so called, claims to be her own lawmaker, she has grieved the Spirit thereby. When a Church claims to itself the right to judge what are to be its own ordinances, instead of willingly and obediently acknowledging that she has no right of choice whatever, but is bound to obey the revealed will of her Great Head, she sins terribly. It is the duty of all Christians to search the Word as to what are the ordinances which God has fixed and commanded, and being once clear as to the rule of the Word, it is ours to obey it. If you see infant baptism in the Word, do not neglect it; if it be not there, do not regard it. Here I must give utterance to a thought which has long followed me. Perhaps the present sad condition of the Christian Church, and the prevalence of the dogma of "baptismal regeneration," may be traceable to the neglect that reigns in the Church almost universally with regard to the great Christian ordinance of believers' baptism. Men laugh at all talk about this, as if the question were of no importance; but I take leave to say that whatever may be the truth upon that ordinance, it is worth every believer's while to find it out. I meet constantly with people who have no sort of faith in infant baptism, and have long ago given it up; and yet, though they admit that they ought to be baptized as believers, they neglect the duty as unimportant. Now mark, when the great day shall reveal all things, I am persuaded it will reveal this, that the Church's supplanting the baptism of believers by that of infants, was not only a great means in the original establishment of Popery, but that the maintenance of the perverted ordinance in our Protestant Church, is the chief root and cause of the present revival of Popery in this land. If we would lay the axe to the roots of sacramentarianism, we must go back to the old scriptural method of giving ordinances to believers only—the ordinances after faith, not before faith. We must give up baptizing in order to regenerate, and administer it to those alone who profess to be already regenerate. When we all come to this, we shall hear no more of "baptismal regeneration;" and a thousand other false doctrines will vanish away. Lay down the rule that unbelievers have no right to

Church ordinance, and you put it out of the power of men to establish the unhallowed institution of a State Church; for, mark you, no National Church is possible on the principle of believers' baptism, a principle much too exclusive to suit the mixed multitude of a whole nation. A State Church *must* hold to infant baptism; necessarily it must receive all the members of the State into its number—it *must,* or else it cannot expect the pay of the State. Make the Church a body, consisting only of professedly faithful men, believers in the Lord Jesus, and let the Church say to all others, "You have no part nor lot in this matter until you are converted," and there is an end of the unholy alliance between the Church and the world, which is now a withering blight upon our land. Errors of doctrine, practice, and polity, may cause the dew of heaven to be withheld. You will say, "Such errors did not hinder revivals in other days?" Perhaps not, but God does not always wink at our ignorance. In these days no one needs to be ignorant about the mystery of "baptismal regeneration," the error has worked itself to its full development, and reached such a climax, that every Christian man ought to give it his most earnest consideration. Guilt will come upon us if we are not earnest in seeking out the roots of an evil which is the cause of such deadly mischief in the land. If, as a Church, we are clear in our testimony on this point, I entreat you to see if there be any other error with which you may be charged. Is there a part of Scripture, which we have not attended to? Is there a truth, which we have neglected? Let us hold ourselves ready to relinquish our most cherished opinions at the command of Scripture, whatever they may be. I say to you what I say to others, if the form of our Church government, if the manner of our administration of Christian ordinances, if the doctrines we hold, be unwarranted by the Word of God, let us be faithful to our consciences and to the Word, and be ready to alter, according to our light. Let us give up the idea of stereotyping anything; let us be ready at any moment and every moment to do just what the Spirit of God would have us to do; for if not, we may not expect the Spirit of God to abide with us. O for a heart to serve God perfectly! O that such a heart were given to all his people, so that they were ready to renounce authority, antiquity, taste, and opinion, and bow before the

Holy Ghost alone! May the Church yet come to walk by the simple rule of God's Book and by the light of God's Spirit, and then shall we cease to grieve the Holy Ghost!

III. Thirdly, and very briefly—much too briefly—THE LAMENTABLE RESULT *of the Spirit's being grieved.*

In the child of God it will not lead to his utter destruction, for no heir of heaven can perish; neither will the Holy Spirit be utterly taken away from him, for the Spirit of God is given to abide with us for ever. But the ill-effects are nevertheless most terrible. You will lose, my dear friends, *all sense of the Holy Spirit's presence;* he will be as one hidden from you—no beams of comfort, no words of peace, no thoughts of love—there will be what Cowper calls, "an aching void which the world can never fill." Grieve the Holy Spirit, and you will lose *all Christian joy;* the light shall be taken from you, and you shall stumble in darkness; those very means of grace which once were such a delight, shall have no music in your ear. Your soul shall be no longer as a watered garden, but as a howling wilderness. Grieve the Spirit of God, and you will lose all *power;* if you pray, it will be a very weak prayer—you will not prevail with God. When you read the Scriptures, you shall not be able to lift the latch and force your way into the inner mysteries of truth. When you go up to the house of God, there shall be none of that devout exhilaration, that running without weariness, that walking without fainting. You shall feel yourself like Samson when his hair was lost, weak, captive, and blinded. Let the Holy Spirit depart, and *assurance* is gone, doubts follow, questionings and suspicions are aroused.

> "Do I love the Lord or no?
> Am I his, or am I not?"

Grieve the Spirit of God, and *usefulness* will cease: the ministry shall yield no fruit; your Sunday School work shall be barren; your speaking to others and labouring for others souls shall be like sowing the wind. Let a Church grieve the Spirit of God, and oh, the blights that shall come and wither her fair garden! Then her days of solemn assembly shall have no acceptance with heaven; her sons, although all of them ordained as priests unto God, shall have no acceptable incense to offer. Let the Church grieve the Spirit, and she

shall fail to bless the age in which she lives; she shall cast no
light into the surrounding darkness; no sinners shall be
saved by her means; there shall be few additions to her
number; her missionaries shall cease to go forth; there shall
be no marriage feasts of communion in her house; darkness
and death shall reign where all was joy and life. Brethren,
beloved in the Lord, may the Lord prevent us from grieving
his Spirit as a Church, but may we be earnest, zealous,
truthful, united, and holy, so that we may retain among us
this heavenly guest who will leave us if we grieve him.

IV. Lastly, there is one PERSONAL ARGUMENT which is
used in the text to forbid our grieving the Spirit—"Whereby
ye are sealed unto the day of redemption."

What does this mean? There are many meanings assigned
by different commentators: we shall be content with the
following—A seal is set upon a thing to *attest its authenticity
and authority.* By what can I know that I am truly what I
profess to be? I am by profession a Christian. How do I know
whether I am really a Christian or not? God sets a seal on
every genuine saint: what is it? It is the possession of the
Holy Spirit. If you have the Holy Spirit my dear friend, that
is God's seal set upon you that you are his child. Do you not
see, then, that if you grieve the Spirit, you lose your seal,
and you are like a commission with the seal rent away: you
are like a note of hand without a signature? Your evidence of
being God's child is the Spirit; for if "any man have not the
Spirit of Christ, he is none of his." If you have not the Spirit
in you, that will be decisive evidence for you that you do not
belong to Christ; for you lack the groundwork of true
assurance, which is the indwelling presence, power, and
enjoyment of the Spirit.

Moreover, I have said a seal is used for *attestation;* and so
it is, not only to you, but to others. You say to the world
around, "I am a child of God." How are they to know it? They
can only judge as you must judge yourself, by looking for the
seal. If you possess the Spirit of God, they will soon see you
to be a Christian; if you have it not, whatever else you have,
you will soon be discovered to be a forgery, for you lack the
seal. Beloved, all Church history proves this, that when the
Christian Church has been filled with the Spirit of God, the
world has confessed her pedigree, because it could not help

doing so; but when the Church has lost her enthusiasm and fervour, because she has lost the heavenly fire, then the world has asked, "What is this Christian Church more than the synagogue of the Jews, or the company of Mahomet?" The world knows God's seal; and if it does not see it, it soon despises that society which pretends to be the Church of God, and has not the mark and proof of it. The same truth holds good in all cases; for instance, in the matter of the Christian ministry. When I first came to minister in London, there was some little talk about my being ordained. "If I am ordained of God, I do not need human ordination; and if, on the other hand, God has not called me to the work, no man or set of men can do it." But it was said, "You must have a recognition service, that others may signify their approbation!" "No," I said, "if God be with me, they will recognise me quickly enough as a man of God; and if the Lord's presence be denied me, human approbation is of little worth." Brethren, if you profess to be called to any form of ministry, your only way of proving your call will be by showing the seal of the Spirit; when that seal is affixed to your labours, you will require no other recognition. The camp of Dan soon recognised Samson when the Spirit came upon him; and when he went among his enemies—the Philistines—with the jaw-bone of an ass, they soon recognised him as they saw him piling the slain heaps upon heaps. This is how the Christian man or minister must compel the recognition of his status and call. Knights of the cross must win their spurs upon the battle-field. The only way for a Christian to be discerned to be a Christian, or for a Church to be manifested as a Church of God, is by having the Spirit of God, and in the name of the Spirit of God doing exploits for God, and bringing glory to his holy name.

Once more, a seal is used for *preserving,* as well as for attesting. The Eastern seals up his money-bags to secure the gold within, and we seal our letters to guard the enclosure. A seal is set for security. Now, beloved, as the only way by which you can be known to be a Christian is by really possessing the supernatural power of the Holy Ghost, so, also, the only way by which you can be kept a Christian, and preserved from going back to the world, is by still possessing that same Holy Spirit. What are you if the Spirit of God be

gone? Salt that has lost its savour, wherewith can you be
salted? "Trees twice dead, plucked up by the roots...
wandering stars, to whom is reserved the blackness of
darkness for ever." The Holy Spirit is not to you a luxury,
but a necessity: you must have him, or you die; you must
have him, or you are damned, ay, and with a double
damnation. Here comes in this choice promise that the Lord
will not leave you, and will not forsake you; but if he did
leave you for ever, there would remain no more sacrifice for
sin; it would be impossible to renew you again unto
repentance, seeing that you would have crucified the Lord
afresh, and put him to an open shame. Grieve not, then, that
Spirit upon whom you are so dependent: he is your
credentials as a Christian; he is your life as a believer. Prize
him beyond all price; speak of him with bowed head, with
reverent awe; rest upon him with childlike, loving
confidence; obey his faintest monitions; neglect not his
inward whispers; turn not aside from his teachings in the
Word, or by his ministers; and be as ready to feel his power
as the waves of the sea are to be moved by the wind, or a
feather to be wafted by the gale. Hold yourselves ready to do
his bidding. As the eyes of the handmaiden are to her
mistress, so let your eyes be unto him. When you know his
will, ask no questions, count no costs, dare all hazards, defy
all circumstances. Let the will of the Spirit be your absolute
law, apart from gain or loss, apart from your own judgment
or your own taste. Let the will of the Spirit, when once
plainly perceived by you, be instantly obeyed, and try to
perceive that will. Do not wilfully shut your eyes to an
unpleasant duty, or close your understanding to an un-
welcome truth. Lean not to your own understanding;
consider that the Holy Ghost alone can teach you, and that
those who will not be taught of him must remain hopelessly
foolish. Oh! if I might but live to see the Church of God
recognise the power of the Holy Ghost; if I could but see her
cast aside the grave clothes which she has so long persisted
in wearing; if I could see her put no confidence in State or
power—rely no longer upon eloquence and learning; if I
could see her depend upon the Holy Ghost, even though her
ministers should again be fishermen, and her followers
should again be the "base things of this world, and the

things that are not;" even though she should have to be
baptized in blood; even though the man-child should excite
the dragon's wrath, and he should pour floods out against
her, yet the day of her final victory would have dawned. If
she did but obey the Spirit—if her directories, creeds, and
rules, her prayer-books, rubrics, and canons, were cast to the
winds, and the free Spirit of the living God ruled
everywhere; if, instead of the decrees of her councils, and the
slavish bondage of priestcraft and ritual, she would only
embrace the liberty wherewith Christ hath made her free,
and walk according to his Word and the teachings of her
heavenly Teacher, then might we hear the shout of the King
in our midst, and the battlements of error would fall! God
send it, and send it in our time, and his shall be praise!

I fear there are some here who do not *grieve* the Spirit, but
do worse than that; they *quench* the Spirit—they *resist* the
Spirit. May the Lord grant them forgiveness of this great
sin, and may they be led to the cross of Christ to find pardon
for every sin! At the cross, and there alone, can everlasting
life be found. God bless you, for Jesus' sake. Amen.

3

The Private Tutor

"He that loveth me not keepeth not my sayings: and the word which ye hear is not mine, but the Father's which sent me. These things have I spoken unto you being yet present with you. But the Comforter, which is the Holy Ghost, whom the Father will send in my name, he shall teach you all things, and bring all things to your remembrance, whatsoever I have said unto you."   John 14:24-26

All through this thrice-blessed chapter man cuts a very sorry figure. Whoever it is that speaks, whether it be Philip, or Judas, or Thomas, each one displays his own ignorance, either by asking an unwise question or by making a mistaken request. Yet, brethren, these apostolic men were by no means inferior persons; but so superior that we sink into insignificance in comparison with them. Jesus made them heralds of his gospel, master-builders of his church; and if *they* displayed such ignorance, even when the Lord Jesus Christ himself had personally spoken to them, *we* must not wonder that we are apt to blunder; neither should we despair if we find ourselves dull and slow. If those fathers of the church so greatly needed to be taught of the Holy Ghost, how much more do we? If they could receive nothing except by the Spirit of God, how can we hope to be wise apart from his instructions? Our position should be sitting with Mary at the Master's feet, varied with bowing into the dust before the Lord under a humble sense of our folly. The chapter before us is well watered with streams of comfort; but yet I confess it is ever a valley of humiliation to me, as I see what poor creatures even the chief of saints are when left to themselves.

But, at the same time, how wonderfully throughout this

passage do we see the lovingkindness of our God in condescending to the weaknesses of his people. In one verse of our text, the twenty-sixth, we have the whole Trinity at work upon the believer: "The Comforter, which is the Holy Ghost, whom the Father will send in my name." There we have the Holy Spirit, the Father, and the Son, uniting their sacred energies for the illumination of the chosen. Each divine person seeks to make the other to be more fully known: the Son speaking what he hears with the Father, and the Spirit taking the things of the Son and revealing them to us; the whole Trinity working in us to will and to do according to the divine pleasure. What *we* are, my brethren, is of small consequence compared with what *he* is who worketh all our works in us. What if we be nothing but clay; the great Potter knows how to fashion us to his praise. The great item is not what the clay is, but what the potter can make out of it. Let us not despond because of what we are by nature, but let us rejoice as we remember the wisdom and power of God who has begun a good work in us, and will not cease from his working till he has perfected his design. Wherefore, comfort one another with these thoughts. Lie low, and be more and more teachable; yet be hopeful, for you shall be taught. Confess your own ignorance, but confide in the Lord's power to teach you. Rest assured that even for you there is a noble destiny; God shall reveal himself to you and in you; and you shall not only know for yourself, but shall declare to principalities and powers in the heavenly places the manifold wisdom of God.

In handling my text at this time I desire to be entirely under the power of the Spirit of God. Not with enticing words of man's wisdom would I preach, not with the garnishings of oratory would I foolishly dream of lending power to the omnipotent word of God; but with all simplicity I would speak plainly that which the Holy Spirit teacheth by our text.

It appears to me that there are three things here worthy of patient observation: one is, *the test of a true believer,*—"He that loveth me not keepeth not my sayings"; a second is, *the need of a true believer*—he needs to be taught of the Holy Ghost, and to have his memory refreshed by the same gracious Spirit,—"He shall bring all things to your remembrance." The best disciple needs help in his understanding, and in his memory. Thirdly, let us think of *the privilege of a true believer*,—"The Comforter, which is the Holy Ghost, shall teach you all things, and bring all things to your remembrance, whatsoever I have said unto you."

I. Let us begin with THE TEST OF A TRUE BELIEVER; and let each one consent to be tested. Let each man put himself into the scale, that he may know his weight; for the Lord pondereth the heart. He who never judges himself will perish in the judgment of the last great day.

I would draw your attention to the fact that in this passage, and elsewhere in Scripture, men are divided into two classes, and not a word is said of a neutral or inter- mediate class. The twenty-first verse says, "He that hath my commandments, and keepeth them, he it is that loveth me"; and the twenty-fourth verse says negatively, "He that loveth me not keepeth not my sayings." Evidently there are two sorts of persons in that part of the world which is visited by the gospel: he that loveth Christ, and he that loveth him not. If you once hear the gospel you can never be indifferent to it; you must either be its friend or its foe, its disciple or its opposer. If once the Lord Jesus Christ crosses the orbit of your life, you can never henceforth be neutral; you must either reject him or receive him; believe him or make him a liar. I would urge home upon each of you that simple but solemn truth, lest any person should think himself omitted from the range of my discourse. I would so spread the net that no fish may remain outside its meshes. The gospel must, in the nature of things, be to you who hear it either a savour of life unto life, or of death unto death. By this gospel you shall be judged, and it shall either bring you where there is no condemnation to them that are in Christ Jesus, or it shall leave you where you are condemned already because you have not believed upon the Son of God. Do not, therefore, hope to live and die as if there were no Christ. Attempt not to say, "He is nothing to me." Though you pass by the cross, and refuse to look on Christ, yet the crucified One looks on you, and casts his shadow on your path. His blood will be upon you, either to cry out against you, as a murderer of the Son of God, or else to be your cleansing from all sin. As to the person of your Lord, it is evident that you

either love him or do not love him; one of the two it must be.
What is your condition at this hour? Sitting among the
people of God in this house on this Sabbath day, are you
lovers of the Lord Jesus, or are you enemies to him?

May God bless that stroke of the winnowing fan, so that by
it the chaff may be separated from the wheat.

But *the test is this, the loving of Christ.* Loving Christ is
not the way of salvation; that can only be ascribed to faith,
as it is written, "He that believeth on me hath everlasting
life." But the flower which comes out of the seed of faith is
love, and faith is not true faith unless it worketh by love,
and so purifieth the heart.

Observe that *the love is personal*: "he that loveth *me* not."
He speaks not here of love to doctrine, but of love to himself;
"he that loveth *me*." There is a personal Christ, and he is to
be loved by each one of us individually. Do not think of
Christ as a historic personage, who came and went away,
whose memory may be dear, but who cannot personally be
the object of a present love. If you are truly his disciple, and
a partaker of his salvation, you love *him*. You realize him as
a living person, as much so as your own self, as your dear
wife or your near friend; and your heart in deed and in truth
is bound to him. The tendrils of your affection must lay hold
on Jesus, climbing upwards toward God by laying hold upon
his Son. You may not always be able to *say* that you are sure
that you love him, because your agony to be right may create
in you a painful anxiety, and even a morbid jealousy as to
your own sincerity; but you do love him if you are called by
his grace, and if you do not love him, neither have you tasted
of his power to save. When I read those words just now, "He
that loveth me not," I felt as if I must repeat the words of
Paul, and say, "Let him be Anathema Maranatha,"—cursed
at the coming of the Lord; for is it not an awful thing for any
heart to refuse to love Jesus? The most lovable of all beings
is Jesus. It is unnatural not to love one so amiable. As
streams of water naturally flow into the lowest part of the
valley, so one would have thought that the condescension of
Jesus for our sakes made it natural for the love of men to
run towards him and concentrate itself within him. Alas, our
nature is now unnatural, and it is only as the Spirit of God
creates a new love in the heart that we yield our love to the

ever-blessed Saviour. If we are not lovers of the Lord Jesus, the Spirit of all grace has not made us to know and trust Christ; for if we knew Jesus and trusted him our heart must be wedded to him. Christ trusted must be Christ beloved. We must love God when once the love of God is shed abroad in our hearts by the Holy Ghost. Judge ye yourselves, then: do you love Jesus truly and supremely? He saith, "He that loveth son or daughter more than me is not worthy of me." He claims the first place in the hearts of his people. He is an all-engrossing Saviour, who will never be satisfied till he has monopolised all our affections and carried our hearts away to abide with him in the treasury above. Let it be a matter, then, of personal trial with each one of you. Hear your risen Lord saying, "Lovest thou me?" Not to Simon alone, but to you, John, and to you, Mary, he saith, "Lovest thou me?" He standeth here this morning, as once he stood by the lake of Galilee, and he puts this loving enquiry to each disciple, "Lovest thou me?" Is his adorable person the object of your intense regard? Can you fall at his feet and say, "Lord, thou knowest all things, thou knowest that I love thee! Show me what thou wouldst have me to do."

Furthermore, as we look at this text we observe that, inasmuch as it is not always possible to gauge the emotions and the affections, *a further test is given us*: "He that loveth me not keepeth not my sayings." I may know, therefore, whether I love the Lord Jesus Christ by answering this further question, Do I keep his sayings? What meaneth this? It means, first, have we *a reverent regard for all the teachings of the Lord Jesus Christ*? Do we receive them as being our standard of doctrine, and our rule of life? Remember that, in effect, all that is in the Old Testament as well as in the New must be considered to be the sayings of Christ; for he says that he came not to destroy the law, but to establish the law. Heaven and earth shall pass away, but not one tittle of the law shall fail. The whole record of inspiration is endorsed by Christ, and may be said to be his sayings. Now, do you accept these sacred Scriptures as your infallible guide? Remember, the sayings of Jesus are the word of the Father. Mark how Jesus says, "The word which ye hear is not mine, but the Father's which sent me." I tremble as I see in this day such a trifling with the Word of God; such a haste to

criticise this and question that. There are degrees of inspiration, so we are told; and if that be so, we can be sure of
nothing, since we have first to decide some subtle question
as to the measure of the inspiration. As well have no Bible
as such a Bible. Brethren, the Word of the Lord shall have
no such treatment from me, and I trust it will not be so
served by any of you, for if so, you will rob yourselves of
comfort, and offer grievous disrespect to your divine Lord. I
hope we can declare concerning all his sayings,—"Thy word
was found, and I did eat it, and it was unto me as my
necessary food." More to be desired are these sayings than
gold, yea, than much fine gold: they are sweeter also than
honey, and the honeycomb. Did a saying come from Christ?
Has Jesus set forth a truth in these Scriptures? Then it is
not ours to judge, not ours to doubt; but ours to accept with
implicit faith. The authority of Jesus stands to us in the
stead of reasoning. We so reverence him that we reverence
his sayings as being truth itself. To keep his sayings means,
further, *to make careful storage of them in the memory.*

To keep these sayings must mean to lay them up in the
heart. The blessed Virgin "kept all these things, and pon-
dered them in her heart," and so doth every Christian. "Thy
word have I hid in my heart that I might not sin against
thee." It is a blessed thing when we are not content to hear
God's Word on the Sabbath, but listen to its echoes every
day in the week. We constantly chew the cud by meditation,
and so we are nourished. We delight to know the meaning of
the Word by keeping it continually before our minds. We
keep the heavenly object long before the sensitive plate of
our mind till it is perfectly photographed thereon, and we
ourselves are changed by it from glory to glory as by the
image of the Lord. Oh, brethren, unless we reverence the
Word, and hoard it up as the choicest of treasures, we have
no proof that we love Christ.

Further than this, to keep Christ's sayings must mean
that, having learned them and retained them in the
memory, we also further keep them in the mind by *frequent
contemplation.* There is a great failure in this respect, I am
afraid, among many professors; but those who fervently love
Jesus, and are sanctified to his service, delight to be much
engaged in meditating upon the sayings of Jesus Our earth-

ly cares are our burden, but our heavenly thoughts are our rest. What are human sciences but glimpses at transient and shadowy things? But spiritual meditation yields us views of eternal and substantial truth. As I walk through my house and rejoice in the comforts of my home, I say to myself, "These are only mine for a little while. God has prolonged my life hitherto, but at any moment these visible things may melt away, and I may be where things are real, though they are now invisible." Everything that has to do with this world is a vain show; but as for the world to come, he that hath a possession therein hath true riches. Should not our thoughts go most after that which is most? Should we not give the best of our consideration to that which is best? the most of our time to that which is not of time, but of eternity? I am sure he that loves Jesus delights to think upon the choice words which fell from his lips. We sit down under his shadow, for he is to us the tree of life, and not a single leaf of his shall wither, nor the least of his sayings fall to the ground.

Still, I have no doubt that the main meaning of keeping Christ's sayings is found in *obeying him*. Dear friends, I do not want to say anything that will be severe, but yet I shall put to you a question which ought to alarm many professors. Did you ever spend a whole day from morning to night in distinctly and resolutely doing that which would honour Christ? I do not mean did you give up your business? did you quit your family? such strange conduct would not honour Jesus, but would do the reverse. But have you day after day thought and acted as if Jesus were your master, and you his servant? Is it habitual with you to say, "I will only do that which Christ would do if he were in my place? His example shall be my law. I will not be ruled by the hope of personal advantage or selfish comfort; but to me the supreme rule shall be,—"What would Jesus do? What would Jesus have me to do?" I am afraid certain professors fancy that to hold a sound creed, and to attend a faithful ministry, and to subscribe now and then to charitable objects, is about the whole of religion. But you utterly miss the mark if you judge such matters to be the chief items of godliness. The chief matter is so to love Christ that we live for him, and honour him by obedience to him. We cannot serve Christ by following out our own whims. He who follows his own vagaries is a

vagrant; only he who obeys Jesus is his follower. By doing
what Jesus bids us, by catching his Spirit, by seeing things
in his way of seeing them, and by acting both towards man
and towards God in his way of acting, we may make men see
what a glorious Saviour we have. We ought so to display the
sweet fruit of the Holy Spirit in our lives that men may be
filled with admiration of our Lord. May God help us to do
this; for if we do not keep our Lord's sayings by our holy
living, we have no proof that we love Christ; and if we do not
love him, then we are not his disciples.

I beg you, my fellow brethren, to apply this text to yourselves. Is the Lord Jesus reverenced by you as your teacher?
Do you bow before the authority of his Word? Do you turn to
the Bible and say of it,—

> "This is the judge that ends the strife,
>   Where wit and reason fail"?

Have you subjected your intellect to his teaching? The loose
thinkers of the present day imagine that they may believe
what they like, and think what they please. But it is not so.
They do as good as say, "Our minds are our own, God shall
never rule over us." But this becometh not a saint. Our Lord
Jesus will be King of our entire nature, or of none of it. I
claim the province of the understanding for my Lord; for it is
a part of his empire which he will not leave in the hand of
the enemy. We are as responsible for our belief as for our
acts. We are never in full subordination to our Lord till we
yield ourselves devoutly and reverently to his instruction,
calling him Master and Lord, because so he is! Brethren, do
you yield your whole lives to Jesus? Do you aim at perfect
obedience? Do you repent your failures? Do you cry to him
daily, "My Master, mould me to thy will, for to bear thine
image is my ambition. I would re-live thy life, and be thy
representative on earth, even as thou art my representative
in heaven. Oh, that I could say of thy Father and my Father,
'I do always the things which please him'"?

II. So far for the test of discipleship. Now, in the second
place, I beg you to follow me while I speak for a minute or
two upon THE NEEDS OF A TRUE BELIEVER.

The believer, though he loves his Lord truly is, nevertheless, a most necessitous person, and sadly full of wants

He does not need any better gospel: the Lord Jesus Christ taught us the best gospel that could be; and, indeed, there can be no other. When Paul spoke of "another gospel," he added, "which is not another; but there be some that trouble you." We desire nothing wiser, fuller, or better, than the doctrine which our Lord once delivered to the saints. I heard of a mother speaking to her boy the other day words of truth and soberness. Her hopeful and eager son was tempted to run after certain novelties of doctrine and practice, and she said to him, "What we have heard from our minister is enough for me, for it is according to Scripture. Your father and mother have lived on this gospel, and it has helped them through a thousand troubles, even to this day; and your dear old grandfather and grandmother lived on the same truth, and died upon it triumphantly; therefore, hold fast by it. We have tried it and proved it, therefore do not depart from it." That was common-sense talk. I am afraid of the new gospel; I have not proved it; but what I have seen of its results in others makes me tremble. Let those who will, go to sea in ships of reed or of card-board, heart-of-oak suffices for me. Such vessels have carried men to the ends of the world and home again for many years, and in these alone will I cross the ocean. Those who seek after the novelties of this conceited century seek to push their Lord from his place, that a philosopher may fill his throne. They seem to say, "Stand thou back, thou Galilean! Thou wast good enough for the dark ages, but we need a brighter light for these brighter times." I return to what I said before,—we need no better gospel than that which God himself has set forth in the person of his Son Jesus Christ.

These disciples to whom our Lord spake did not need any better preacher: they could not imagine a better. "Never man spake like this man." What power and authority there was in him, and what an unction of the Holy One was upon him. I cannot say that of you; for you, beloved friends, might often sigh for an abler preacher, and it may be that in some places where you live your Sabbaths are a bondage to you, because the pure gospel is not declared, and the sheep are not fed. But in the case of these apostles, they could not have had a better preacher; and yet, for all that, because the Holy Spirit was not yet fully given, and was not dwelling in them, they had really learned very little. You see the Lord Jesus Christ says of himself, "These things have I spoken unto you." He does not say that he had actually *taught* them. The last words of my text are, "All things whatsoever I have *said* unto you." All that Jesus had done, if we view him merely as a preacher, was to speak and to say; but he could not teach the heart apart from the Holy Ghost. Between Christ on earth and his disciples what a distance there was! In his condescension he came very near to them; but yet you always perceive a gulf between the wise Master and the foolish disciples. Now the Holy Ghost annihilates that distance by dwelling in us.

The best instructed of the apostles failed to understand his Lord while he merely spake to them. Often the disciples ran away with the words which he had uttered, and dwelt upon their letter, altogether missing their spiritual meaning. Frequently when they obtained a glimpse of the spiritual meaning, they beclouded it with some prejudice or tradition of their own, which, like smoke, obscured their vision. As to memory, they displayed but little of that faculty towards spiritual things; they were constantly forgetting what the Lord had told them, and acting in a manner directly the opposite of his precept and example. Externally, all was provided, outward ministries of the noblest order were vouchsafed; but they needed something within them; an inward and effectual teacher, a secret and powerful remembrancer. Yea, more, they required to be caused to enjoy what they knew and remembered; they needed the Comforter to extract for them the honey of consolation from the honeycomb of doctrine. Their Lord had taught them all manner of comfortable truths, and yet he had to say to them, "Let not your heart be troubled." He had supplied them with the best arguments for courage, and yet they were afraid. They required a helper who would make them understand the truth, remember the truth, and enjoy the truth; and this is just what you and I stand in need of every hour; for we may sit under the most edifying preacher and remain unedified if we look to his words only. We may hear the best doctrine and yet be unable to get at it so as to receive it and feel the power of it. Truth without the Spirit of God profiteth not the soul.

Even if you understand you may forget. I dare say you have often to lament that the good word slips away from you, and this is a great evil. Why do we forget? Is it not largely through ignorance and want of understanding? When a child does not understand his lesson he soon forgets it. He who does not obtain a clear view of the truth will fail to remember it, just as you soon forget a person whom you have only seen casually for a few moments, and in a dim light. We cannot easily hold in the memory that which we have not firmly grasped with the mind. Again, we forget heavenly things because we are so occupied with worldly things: our cares, our joys, our pleasures, our pursuits often crowd the things of God into a corner, and even tread them down with heedless fury. We forget our eternal prospects because we are thinking of our immediate interests. Our circumstances compel us to think of lower objects, but we need divine help to abide in communion with the higher matters. We need some one to bring these things to our remembrance, and to elevate us to a superior region of mind and heart.

At times we forget our Lord's sayings, and become bewildered by many afflictions. Trouble follows trouble: we go from darkness to deeper darkness in our experience, and we are so worried that we forget. When we most need the promise we are most apt to forget it. There are good solid steps all through the Slough of Despond; but when a man is passing through that horrible place he is usually so hurried and confused that he cannot see the stepping-stones, but slips into the deep mire where there is no standing. It is ill for us to be in a storm and our anchor at home. The promise is admired when we do not require it; but how often is it forgotten when it would be of the utmost service. We need a prompter, a friend out of sight to suggest the proper word, or else we blunder and flounder, and do not act our parts aright. It is the work of the Holy Spirit to refresh our memories.

Sometimes, I am afraid, our memories fail us because we are not particularly anxious to recollect. Certain precepts are so contrary to the carnal mind that if we can forget them we are sure to do so. You know how easy it is in your family reading to omit parts of God's word which are too close and personal. We are afraid of the razor which cuts too close to the skin. Have you not felt on a morning when your servants have been gathered together, that you could not well read a certain passage because you had been out of temper, or unkind, or in some other way out of proper form? You feared that they would say, "Our master and the Bible do not agree." In your own private thoughts a precept occurs to you, but you feel it convenient to ignore it because it would stand in the way of a design which you are cherishing. You intend to go through with your purpose, and therefore you shut your eyes to an inconvenient text. But if we are under the guidance of the Spirit of God, he will bring to our remembrance the duty in its proper time, and we shall bring forth our fruit in its season. It is extremely easy to be wise after folly, and to be calm after the danger is over. We find the candle when the night is ended. We cry, "Dear me, if I had felt yesterday what I feel to-day, how differently I would have acted." We are so often a little behind the market. We lock the door after the horse is stolen. Fruit out of season is always deficient in flavour; never are the scent and the taste so perfect as in the middle of the season. Oh, that we may bring forth our fruit in its due season,—patience in tribulation, courage in danger, holiness in life, and hope in death. We fail to do this because that evil nature which is in us makes us forget at the precise moment what we ought to remember. It is the office of the Holy Spirit to bring before us the sayings of Christ in their due order and time. Do you not need this?

III. Hoping to retain your prayerful attention, I proceed to notice, THE PRIVILEGE OF THE TRUE BELIEVER. It is the true disciple's privilege to possess in the Holy Spirit a private tutor, a prompter, and a Comforter.

The Lord Jesus says, "The Comforter, which is the Holy Ghost, whom the Father will send in my name, he shall teach you all things." Christ in his sayings gave us our class-book, complete and infallible; but through our dulness we need more. That young man has gone to college: he has with him all necessary books, and in them is to be found all that he will need to learn; even thus the Lord Jesus has given us in his sayings all that we need to know. But the young man's father wishes him to become a learned man, and therefore he engages for him a private tutor, who will teach him what the books contain. With his tutor's help his book is of far greater use to him than before. If any passage is difficult the tutor explains it; he puts the youth into the way of reading his class-books, so as to get the full value of them. Spiritually this is the office of the Holy Ghost: he finds us the key wherewith to open up the mystery which else would be out of our reach.

He really teaches us. To *teach* you is a very different thing from speaking to you. A person may speak to a company of young people, and yet teach them nothing. If I am anxious to instruct a brother on any point, I do not merely speak to him, but I go over the ground carefully, set out each point distinctly, repeat my statements deliberately, and illustrate them appropriately. The Spirit of God, when he takes the child of God out of the company, and speaks privately to his heart, goes over the truth with him till it is made clear, and happily apprehended. We need to have truth opened up to the understanding, impressed upon the heart, made real to the apprehension, applied to the mind, wrought into the affections, and endeared to the soul. It is one thing to hear the Word, but it is another thing to learn the Word: it is one thing to be told, but quite another thing to be taught.

The Spirit teaches the saints, either at once or by degrees, all the truth of Christ. Some parts of that whole you will never learn, except upon a sick bed, or in deep depression of spirit, or in bereavement and adversity; while other truths will only be learned on the bright mountains of assurance and communion with God. It is the Spirit's province to burn truth into the soul, to engrave it upon the renewed heart, and make the mind sure and certain as to what it knows. No knowledge is so sure as that which the Holy Spirit communicates to our spirit. Inward teaching is effectual teaching. A man taught of God knows, and cannot be made to question what he knows. Time was, whenever I heard a sceptical remark, I felt wounded and somewhat shaken. I am no longer shaken by these wandering winds. There are certain things of which I am as sure of as my own existence; I have seen, tasted, and handled them, and I am past being argued out of them by those who know nothing about them. I am a lost man if the old, old gospel is not true; there is no way of salvation for me if it be not of grace through faith in the atoning sacrifice; and as I know that I am not lost, but am surely a saved man, I know that the Word which has saved me is the truth of God. Those who are familiar with spiritual realities defy denial: they set their inward consciousness against ten thousand scepticisms; if they cannot convince others, they are convinced themselves. We must be taught by the Spirit of God in a secret, personal, unquestionable, effectual manner. We must be made to feel the power of the truth by a spiritual inoculation with it, so that it enters into our very life, and becomes part and parcel of ourselves.

It is promised us that the Comforter will teach us *all things*—that is, all the things which Jesus said and did. Have we realized this far-reaching privilege? There is a great variety in the knowledge of Christ. Nobody need think that he will exhaust it. There is, moreover, a proportion in the things of Christ, and we need to know all that our Lord has set forth. Jesus does not teach doctrine only, though some professors crave doctrine, and doctrine alone. Jesus does not teach all practice: he teaches practice wondrously, but he also declares doctrine. Our Lord does not teach either doctrine or practice without experience, but he makes a perfect blend to our edification. The way with some of God's people is either to have nothing but doctrine, or else nothing but practice, or else nothing but experience, and this warps and spoils them. Give yourself up to the Spirit of God, and he will teach you all things: here a little, and there a little, —here a little of what you should know, there a little of what you should feel, and then again a little of what you should do.

Do remember that especially in the doing part of it the Spirit of God must be your teacher. A lad is put apprentice to a handicraft. How does he learn it? Why, by seeing how his master does it, and by doing it himself. At first he spoils the material, and his master needs to have much patience with him; but at last practice makes perfect, and the apprentice becomes a journeyman. The Spirit of God with wonderful condescension puts us to practise a little patience. We soon get weary of that task. When he gives us an opportunity of producing love—love to some poor wretched waif on life's rough sea; we are apt to grow chilled by his ingratitude, and wearied with our non success. The Holy

Spirit drills us in heavenly marching till we keep step with our Lord, and men take knowledge of us that we have been with Jesus, and have learned of him.

Brethren, you are to keep your Lord's sayings and never go beyond them; but to do this will need the private tuition of the Holy Ghost, and you must not be satisfied unless he wakeneth you morning by morning, and openeth your ear to hear what he hath to say, bringing home to your heart and conscience the things that make you wise unto salvation.

As we need something beside this, it is a mercy that we have it. We require that our memories be strengthened. What wretched memories we have as to divine things. As I have already said, we recollect when it is too late, and thus our memories serve rather to minister to our regret than to our improvement. It should not be so, and if we will put ourselves under the teaching of the Spirit of God it shall not remain so; he will strengthen our memories spiritually. He often brings truth to our minds; do you not find it so? While you are sitting here this morning flashes of light have been around you. Branch roads have opened up as we have proceeded; vistas of truth have rejoiced your vision. You have cried with wonder, "I never saw that before!" That is the Spirit of God. Frequently a doctrine comes home to you with the force of a new discovery; you had heard the truth before, but you had never seen it; but the Spirit brings it to your remembrance with singular vivacity and force.

He refreshes the mind by vivid recollections. He refreshes the heart by melting gratitude. I have known times when my memory of the love of Christ has made me sit down and weep for very joy. Oh, what gratitude wells up in the heart when the Holy Spirit brings all that Christ did to remembrance, and we hear him say from his cross, "I did all this for thee, what hast thou done for me?" It is the Spirit's work to refresh the memory of the heart as well as the memory of the mind. Ofttimes he refreshes the memory of the conscience—not quite so pleasant an operation. I have been doing for years wrong things without knowing them to be wrong. I have been neglecting a manifest duty for a long time, but all of a sudden that duty has been brought to my remembrance as one of the things which Jesus told me. I bless the Holy Ghost for thus sanctifying me by giving me a

higher standard of holiness, and making me more particular
about things which I glossed over with but slight attention.
This is a part of the work of the Holy Spirit of God, to bring
all things to your remembrance whatsoever he hath told
you.

I am sure the Spirit of God often blesses us by bringing
things to the memory of our hope. Perhaps this is an odd
way of putting it; for how can hope have a memory? But I
mean this, that hope seems to forget that the Lord hath said,
"I will never leave thee, nor forsake thee," Hope seems to
forget that

> "There is a land of pure delight,
> Where saints immortal reign."

And sometimes the Spirit of God brings all that glorious
revelation of the world to come before our minds. Have you
never felt glory begun below? Have not the pearly gates
seemed to stand, not ajar, but wide open, and have you not
in spirit walked down the streets of gold, and worn your
crown, and cast it at your Saviour's feet? Then you have said
to yourself, "I can bear this pain, I can put up with these
depressions and these inconveniences, for I know that there
is laid up for me in heaven a crown of life that fadeth not
away." The Spirit of God thus brings all things to our remembrance.

I shall say no more, but pray the Spirit of God to come
upon you this very day, and bring to your remembrance all
things that Christ has ever said to you. There will be a
mixture of sunny memories and sorrowing memories; but
they will be blessed memories, all of them. I thought when I
was trying to prepare a subject for this morning, "All that I
have preached for these many years is taken from me and
printed, so that I cannot repeat it,—what shall I do?" and
then this truth came to me, "He shall teach you"; "He shall
teach you," and I begged him to teach *me* that I might teach
you. I thought, "Alas, I have had many bright and sparkling
thoughts at times, but they do not come just now." I sat still
waiting, and then the fact came to me that the Holy Ghost
would bring all things to my remembrance whatsoever the
Lord Jesus had said. I find my natural memory to be less
powerful than it used to be in the days of my youth: shall I,

therefore, be allowed to forget when I am teaching? No, "He shall teach you, and bring all things to your remembrance." How beautiful! I have noticed old people whose memories have been sadly feeble. I knew one who forgot his children. But I never knew an old saint yet who forgot the name of the Saviour, or failed to remember his love. Sometimes the Holy Ghost bears such witness in the heart that the memory is very strong about divine things even when it fails about natural things. So, my dear old friend, you that the youngsters sometimes amuse themselves with because your memory has got to be like an old sieve that lets everything through; it will not let your Lord through, you will always feel the music of his name. You will never forget your Well-Beloved if you live to be as old as Methuselah. Memory, though it leaves no other name, shall leave that name recorded there. Christ's love is not hung upon us like a garland on a tree, but it is cut into us, and as the tree grows the letters grow deeper and broader every day. The Holy Ghost, who is the life of believers, writes more and more clearly upon that life the glorious and blessed name of Jesus. I wish that any here who do not know Christ would cry for the Spirit of God to teach him to them. If you long to be saved, pray that by his Spirit the Lord Jesus may bring you into the bond of the covenant, for his love's sake. Amen.

4

The First Fruit Of The Spirit

"But the fruit of the Spirit is love..."   Galatians 5:22

The worst enemy we have is the flesh. Augustine used frequently to pray, "Lord, deliver me from that evil man, myself." All the fire which the devil can bring from hell could do us little harm if we had not so much fuel in our nature. It is the powder in the magazine of the old man which is our perpetual danger. When we are guarding against foes without, we must not forget to be continually on our watchtower against the foe of foes within. "The flesh lusteth against the Spirit." On the other hand, our best friend, who loves us better than we love ourselves, is the Holy Spirit. We are shockingly forgetful of the Holy Ghost, and therein it is to be feared that we greatly grieve him; yet we are immeasurably indebted to him: in fact, we owe our spiritual existence to his divine power. It would not be proper to compare the love of the Spirit with the grace of our Lord Jesus Christ, so as even by implication to set up a scale of degrees in love; for the love of the regenerating Spirit is infinite, even as is the love of the redeeming Son. But yet for a moment we will set these two displays of love side by side. Is not the indwelling of the Spirit of God equal in loving-kindness to the incarnation of the Son of God? Jesus dwelt in a pure manhood of his own; the Holy Spirit dwells in our manhood, which is fallen, and as yet imperfectly sanctified. Jesus dwelt in his human body,

having it perfectly under his own control; but, alas, the Holy
Spirit must contend for the mastery within us, and though
he is Lord over our hearts, yet there is an evil power within
our members, strongly intrenched and obstinately bent on
mischief. "The flesh lusteth against the Spirit, and the Spirit
against the flesh." Our Lord Jesus dwelt in his body only for
some thirty years or so; but the blessed Spirit of all grace
dwelleth in us evermore, through all the days of our pilgrimage: from the moment when he enters into us by
regeneration he continueth in us, making us meet to be
partakers of the inheritance of the saints in light. You sing

> "Oh, 'tis love, 'tis wondrous love,"

in reference to our Lord Jesus and his cross: sing it also in
reference to the Holy Spirit and his long-suffering. He looks
at us from within, and therefore he sees the chambers of
imagery where hidden idols still abide. He sees our actions;
not from without, for therein, perhaps, they might be judged
favourably; but he discerns them from within, in their
springs and in the pollution of those springs, in their main
currents and in all their side eddies and back waters. O
brethren, it is wonderful that this blessed Spirit should not
leave us in indignation; we lodge him so ill, we honour him
so little. He receives so little of our affectionate worship that
he might well say, "I will no longer abide with you." When
the Lord had given up his people to the Roman sword, there
was heard in the temple at Jerusalem a sound as of rushing
wings, and a voice crying, "Let us go hence." Justly might
the divine presence have left us also because of our sins. It is
matchless love which has caused the Holy Spirit to bear with
our ill manners, and bear our vexatious behaviour. He stays
though sin intrudes into his temple! He makes his royal
abode where evil assails his palace! Alas, that a heart where
the Spirit deigns to dwell should ever be made a thorough-
fare for selfish or unbelieving traffic! God help us to adore
the Holy Ghost at the commencement of our discourse, and
to do so even more reverently at its close!

The Holy Ghost when he comes into us is the author of all
our desires after true holiness. He strives in us against the
flesh. That holy conflict which we wage against our
corruption cometh entirely of him. We should sit down in

willing bondage to the flesh, if he did not bid us strike for
liberty. The good Spirit also leads us in the way of life. If we
be led of the Spirit, says the apostle, we are not under the
law. He leadeth us by gentle means, drawing us with cords
of love, and bands of a man. "He leadeth me." If we take a
single step in the right road, it is because he leadeth us, and
if we have persevered these many years in the way of peace,
it is all due to his guidance, even to him who will surely
bring us in and make us to enjoy the promised rest.

> "And every virtue we possess,
> And every victory won,
> And every thought of holiness,
> Are his alone."

The Holy Ghost not only creates the inward contest
against sin, and the agonizing desire for holiness, and leads
us onward in the way of life, but he remains within us,
taking up his residence, and somewhat more: for the text
suggests a still more immovable steadfastness of residence
in our hearts, since according to the figure, the Spirit strikes
root within us. The text speaks of "fruit," and fruit cometh
only of a rooted abidance; it could not be conceived of in
connection with a transient sojourning, like that of a
wayfaring man. The stakes and tent pins that are driven
into the ground for an Arab's tent bear no fruit, for they do
not remain in one stay; and inasmuch as I read of the "fruit
of the Spirit," I take comfort from the hint, and conclude that
he intends to abide in our souls as a tree abides in the soil
when fruit is borne by it. Let us love and bless the Holy
Ghost! Let the golden altar of incense perfume this earth
with the sweet savour of perpetual adoration to the Holy
Ghost! Let our hearts heartily sing to him this solemn
doxology:—

> "We give thee, sacred Spirit, praise,
> Who in our hearts of sin and woe,
> Makes living springs of grace arise,
> And into boundless glory flow."

I. Now, coming to our text, I shall notice the matters
contained in it, and the first thing which my mind perceives
is A WINNOWING FAN. I would like to be able to use it, but it

is better far that it should remain where it is, for "the fan is in *his* hand, and *he* will thoroughly purge his floor." The handle of this winnowing fan is made of the first word of the text, that disjunctive conjunction, that dividing mono-syllable, "*But.*" "*But* the fruit of the Spirit is love"!

That "but" is placed there because the apostle had been mentioning certain works of the flesh, all of which he winnows away like chaff, and then sets forth in opposition to them "the fruit of the Spirit." It you will read the chapter, you will notice that the apostle has used no less than seventeen words, I might almost say eighteen, to describe the works of the flesh. Human language is always rich in bad words, because the human heart is full of the manifold evils which these words denote. Nine words are here used to express the fruit of the Spirit; but to express the works of the flesh,—see how many are gathered together!

The first set of these works of the flesh which have to be winnowed away are the *counterfeits of love to man.* Counter-feited love is one of the vilest things under heaven. That heavenly word, *love,* has been trailed in the mire of unclean passion and filthy desire. The licentiousness, which comes of the worship of Venus, has dared to take to itself a name which belongs only to the pure worship of Jehovah. Now, the works which counterfeit love are these: "*Adultery*, forni-cation, uncleanness, lasciviousness." To talk of "love" when a man covets his neighbour's wife, or when a woman violates the command, "Thou shalt not commit adultery," is little less than sheer blasphemy against the holiness of love. It is not love, but lust; love is an angel, and lust a devil. The purities of domestic life are defiled, and its honours are disgraced when once the marriage bond is disregarded. When men or women talk of religion, and are unfaithful to their marriage covenant, they are base hypocrites. Even the heathen condemned this infamy, let not Christians tolerate it. The next fleshly work is "*fornication*," which was scarcely censured among the heathen, but is most sternly condemned by Christianity. It is a wretched sign of the times that in these corrupt days, some have arisen who treat this crime as a slight offence, and even attempt to provide for its safer indulgence by legislative enactments. Has it come to this? Has the civil ruler become a panderer to the lusts of corrupt minds? Let it not be once named among you, as it becometh saints. "*Uncleanness*" is a third work of the flesh, and it includes those many forms of foul offence which defile the body and deprive it of its true honour; while to bring up the rear we have "*lasciviousness*," which is the cord which draws on uncleanness, and includes all conversation which excites the passions, all songs which suggest lewdness, all gestures and thoughts which lead up to unlawful gratification. We have sadly much of these two evils in these days, not only openly in our streets, but in more secret ways. I loathe the subject. All works of art which are contrary to modesty are here condemned, and the most pleasing poetry if it creates impure imaginations. These unclean things are the works of the flesh in the stage of putridity—the very maggots which swarm within a corrupt soul. Bury these rotten things out of our sight! I do but uncover them for an instant that a holy disgust may be caused in every Christian soul; and that we may flee therefrom as from the breath of pestilence. Yet remember, O you that think yourselves pure, and imagine you would never transgress so badly, that even into these loathsome and abominable criminalities high professors have fallen; ay, and sincere believers trusting in themselves have slipped into this ditch, from whence they have escaped with infinite sorrow, to go with broken bones the rest of their pilgrimage. Alas, how many who seemed to be clean escaped from pollution have so fallen that they have had to be saved so as by fire! Oh, may we keep our garments unspotted by the flesh; and this we cannot do unless it be in the power and energy of the Spirit of holiness. He must purge these evils from us, and cause his fruit so to abound in us that the deeds of the flesh shall be excluded for ever.

The winnowing fan is used next against the *counterfeits of love to God*; I refer to the falsities of superstition—"Idolatry and witchcraft"—"but the fruit of the Spirit is love." Alas, there are some that fall into *idolatry*; for they trust in an arm of flesh, and exalt the creature into the place of the Creator; "their God is their belly, and they glory in their shame." The golden calf of wealth, the silver shrines of craft, the goddess of philosophy, the Diana of fashion, the Moloch of power, these are all worshipped instead of the living God. Those who profess to reverence the true God, yet too generally worship him in ways which he has not ordained. Thus saith the Lord, "Thou shalt not make unto thee any graven image, or any likeness of anything that is in heaven above, or that is in the earth beneath, or that is in the water under the earth: thou shalt not bow down thyself to them, nor serve them." Yet we have Christians (so called) who say they derive help in the exercise of devotion from images and pictures. See how their places of assembly are rendered gaudy with pictures, and images, and things which savour of old Rome. What idolatry is openly carried on in certain buildings belonging to the National Church! What sensuous worship is now approved! Men cannot worship God now-adays unless their eyes, and ears, and noses are gratified: when these senses of the flesh are pleased, they are satisfied with themselves; "but the fruit of the Spirit is love." Love is the most perfect architecture, for "love buildeth up;" love is the sweetest music, for without it we are become as a sounding brass or a tinkling cymbal; love is the choicest incense, for it is a sacrifice of sweet smell; love is the fittest vestment,—"Above all things put on charity, which is the bond of perfectness." Oh, that men would remember that the fruit of the Spirit is not the finery of the florist, the sculptor, or the milliner, but the love of the heart. It ill-becomes us to make that gaudy which should be simple and spiritual. The fruit of the Spirit is not idolatry,—the worship of another god, or of the true God after the manner of will-worship. No, that fruit is obedient love to the only living God.

"*Witchcraft*," too, is a work of the flesh. Under this head we may rightly group all that prying into the unseen, that rending of the veil which God has hung up, that interfering with departed spirits, that necromancy which calls itself spiritualism, and pays court to familiar spirits and demons—this is no fruit of the Spirit, but the fruit of a bitter root. Brother Christians, modern witchcrafts and wizardry are to be abhorred and condemned, and you will be wise to keep clear of them, trembling to be found acting in concert with those who love darkness rather than light, because their deeds are evil. Idolatry and witchcraft are caused by a want of love to God, and they are evidences that the Spirit's life is not in the soul. When you come to love God with all your heart, you will not worship God in ways of your own devising, but you will ask, "Wherewithal shall I draw near unto the most high God?" and you will take your direction from the Lord's inspired word. The service which he prescribes is the only service which he will accept. The winnowing fan is at work now: I wonder whether it is operating upon any here present?

But next, this great winnowing-fan drives away with its "but" all _the forms of hate_. The apostle mentions "_hatred_," or a habitual enmity to men, usually combined with a selfish esteem of one's own person. Certain men cherish a dislike to everybody who is not of their clique, while they detest those who oppose them. They are contemptuous, to the weak ready to take offence, and little careful whether they give it or no. They delight to be in minorities of one, and the more wrongheaded and pugnacious they can be, the more are they in their element. "_Variance_," too, with its perpetual dislikes, bickerings, and quarrellings, is a work of the flesh. Those who indulge in it are contrary to all men, pushing their angles into everybody's eyes, and looking out for occasions of faultfinding, and strife. "_Emulations_,"—that is, jealousy. Jealousy in all its forms is one of the works of the flesh: is it not cruel as the grave? There is a jealousy which sickens if another be praised, and pines away if another prospers. It is a venomous thing, and stingeth like an adder: it is a serpent by the way, biting the horse's heels, so that his rider shall fall backward. "_Wrath_" is another deed of the flesh: I mean the fury of angry passion, and all the madness which comes of it. "But I am a man of very quick temper," says one. Are you a Christian? If so, you are bound to master this evil force, or it will ruin you. If you were a saint of God to the very highest degree in all but in this one point, it would pull you down; ay, at any moment an angry spirit might make you say and do that which would cause you life-long sorrow. "_Strife_" is a somewhat milder, but equally mischievous form of the same evil; if it burns not quite so fast and furiously, yet it is a slow fire kindled by the self-same flame of hell as the more ardent passion. The continual love of contention, the morbid sensitiveness, the overweening regard to one's own dignity, which join together to produce strife, are all evil things. What is the proper respect which is due to poor creatures like ourselves? I ween that if any one of us did get our "proper respect," we should not like it long: we should think that bare justice was rather scant in its appreciation. We desire to be flattered when we cry out for "proper respect." Respect, indeed! Why if we had our desert, we should be in the lowest hell! Then our apostle mentions "*seditions*," which occur in the state, the church, and the family. As far as our church life is concerned, this evil shows itself in an opposition to all sorts of authority or law. Any kind of official action in the church is to be railed at because it is official; rule of any sort is objected to because each man desires to have the preeminence, and will not be second. God save us from this evil leaven! *Heresy* is that kind of hate which makes every man set up to create his own religion, write his own Bible, and think out his own gospel. We have heard of "Every man his own lawyer," and now we are coming to have "Every man his own God, every man his own Bible, every man his own instructor." After this work of the flesh, come "*Envyings*," not so much the desire to enrich one's self at another's expense, as a wolfish craving to impoverish him, and pull him down for the mere sake of it. This is a very acrid form of undiluted hate, and leaves but one stronger form of hate. To desire another's dishonour merely from envy of his superiority is simply devilish, and is a sort of murder of the man's best life. The list is fitly closed by "*murders*," a suitable corner-stone to crown this diabolical edifice; for what is hate but murder? And what is murder but hate bearing its full fruit? He who does not love has within him all the elements that make a murderer. If you have not a general feeling of benevolence towards all men, and a desire to do them good, the old spirit of Cain is within you, and it only needs to be unrestrained and it will strike the fatal blow, and lay your brother dead at your feet. God save you, men and brethren, every one of you, from the domination of these dark principles of hate, which are the works of the flesh in its corruption. "But the fruit of the Spirit is love."

Next time you begin to boil over with wrath, think you feel a hand touching you and causing you to hear a gentle voice whispering, "But the fruit of the Spirit is love." Next time you say, "I will never speak to that man again, I cannot endure him," think you feel a fresh wind fanning your fevered brow, and hear the angel of mercy say, "But the fruit of the Spirit is love." Next time you are inclined to find fault with everybody, and set your brethren by the ears, and create a general scuffle, I pray you let the chimes ring out, "But the fruit of the Spirit is love." If you wish to find fault, it is easy to do so; you may begin with me and go down to the last young member that was admitted into the church, and you will not have to look long before you can spy out something which needs improvement; but to what end will you pick holes in our coats? Whenever you are bent on the growling business, pause awhile and hear the Scripture admonish you, "The fruit of the Spirit is love." When you wax indignant because you have been badly treated, and you think of returning evil for evil, remember this text, "The fruit of the Spirit is love." "Ah," you say, "it was shameful!" Of course it was: and therefore do not imitate it: do not render railing for railing, but contrariwise blessing, for "the fruit of the Spirit is love."

The winnowing-fan is at work: God blow your chaff away, brethren, and mine too!

The next thing which the winnowing-fan blows away is *the excess of self-indulgence*—"drunkenness, revellings, and such like." Alas, that Christian people should ever need to be warned against these animal offences, and yet they do need it. The wine-cup still has its charms for professors. Nor is this all: it is not merely that you may drink to excess, but you may eat to excess, or clothe your body too sumptuously, or there may be some other spending of money upon your own gratification which is not according to sober living. Drunkenness is one of those trespasses of which Paul says, "that they which do such things shall not inherit the kingdom of God." The revelling which makes night hideous with its songs so called,—call them howlings and you are nearer the mark,—the revelling which spends hour after hour in entertainments which heat the blood, and harden the heart, and chase away all solid thought, is not for us who have renounced the works of darkness: for us there is a better joy, namely, to be filled with the Spirit, and "the fruit of the Spirit is love."

II. The second thing which I see in the text is A JEWEL,— that jewel is *love*. "The fruit of the Spirit is love." What a priceless Kohinoor this is! It is altogether incalculable in value. What a heavenly grace love is! It has its centre in the heart, but its circumference sweeps, like omnipresence, around everything. Love is a grace of boundless scope. We love God: it is the only way in which we can embrace him fully. We can love the whole of God, but we cannot know the whole of God. Yes, we love God, and even love that part of God which we cannot comprehend or even know. We love the Father as he is. We love his dear Son as he is. We love the ever-blessed Spirit as he is. Following upon this, for God's sake we love the creatures he has made. It is true in a measure that

> "He prayeth best that loveth best,
> Both man and bird and beast."

Every tiny fly that God has made is sacred to our souls as God's creature. Our love climbs to heaven, sits among the angels, and anon bows among them in lowliest attitude; but in due time our love stoops down to earth, visits the haunts of depravity, cheers the garrets of poverty, and sanctifies the dens of blasphemy, for it loves the lost. Love knows no out-cast London, it has cast out none. It talks not of the "lapsed masses," for none have lapsed from its regard. Love hopes good for all, and plans good for all: while it can soar to glory it can descend to sorrow.

Love is a grace which has to do with eternity; for we shall never cease to love him who first loved us. But love has also to do with this present world, for it is at home in feeding the hungry, clothing the naked, nursing the sick, and liberating the slave. Love delights in visiting the fatherless and the widows, and thus it earns the encomium,—"I was an hungered, and ye gave me meat: I was thirsty, and ye gave me drink: I was a stranger, and ye took me in: naked, and ye clothed me: I was sick, and ye visited me: I was in prison, and ye came unto me." Love is a very practical, home-spun virtue, and yet it is so rich and rare that God alone is its author. None but a heavenly power can produce this fine linen; the love of the world is sorry stuff.

Love has to do with friends. How fondly it nestles in the parental bosom! How sweetly it smiles from a mother's eye! How closely it binds two souls together in marriage bonds!

How pleasantly it walks along the ways of life, leaning on the arm of friendship! But love is not content with this, she embraces her enemy, she heaps coals of fire upon her adversary's head: she prays for them that despitefully use her and persecute her. Is not this a precious jewel indeed? What earthly thing can be compared to it?

You must have noticed that *in the list of the fruits of the Spirit it is the first*—"The fruit of the Spirit is love." It is first because in some respects it is best. First, because it leads the way. First, because it becomes the motive principle and stimulant of every other grace and virtue. You cannot conceive of anything more forceful and more beneficial, and therefore it is the first. But *see what followeth at its heel*. Two shining ones attend it like maids of honour, waiting upon a queen. "The fruit of the spirit is love, joy, peace": he that hath love hath joy and peace. What choice companions! To love much is to possess a deep delight, a secret cellar of the wine of joy which no man else may taste. He that loveth is like to God, who is the God of peace. Truly the meek and loving shall inherit the earth, and delight themselves in the abundance of peace. He is calm and quiet whose soul is full of love; in his boat the Lord stands at the helm, saying to the winds and waves, "Peace; be still!" He that is all love, though he may have to suffer, yet shall count it all joy when he falleth into divers trials. See then what a precious jewel it is that hath so many shining brilliants set at its side.

Love has this for its excellence, that it fulfils the whole law: you cannot say that of any other virtue. Yet, while it fulfils the whole law, it is not legal. Nobody ever loved because it was demanded of him; a good man loves because it is his nature to do so. Love is free—it bloweth where it listeth, like the Spirit from which it comes. Love, indeed, is the very essence of heart liberty. Well may it be honoured; for while it is a true grace of the gospel, it nevertheless fulfils the whole law. If you would have law and gospel sweetly combined, you have it in the fruit of the Spirit, which is love.

Love, moreover, is Godlike, for God is love. Love it is which prepares us for heaven, where everything is love. Come, sweet Spirit, and rest upon us till our nature is transformed into the divine nature by our becoming burning flames of love. Oh, that it were so with us this very day!

Mark, beloved, that the love we are speaking of is not a love which cometh out of men on account of their natural constitution. I have known persons who are tenderly affectionate by nature; and this is good; but it is not spiritual love: it is the fruit of nature and not of grace. An affectionate disposition is admirable, and yet it may become a danger, by leading to inordinate affection, a timid fear of offending, or an idolatry of the creature. I do not condemn natural amiability; on the contrary, I wish that all men were naturally amiable: but I would not have any person think that this will save him, or that it is a proof that he is renewed. Only the love which is the fruit of the Spirit may be regarded as a mark of grace. Some people, I am sorry to say, are naturally sour; they seem to have been born at the season of crab apples, and to have been fed on vinegar. They always take a faultfinding view of things. They never see the sun's splendour, and yet they are so clear-sighted as to have discovered his spots. They have a great speciality of power for discerning things which it were better not to see. They do not remember that the earth has proved steady and firm for centuries, but they have a lively recollection of the earthquake, and they quake even now as they talk about it. Such as these have need to cry for the indwelling of the Spirit of God, for if he will enter into them his power will soon overcome the tendency to sourness, for "the fruit of the Spirit is love." Spiritual love is nowhere found without the Spirit, and the Spirit is nowhere dwelling in the heart unless love is produced. So much for this jewel!

III. I see in the text a third thing, and that is A PICTURE: a rich and rare picture painted by a Master, the great designer of all things beautiful, the divine Spirit of God. What doth he say? He saith, "The fruit of the Spirit is love." We have seen many fine fruit pictures; and here is one. The great artist has sketched fruit which never grows in the gardens of earth till they are planted by the Lord from heaven. Oh, that every one of us might have a vineyard in his bosom, and yield abundance of that love which is "the fruit of the Spirit."

What does this mean? "Fruit," how is love a fruit? The metaphor shows that love is a thing which comes out of life. You cannot fetch fruit out of a dead post. The pillars which support these galleries have never yielded any fruit, and they never will; they are of hard iron, and no life-sap circulates within them. A dead tree bringeth forth no fruit. God implants a spiritual life in men, and then out of that life comes love, as the fruit of the Spirit.

Love appears as a growth. Fruit does not start from the tree perfectly ripe at once: first comes a flower; then a tiny formation which shows that the flower has set; then a berry appears, but it is very sour. You may not gather it. Let it alone a little while, and allow the sun to ripen it. By-and-by it fills out, and there you have the apple in the full proportions of beauty, and with a mellow flavour which delights the taste. Love springs up in the heart, and increases by a sure growth. Love is not produced by casting the mind in the mould of imitation, or by fastening the grace to a man's manner as a thing outside of himself. Little children go to a shop where their little tastes are considered, and they buy sticks upon which cherries have been tied; but everybody knows that they are not the fruit of the sticks, they are merely bound upon them. And so have we known people who have borrowed an affectionate mannerism and a sweet style; but they are not natural to them: they are not true love. What sweet words! What dainty phrases! You go among them and at first you are surprised with their affection, you are a "*dear* sister" or a "*dear* brother," and you hear a "*dear* minister," and you come to the "*dear* Tabernacle," and sing *dear* hymns to those *dear* old tunes. Their talk is so sweet that it is just a little sticky, and you feel like a fly which is being caught in molasses. This is disgusting; it sickens one. Love is a fruit of the Spirit, it is not something assumed by a man, but something growing out of his heart. Some men sugar their conversation very largely with pretentious words because they are aware that the fruit it is made of is unripe and sour. In such a case their sweetness is not affection but affectation. But true love, real love for God and man, comes out of a man because it is in him, wrought within by the operation of the Holy Ghost, whose fruit it is. The outcome of regenerated manhood is that a man lives no longer unto himself but for the good of others.

Fruit again calls for care. If you have a garden you will soon know this. We had a profusion of flowers upon our pear trees this year, and for a few weeks the weather was warm beyond the usual heat of April, but nights of frost followed and cut off nearly all the fruit. Other kinds of fruit which survived the frost are now in danger from the dry weather which has developed an endless variety of insect blight, so that we wonder whether any of it will survive. If we get over this trial and the fruit grows well we shall yet expect to see many apples fall before autumn, because a worm has eaten into their hearts and effectually destroyed them. So is it with Christian life: I have seen a work for the Lord prospering splendidly, like a fruitful vine, when suddenly there has come a frosty night and fond hopes have been nipped: or else new notions, and wild ideas have descended like insect blights and the fruit has been spoiled; or if the work has escaped these causes of damage, some immorality in a leading member, or a quarrelsome spirit, has appeared unawares like a worm in the centre of the apple, and down it has fallen never to flourish again. "The fruit of the Spirit is love." You must take care of your fruit if you wish to have any laid up in store at the end of the year; and so must every Christian be very watchful over the fruit of the Spirit, lest in any way it should be destroyed by the enemy.

Fruit is the reward of the husbandman and the crown and glory of the tree. The Lord crowns the year with his goodness by giving fruit in due season: and truly the holy fruit of love is the reward of Jesus and the honour of his servants.

How sweet is the fruit of the Spirit! I say "fruit" and not fruits, for the text says so. The work of the Spirit is one, whether it be known by the name of love, or joy, or peace, or meekness, or gentleness, or temperance. Moreover, it is constant; the fruit of the Spirit is borne continually in its season. It is reproductive, for the tree multiplies itself by its fruit; and Christianity must be spread by the love and joy and peace of Christians. Let the Spirit of God work in you, dear brethren, and you will be fruitful in every good work, doing the will of the Lord, and you will rear others like you, who shall, when your time is over, occupy your place, and bring forth fruit to the great Husbandman.

IV. Lastly, you see in my text A CROWN. "The fruit of the Spirit is love." Let us make a diadom out of the text, and

lovingly set it upon the head of the Holy Spirit, because he
has produced in the people of God this precious thing which
is called "Love."

How comes heavenly love into such hearts as yours and
mine? It comes, first, because the Holy Ghost has given us a
new nature. There is a new life in us that was not there
when we first came into the world, and that new life lives
and loves. It must love God who has created it, and man who
is made in his image. It cries, "My Father," and the essence
of that word, "My Father," is love.

The Spirit of God has brought us into new relationships.
He has given us the spirit of adoption towards the Father; he
has made us to feel our brotherhood with the saints, and to
know our union with Christ. We are not in our relationships
what we used to be, for we were "heirs of wrath even as
others"; but now we are "heirs of God, joint heirs with Jesus
Christ"; and consequently we cannot help loving, for love
alone could make the new relation to be fully enjoyed.

The blessed Spirit has also brought us under new
obligations. We were bound to love God and serve him as
creatures, but we did not do it: now the Holy Spirit has made
us to feel that we are debtors to infinite love and mercy
through redemption. Every drop of Jesus' blood cries to us to
love; every groan from yonder dark Gethsemane cries love.
The Spirit of God works in us, so that every shiver of yonder
cross moves us to love. The love of Christ constraineth us: we
must love, for the Spirit hath taken of the things of the
loving Christ and hath revealed them unto us.

The Spirit of God has so entered into us that he has caused
love to be our delight. What a pleasure it is when you can
preach a sermon full of love to those to whom you preach it,
or when you can visit the poor, full of love to those you
relieve! To stand in the street corner and tell out of Jesus'
dying love—why, it is no irksome task to the man who does
it lovingly; it is his joy, and his recreation. Holy service in
which the emotion of love is indulged is as pleasant to us as
it is to a bird to fly, or to a fish to swim. Duty is no longer
bondage, but choice; holiness is no longer restraint, but
perfect liberty; and self-sacrifice becomes the very crown of
our ambition, the loftiest height to which our spirit can
aspire. It is the Holy Ghost that does all this.

Now, my dear hearer, have you this love in your heart?
Judge by your relation to God. Do you live without prayer?
Do you very seldom read God's word? Are you getting
indifferent as to whether you go and worship with his
people? Ah, then, be afraid that the love of God is not in you.
But if you feel that everything that has to do with God you
love—his work, his service, his people, his day, his book—
and that you do all that in you lies to spread his kingdom,
both by prayer, by word of mouth, by your liberality, and by
your example; if you do love you can easily see it, I think,
and there are many ways by which you can test yourself.

Well, suppose that to be satisfactorily answered, then I
have this further question:—Do you and I,—who can say,
"Lord, thou knowest that I love thee,"—do we sufficiently
bless the Holy Spirit for giving us this jewel of love? If you
love Christ, then say, "This love is given to me, it is a rare
plant, an exotic, it never sprang out of my natural heart.
Weeds will grow apace there, but not this fair flower." Bless
the Holy Spirit for it. "Oh, but I do not love God as I ought!"
No, brother, I know you do not, but bless him that you love
him at all. Love God for the very fact that he has led you to
love him; and that is the way to love him more. Love God for
letting you love him. Love him for taking away the stone out
of your heart, and giving you a heart of flesh. For the little
grace that you see in your soul, thank God. You know when
a man has been ill, the doctor says to him, "You are not well
by a long way, but I hope you are on the turn." "Yes," says
the man, "I feel very ill; but still I think I am a little better:
the fever is less, and the swelling is going down." He
mentions some little symptom, and the doctor is pleased,
because he knows that it indicates much: the disease is past
the crisis. Bless God for a little grace! Blame yourself that
you have not more grace, but praise him to think you have
any. Time was when I would have given my eyes and ears to
be able to say, "I do love God;" and now that I do love him, I
would give my eyes and ears to love him more. I would give
all I have to get more love into my soul; but I am grateful to
think I have a measure of true love and I feel its power. Do
be grateful to the Holy Ghost. Worship and adore him
specially and peculiarly. You say, "Why specially and peculiarly?" I answer—Because he is so much forgotten. Some

people hardly know whether there be any Holy Ghost. Let the Father and the Son be equally adored; but be careful in reference to the Holy Spirit, for the failure of the church towards the Holy Trinity lies mainly in a forgetfulness of the gracious work of the Holy Spirit. Therefore I press this upon you, and I beg you to laud and magnify the Holy Ghost, and sedulously walk in all affectionate gratitude towards him all your days. As your love increases, let your worship of the Holy Spirit become daily more and more conspicuous, because love is *his* fruit although it be *your* vital principle. To the God of love I commend you all. Amen.

5

The Heavenly Wind

"The wind bloweth where it listeth, and thou hearest the sound thereof, but canst not tell whence it cometh, and whither it goeth: so is every one that is born of the Spirit."   John 3:8

The Holy Spirit is to be admired, not only for the great truths which he teaches us in Holy Scripture, but also for the wonderful manner in which those truths are balanced. The word of God never gives us too much of one thing or too little of another: it never carries a doctrine to an extreme, but tempers it with its corresponding doctrine. Truth seems to run at least in two parallel lines, if not in three, and when the Holy Spirit sets before us one line he wisely points out to us the other. The truth of divine sovereignty is qualified by human responsibility, and the teaching of abounding grace is seasoned by a remembrance of unflinching justice. Scripture gives us as it were the acid and the alkali; the rock and the oil which flows from it; the sword which cuts and the balm which heals. As our Lord sent forth his evangelists two and two so doth he seem to send out his truths two and two, that each may help the other, for the blessing of those who hear them. Now in this most notable third of John you have two truths taught as plainly as if they were written with a sunbeam, and taught side by side. The one is the necessity of faith in the Lord Jesus Christ, and the fact that whosoever believeth in him is not condemned. This is a vital doctrine, but there is a possibility of preaching it so baldly and so out of relation to the rest of God's word that men may be led into serious error. Justification by faith is a most precious truth, it is the very pith and heart of the gospel, and yet you can dwell so exclusively upon it that you cause many to forget other important practical and experimental truths, and so do them serious mischief. Salt is good, but it is not all that a man needs to live upon, and even if people are fed on the best of dry bread and nothing else they do not thrive; every part of divine teaching is of practical value and must not be neglected. Hence the Holy Ghost in this chapter lays equal stress upon the necessity of the new birth or the work of the Holy Spirit, and he states it quite as plainly as the other grand truth. See how they blend—"Ye must be born again;" but "whosoever believeth in him shall not perish, but have everlasting life;" "Except a man be born of water and of the Spirit, he cannot enter into the kingdom of God;" but "he that believeth on him is not condemned." Two great truths are written in letters of light over the gate of heaven, as the requisites of all who enter there—*Reconciliation by the blood of Jesus Christ;* and *Regeneration by the work of the Holy Ghost.* We must not put one of these truths before the other, nor allow one to obliterate or hide the other: they are of equal importance, for they are revealed by the same divine Spirit, and are alike needful to eternal salvation. He who cares to preach either of these ought also diligently to teach the other, lest he be found guilty of violating that salutary precept, "What God hath joined together let no man put asunder." Avoid all neglect of faith, and equally shun all undervaluing of the work of the Holy Ghost, so shall you find that narrow channel in which the way of truth doth lie. You must rest in Christ that you may be accepted before God, but the work of the Holy Spirit within you is absolutely needful that you may be able to have communion with the pure and holy God. Faith gives us the rights of the children of God, but the new birth must be experienced that we may have the nature of children: of what use would rights be if we had not the capacity to exercise them?

Now it is of the work of the Spirit of God, and of the man in whom the Spirit of God has worked, that I shall speak this morning, according to the tenor of the text. The text may be read two ways. First, it may evidently refer *to the Holy Spirit himself.* Do you not expect the text to run thus—

"The wind bloweth where it listeth, and thou hearest the
sound thereof, but canst not tell whence it cometh, and
whither it goeth: so also is the Spirit of God"? Is not that the
way in which you naturally expect the sentence to end? Yes,
and I doubt not that such was really the Saviour's meaning;
but frequently according to the New Testament idiom the
truth is not stated as our English modes of speech would
lead us to expect: for instance, "The kingdom of heaven is
like unto a man that sowed good seed in his ground." Now
the kingdom is not like the man, but like the whole trans-
action of the parable in which the man is the principal actor.
"The kingdom of heaven is like unto a merchantman seeking
goodly pearls," but the kingdom is not like the man, but the
comparison runs into all that the man does. So here the Lord
Jesus lays hold of one grand sphere of the Spirit's operations
and puts it down, intending, however, a wider sense. There
are certain readings of our text which would make this more
clear if we could think them allowable, as for instance that
which does not render the Greek word by "wind" at all, but
translates it "spirit," and makes it run, "The Spirit bloweth
where he listeth, and thou hearest the sound thereof." I do
not adopt that reading, but there are several great
authorities in its favour, and this tends to show that our first
head is correct. When we have spoken upon that we will take
the language in its second sense, in reference *to the
regenerate man,* and then we read, "The wind bloweth where
it listeth, and thou hearest the sound thereof, but canst not
tell whence it cometh, and whither it goeth: so is every man
that is born of the Spirit": he himself, like the Spirit of which
he is born, is free, and is mysterious in his ways, but
discerned by the sound of his works and life.

I. Take the text in reference to THE HOLY SPIRIT HIMSELF.
The figure is the wind, and, as most of you know, the
Hebrew word for "wind" and for "spirit" is the same; and it is
interesting to note that the same is true with the Greek word
"pneuma," which signifieth both "breath" and "spirit," so that
the figure which the Saviour used might very naturally grow
out of the word which he employed. The wind is air in
motion, and is, of course, material; but air is apparently
more spiritual than any of the other elements, except fire,
since it is not to be grasped by the hand nor seen with the

eye. It is certain that wind really exists, for we hear the sound thereof and observe its various effects, but it is not to be touched, handled, or gazed upon; men cannot traffic in it, or measure it in scales, or weigh it in balances. We may watch for hours, as we will the clouds as they hasten along like winged fowl, but the wind which driveth them is out of our sight; we observe the waves roused to fury in the tempest, but the breath which so excites them we cannot see. Hence the word becomes all the more excellent a figure of that mighty power, the Holy Ghost, of whose existence no man ever doubts who has come under his influence, but who, nevertheless, is not to be tracked in his movements, nor to be seen as to his divine person; for he is mysterious, incomprehensible, and divine.

The metaphor of the wind cannot fully set forth the Holy Spirit, as you know; and, consequently, many other natural figures are employed, such as fire, dew, water, light, oil, and so on, in order to exhibit all the phases of his influence; but still the wind is a most instructive metaphor as far as it goes, and as we cannot draw forth all its teaching in one sermon let us be content to keep as closely as we can to the text.

First, the wind is a figure of the Holy Ghost in *its free-ness*—"the wind bloweth where it listeth." We speak of the wind as the very image of freedom: we say to those who would enthral us, "go bind the winds," as for ourselves, we claim to be "free as the winds which roam at their own will." No one can fetter the wind. Xerxes threw chains into the Hellespont to bind the sea, but even he was not fool enough to talk of forging fetters for the winds. The breezes are not to be dictated to. Cæsar may decree what he pleases, but the wind will blow in his face if he looks that way. The Pope may command the gale to change its course, but it will blow around the Vatican neither less nor more for the holy father and the cardinals. A conference of plenipotentiaries from all the powers of Europe may sit for a week and resolve unanimously that the east wind shall not blow for the next six months, but it will take no heed of the arrangement, and will cast dust into the counsellors' eyes, and whistle at their wisdom. No proclamation nor purpose under heaven will be able to affect the wind by so much as half a point of the compass. It will blow according to its own sweet will, where it pleases, when it pleases, how it pleases, and as it pleases, for "the wind bloweth where it listeth." So is it, only in a far higher and more emphatic sense, with the Holy Spirit, for he is most free and absolute. Ye know that the wind is in the hand of God, and that he ordaineth every zephyr and each tornado: winds arise and tempests blow by order from the throne supreme; but as for the Holy Spirit, he is God himself, and absolutely free, and worketh according to his own will and pleasure amongst the sons of men. One nation has been visited by the Holy Spirit and not another—who shall tell me why? Why lie yon heathen lands in the dense darkness while on Britain the light is concentrated? Why has the Reformation taken root in England and among the northern nations of Europe, while in Spain and Italy it has left scarce a trace? Why blows the Holy Spirit here and not there? Is it not that he doeth as he wills? "I will have mercy on whom I will have mercy, and I will have compassion on whom I will have compassion" is the declaration of the divine sovereignty, and the Spirit of God in his movements confirmeth it. Among the nations where the Spirit of God is at work how is it that he blesseth one man and not another? How is it that of two men hearing the same sermon, and subject to the same influences at home, one is taken and the other left? Two children nursed at the same breast, and trained by the same parents, grow up to different ends. He who perishes in sin has no one to blame but himself, but he who is saved ascribes it all to grace—why came that grace to him? We never dare to lay the fault of man's not repenting and believing upon God—that resteth with the evil will which refused to obey the gospel; but we dare not ascribe the saving difference in the case of the one who believes to any natural goodness in himself, but we attribute it all to the grace of God, and believe that the Holy Spirit worketh in such to will and to do according to his own good pleasure. But why works he in us? Why in any of the chosen? Ah, why? "The wind bloweth where it listeth."

So, too, is it with the blessing which rests upon ministries. One man winneth souls to God, and as a joyous reaper returneth with full sheaves, but another who goeth forth with strong desires, and seems at least to be as earnest as his fellow, comes home with a scanty handful of ears, which he has painfully gleaned. Why is one man's net full of fish and another's utterly empty? One servant of the Lord seems, whenever he stands up to preach the gospel, to attract men to Jesus as though he had golden chains in his mouth which he did cast about men's hearts to draw them in joyful captivity to his Lord, while another cries in bitterness of soul, "Who hath believed our report?" Truly, "the wind bloweth where it listeth." Ay, and these changes happen to each man severally: one day the preacher shall be all alive, his spirit shall be stirred within him, and he shall speak evidently with the Holy Ghost sent down from heaven; and to-morrow he shall find himself dull and heavy, even to his own consciousness, and even more so to his people's experience, for the power rests not upon him. One day he speaketh like the voice of God, and another day he is but as a reed shaken of the wind. His fat kine of years gone by are devoured by the lean cattle of the present. He has his famine as well as his plenty. You shall see him come forth to-day with the unction of the Lord upon him, and his face shining with the glory of fellowship with the Most High, and to-morrow he shall say, "Look not upon me, for I am black," for the glory shall have departed. We know what it is to come forth like Samson when his locks were shorn; and to shake ourselves as at other times and discover that the Lord is not with us. Why all this? Is it not because "the wind bloweth where it listeth"? The Holy Spirit, for his own wise reasons, puts not forth an equal power upon any man at all times. We cannot control nor command the Spirit of the living God: he is in the highest sense a free agent. "Thy free Spirit" is a name which David gave him, and a most appropriate name it is.

Yet, beloved, do not fall into a misapprehension. The Holy Ghost is absolutely free in his operations, but he is not arbitrary; he doeth as he wills, but his will is infallible wisdom. The wind, though we have no control over it, hath a law of its own, and the Holy Ghost is a law unto himself; he doeth as he wills, but he willeth to do evermore that which is for the best. Moreover, we know with regard to the wind that there are certain places where you will almost always find a breeze: not here, in the teeming city, nor down in the valley shut in by the mountains, nor on yonder steaming marsh; but lift up your eyes to the hills, and mark how the breeze courses along the downs, and sweeps the summits of the mountain ranges. In the morning and the evening, when the inland air is hot as an oven, gentle winds come to and from the sea and fan the fisher's cheek: you may find places where the air seems always stagnant and men's hearts grow heavy amid the feverish calm, but there are elevated hillsides where life is easy, for the air exhilarates by its perpetual freshness. Brethren, among lively saints, in the use of the means of grace, in private prayer, in communion with the Lord, you will find the wind that bloweth where it listeth always in motion.

The wind too hath at least in some lands its times and seasons. We know that at certain times of the year we may expect winds, and if they come not to a day or two, yet, as a rule, the month is stormy; and there are also trade winds, monsoons which blow with remarkable regularity and are counted upon by mariners. And so with the Spirit of God. We know that at certain times he visits the churches, and under certain conditions puts forth his power. If, for instance, there is mighty prayer, you may be sure the Spirit of God is at work; if the people of God meet together and besiege the throne of grace with cries and tears, the spiritual barometer indicates that the blessed wind is rising. Besides, the Holy Spirit has graciously connected himself with two things, truth and prayer. Preach the truth, publish the gospel of Jesus Christ, and it is the habit of the Holy Spirit to make the word quick and powerful to the hearts of men. If we falsify his word, if we keep back part of the truth, if we become unfaithful, we cannot expect the Holy Spirit to bless us; but if our teaching be Christ crucified, lovingly set forth, and if the grace of God in its fulness be really declared, the Holy Spirit will attend the truth and make it the great power of God. I will not say that it is always, and without exception so, but I think exceptions must be rare; almost invariably the Spirit beareth witness with the truth in the conversion of men. So too with prayer, the Holy Spirit is pleased to connect himself with that also, if it be believing prayer. Here the connection is exceedingly intimate, because it is the Spirit of God who himself gives the believing prayer, and it is not only true that the Spirit will be given in answer to prayer, but the Spirit is already given or the believing prayer would never have been offered. The spirit of prayerfulness, the spirit of anxiety for the conversion of men is one of the surest indications that the Holy Spirit is already at work in the minds of his people.

Coming back, however, to the great fact that we cannot command the Holy Spirit, what influence ought that truth to have upon us? Should it not be just this? It should lead us to be very tender and jealous in our conduct towards the Holy Ghost, so that we do not grieve him and cause him to depart from us. Vex not the Spirit. When you enjoy his gracious operations be devoutly grateful, and walk humbly before God, that you may retain them; and when he is at work let not negligence on your part cause you to receive the grace of God in vain. The wind blew, but the sailor was asleep; it was a favourable breeze, but he had cast anchor and his barque moved not. If he had but known it all through the night he would have spread his sail and have made good headway towards his port; but he slumbered, and the blessed wind whistled through the cordage and the ship lay idle at its moorings. Let it not be so with us. Never suffer the Spirit of God to be with us and find us regardless of his presence. In the olden times, when country people depended more than they do now on the use of the windmill to grind their corn, some parishes would be half-starved, when week after week there had been no wind. The miller would look up anxiously, and everybody in the parish would become a watchman for his sails, hoping that they would soon be set in motion. If the breeze stirred at the dead of night, and the miller was sound asleep, somebody or other would run and knock him up. "The wind is blowing, the wind is blowing, grind our corn." So it ought to be whenever the Spirit of God is vigorously working in his church, we should eagerly avail ourselves of his power. We should be so anxious for his divine operations that all should be on the watch, so that if some did not discover it others would, and observant ones would cry, "The Holy Ghost is working with us; let arise and labour more abundantly." Hoist sail when the wind favours; you cannot command it, therefore carefully value it.

But we must pass on. The Holy Spirit is described as being

like the wind as to *his manifestations*. "Thou hearest," says
Jesus, "the sound thereof." It has been suggested, and some
have enlarged upon it, that there are many other manifestations of the presence of wind: you can feel it, you can
see its results upon the trees and the waves, and sometimes
you can be sure that the wind has been at work by the
devastation which it has caused: but in this place our
Saviour was not so much alluding to a great wind as to the
gentler breezes. The Greek word *"pneuma"* is translated
"breath," and can hardly be made to mean a tempest. It was
a gentle wind like a zephyr of which the Lord was here
speaking. The great winds, as I have already said, can be
somewhat calculated upon, but if you sit in the garden in the
cool of the evening it is utterly impossible for you to tell
whence the zephyrs come and where they go; they are so
volatile in their movements and untrackable in their course;
here, there, everywhere the soft breezes of evening steal
among the flowers. Our Lord tells us that such gentle
zephyrs are heard: Nicodemus in the stillness of the night
could hear them. "Thou hearest the sound thereof." The
leaves rustle, and that is all; you hear a gentle movement of
branch and stem, and as it were the tinkling of flower-bells,
and so you discover that the wind is flitting among the beds
and borders. Now, beloved, this shows us that the hearing
ear is intended by God to be the discerner of the Spirit to
men, to the most of men the only discerner that they have.
"Thou hearest the sound thereof." What a wonderful dignity
the Lord has been pleased to put upon this little organ, the
ear. The Romish church gives the preference always to the
eye; her priests are always for astonishing men into grace
with their wonderful performances; but God's way is "Faith
cometh by hearing," and the first detector of the Holy Ghost
is the ear. To some men this is the only revealer of his
mysterious presence, as I have already said: they hear the
sound thereof, that is to say, they hear the gospel preached,
they hear the word of God read. Truth when it is couched in
words is the rustling of the holy wind, it is the footstep of the
Eternal Spirit as mysteriously he passes along a congregation. Oh, what grief it is that some never get any
further than this, but abide where Nicodemus was at the
first: they hear the sound thereof and nothing more. Some of

you are now daily hearing truth which has saved thousands, but it does not save you; you are hearing the very truth which peoples heaven, but yet it leaves you without a hope of eternal life; yet be ye sure of this, the kingdom of God has come nigh unto you. "Thou hearest the sound thereof," and that wind whose whispers you hear is not far off thine own cheek. When thou hearest the rustling amongst the boughs of the trees the breezes are not far to seek, nor is the Spirit of God far away when his sound is heard.

Some hearers, however, go further, for they hear the sound of the Spirit in their consciences and it disturbs them; they would sleep as do others, but as the wind sometimes comes whistling through the keyhole or howls down the chimney and wakes the sluggard, or if the man be lying in a garden asleep the breezes play around his ears and face and startle him, so is it with many unconverted people; they cannot be quiet, for they hear the sound of the Holy Spirit in their consciences, and are troubled and perplexed. There is a revival and they are not saved, but they are startled and alarmed by it; their sister is converted, they are not, but still it comes very near them, and they feel as if an arrow had gone whizzing by their own ear. It is hard living in a careless state in the midst of revival. "Thou hearest the sound thereof." But some of you in your conscience are hearing the sound now in your family circle, from the fact that one after another of your relatives have been brought to know the Lord; you cannot avoid feeling that there is something powerful abroad, though it has not yet exerted its regenerating power upon you.

As for the man who is saved, he hears the Holy Spirit in the most emphatic sense, and with what variety that sound comes to him. At first he heard it as a threatening wind, which bowed him in sadness and seemed to sweep all his hopes to the ground, as the sere leaves of the forest are carried in the autumn's wind. When the Spirit's voice sounded in mine ears at the first it was as a wail of woe, as a wind among the tombs, as a sigh among faded lilies. It seemed as if all my hopes were puffed away like smoke, or as the night mists in the morning breeze; nothing was left me but to mourn my nothingness. Then I heard a sound as of the hot sirocco of the East, as if it issued from a burning oven. You know the text, "The grass withereth and the flower thereof fadeth away, because the Spirit of the Lord bloweth upon it: surely the people is grass." In my soul there had bloomed a fair meadow of golden kingcups and fair flowers of many dainty colours, but the Spirit of God blew thereon and withered it all, and left it as a dry, brown, rusty plain, whereon was neither life nor comeliness. So far the sacred wind destroys that which is evil, but it ends not there, for we thank God we have heard the sound of the Spirit as a quickening wind. The prophet cried, "Come from the four winds, O breath, and breathe upon these slain that they may live"; the wind came and the dead arose an exceeding great army. The like miracle has been wrought on us. The sere bones of our own death have crept together, bone unto his bone, and flesh has come upon them, and now because of the divine breath we have begun to live. Now, also, when the Holy Spirit visits us he renews our life and energy, and we have life more abundantly. The Holy Spirit has since then been to us full often a melting wind, "He causeth his wind to blow and the waters flow." Locked up in the chains of ice all through the winter the waters are still as a stone, but the spring-winds come, the brooklets find liberty and leap away to the rivers, and the rivers flow in all their free force to add their volume to the sea. So hath the Spirit of God oftentimes broken up our frost, and given our spirits joyous liberty. He melts the rocky heart and dissolves the iron spirit, at the sound of his goings men are moved to feeling. We know the sound of this wind also as a diffusive breath, drawing forth and diffusing our slumbering graces. "Awake, O north wind; and come, thou south; blow upon my garden, that the spices thereof may flow out." Oh, what a sweet unloosing of holy gratitude, and love, and hope, and joy has there been in our heart when the Spirit of God has visited us. As sweet essences lie hidden in the flowers, and come not forth until the loving wind doth entice them to fly abroad, so do sweet graces lie within renewed spirits until the Holy Ghost cometh and speaketh to them, and they know his voice and come forth to meet him, and so sweet fragrances are shed abroad.

Yes, my brethren, all this we know, and we have heard the sound of the Holy Spirit in another sense, namely, as going

forth with us to the battle of the Lord. We have heard that
sound of a going in the tops of the mulberry trees which
David heard, and we have bestirred ourselves, and victory
has been ours. If we have not heard that rushing mighty
wind which came at Pentecost, yet have we felt its divine
effect, which ceaseth not, but still bringeth life, power,
energy, and all that is wanted for the conversion of the sons
of men to us who are bidden to go forth and preach the
gospel amongst the nations. In all these respects the Holy
Ghost has manifested himself, as wind does, by his sound.
"Thou hearest the sound thereof." "Their sound went into all
the earth, and their words unto the ends of the world."

A third likeness of the Spirit to the wind is set before us in
the point of *mystery*. "Thou canst not tell whence it cometh
nor whither it goeth." Of the wind we may tell that it comes
from such and such a quarter or point, but you cannot put
your finger on the map and say, "The north wind began in
this region," or "here the west wind was born." Indeed, we
know very little about the winds, their origin, or their laws.
One of the best and most accurate observers of the wind
during thirty years recorded every wind in his region, until
at the end of the term he abandoned the few rules which he
had laid down during the first two or three years, for he
found that no rule held good. No man can say whence the
wind leapeth forth. The heathen dreamed of a certain cave
wherein the winds were enclosed as in a prison, and suffered
to go abroad one by one: it was but a fable; we know not
where the winds first spread their wings, or where they
sleep when all is still. So is it with the Holy Spirit in the
mind of man, his first movements are hidden in mystery.
You know that you are converted, my dear friend, and you
know somewhere about the time, and probably you
remember somewhat as to the means which the Lord used
for your salvation. Those outward circumstances you do
know, but how the Holy Spirit operated upon you you do not
and cannot tell any more than you can tell how swells the
life within the seed until it springs up and becomes the full
corn in the ear, or how the sap in the trees first descendeth
in the winter and afterwards climbeth again in the spring.
There are secrets which nature doth not reveal, and the
work of the Spirit is even more a secret, and assuredly no

man can explain it to his fellow or to himself. Why is it, my friend, that you obtained a blessing under one sermon but not under another, and yet when you spoke to your sister she had been more blessed under the second than the first? The power does not come from the preacher, then, it is clear, and "thou canst not tell whence it cometh." There are times in which you feel not only that you can pray but that you must pray; how came you to be in that state? I know what it is to feel in a very ecstacy of delight in the Lord, for which I can scarcely account, for at another time when I have been engaged in the same work, and I think with the same earnestness, I have not been conscious of any such exceeding delight in God. At one time the heart will be full of penitence as if it would break for sin, and at another season it will overflow with such delight in Christ that the sin seems almost forgotten in the pardoning sacrifice. Why these diverse operations? We know what it is at times to feel such a sense of death upon us as to be earnestly preparing for our last hours; and at another time to be altogether forgetful of death, and to be living, as it were, the immortal life already, raised up together and made to sit together with Christ. But how these various modes and forms and workings of the Spirit come who among us shall tell? Go trace the dewdrops, if ye can, to the womb of the morning, and discover which way went the lightning's flash, or how the thunder rolled along the mountain tops, but ye cannot tell nor can you guess whence cometh the Spirit of God into your souls.

Nor can we tell whither it goeth. Here, again, is another mystery. Oh, it charms me to think that when we let loose the truth in the power of the Spirit we never know where it will fly. A child takes a seed, one of those little downy seeds which has its own parachute to bear it through the air; the little one blows it into the air, but who knows where that downy seed shall settle, and in whose garden it shall grow? Such is truth, even from the mouths of babes and sucklings. Whole continents have been covered with strange flowers simply by the wind wafting foreign seeds thither, and mariners have discovered sunny islets out there in the Southern Sea, where foot of man has never trodden, covered with abundance of vegetation which the wind has by degrees wafted thither. Scatter the truth on all sides, for you cannot tell where the Spirit will carry it. Fling it to the winds, and you shall find it after many days. Scatter the living seed with both hands, send it north, south, east, and west, and God will give it wings.

> "Waft, waft ye winds the story,
>   And you, ye waters roll,
>   Till like a sea of glory,
> It spreads from pole to pole."

I had a letter but the other day when I was sore sick: it was written by a sister in Christ in the very heart of the empire of Brazil. She said that she had met with a copy of my "Morning Readings," and had found thereby the way of peace, and, therefore, she wrote me such a loving, touching letter, that, as I read it, it brought tears to my eyes. There was something more affecting yet, for at the end was written in another hand, some words to the effect that his dear wife who had written the above letter had died soon after finishing it, and with a bleeding heart the lone husband sent it on to me, rejoicing that ever the word came to his wife's soul in the far-off land. Brethren, you do not know where the word will go and the Spirit with it. In Bohemia the papists thought they had stamped out the gospel, and with cruel edicts they kept down all thought of Protestantism, but just lately, since the toleration, the gospel has been preached in that country, and to the surprise of everybody there have come forward men and women from lone cottages in the woods and from different corners of the great cities of Bohemia, bringing with them ancient copies of the word of God, themselves being eager to know the precious truth for which they remember that their fathers died. A truth will go adown the centuries: like the river, it sings

> "Men may come and men may go,
>   But I go on for ever."

"Thou canst not tell whither it goeth," it will travel on till the millennium. Send that saying abroad that the truth cannot die. The persecutor cannot kill it, it is immortal, like the God who sent it forth; the persecutor cannot even stay its course, it is divine. Popery will always be in danger so long as there is one leaf of the Bible upon earth, or one man living who knows the Saviour. Antichrist cannot triumph; the Holy Spirit wars against it with the sword of the word, and thou canst not tell how far into the heart of error any truth may be driven. To the overthrow of falsehood and the death of sin the Spirit speeds on, but thou knowest not how.

"Thou canst not tell whither it goeth" either in any one heart. If you have received the Holy Spirit into your heart, you cannot tell whither he will carry you. I am sure that William Carey, when he gave his young heart to Christ never thought the Spirit of God would carry him to Serampore to preach the gospel to the Hindoos; and when George Whitefield first drank of the life-giving spirit it never occurred to him that the pot-boy at the Bell Inn at Gloucester would thunder the gospel over two continents and turn thousands to Christ. No! You know not to what blessed end this wind will waft you. Commit yourselves to it: be not disobedient to the heavenly vision; be ready to be borne along as the Spirit of God shall help you, even as the dust in the summer's breeze. And O child of God, you do not yourself know to what heights of holiness and degrees of knowledge and ecstacies of enjoyment the Spirit of God will bear you. "Eye hath not seen nor ear heard the things which God hath prepared for them that love him," and though he hath revealed them by his Spirit (for the Spirit searcheth all things, even the deep things of God), yet even to the best taught child of God it is not yet known to the full whither the Spirit of God goeth. "Trust ye in the Lord for ever, for in the Lord Jehovah there is everlasting strength," and he will bear you onward and upward, even to perfection itself, and you shall be with Jesus, where he is, and behold his glory.

II. I have but a few minutes left for my second head, but I do not need many, since I do not wish to say much upon it. The text relates TO THOSE WHO ARE BORN OF THE SPIRIT. "The wind bloweth where it listeth, and thou hearest the sound thereof, but canst not tell whence it cometh, and whither it goeth: so is every one that is born of the Spirit." The birth partakes of the nature of the parent. That which is born of the Spirit is like unto the Spirit of which it is born, even as that which is born of the flesh is flesh, and is similar to the flesh by which it is begotten. The twice-born man is like the Holy Ghost who produced him, and he is like him in

each of the points which we have already dwelt upon. As to
freedom, you may say of him, "He bloweth where he listeth."
The Spirit of God makes the believer a free man, bestows on
him the freedom of his will which he never had before, and
gives him a delightful consciousness of liberty. "If the Son
make you free ye shall he free indeed." I do not affirm that
every spiritual man does as he lists, because, alas, I see
another law in our members warring against the law of our
mind, and bringing us into captivity to the law of sin and
death: but still, "where the Spirit of the Lord is, there is
liberty." Now you can pray, which you could not do before;
now you can praise, though you could not extract a note of
praise from your ungrateful heart before; now you can cry,
"Abba, Father;" now you can draw near to God. You are no
longer under man's control, you blow where you list; you are
not now ruled by priestcraft, nor domineered over by the
opinion of your fellow-man. The Lord has set you free, and
you list to go where God's word bids you go, and you find the
utmost liberty in going that way. Oh, brethren, I cannot tell
you the change which is felt by a regenerate man in the
matter of spiritual liberty. When you were under the
bondage of the law, of custom and of sin, and of fear of death
and dread of hell, you were like a man shut up in one of
those cells in Venice which lie below the level of the water
mark, where the air is foul, and the poor prisoner can only
stir half-a-dozen feet and then walk back again in the
darkness; but when the Spirit of God comes he brings the
soul from darkness into light, from clammy damp into the
open air; he sets before you an open door, he helps you to
run in the ways of God's commands, and as if that were not
enough, he even lends you wings, and bids you mount as the
eagle, for he has set you free.

Again, the man who is born of the Spirit is somewhat
manifested; and is known by his sound. "Thou hearest the
sound thereof." The most ungodly man if he lives near a
Christian will hear the sound of him. The secret life within
will speak; words there will be, for Christians are not dumb,
but actions will speak more loudly still; and even apart from
actions the very spirit and tone of the man who is really
regenerated will speak, and the ungodly man will he
compelled to hear it. "Thou hearest the sound thereof."

And now notice *the mystery* there is about a Christian. Thou knowest nothing, if thou art unregenerate, about the life the believer leads, for he is dead, and his life is hid with Christ in God. Thou knowest not whence he cometh forth in the morning; those beds of spices which have made his garments fragrant thou hast not seen; that weeping in prayer or that rejoicing in fellowship with which he opened the morning thou knowest nothing of, and thou canst not know until thou art thyself born of the Spirit. Neither canst thou tell whither the spiritual man goeth. In the midst of his trouble thou seest him calm; dost thou know where he went to win that rare quietude? In the hour of death thou seest him triumphant; dost thou know where he has been to learn to die so joyously? No, the unregenerate man knows not whither the believer goes. There is a secret place of the Most High, and they shall abide under the shadow of the Almighty who have once learned to enter there, but carnal men come not into this secret chamber. The Christian life is a mystery all through, from its beginning to its end: to the worldling all a mystery, and to the Christian himself a puzzle. He cannot read his own riddle, nor understand himself. This one thing he knoweth, "Whereas I was once blind, now I see"; this also he knoweth, "O Lord, I am thy servant, I am thy servant, and the son of thine handmaid: thou hast loosed my bonds"; this also he knoweth, that when his Lord shall be revealed then will he also shine forth as the sun. The life within him in its coming and going is all a mystery to him, but he blesses God that he has fellowship therein. He goes on his way feeling that though men know not whence he is, nor whither he is going, yet the Lord knows him, and he himself is sure that he is going to his Father and his God. O that every one of you had so delightful a hope. The Lord grant it to you, for Jesus' sake.

6

Intimate Knowledge Of The Holy Spirit

"Even the Spirit of truth; whom the world cannot receive, because it seeth him not, neither knoweth him: but ye know him; for he dwelleth with you, and shall be in you."   John 14:17

The part of the text on which we shall meditate is this:— "The Spirit of truth; ye know him; for he dwelleth with you, and shall be in you." Observe that the Holy Spirit is here called the Spirit of truth. There is much meaning in this expression. He is the teacher of truth, unalloyed truth, practical, divinely effective truth. He never teaches anything but the truth. If it comes from the Spirit of God, we may receive it from him without any hesitation. It is he that takes of the things of Christ, and shows them unto us; and these things are true, and he thus proves himself to be the Spirit of truth. He is the very Spirit and soul of truth, the essence, the life and power of it. Divine truth, when merely heard, takes no effect upon the mind until the Spirit of God enlivens it, and then it becomes a quickening force. He makes the truth itself, in its reality and substance, to enter the soul, and affect the heart. He is the teacher of truth, and he is himself the active power that makes truth to be truth to us in the assurance of our inmost souls.

He is the Spirit of truth in this sense, too, that he works truthfulness in his people. In those with whom the Holy Ghost works effectually "there is no guile"; they are openhearted, honest, sincere, and true; they have an intense affection for the truth, and a zeal for it. They are by his truthful influence preserved from deadly error. If it were possible, false teachers would deceive even the elect; but where the Spirit of God dwells, he detects for us the false from the true, and he gives us the spirit of a sound mind, by which we reject that which is false, and cleave only to that which is revealed of God. In this sense he is the Spirit of truth; and as he works truthfulness in his people, so the work that he does is always true and real work. You may get up an animal excitement, and your converts will, in due time, fail: but the Spirit of God worketh true conversion, sincere repentance, and saving faith, such as no sun of persecution can dry up and wither. He worketh deep conviction of sin, and simple faith in the Lord Jesus; and these things abide in the heart. The new birth, as he works it, is not after the fancied manner of baptismal regeneration, but after an effective spiritual manner, so that a divine life is imparted, and the man becomes a child of God. He produceth real sanctification: not the pretence of perfection, but the reality of holiness. Everything the Spirit of God does is substance, and not shadow. The baseless fabric of a vision is the work of man; but the eternal, abiding, everlasting work of grace is wrought by the Spirit of truth alone.

As he is the Spirit of truth, we may be sure that, whatever he sets his seal upon is true. He will only bear witness to truth; but he will not assist in maintaining error. Mark this word: careful observation will show, that in proportion as the nominal church of the present day has departed from the truth of God, the Spirit of God has departed from her. He can never set his seal to a lie; the testimony of his sacred operation, in "signs following," is borne only to the truth of God. If I preach to you that which is not the Word of the Lord, it will not be followed by the work of the Spirit of truth; there will be no conversions among sinners, and there will be no edification for the people of God. It is by the truth as his instrument that the Spirit of God works; and we must be very careful that we do not bring forth any other instrument. Let us not talk, as some do, as if Scriptural doctrine were of little or no consequence; for where the doctrine is not of God, the Spirit of truth is grieved, and he will depart from such a ministry. Except we keep close to the words of the Lord Jesus, and the revelation of the inspired Book, the

Spirit of truth will show his displeasure by refusing to use
our utterances. In vain your music, your architecture, your
learning, and your "bright services" if the truth be given up.
Farewell to the witness of the Spirit in the hearts of men
when men are taught the inventions of men in the place of
the revelation of God.

If the Holy Spirit is bearing witness in your spirit that you
are the children of God, then you are truly born of God; the
presence of the divine Paraclete is the seal of your adoption.
If he dwells in you, this is the token of your sonship; for he
does not dwell in the unregenerate. If he helps, strengthens,
comforts, guides, illuminates, and sanctifies you, you have a
seal which you need not question, the seal of God upon you,
that you are his chosen, and shall be his in the day when he
makes up his jewels.

This brings me to the doctrine upon which I shall enlarge
this morning. This is *the* distinction between the men of the
world and the disciples of Christ. The world knows nothing
of the Holy Spirit; but the disciples of Christ know him; for
the Lord Jesus saith, "He dwelleth with you, and shall be in
you." There are a great many distinctions in the world of a
religious kind: one man weareth his phylacteries, another is
girt with camel's-hair; one man comes with multiplied
ceremonies, another with none at all. You cannot judge who
are the people of God by these external things. Forms of
church government, and modes of worship, may be important in their own place; but before the Lord the infallible test
is this—Do you bear the fruit of the Spirit of God in you?
Doth he indwell you? "If any man have not the Spirit of
Christ, he is none of his"; but he that hath the Spirit dwelling within his soul, he it is that is a trueborn heir of heaven.

We have raised a solemn question to begin with, have we
not? But, dear friends, I do not desire it to remain a
question. I pray that it may be no question with any one of
you, but that you may know that it is so, and may go on to
enjoy the blessed privilege of being on intimate terms with
the Holy Ghost: "But ye know him; for he dwelleth with you,
and shall be in you."

I. To come close up to my subject, the first head will be
BELIEVERS IN JESUS CHRIST KNOW THE HOLY SPIRIT. They
know him, to begin with, *by believing what has been taught*

them concerning the Comforter by the Lord Jesus Christ.
When Jesus Christ had taught his people concerning the
Holy Spirit, and they had received his teaching, he said, "Ye
know him; for he dwelleth with you, and shall be in you." If
they had refused the sayings of Christ, if they had possessed
no love, if they had not kept his commandments, if they had
arrogantly resolved to find out this mystery for themselves
by their own thinking, apart from the instruction of their
Master, they would not have known the Spirit of God. We
must begin our acquaintance with the Spirit by sitting at the
feet of Jesus, and accepting his testimony as sure.

But, more than this, we know the Holy Spirit *by knowing
our Lord Jesus, and by him knowing the Father.* There is
such an intimate union between the Holy Spirit, the Father,
and the Son, that, to know the Holy Spirit, we must know
the Son of God, and know the Father. If we know the Lord
Jesus, we have the Spirit of God; for by no one else could the
things of Christ be revealed to us. Beginning, then, at the
very beginning, do you know the Lord Jesus Christ? You
know something about him, but do you know *him?* Is he your
near friend, your acquaintance? Are you on personal terms
of fellowship with him? If so, then you see the Father in his
face. Jesus says, "He that hath seen me hath seen the
Father"; and he tells his people, "From henceforth ye know
him, and have seen him." You are, therefore, acquainted
with God the Father through Jesus Christ the Son, and you
have seen the glory of his grace beaming in your Saviour's
face. In this way you have become acquainted with the Holy
Spirit, who is not divided from the Father and the Son. As
you know the Son you know the Father, and in this way you
come to know the Holy Spirit. No man cometh to the Father
but by the Son, and he that cometh to the Father receiveth
of the Spirit.

We know the Holy Spirit, next, *by his operations upon us.*
We not only know about his operations, but we have been
the subjects of them. All those who are true disciples of
Christ have felt a divinely supernatural power working upon
them. First, the Holy Spirit operates to our spiritual quickening. There was a time when we were dead in trespasses
and in sins: holy feeling was unknown to us, and the life of
faith was far from us. At that time we did not desire, nor

even know spiritual things: we were carnally minded, and the carnal mind knoweth not the things which be of God. The Spirit of God came upon us, and we were awakened, aroused, and made to live. Do you remember that? Many of us can distinctly remember when we passed from death unto life. With others the visible life may have been made manifest more gradually, but even in them there was a moment when the vital force entered the soul, and they can now rejoice that they have been quickened who were once spiritually dead. You know the Spirit in measure when he breathes upon your dead heart, and it begins to throb with the heavenly life. In connection with that quickening there was conviction of sin. In what a powerful light does the Holy Spirit set our sin! In my discourses to you about sin I try to show you how heinous it is, and how terrible are its consequences; but when a single beam from the Spirit of truth shines upon sin, it makes it appear "exceeding sinful." I remember how Mr. Bunyan says, when under conviction, "I thought none but the devil himself could equal me for inward wickedness and pollution of mind." When the Spirit of God revealed him to himself, he would have willingly changed places with toads and serpents, for he esteemed the most loathsome objects to be better than himself. This revelation of darkness is the effect of light, the light of the Spirit of God; and when he convinces us of sin we begin to know him.

When, after having convinced us of sin, he leads us to repentance and to faith in Jesus Christ, then, we know him! How many a promise did some of you hear, but you could not receive it! How many a comforting discourse did you listen to, and yet it did not comfort you! but when the Spirit of God came, as in a moment, you saw Jesus as the consolation of Israel, the Friend of sinners, the atoning Sacrifice, the Surety of the covenant of grace, and sweet peace came streaming into your soul! At that time you did not only know that the Holy Spirit leads to Jesus Christ, but you knew that he was leading *you*. In that respect you knew him by an experimental acquaintance, which is the best of knowledge.

Since that time, beloved brethren, we have known the Holy Spirit in many ways: restraining from evil, stimulating to good, instructing, consoling, directing, and enlivening. He has been to us, full oft, the Spirit of reviving; we have grown dull, and cold, and sleepy, till that verse of the hymn has been verified:

"In vain we tune our formal songs,
In vain we strive to rise,
Hosannas languish on our tongues,
And our devotion dies."

But no sooner has the Spirit visited us, than we have felt all alive—bright, cheerful, and intense. Then our whole heart has run in the ways of God's commands, and we have rejoiced in his name. How true is that word, "He restoreth my soul"! Thus have we known the Holy Spirit by his operations within us.

Oftentimes he has acted as an illuminator. A difficult Scripture or mysterious doctrine has been before me: I have looked at the original, and I have examined what the best Biblical students have written upon it; and yet, when I have thus used all the helps within reach, the point has remained in the dark. My best aid has ever been to resort to the great Author of the sacred Word, even the Holy Spirit himself. He can, by blessing the means which we are using, or by directly leading the mind in the right track, put an end to all difficulty. He has the clue of every maze, the solution of every riddle; and, to whom he wills, he can reveal the secret of the Lord. Dear young believers, you who wish to understand the Scriptures, seek this light from above, for this is the true light. Other lights may mislead, but this is clear and sure. To have the Spirit of God lighting up the inner chambers of truth, is a great boon. Truth of the deeper sort is comparable to a cavern, into which we cannot find our way except by a guide and a light. When the Spirit of truth is come, he pours daylight into the darkness, and leads us into all truth. He does not merely show the truth, but he leads us into it, so that we stand within it, and rejoice in the hid treasure which it contains. Then we know him as our sacred illuminator.

I specially note that we also know him as the Comforter. Alas for the disturbance of heart which we receive in the world; perhaps even in the family! Few things, it may be, are as we could wish, and therefore we are oole troubled; but when the Spirit of God comes, peace flows to us like a river, and Jesus breathes on us, and says, "Peace be unto you." Do you know that peace? Many saints of God have enjoyed a heavenly calm upon their sick beds: when pain would else have distracted them, the Spirit of God has rested them in Jesus. I have heard of one saint, near his end, who asked, "Is this dying? Then I should like to keep on dying for ever." He felt so much comfort, such an inbreaking of the floods of joy which the Holy Spirit creates, that death itself had not only lost its sting, but had even become a joy to him. The comforts of the Holy Ghost take bitterness out of wormwood and gall, and the sting out of the last enemy. May God give us to know the Holy Spirit as our Comforter! Happy knowledge!

I trust that we have oftentimes known the Holy Spirit as guiding us in various ways. I will not speak largely on this, for some might not understand it; but I know of a surety that the Holy Spirit does give to his favoured people hints as to things to come. I say not that any man is inspired to tell the future; but I do say that choice saints have received preparations for the future, and foreshadowings of their coming experiences. When believers come into difficult circumstances, they bow the knee, and cry for guidance, even as David said, "Bring hither the ephod." The oracle is not dumb, but in some way, not always to be explained, the Spirit of God guides our steps through life, if we are willing to obey his monitions. Is it not written, "Thine ears shall hear a word behind thee, saying, This is the way, walk ye in it"? The divine communications of the Holy Spirit are the precious heritage of true saints; but they are a peculiar voice to their own souls, and are not to be repeated in words. If you know these divine workings, as I am sure many of you do, then through his operations you are made to know the Holy Spirit. That deep calm; that peace which only he can give; that exhilaration, that superlative joy as of heaven begun below which only the Lord can work; that steadfast courage, that holy patience, that fixedness of heart, that gentleness of manner and firmness of purpose, which come only from above—these all introduce you to the wonder-working Spirit who takes pleasure thus to operate upon the minds of the heirs of eternal glory. Thus we know the Holy Spirit by his works, and gifts, and revelations.

But I do not think we have entered the centre of the text
even yet. "Ye know *him,*" says the text: *ye know not only his
work, but himself.* I may know the great achievements of an
artist in marble, but I may not know the sculptor himself. I
may know a man's paintings, and therefore I may guess
somewhat of his character, but yet I may not know the man
himself. "Ye know him," says our Lord; and truly we know
the Holy Ghost as to his personality. If the Holy Ghost were
a mere influence, we should read, "Ye know *it.*" Let us
always shun the mistake of calling the Holy Ghost "*it.*" *It*
cannot do anything. *It* is a dead thing: the Holy Ghost is a
living, blessed person, and I hope we can say that we know
him as such. Others may doubt his personality; but we
believe in the teaching of our Lord Jesus Christ, and behold,
in the names given to him, the emotions ascribed to him,
and the acts performed by him, abundant proofs of his
sacred personality. In our hearts we know *him.*

As we know his personality, so we know also his divinity,
because the Holy Ghost works in us effects which none but
God could work. Who can give life to the spiritually dead?
Who but the Lord and giver of life? Who can instruct and
illuminate as the Holy Spirit does? Only because he is divine
can he guide us into all truth, and purify us unto perfect
holiness. There have been things wrought in us, in our
experience, in which we have beheld, not only the finger of
God, but God himself working in our hearts to will and to do
of his own good pleasure. Oh, worship the Holy Spirit! The
greatest crime of sinners is to blaspheme the Holy Ghost,
and the greatest fault of saints is to neglect the Holy Ghost.
Let us adore him, yield to him, confide in him, and pray that
we may know him to the full.

So it comes to this, that as we know the Holy Spirit's
personality and Godhead, we have come to know *him.* I
mean this—that there is now a personal intercourse between the believer and the Holy Ghost, a conscious and clear
fellowship and communion. The communion of the Holy
Ghost is one of the three choice blessings of the great
Benediction. Do we not enjoy it? We speak with him, and he
speaks with us. We trust him, and he puts us in trust with
many a precious truth. We are not strangers now; we do not
talk of him as a personage a long way off of whom we have

heard, a divine mystery with which prophets and apostles were acquainted in remote ages; but we know him. Come, let me look into your faces, my beloved in the Lord, and let me ask you, Is this true or not? If you are obliged to say, "We do not know whether there be any Holy Ghost, for we are utter strangers to him," then I pray the Lord to deal graciously with you, and manifest his Son Jesus Christ to you by the power of that same Holy Spirit of whom we speak. The Spirit of truth is to those of us who trust in the Lord Jesus our present help; he is more familiar with us than any other person; for he enters within, where none else find admission. "Ye know him; for he dwelleth with you, and shall be in you." Thus much upon our first head; now I will take you to another, exceedingly important and interesting. May the Holy Ghost help me!

II. The second head is this: BELIEVERS KNOW THE HOLY SPIRIT THROUGH HIMSELF. Let us read the text again: "Ye know him; for he dwelleth with you, and shall be in you." It is not, "Ye know him; for ye have heard gracious preaching;" nor, "Ye know him; for ye have read about him in the Scriptures." No—"Ye know him; for he dwelleth with you, and shall be in you." The moon cannot help us to see the sun, nor can man reveal God. God can only be seen in his own light. No one can reveal the Holy Spirit but the Holy Spirit. I thought this morning, coming along—I have to preach about the Holy Spirit; but what can I do without the Holy Spirit himself? I can only preach aright concerning him by his own presence with me; and if he be not there, I shall only darken counsel by words without knowledge. Why is it that we know the Holy Ghost only by the Holy Ghost?

I answer, first, on account of *the inadequacy of all means.* By what methods can you make a man know the Holy Ghost? He is not to be discerned by the senses, nor perceived by eyes or ears. What if the preacher should be as eloquent as an angel, in what way would that make you know the Holy Ghost? You would probably remember more of the man than of his subject. Nothing is more to be deplored than a hungering after mere oratory. It would be infinitely better to speak stammeringly the truth than to pour forth a flood of words in which the truth is drowned. Words are nothing but air and wind, and they cannot possibly reveal the Holy

Spirit. No outward ordinances can reach the point any more than human speech. We greatly rejoice in the baptism of believers, and in the breaking of bread, in which the death of the Lord Jesus is set forth before us; but in what symbol could we fully see the Holy Spirit? If he were even to descend upon us as a dove, we should see the visible shape, but we should not necessarily discern the Spirit. The Spirit himself must reveal himself. Beloved, there is no chariot in which God can ride to us: the axles of creation itself would break beneath the enormous load of Deity. It is not possible for God to reveal himself fully by his works: he is seen only by himself. Hence the Son of God himself has come to us as "God with us." In him we see God. The Holy Spirit must himself come into the heart to which he would make himself known.

This is even more clear from *the inability of our nature to discover the Holy Spirit.* We are dead by nature, and how can we know anything until he makes us alive? Our eyes are spiritually blinded: how can we see him until he opens our eyes? We are altogether without strength by nature: how can we run after him until he first comes to us and gives us the power to do so? We are unable to perceive the Holy Spirit; for the carnal man knoweth not the things which are of God, for they are spiritual, and must be spiritually discerned. We must be endowed with a spirit before we can discern the great Spirit. Flesh cannot transform itself into spirit. No, it is the Lord himself who must come and breathe into us the Spirit of life, and then we perceive him who is the Spirit of truth.

The Holy Spirit must reveal himself to us if we are to know him: this is clear *from the nature of the case.* How do I know a man but by the man himself appearing to me, and speaking to me, and manifesting himself to me? You cannot with accuracy judge a man by his writings. It is a curious circumstance, that Mr. Toplady, who wrote very bitterly on behalf of truth, was, in temper, the sweetest of men. On the other hand, Mr. Romaine, of Blackfriars, who, in his writings, seems to be the gentlest of beings, was by no means free from harshness. You must see a man, nay, more, you must live with a man in order to know him. You must live with the Holy Spirit, and he must dwell with you, and be in you, before you can speak of knowing him at all.

The facts of the case prove this. I shall put it to any believer here who can humbly say, "I know him; for he dwelleth with me, and is in me." How do you know the Holy Ghost but by the Holy Ghost? Did you learn your religion of me? Then you have it all to unlearn. Did you learn it out of a book? You have need to begin again. Did you inherit it from your parents, or borrow it from your friends? Then you are still ignorant of the vital point. God is only known through himself; the Holy Spirit by the Holy Spirit. Have you not found it so in your own case? Why, you have sat and heard a sermon which was in itself cheering, comforting, and quickening; for your neighbour said, "What a happy time we have enjoyed!" Alas! you thought you had never felt more stupid and lifeless. Have you not gone down the Tabernacle steps, and said to yourself, "I am as hard as stone, and as cold as a winter's fog? What shall I do?" Thus are you without the Spirit of God; but when the divine Spirit comes upon you, such complaints are at an end; then doth the lame man leap as an hart, and the tongue of the dumb is made to sing. Then are you full of living joy in listening to the gospel; every word you hear seems to be on wheels; and towards you the cherubim fly swiftly, bringing live coals from off the altar.

III. My third head is, BELIEVERS ENJOY A SACRED INTIMACY WITH THE SPIRIT OF GOD. I am not going to withdraw that word intimacy. It is warranted by the language of our Lord; for he says, "Ye know him; for he dwelleth with you, and shall be in you."

First, he says, *"He dwelleth with you."* Is not that a wonderful sentence? The Holy Ghost is God, and therefore the heaven of heavens cannot contain him, and yet behold the condescending fact! "He dwelleth with you." The Holy Spirit is now upon earth, the vicar and representative of the Lord Jesus Christ, who said, "I will send you another Comforter"—that is, another Helper and Advocate, like himself. Consider how our Lord dwelt with his disciples; for after the same fashion the Spirit of truth dwells with us. Jesus permitted to his disciples the most intimate intercourse with himself: they ran to him with their troubles, they told him their difficulties, they confessed their doubts. He was their master and Lord, and yet he washed

their feet. He ate and drank with them, and permitted the
freest intercourse. You never find our Lord repelling their
approaches, or resenting their familiarities. He did not draw
a ring round himself and say, "Keep your distance." Now, in
the same manner, the Spirit of truth deals with believers.
"He dwelleth with you." You may go to him at any time, you
may ask what you will of him, you may speak to him as a
man speaketh with his friend. You cannot see him, but he
sees you, which is much better; you cannot hear his voice,
but he hears your voice, nay, he hears your thoughts without
a voice. He is most near to those who are in Christ. "He
dwelleth with you."

Dwelling with us, he is in our assemblies. It is he who fulfils the promise of our Lord, "Lo, I am with you alway, even
unto the end of the world." It is by the Holy Spirit that the
Lord Jesus is with us: that we might enjoy that sacred
presence, it was expedient for our Lord to go away. Beloved,
what a mercy it is when the Holy Ghost is in our assembly!
What a dreary business it is when the Holy Ghost is gone
from the congregation! The people come and go, and perhaps
there may be fine music, splendid millinery, admirable
eloquence, a vast crowd, or a wealthy congregation. But
what of these things? They are a bag of wind! If the Holy
Spirit is not in the congregation, it is gathered together in
vain. Behold, the people spend themselves for very vanity if
the Lord is not among them. But the Comforter does come
into our assemblies; for it is written, "He dwelleth with you."

He also comes into our homes—"He dwelleth with you."
Where do you dwell, O true believer? Is it in a very poor
lodging? "He dwelleth with you." It may be, dear friend, you
live on board ship, and are tossed upon the sea; but "He
dwelleth with you." Perhaps you go to work in a mine, far
beneath the surface of the earth; still, "He dwelleth with
you." Many choice saints are bed-ridden, but the Spirit
dwells with them. I commend to all of you who love the Lord
these gracious words: "He dwelleth with you." The first
disciples said to the Lord Jesus, "Master, where dwellest
thou?" He answered, "Come and see." So do I bid you note
where the divine Spirit deigns to dwell. Behold and wonder:
he dwells with his people wherever they are; he does not
leave them alone, but he abides with them as a shepherd

with his flock.

Well may we know him, for he takes up his abode with us; and he does this, not as a latent, inoperative influence, but he works in the place where he dwells. He makes our members instruments of his working, and sanctifies the faculties of our nature as vessels of a temple wherein he dwells. He perfumes every chamber of the house of man-hood, and consecrates every corner of our being. O believer, "He dwelleth with you" in all the might of his Godhead, and you are made strong in the inner man by his strengthening. Fall back upon the Holy Ghost in the moment of your weakness. Alas, my brethren! are there any moments when we are not weak? Fall back, therefore, upon the Holy Spirit at all times. Even in the prayer in which you seek strength, ask that the Spirit may help your infirmities. Even for the faith which brings you all grace, ask for the Spirit of God to work faith in you. "He dwelleth with you," for you are unable to live without his constant presence, and you need not attempt the perilous experiment.

The second sentence runs, *"He shall be in you."* This is a greater marvel. "Know ye not that your bodies are the temples of the Holy Ghost?" Take care of them; never defile them; let not the idea of drunkenness, gluttony, or lust, come near you; for it is written, "If any man defile the temple of God, him shall God destroy." With what reverence should we look upon the body, now that it has been redeemed by the Lord Jesus, and is indwelt by the Holy Spirit! The Spirit also dwells within your minds. We possess him, and he possesses us. "He shall be in you," as a king in his palace, or a soul in its body. I am afraid that many professors know nothing about this. I must be talking nonsense in the esteem of some of you: if it seems nonsense, let that fact condemn you. You cannot be right before God unless the Spirit of God be in you, in your mind, your heart, your desires, your fears, your hopes, your inmost life. The Spirit must permeate your entire being, filling it full with his floods, even as the waters cover the channels of the deep. "He shall be in you." It is a wonderful fact, but believers realize it. The Spirit shall be in you as the source of your life, and the force of your life. What cannot a man do when the Holy Spirit is in him? His weakest endeavour will prosper when the Holy Spirit is pouring his

life into him; for he shall be like a tree planted by the rivers
of water, that bringeth forth his fruit in his season; his leaf
also shall not wither; and whatsoever he doeth shall prosper. But, without the Holy Spirit, what barren and withered
trees we are! May we never know the awful drought which
comes of the absence of the Spirit!

Brethren, when our Lord Jesus Christ came upon the
earth, and was beheld as God in human flesh, that was to us
the pledge of the indwelling of the Holy Ghost in us: for, as
God dwelt in the human person of the Lord Jesus Christ,
even so doth the Spirit abide in our humanity. Our Lord's
life on earth was *the picture* of the Spirit's indwelling. As he
was anointed of the Spirit, even so are we in our measure.
"He went about doing good." He lived consecrated to God,
loving the sons of men; and thus will the Spirit of God within
us cause us to live: we shall imitate the Christ of God
through the Spirit of God. The death of Christ was *the way*
by which the Spirit was enabled to come to sinful men. By
his great sacrifice the stone is rolled away which once
blocked the road.

> "'Tis through the purchase of his death,
> Who hung upon the tree,
> The Spirit is sent down to breathe
> On such dry bones as we."

When our Lord rose from the dead we had *the guarantee*
that even so the Spirit of God would quicken our mortal
bodies, and renew us into newness of life. But it was when
our Lord ascended up on high, leading captivity captive, that
the Holy Spirit was, *to the full, actually given.* When our
Redeemer returned to his Father's throne, he scattered the
largess of heaven: he gave the Holy Spirit to men of various
offices, and to his whole church; then were the days of
refreshing by divine visitation. Your ascended Lord gives
you this token of his love—the indwelling of the Holy Ghost
in you: prize it above all things. Do you know it? It seems
like an impertinence for me to put this question to some of
you, who are grey-headed, and yet there is need. I trust you
knew the Holy Spirit before I was born; but yet I cannot help
pressing the enquiry, for you may not know him even now. I
have urged the question upon myself, and therefore I urge it

upon you. Does the Spirit of truth dwell in you? If not, what will you do?

IV. I come to a conclusion with one more observation. BELIEVERS SHALL HAVE A CONTINUANCE AND AN INCREASE OF THE SPIRIT'S INTIMACY. "He dwelleth with you, and shall be in you."

Mark well the increase. Is it not a blessed step from *with* to *in?* "He dwelleth with you"—that is, a friend in the same house; "and shall be in you," that is, a spirit within yourself; this is nearer, dearer, more mysterious, and more effective by far. The bread yonder is *"with"* me. I eat it, and now it is *"in"* me. It could not nourish me until it advanced from "with" to "in." What a distinct advance it is for the child of God when he rises from the Spirit of God being *with* him to the Spirit of God being *in* him! When the Spirit of God helped the apostles to work miracles, he was *with* them; but when they came to feel his spiritual work in their own souls, and to rejoice in the comfort which he brought to them, then he was *in* them. Even if you could obtain miraculous gifts, you ought not to be satisfied to speak with tongues, nor to work miracles; but you should press on to know the Spirit with yourself—indwelling, communing, quickening you.

"He shall be in you." Notice, that in consequence of this, we know him. If a person dwells with us, we begin to know him; but if he dwells within us, and has become intertwined with our being, then we know him indeed. "He shall be in you" is a high degree of intimacy.

As we have noticed the increase, so remark the continuance: "He *shall be* in you." There is no period in which the Holy Spirit will have finished his work so as to go away and leave the believer to himself. Our Saviour says of the Comforter, that he "shall abide with you for ever." Grieve not the Spirit of God, I pray you; quench him not, resist him not, but carefully cherish in your hearts this divine word, "He shall be in you." What comfort is here! You dread the days of age and infirmity, but "He shall be in you." You tremble before that trial which threatens you, but "He shall be in you." You do not know how you will answer the gainsayer: take no thought what you shall speak, it shall be given you in the self-same hour what you shall speak, for he shall be in you. And when the last moment approaches, when you must breathe out your soul to God, the living Spirit who dwelleth with you, even as the nurse sitteth at your bedside, shall then be *in* you, and by his living power within shall transform death into the gate of endless life. "He dwelleth with you, and shall be in you." O child of God, your Comforter will not leave you; he will continue still to take up his residence within you until you shall be taken up to dwell where Jesus is for ever and ever.

This is our great reliance for the future upholding of the church as a whole, and of each individual believer: the Spirit of God dwelleth with us, and shall be in us. The church of God will never be destroyed; the gates of hell shall not prevail against her; for the Holy Ghost dwelleth with us, and shall be in us to the end of the world. This is the reliance of the child of God personally for his perseverance in grace. He knows that Jesus lives, and therefore he shall live; and the Holy Spirit is within him, as the life of Christ, which can never die. The believer pushes on, despite a thousand obstacles, knowing that God gives him the victory, through the Lord Jesus Christ, out of whose hand none can pluck him.

I have done; and yet I have done nothing unless the Spirit of God shall bless the word spoken. Oh, that some of you, who have never known the Spirit of God, may feel his power coming upon you at this moment! You may be sitting in the pew very careless even now, and yet before you leave he may descend, and soften your hard heart. The other day the ground was hard as iron, and the water was turned to ice; but there came a breath from the south, and soon a thaw set in, the snow vanished, and the ice was gone: even so the Holy Spirit breathes on us, and our inward frost disappears at once. Come, Holy Spirit. Come even now. Let us implore his presence and power. Pray for a closer, clearer knowledge of him, O ye children of God. Pray also that sinners may be met with by his grace. The first token of the Spirit's work will be that they will begin to feel their sin, and cry for mercy; and when that is done, the glad tidings of pardon are for them. To them we say, "Believe on the Lord Jesus Christ, and thou shalt be saved, and thy house." The Lord make the word effectual, for Jesus Christ's sake. Amen

7

Filled With The Spirit, And Drunkenness With Wine

"And be not drunk with wine, wherein is excess; but be filled with the Spirit." Ephesians 5:18

While I was reading to you just now, in the fourth and fifth chapters of Paul's letter to the Ephesian believers, I could not help feeling that you could little understand the elevation and the purity of the precepts of the apostle, as they must have appeared to the inhabitants of such a wicked city as Ephesus. When first read, these precepts must have seemed like an unearthly light. We have now a public sentiment which condemns drunkenness, lying, and many other vices, which were scarcely considered worthy of censure by that degraded people. Christianity had not affected public sentiment at the time: that sentiment was distinctly immoral. The sin of fornication was scarcely judged to be sinful; theft was most common, as, indeed, it is in the East to this day; lying was universal, and only blamed if committed so clumsily as to be found out. I may say of drunkenness, that, although it was not regarded as a commendable thing, yet it was looked upon as a failing of great minds, not to be too much condemned. Alexander the Great, as you know, died through drink. He offered a prize on one occasion to those who could drink the most, and in that famous drinking-bout, large numbers of his chieftains and nobility died in the attempt to rival others. Even of such a man as Socrates it is said (though I know not with what truth) that he was famous for the quantity that he could drink. The stories of the feasts of that age I would be ashamed to repeat; and you certainly would not have the patience to hear them. Drunkenness, and gluttony, and such like, were the common faults both of the great and of the small; for while some had no opportunity for gluttony, for they did not get enough to eat, they only failed to be gluttons for that reason, and not from principle. The apostle sets before his new converts, not a modified system of right and wrong, but the purest virtues and the most heavenly graces. As the ages have rolled on, we have seen the wisdom of holding up from the first an elevated standard, both of doctrine and practice. We must not bring the standard down to the men, but the men up to the standard. We may not, with the design of making converts more rapidly, alter the pure Word with which our Lord has entrusted us.

Brethren, I am not going to speak to you to-night about the sin of drunkenness. Many of you feel an intense aversion to that degrading vice. If there are any here who require a homily upon drunkenness, they have only to let conscience speak, and it will tell them how base a sin it is. If they do not know the shamefulness of their wicked habit, there are plenty round about them who will let them know in indignant language. Perhaps of all the sins that are rife in our country to-day, drunkenness brings the most present misery upon mankind. A very large proportion of the want from which people suffer is due to wasteful excess in drink. You know it is so, if you are intelligent observers. Other sins may seem to go deeper into the soul, and are more subject to punishment by law; but for creating widespread suffering, suffering brought upon the innocent, upon the wife, and upon the child, this vice raises its head above all others. This throngs our workhouses, fills our jails, and crowds our lunatic asylums; ay, and fats our cemeteries with carcases of men and women who die before their time. This is the Moloch of the nineteenth century. I am not going to preach about that one particular vice to-night, as though I would saw off a big limb from the tree of evil. It is my custom to lay the axe at the root of the tree, aiming my blows at the very nature which bears this evil branch. Still, this is a very farspreading bough; and, as I have seen the woodmen

lopping the tree before they cut it down, there will be no
waste of time if I aim a blow or two at this huge branch of
the tree of evil, this bough of drunkenness. It is far too
common to this day; but, thank God, through the efforts of
temperance friends, and, I hope, through the power of the
Spirit of God upon many, it is not as it used to be; and it is
regarded now in a very different light from that in which it
was viewed even by Christian people years ago.

The apostle has been pleased, in this passage, guided by
the Holy Spirit, to put in apposition, and, in some respects,
in opposition, a prohibition and a command: *"Be not drunk
with wine,* wherein is excess, but *be filled with the Spirit."*
He had a reason for putting these two things together. There
is a very, very, very wide and deep abyss between being
drunk with wine and being filled with the Spirit. Drunkenness is down, down, down to the depths of the brute, and far
lower still; fulness with the Spirit is up, up, up, to the very
heights of God. However did it happen that in the *same*
verse, without a break, Paul should put the two together—
the prohibition and the command? There was a reason, and
a very good reason, for this conjunction of things so far apart
in character. I think that I see two reasons. The first is
because *there is a parallel between them*—a degree of similarity amid their infinite difference. Secondly, he so placed
them because *there is a contrast between them* of a very
striking kind. The contrast is as instructive as the parallel.
"Be not drunk with wine"; but hasten to the very opposite
extreme, and "Be filled with the Spirit."

I. First, LET ME DRAW THE PARALLEL. Why do men become
drunk with wine, or other alcoholic liquors? There are
several reasons. I shall not mention them all, for they are
innumerable, and many of them too ridiculous to be
mentioned in a sermon.

One motive is *to find in wine an exhilaration.* It is a feast-
day; let us have wine, that we may warm our hearts, and
laugh, and sing, and make merry. It is a marriage-day; it is
a birthday; it is a royal holiday; it is something out of the
common; bring forth the winecup! So say the sons of men.
When the man has drunk what he ought to think enough,
feeling already a little elevated, he must drink yet more,
with the same view. He would rise higher, and higher, and

higher, and be filled with glee, and jollity, and make uproar-
ious laughter, and be lord of misrule for the day. Strong
drink is taken to exhilarate; and for a while it has that
effect. How some men are carried away when intoxicated!
How lifted up they are! What a great man the least becomes!
What a divine the man who never looked into his Bible!
What a philosopher the boor that does not know his letters!
What a lord of creation the loon who has not two shirts!
What a hero, every way, the coward who is afraid of his
shadow! He is exhilarated when he has taken wine.

I grant you, that it is natural that we should all wish to be
somewhat exhilarated. We like to have stirring times, in
which we do not lie still and stagnant: we would have our
whole nature stirred with pleasure. We like to have our
high-days and holidays, even as others. "Now," says the
apostle, "that you may enjoy the most exquisite exhilaration,
be filled with the Spirit." When the Spirit of God comes into
a man with extraordinary power, so as to fill his soul, he
brings to his soul a joy, a delight, an elevation of mind, a
delightful and healthful excitement, which lifts him up
above the dull dead-level of ordinary life, and causes him to
rejoice with joy unspeakable and full of glory.

This is safe delight, and hence I commend it to you. It is
safe delight, because it is holy delight; holy delight, because
it is the Holy Spirit that works it in you, and he makes you
to delight in everything that is pleasing to the Holy God.
Seek no longer the excitement which comes from the
flowing-bowl; for here is for you something more safe, more
suitable, more sacred, more ennobling: "Be filled with the
Spirit." I know there are some Christians who never have
much joy. You remember one, an old acquaintance of yours,
the elder brother. His experience was expressed to his father
in grumbling tones: "Lo, these many years do I serve thee,
neither transgressed I at any time thy commandment: and
yet thou never gavest me a kid, that I might make merry
with my friends." Far too many Christians are of that order.
Hear what they say: "I have always been regular in my
attendance on the means of grace, have read my Bible, have
acted consistently with my profession; yet I know nothing of
delight in God." Now, my dear friend, take this advice, "Be
filled with the Spirit." You have, as yet, received only a few

drops from the divine shower of his sacred influences. Ask for the rivers, the floods, the torrents of his sacred power. Let the heavenly floods come in and fill you up to the brim, and then will you have a joy which shall rival the bliss of those who are before the throne of God.

Furthermore, I have known people take wine with the idea of being *strengthened* thereby. There are such individuals still alive in the light of this advanced century. Many of the best physicians tell us that there is no strength whatever in strong drink. At any rate, whatever strength there is in the drink, it does not give any strength to the man. I am not going into physical or metaphysical discussions to-night. There is no doubt that many indulge in wine to an extreme, with the object of getting strength thereby. I believe their action to be founded on a very grave mistake. But to you Christian people instruction comes in here. "Be not drunk with wine," with the view of gaining strength thereby; "but be filled with the Spirit," for the Spirit of God can give you strength to *the* highest degree. He can gird you with spiritual strength—the strength of faith; and there is no strength like it; for all things are possible to him that believeth. He can give you the strength that wrestles in prayer, that lays hold upon the angel of the covenant, and will not let him go, except he grant a blessing. The Spirit of God gives the strength to suffer and the strength to labour; the strength to receive and the strength to give out again; the strength to hope, the strength to love, the strength to conquer temptation, the strength to perform holy action. When you are filled with the Spirit, how strong you are! There is no influence about us for good when the Holy Spirit has departed. But when a man gets the Spirit of God to fill him to the full, his presence has a mystic power about it:—

"'Tis e'en as if an angel shook his wings."

Though such a man tarrieth but for a short time in a place, he leaves a savour behind him that will not be forgotten. Dear brothers and sisters, whether you are preachers, or teachers, or parents, or persons engaged in the service of God in your ordinary labour, if you want strength with which to bring glory to the Most High, be ye filled with the Spirit. Oh, that we had in our midst many that were strong because of this!

In the next place, wine has been taken by a great many, and taken to excess, to *embolden* them; and it does embolden them to a very high degree. A man under the influence of liquor will do what he would never think of doing at any other time: he will be rash, fool-hardy, and daring to the last degree. We have heard of foreign nations whose troops have been so afraid of the fight that they have dosed them with strong drink to induce them to march into the battle. We used to hear the expression, "Dutch courage," which meant the boldness which came of ardent spirits; though I do not suppose the Dutch had more of it than the English. No doubt many a man under the influence of drink has risked his life, and performed what looked like feats of valour, when, indeed, he was simply beyond himself, and out of his right mind, or he would not have been so foolhardy. Wine does embolden many men in a wrong way. Beloved friends, we are not to make ourselves ridiculous with fanaticism; but bold with the spirit of truth. "Be not drunk with wine, wherein is riot," in order to be emboldened to do anything; but be ye filled with the Spirit of the living God, wherein is quietness, and whereof cometh a courage which is to be admired, and not derided. Oh, how brave a man is when he is filled with the Spirit of God! Then, knowing a thing to be right, he resolves to do it, and he never counts the cost. He has counted that cost long ago, and reckoned that the light suffering that would come by doing right was no longer worthy to be compared with the glory of being found a faithful servant of God. When a man has little of the Spirit of God he begins calculating the pence. "Will it pay? The thing is right enough," he says, "but then I cannot afford it. I know that what I am doing is wrong; but, still, I could not give it up. It would involve too much sacrifice." That man has little, if any, of the Spirit of God; for the Spirit destroys selfishness, and all that love of gain which eats as doth a canker. A man in whom the Spirit of God dwells abundantly says, "I shall never think, from this day forth, what may be to me the consequences of any course of action which the Lord my God commands me to follow. If it is right in the sight of God, I will do it. If God approves it, so shall it be; but if it be wrong, not a world made of gold, if it could all be

mine, should tempt me to parley for a moment." Be ye filled
with the Spirit. It will make you bold in the cause of the Lord
Jesus. How bold the martyrs were! How bravely humble
women were wont to speak up for Christ! How slaves,
peasants, persons of no education, faced the Roman governors—ay, stood before the Roman Emperor himself, and
were not in the least afraid! When they cried, "To the lions
with them!" they flinched not from so cruel an end. They
were a brave people, those early Christians, for they were
filled with the Spirit. And our men and women in England,
in the days of Mary, how bold they were when filled with the
Spirit! The Holy Spirit is the creator of heroes. If the Spirit
of God be gone, we are a cowardly set; but if the Spirit of God
shall come down upon us, as I hope he may, then every man
and woman here, however timid by nature, will be able to
bear witness for Christ, according as Christ shall call him to
that work. O my beloved, for whom I long and pray that you
may be an army for the Lord, "Be filled with the Spirit."

Wine has been also taken in large quantities, for *the destruction of pain,* for the drowning of misery, for support in
the agony of a cruel death. Solomon says, "Give strong drink
unto him that is ready to perish, and wine unto those that be
of heavy hearts. Let him drink, and forget his poverty, and
remember his misery no more." It was an old custom, that
when a man was doomed, and about to die, they gave him
some narcotic cup that he might be somewhat stupefied and
suffer the less. There was some mercy in this; though truly,
"the tender mercies of the wicked are cruel." No doubt many
persons have most foolishly taken to drink in order to forget
their grief and assuage their sorrow. We must earnestly
condemn such wicked conduct; but still, so it is; and the
apostle puts it, "Be not drunk with wine, wherein is excess;
but be filled with the Spirit"; for that will remove depression
and sustain under anguish in a most wonderful way; indeed,
in a holy and perfect way. If you want to forget your misery,
remember to apply for a sweet visitation of the Comforter. If
there has lately happened some great calamity to you, and
you are saying, "How shall I bear it?" the answer is, "Be
filled with the Spirit of God." Here shall you drink oblivion of
the heavy trial; or, better still, you shall forget the sharpness
of the trial, in your knowledge that it worketh patience, and

patience experience, and experience hope, which maketh not
ashamed. O beloved friend, do not kick at the trial, be
willing to bear it; but get more of the indwelling of the
sacred Comforter. "Be filled with the Spirit." Perhaps this
may be a direction to some dear friend here who has lately
been called to tread a more trying path than usual. "How
shall I bear it, sir? How shall I bear it? I never was so tried
before." Seek earnestly for more of the Spirit of God than
you ever had before. He will give you in proportion to your
necessity. He is fully equal to every emergency. His consolations can balance your tribulations. Wait upon him for
the comfort of the Spirit. The day may come when you will
glory in your infirmities and afflictions, because God used
them to make room for more of his Spirit to dwell in you.
Certain I am that if you have to go home to-night to lie for
the next twenty years upon a sick bed—and certain of God's
saints have not been off the sick-bed for all that time—or if
all your property is gone, and you are called to endure
poverty during the rest of your pilgrimage; or if you shall
hear of the death of the dearest one you have, if the Holy
Spirit be but given in a larger measure to you, you will have
more happiness and more contentment, and be a better man
by reason of all this affliction that has come upon you. God
grant that you may find it to be true that you may forget
your poverty and misery, and discover no gall in your
bitterest cup! May you drink deep draughts of the joy of the
Lord till you are filled with the Spirit of God! Touch not the
wine-cup, lest in this you dishonour the Holy Ghost, who by
his own power is able to cheer your heavy heart.

Again, I think a fifth reason why some have been drinking
is to *arouse themselves*. They feel flat, they say. Ah, ah! if I
were lecturing to-night, I could give you some of those abundant excuses for drinking which tipplers so readily invent.
You can always find reasons, such as they are, when you
want to pursue a career of self-indulgence. You may find
them of every colour—black, white, red, blue and grey, at
every time, every day. The most unreasonable reasons will
come cropping up if you want to do what your flesh desires.
But there are some who feel, "I want a pick-me-up. I am
rather down, seedy, dull. I want something that will brace
me, so that I may be up to the mark." By the time the man

has had enough of his stimulant he is worse than before. Many have most effectually knocked themselves down in their desire to set themselves up. But, Christian man, if ever you feel dull, "be filled with the Spirit." "If ever I feel dull!" cries one, "Why, I often do, even at this time I have come into the house of prayer, and do not feel as if I could worship." Well, then, go where life and strength are to be had. One of our brethren observed to me, the other day (I do not think he meant to flatter me), "I often go into the Tabernacle feeling that I cannot worship as I should; but," said he, "you always seem to be lively and all right." I thought—Ah, dear brother! you do not know much about me, or you would not praise me; for I often feel the reverse of lively: but I cannot bear to have it so, lest others should be injured by it. There is not a more dull or stupid head than mine in this place. But I have a remedy, and I fly to it: I wish you would all do so. I go to him, you know his glorious name: he is the Resurrection and the Life. I look to him for quickening, and it comes. May that be an example to some of you whenever you feel dull! Do not say, "I cannot pray to-day; I cannot sing to-day." No, but go to the Lord to help you to present acceptable worship. It would be a great relief to me if I could be excused from preaching to you when I do not feel like preaching. Yet, it would not be a blessing to me, for it would encourage me in dulness, and that would be a curse. If you do not pray except when you feel like praying, you will not pray much, nor pray when you most need it. My brethren, when you do not feel like praying, you ought to pray all the more, and go to the Lord to help you to pray. When one does not feel like doing the Lord's work, he must say, "Out with you, Mr. Sluggard! You must get to your work. Stir yourself up"; and here is the hallowed power which will effectually help you therein— "Be filled with the Spirit." Oh, if the Spirit of God makes us feel what poor creatures we are, and what a great Saviour we have; if the Spirit of God makes us feel the love of God shed abroad in our hearts; if we burn with love to the souls of men; if we rejoice in pardon bought with blood; if we see our justification and realize it; if we feel the Spirit of God melting us to tenderness or bracing us to holy bravery—then it is that we are refreshed and stimulated after the best manner. We have found the true arousing; and there will be no reaction after it, no falling back into a deeper depression. I wish that those who feel dull to-night, may be so filled with the Spirit that they will not be content to go to sleep till they have spoken to a poor sinner about salvation and eternal life.

Once more, many men, no doubt, become drunkards from love of what is called *good fellowship.* "Look," said a wife to her husband, "how can you drink at the rate you do? Why, a hog would not do so." The wretched man replied, "No, I do not suppose that it would. It would be more sensible than I am, no doubt; but," he said, "if there was another hog at the other side of the trough that said, 'I drink your health,' this hog would be obliged to do the same; and if there were half-a-dozen of them together, and they kept on toasting one another, I expect the hog would get as drunk as I am." Sad are the effects of evil fellowship. The fellowship in which people indulge, and which they think it necessary to stimulate by drink, has led many into drunkenness. Now see the beauty of this expression, "Be not drunk with wine, wherein is excess; but be filled with the Spirit." When the Spirit of God comes upon Christian men, what fellowship they have with one another, what delight they take in holy conversation, what joy there is in meeting together for solemn worship! I do not wonder that it is added immediately after, "Speaking to yourselves in psalms and hymns and spiritual songs, singing and making melody in your heart to the Lord; giving thanks always for all things unto God and the Father in the name of our Lord Jesus Christ." See the effect of being filled with the Spirit. It brings a fellowship of holy music, sacred gratitude, and heavenly thanksgiving. It makes us feel concerning the house of prayer—

> "I have been there, and still would go,
> 'Tis like a little heaven below."

It makes us sing with rapture:

> "Hail, ye days of solemn meeting!
> Hail, ye days of praise and prayer!
> Far from earthly scenes retreating,
> In your blessings we would share:
> Sacred seasons,
> In your blessings we would share."

The Lord grant us grace to seek our fellowship where he
finds it, with holy men and holy women; that among them in
joyous fellowship we may rejoice and praise his name.

II. I cannot stay longer on this parallel, I have already
been too long: now, LET ME POINT OUT THE CONTRAST. I do
not think that Paul was running the parallel only, for it
would dishonour the work of the Holy Spirit to think that his
operations could be in all things likened to the influence of
alcohol. No, the divine afflatus far excels anything that
earthly excitements can produce.

"Be not drunk with wine, wherein is riot; but be filled with
the Spirit." The contrast is at the very beginning; for it is
written, "Be *filled* with the Spirit." Wine does not fill. No
man is satisfied with all that he drinks. He is still thirsty.
His thirst is often increased by that which was supposed to
quench it. The Spirit of God has a satisfying, satiating, never
nauseating influence upon the heart. It fills it to the very
brim, until the man delights himself in God, and cries, "My
cup runneth over." Then the saint becomes like the tribe of
which we read, "O Naphtali, satisfied with favour, and full
with the blessing of the Lord." Wine ministers to lust, and
lust is a burning sense of want; but the Spirit of the Lord
brings fulness with it, and a perfect rest of heart.

"Wine creates *riot*," says the apostle; and that is the second
point of contrast. When men are drunken, what a noise they
will make! They are ready for any disturbance; but the Holy
Spirit, when you are full of him, makes you quiet with a
deep, unutterable peace. I do not say that you will not sing
and rejoice, but there will be a deep calm within your spirit.
I wish that some Christian people were filled with the Spirit,
if there were no other effect produced upon them but that of
peace, self-possession, restfulness, and freedom from passion. Our friends, the members of the Society of Friends,
who speak much of the Spirit of God, whatever virtues they
may not have, certainly have this one—that they are,
usually, a very quiet, unexcitable, peaceable people. We
want more Christians of this sort. We can put up with all the
uproar of the Salvation Army, if it comes in very deed from
warm hearts and genuine zeal. I will not find any fault with
them for a little noise, though the less of it the better. If your
genius goes that way, sing unto the Lord, and blow your

trumpet; but at the same time, the solid people in the church are those who possess their souls, who go about their business, who suffer, and who labour with an inward peace which is not disturbed, a holy calm which is not ruffled. Do not create riot, but abide in holy peace by being filled with the Spirit. May the Lord keep you in perfect peace with your minds stayed on him.

The next point of contrast is, that wine causes *contention*. When men are drunken with it, how ready they are to quarrel! They make a harmless word to be an insult. Many a man, when full of wine, will bear nothing at all: he is ready to fight anybody and everybody: he cannot have his fill of fighting. But when you are filled with the Spirit, what is the result? Why, peaceful submission. Listen to this: "Submitting yourselves one to another in the fear of God. Wives, submit yourselves unto your own husbands, as unto the Lord." Human nature likes rule; but the Spirit of God works submissiveness of mind. Instead of wanting to be first, the truly spiritual man will be satisfied to be last, if he can thus glorify God. That man who must be always king of the castle, is not filled with the Spirit of God; but he that is willing to be a door-mat, on which the saints may wipe their feet, is great in the kingdom of heaven. Be filled with the Spirit, and you will soon submit to inconvenience, misapprehension, and even exaction for the sake of doing good to those who are out of the way, and in the hope of edifying the people of God. Wine causes riot; the Spirit causes peace. Drunkenness causes contention; the Spirit of God causes submission.

Furthermore, drunkenness makes men *foolish;* but the Spirit of God makes them wise. I am keeping to the connection of my text. Read the fifteenth verse, "See then that ye walk circumspectly, not as fools, but as wise." The drunken man cannot walk at all, because he has not made up his mind as to which way he will go. He attempts to go two ways, and ends in staggering till he falls. The man filled with the Spirit has a very definite idea of which way he is going. He knows the right, and he deliberately chooses it; he perceives the strait and narrow way, and he steadfastly follows it; for God has made him wise. Folly clings to the wine-cup; but wisdom comes with the Holy Spirit.

Drunkenness *wastes time;* but the Spirit of God, when we are filled with him, makes us save it. Read the sixteenth verse: "Redeeming the time, because the days are evil. Wherefore be ye not unwise, but understanding what the will of the Lord is. And be not drunk with wine, wherein is riot." How much of time is wasted over the unholy cup! But the child of God, when the Spirit of God enters into him, makes a conscience of his odd moments and leisure minutes. As goldsmiths sweep up the very dust of their shops, that no filings of the precious metal may be lost, so does the Christian man, when filled with the Spirit, use his brief intervals. It is wonderful what may be done in odd minutes. Little spaces of time may be made to yield a great harvest of usefulness, and a rich revenue of glory to God. May we be filled with the Spirit in that respect!

In the next place, drunkenness makes men *forget their relationships,* but the Holy Spirit makes us remember them. The rest of the chapter goes on to mention our domestic conditions as wives, husbands, children, fathers, servants, masters. The drunken man is bad in every relation, and the drunken woman is, if possible, worse. The drunken man ought never to be a husband, but he sometimes wears that name, and then he has a power to inflict misery which he is sure to use to the utmost. The drunken man will often do towards his wife what I will not trust my lips to speak of—it would be a libel on the brutes of the stall or the beasts of the jungle to liken him to them. A drunken father! Is he worth calling "father"? And it is even worse, if worse can be, when it is a drunken wife or a drunken mother. A special infamy hovers around womanhood soaked in liquor: relationships, in such instances, are quite forgotten under the influence of the accursed drink. Selfishness eats up the very heart of those who else might have been the objects of reverence and love. The contrast to this is the fact that when filled with the Spirit the husband is the tenderest of husbands, the wife the best of wives. No master is so just as the man that is mastered by the Spirit of God; no servant so diligent as he that serves the Lord. By the Holy Spirit our relationships become ennobled; and what was but a common-place position wears a glory of holiness about it. We are transfigured by the Spirit of God, and we transfigure every-

thing we touch. Dear friends, you see that the contrast is a
very vivid one. Look into it very narrowly, and it will repay
the inspection.

Lastly, excess of drink *leaves a man weak and exposed to
peril*. But to be filled with the Spirit!—listen to what comes
of it according to the tenth verse of the next chapter:
"Finally, my brethren, be strong in the Lord, and in the
power of his might. Put on the whole armour of God, that ye
may be able to stand against the wiles of the devil. For we
wrestle not against flesh and blood, but against principalities, against powers, against the rulers of the darkness
of this world, against spiritual wickedness in high places.
Wherefore take unto you the whole armour of God, that ye
may be able to withstand in the evil day, and having done
all, to stand. Stand therefore, having your loins girt about
with truth." When filled with the Spirit the man is no longer
naked, like the drunkard. He no longer lies upon the ground
in danger as one overcome with wine. He is no longer open
to the attack of adversaries, as one who sleeps through
strong drink. God hath made him strong, and armed him,
and now he goes forth to fight in the service of his Master. I
think that you will see the contrast. It is as evident as the
parallel.

I shall keep you no longer except to say this. My beloved
Christian friends, our heart's desire is, that the members of
this church, and, indeed, all the members of Christ's
mystical body, should be filled with the Spirit, Oh, that you
may come absolutely under the sway of the Holy Ghost, and
may abide under his most powerful inspirations! Do you ask
how this is to be? First, *reverently regard him*. Worship him.
Speak not of the Holy Ghost as *it*. Talk not of the Third
Person of the adorable Trinity as *an influence*. He is very
God of very God. God has guarded the sanctity of the Holy
Spirit by causing a certain sin to be specially condemned,
and excepted from pardon—the sin against the Holy Ghost.
Honour him much, then: worship him, and adore him, and
look to him for help.

Next, *do not grieve him*. If there be anything that would
grieve the Holy Spirit, let it grieve *you*, so that you may keep
clear of it. Put away every thought, idea, principle, and act
that is not agreeable to his mind. Neither live in sin, nor

trifle with evil, nor fall into error, nor neglect the reading of
the Word of God, nor fail to obey the commands of the Lord.
Do not grieve the Comforter, but welcome him as your best
Friend. Open your heart to his influences. Watch each day to
hear his monitions. Pray every morning, "Holy Spirit, speak
with me, bedew me, enlighten me, set me on fire, dwell in
me"; and during the day lament to yourself if you do not feel
the Spirit of God moving in you, and ask why it is. "Has he
left me? Is he grieved with me?" Say—

> "Return, O holy Dove! return,
> Sweet messenger of rest!
> I hate the sins that made thee mourn,
> And drove thee from my breast."

As you welcome him when he comes, so *be fit for him to come*
to you and dwell in you. Be clean, for he is pure. Do not
expect the Holy Ghost to dwell in a foul chamber. You cannot
make that chamber like Solomon's temple, wherein the
cedar-wood was overlaid with pure gold; but you can take
care that it is well cleansed. Only the pure in heart shall see
God. Oh, for a clean life, a clean tongue, a clean hand, a
clean ear, a clean eye, a clean heart! God give you these, and
then you shall be ready for the Spirit of God to dwell in you.

And when he does come, learn this thing. *If you would
have him fill you, obey him.* If you believe that an impulse is
from the Spirit of God, follow it out. Never trifle with
conscience—especially you that are beginning life. Mind you
set the tune for the whole of your life by the tenderness of
your consciences at the first. When I was a lad I learned a
certain truth, which my friends and relatives did not know,
but I had to follow my conscience. It looked very egotistical
and wayward for a lad to set up his opinion against older
people; but I could not help it. I saw believer's baptism in the
Bible, and therefore the highest law compelled me to be
obedient to that ordinance. I looked over the matter again
and again, to see if it was not so; and I became more and
more assured as to the mind of the Lord. Therefore I was not
disobedient. It is true that it was suggested to me that if I
did follow out my views, I should have to cut out quite
another career for myself from the one anticipated; but I
could not help *that*. I must do the Lord's will, whatever

might be the consequences. From that day to this I have never had cause to regret my youthful decision. The trial was severe at the time, but it was beneficial to my whole character. It taught me to follow truth wherever it might lead me, and to expect the Spirit of God to abide with me in so doing. Since then I have often come to a place where interest has gone one way and principle has gone another; but it has not cost me half-a-minute's thought which should be my way. I must follow what I believe to be right and true, and preach what I believe to be God's Word; and I will do so whether men hear or whether they forbear. Young men, young women, mind you begin straight. Do not begin with truckling and making compromises. If you take your hats off to the devil to-day, you will have to take your shoes off to him soon; and by-and-by you will become utterly his slaves. Be strong for the truth. Quit yourselves like men. Stand fast for God and holiness. You will be filled with the Spirit if you are obedient to him.

If you are filled with the Spirit of God, and wish to retain his gracious presence, *speak about him*. Note this, "Be not drunk with wine, wherein is riot; but be filled with the Spirit; speaking." That is a curious word to follow so soon. The Holy Ghost is not a dumb Spirit; he sets us speaking. "Speaking to yourselves"; it is a poor audience; but still it is a choice audience if you speak to your brethren. "Speaking to yourselves in psalms and hymns and spiritual songs, singing and making melody in your heart to the Lord." Beloved, when the Spirit of God fills you, you will not only speak, but sing. Let the holy power have free course: do not quench the Spirit. If you feel like singing all the while, sing all the while, and let others know that there is a joy in the possession of the Spirit of God which the world does not understand, but which you are feeling, and to which you wish to bear witness. Oh, that the Spirit of God would come upon this entire church, and fill you all to overflowing! May the members of other churches that are here to-night take home fire with them, and set their churches on flame! The Lord bless you, for Jesus Christ's sake! Amen.

8

Covenant Blessings

"A new heart also will I give you, and a new spirit will I put within you: and I will take away the stony heart out of your flesh, and I will give you an heart of flesh. And I will put my spirit within you, and cause you to walk in my statutes, and ye shall keep my judgments, and do them."

Ezekiel 36:26-27

Luther has well said that the experience of the minister is the best book in his library. I am persuaded it is so, and that God often leads his servants through peculiar states of mind, not so much for their own benefit as for the sake of those to whom they may afterwards minister. It is not long ago since I felt myself when engaged in devotion cold and dead, and in looking into my own heart I saw no ground of comfortable assurance as to my being a possessor of the grace of God: my feelings towards the great Father in heaven were not, as far as I could judge, those of a child: my love towards Jesus Christ for his redemption was almost extinct. I thought over the story of his cross without emotion, and I recalled to my mind the history of his everlasting love without gratitude. My soul was not, as it sometimes is, like the crystal lake which is ruffled with every passing breath of the breeze, but like some northern sea hardened into iron by the fierce reign of endless winter; the sublime truths of infinite grace stirred not my soul. My heart sank within me for a moment, but only for a moment, for there flashed across me this thought,—"The Holy Spirit can produce within your heart all those emotions you are seeking for, all those desires you fain would feel, all the meltings, and the movings, and the yearnings, and the rejoicings, which are significant of the grace of God." Under the influence of that truth, as in a moment, my deadness and coldness were driven away, and I was filled with adoring love. Then I wondered greatly that the Lord should deign to handle such coarse material as our nature, that he should condescend to work upon such gross spirits, such grovelling minds, such carnal understandings as ours. And when, by faith, I perceived that he could not only there and then give me to feel spiritual life, but could maintain it against all hazards, and perfect it beyond all imperfections, and bring me safe into his eternal kingdom and glory; an act of faith exerted upon the Holy Spirit through the cross of Christ made my soul eager for prayer, and my joy and peace in believing were more than restored to me. Then I said within myself, there may be others in a like case, and especially there may be seeking souls who, seeing what must be wrought in them before they can hope to be partakers of the eternal rest, may despair that such a work should ever be done, and looking only to themselves, may be inclined to give up all hope, and conclude that within the pearly gates they can never enter. Perhaps, I thought, if I remind them that "the Spirit also helpeth our infirmities," that Jesus Christ's bequest to us, in virtue of his having gone to heaven, is an Omnipotent One, who can work all our works in us, causing us to will and to do of his own good pleasure,—the thought may encourage their hearts, and enable them to look with restful confidence to him who works all our works in us.

Our text is a portion of that delightful rendering of the covenant of grace which is given us by Ezekiel, and we will, for a single moment, ask you to remember the persons with whom the covenant of grace was made. An early version of the covenant of grace was given to Abraham, and this in Ezekiel is a repetition, expansion, or explanation of the same. This covenant, and that form of it made with Abraham, concern the same individuals. Let us then remind ourselves that the covenant was not made with the fleshly seed of Abraham. If it had been, it would have run in the line of Ishmael as well as that of Isaac; but it was not made with Ishmael, for what saith the Scriptures, "Cast out the bondwoman and her son, for the son of the bondwoman shall not be heir with my son, even with Isaac." The covenant of grace was not made with the children who are born after the flesh as was Ishmael, but with those who are born according to the promise as was Isaac, who was not born by virtue of the energy of the flesh, for of Abraham it was said that he was as good as dead, and as for Sarah that she was long past bearing; but Isaac, the child of laughter, the child of joy, the heir of the promise, was born according to the power of God, and not after the energy of nature. Isaac evidently typifies not the man of works but the man of faith. The man of works is born after the flesh, he has reformed himself, he has done his best, he continues to do his best, he is the child of his own energy, he is the result of human power, he is under the law, for he tries to save himself by the law, he is, therefore, the son of Hagar the bond-woman, and he is under bondage, and his destiny may be learned from the words, "Cast forth the son of the bondwoman, he shall not be heir with my son." But the man of faith has received his faith supernaturally, it has been wrought in him by the Holy Spirit; it is not the fruit of the creature's power, it is the gift of God: it is the child of promise and it is the child of joy and laughter to him; it is a fresh spring of joy within his soul. The man of faith, therefore, is the heir of the promise, and the partaker of the covenant, since he believes in Jesus, whom God raised from the dead. The man who rests upon the grace of God, and believes in God as holy Abraham did, he is a faithful man, and, consequently, he is one of the sons of the father of the faithful.

Let every man, therefore, who believes in Jesus Christ this morning know assuredly that every word of this text belongs to him, and shall be fulfilled to him. I earnestly pray that many a poor sinner may put in his claim and say, "I have no works, but I believe in Jesus Christ; I come now and rest myself upon the bloody sacrifice offered upon Calvary, and I humbly receive the mercy of God through Jesus Christ, by simply depending on him." To every one who exercises faith in God, even though it be but a weak and struggling faith, the precious promise we are about to expound is a heritage which cannot be taken away from him.

The main promise of the text before us is the indwelling of the Holy Spirit; but observe that the text divides itself thus: first, it contains *an assured promise of preparation for the*

Spirit's indwelling; secondly, *a plain promise of that indwelling;* and, thirdly, *the blessed results which flow therefrom.*

I. Observe, first, we have here to all God's covenanted people, or in other words, to all believers, a promise of PREPARATION FOR THE SPIRIT'S INDWELLING. "A new heart also will I give you, and a new spirit will I put within you; I will take away the stony heart out of your flesh, and I will give you a heart of flesh." This promise is as a cluster of nuts, or a bough with many golden apples. Like the cherubim of Ezekiel it has four faces, all smiling upon the heirs of salvation. Like the new Jerusalem it lieth four-square. It is a quadruple treasure worthy of four-fold consideration.

The first of the four blessings is *the gift of a new heart.* "A new heart also will I give you." The Holy Spirit cannot dwell in the old heart; it is a filthy place, devoid of all good, and full of enmity to God. His very first operation upon our nature is to pull down the old house and build himself a new one, that he may be able to inhabit us consistently with his holy spiritual nature. A new heart is absolutely essential, we must be born again or the Spirit of truth cannot abide within us.

Observe where the inward work of grace begins. All man's attempts at the betterment of human nature begin from without, and the theory is that the work will deepen till it reaches that which is within. They profess to emancipate the man from the grosser vices, trusting that the reform will go further, that he will be brought under superior influences, and so be elevated in mind and heart. Theirs is an outward ointment for an inward disease, a bandage upon the skin to stay the bleeding of the heart. Miserable physicians are they all. Their remedies fail to eradicate the deep-seated maladies of humanity. God's way of dealing with men is the reverse. He begins within and works towards the exterior in due course. He is a mere quack who, seeing in a man the signs of disease, operates upon the symptoms, but never looks to the root of the mischief. It is very possible that by potent poisons an empiric may check unpleasing indications, and he may kill the man in doing so; but the wise physician looks to the fountain of the disease, and if it be possible to touch the core and centre of it, he leaves the symptoms to right themselves. If your watch be out of order the watchmaker does not consider it sufficient to clean the silver case, or to remove dust from the face; but he looks within and discovers that this wheel is broken, this cog out of order, or the main spring needing to be renewed; he is not much concerned about setting the hands accurately at first, for he knows that the external manifestations of the correct time will follow from the setting to rights the time-keeping machinery within. Look at our brooks and rivulets which have been by a lax legislature so long delivered over to the tormentors to be blackened into pestiferous sewers; if we want to have them purged it is of small avail to cast chloride of lime and other chemicals into the stream; the only remedy is to forbid the pollution, to demand that manufactories shall not poison us wholesale, but shall in some other manner consume their useless products. The voice of common sense bids us go to the original cause of the defilement and deal with it at its sources. That is just what God does when he saves a sinner, he begins at the origin of the sinner's sin and deals with his heart.

My brethren, what a difficult work this is: "A new heart also will I give you." If it had been said, "A new garment will I give you," many of us could have conferred the same boon. If it had been said, "A new speech will I teach you," this also, with a little skill, might have been arranged; and, if the promise had been, "New habits will I create in you," this also we could have attempted, and perhaps successfully, to imitate, for habits are to be engendered: but a new heart— ah, here human power and wit are non-plussed. Jannes and Jambres in Egypt could imitate some of the miracles, they "did so with their enchantment," and there is much in true religion which men can successfully counterfeit; but, as in Egypt, a point was reached wherein the magicians were foiled, so that they confessed, "This is the finger of God," so in the regeneration of our nature, in the changing the heart, the Lord alone is seen. Who shall pretend to give another a new heart? Go, boaster, and suspend the laws of gravitation, recall the thunderbolt, reverse the chariot of the sun, transform the Atlantic to a lake of fire, and then attempt to change the nature of the heart of man. This God alone worketh, for he only doeth wondrous things. The affections are the most powerful part of our nature, they to a great extent mould even the understanding itself, and if the heart be defiled all the mental faculties become disturbed in their balance. God, therefore, commences at the heart, and therein begins a work in which man cannot compete with him, nor can he even help him. God must do it. The same God who made men must new make them, if the new-making is to begin with a change of heart. Blessed be God, he is omnipotent enough to give us new hearts, he has wisdom enough to renew us, he has purity sufficient to cleanse us, he has abounding mercy to bear with us. Mark, he gives us "a *new* heart," not an old heart touched-up and mended; not an old heart a little purified and improved; but a new heart which enters into a new life, receives new inspirations, feeds on new food, longs for new happiness, performs new actions, and is, in fact, an inhabitant of the new heavens and the new earth wherein dwelleth righteousness.

Brethren, I will read this sentence over again, "A new heart also will I give you;" and I would call your attention to the style of the language. It is "I will," and yet again, "I will." Jehovah's Ego is the great word. It is not "I will if," or "I will perhaps," or "I will upon certain conditions," but—"I *will* give." He speaks in a Godlike tone. It is royal language, the very word of Him who of old said, "Light be," and light was. He who spoke the world into being now speaks the new world of grace into being in the self-same majestic voice.

Turn, now, to the second blessing—*"A new Spirit will I put within you."* Perhaps this clause may be explained as an interpretation of the former one. It may be that the new heart and the new spirit are intended to represent the same thing. But, I conceive there is more than this. "A new spirit,"—does not the term indicate that a new vital principle is implanted in men? We have often explained to you that the natural man is correctly and strictly speaking a compound of soul and body only. The first man, Adam, was made a living soul; and, as we bear the image of the first Adam, we are body and soul only. It is our own belief that in regeneration something more is done than the mere rectifying of what was there: there is in the new birth

infused and implanted in man a third and more elevated
principle,—a spirit is begotten in him; and, as the second
Adam was made a quickening spirit, so in the new birth we
are transformed into the likeness of Christ Jesus, who is the
second Adam. The implantation, infusion, and putting into
our nature the third and higher principle is, we believe, the
being born again. Regarded in this light, the words before us
may be regarded as an absolute and unconditional promise
of the covenant of grace to all the seed that a new spirit shall
be put within them. But, if we view it as some do, we shall
then read it thus—the ruling spirit of man's nature shall be
changed. The spirit which rules and reigns in Godless,
Christless men, is the spirit of a rebellious slave, the spirit of
self. Every natural man's main motive is himself, even in his
religion he only seeks self. If he be attentive to prayers and
sermons, it is that he himself may be saved; and if he fears
God, and dreads the terrors of his law, it is on his own
account—not that he cares for God's glory, God's honour, or
the rights of God—not one whit; he has no more interest in
God than a rebellious slave has in the property of his
master. He wears the yoke, but he groans under it; he would
gladly enough escape from it if he could; he is only happy
when he is breaking his master's laws and fulfilling his own
selfish will. But, when the Spirit of God comes upon us, to
make our spirit a fit place for his residence, he takes away
the spirit of the slave, and gives us the spirit of a child, and
from that moment the service of God becomes a different
thing: we do not serve him now because we are afraid of the
whip, but nobler motives move us; gratitude binds us to the
Lord's service, and love gives wings to the feet of obedience.
Now the Lord is no more regarded as a tyrant, but as a wise
and loving parent. Whatever he may do with us, we rejoice
in his wisdom and goodness. We view him no longer with
suspicion and dread, but with confidence and joy. No more
do we ask "whither shall I go from thy presence?" but we
desire to come near to him, and in our sorrows our cry is,
"Oh, that I knew where I might find him, that I might come
even to his seat." It is a revolution indeed, when the hatred
and dread of a slave are exchanged for the loving subjection
of a son. This is one of the precious privileges of the covenant
of grace, which I trust, beloved, many of you have already

received, and which I hope others who have not received it will seek after. If they have believed in Jesus, a new spirit, a spirit of sonship is their privilege; let them not be content unless they have it now.

A third and further blessing of the text is the *removal of the stony heart*. "I will take away the stony heart out of your flesh." I do not think the Lord removes at once the *evil* heart out of any man's flesh; there it remains to be fought with, like the Canaanites in Canaan when Israel had entered there, to prove us and to try us, but he does take away the stony heart at once. The stony heart is a hard heart. The moment anything strikes a stone it repels the blow; when the gospel is heard by a hard heart it throws it off again, it is not moved by it, it is not affected by it. You might as well throw feathers at a wall as preach gospel sermons to hard hearts, if your confidence be in the sermon itself; only God's power can make the feather-like sermon to penetrate the heart of stone. The Lord can do it, but the thing itself cannot be done by nature. The natural heart is an impenetrable heart; you may make scratches upon the surface, but you cannot enter within it to reach its inner core. What a marble heart by nature each one of us has. Till grace visits us the truth cannot enter us any more than light can shine into a stone. A stony heart is unfeeling, you can make no impression upon it: it cannot smart, it cannot breathe, it cannot sigh, it cannot groan,—a stony thing because it is a dead thing. Bruise it, and that which would make flesh black and blue does not affect the stone. Cut it, and that which would cause an agony to living flesh makes no disturbance in its granite mass. A cold, insensible thing, not to be warmed even by the rehearsal of the love of Calvary, such is our heart by nature. Dear hearers, such is the heart of every one of you till God deals with you;—just a lump of stone. Of course we speak not literally but spiritually, yet what we assert is a solemn fact. God says "I will take away the stony heart." What a wonderful operation to take a stone out of the heart. How much more wonderful to take the stony heart itself right away and create a fleshy heart in its stead.

I would ask you again, though it may look like a repetition, to notice how royally the Lord speaks. He does not say, "Perhaps I will." He does not say, "If you are willing I will," but, *"I will,"* saith he. Oh, it is gloriously worded, "I will take away the stony heart out of your flesh." The Lord's omnipotence can accomplish it. We have heard of many expedients for softening hard hearts, but none of them are of any avail. I know preachers who delight in talking of a mother's tears, and a father's grey hairs, of dying children and consumptive sisters, and I believe these are all legitimate topics; but, no hearts are ever turned from stone to flesh merely by natural emotion. You may make a man weep over his dead child or his dead wife, till his eyes are red, but his heart will be black for all that. Men's hearts are changed by quite another agency than oratorical or rhetorical appeals to the natural affections. I readily admit that such appeals have their own sphere, but for the renewing of the heart something much more effectual is wanted than natural emotion. It is written, "I will take away the heart of stone out of your flesh," and there is the secret of the matter.

The fourth promise of the preparation of the heart for the indwelling of the Spirit is this: *"I will give you a heart of flesh,"* by which is meant a soft heart, an impressible heart, a sensitive heart, a heart which can feel, can be moved to shame, to repentance, to loathing of sin, to desiring, to seeking, to panting, to longing after God; a tender heart, a heart that does not require a thousand blows to move it, but, like flesh with its skin broken, feels the very faintest touch,—such is the heart which the Holy Spirit creates in the children of God. It is a teachable heart, a heart willing to be guided, moulded, governed by the divine will: a heart which, like young Samuel, cries, "Speak, Lord, for thy servant heareth":—an obedient heart, ready to be run into the mould, plastic beneath the sacred hand, anxious to be conformed to the heavenly pattern. This is an early work of grace in the soul, for as soon as ever the gospel is heard in power, and the Spirit of God comes upon a man, long before he enters into the liberty wherewith Christ makes men free, he ceases to have a heart of stone: long before he can say, "Christ is mine," he becomes tender and impressible under the truth, and it is a great mercy it is so; it is a blessed sign of a work begun which will be effectually carried on, where the heart trembles at God's word, where there are earnest desires towards Christ, and the man is no longer a braggart

rebel, but a trembling child come back to his father, and
longing to cry, "Father, I have sinned against heaven and
before thee."

Beloved, it is meet here to add a word of caution to some of
you. Do not mistake natural tenderness for that heart of
flesh which God gives. There are many persons who are
naturally very impressible, many amongst women, and some
amongst men. For this characteristic they are rather to me
admired than censured; but, let them not mistake this for a
work of grace. A heart of wax is soft, but it is not a heart of
flesh. The softness of nature is not the sensitiveness of
grace. It is often the case that some persons who are
religiously sensitive are equally sensitive the other way,
and, while you can influence them for good, others can as
easily influence them for evil. They happen to be just now
religious because the associations surrounding them have
that tendency, but were they under other influences they
would be sceptical if not utterly irreligious. They would have
been lovers of the pleasures which others pursue had not
home habits sobered their minds, for their hearts are still
unrenewed. Mere religious impressibility is not grace, it is
nature alone, and I even fear that to some it is a temptation
to be so extremely impressionable. I am not always sanguine
concerning persons who are readily excited, for they so soon
cool down again. Some are like india-rubber, and every time
you put your finger on them you leave a mark, but it is
wasted time, because they get back into the old shape again
as soon as you have done with them. I was preaching once in
a certain city, and a very worthy but worldly man went out
of the congregation while I was in the middle of the sermon,
the third sermon he had been hearing from me during the
week. One who followed him out asked him why he left, and
he frankly replied that he could not stand it any longer,
"for," said he, "I must have become religious if I had heard
that sermon through. I was nearly gone." "I have been,"
added he, "like an india-rubber doll under this man, but
when he goes away I shall get back into the old shape
again." Very many are of the same quality; they have so
much natural amiability, good sense, and conscientiousness,
that the gospel ministry has a power over them, and they
feel its influence, though, not so as to be saved by it. Beware,

then, that you do not mistake the gilding of nature for the solid gold of grace. When God's grace helps the preacher to wield the gospel hammer, and it comes down with power upon a piece of flint, how speedily the stone flies to shivers, and what a glorious work of heart-breaking is done, and then the Lord comes in and gives, by his own almighty grace, a heart of flesh. This is the change we want, the taking away of the stone, the giving of the heart of flesh.

Let us read these four promises again, and I hope they will reach any poor trembling soul who may be saying, "I would but cannot repent, I would but cannot feel; if ought is felt 'tis only pain to find I cannot feel. My heart is so bad, so hard, so cold, I can believe in Christ but I cannot change my nature." Poor soul, there is no need you should, for there is one who can do the work for you, and these are his absolute promises to you if you are now looking to Christ upon the cross and resting all your hopes in him. "A new heart also will I give you, and a new spirit will I put within you; and I will take away the stony heart out of your flesh, and I will give you a heart of flesh."

II. But time flies, and therefore let us consider, in the second place, THE INDWELLING OF THE HOLY GHOST. When the Spirit has thus prepared his habitation, he comes to reside within the renewed man. I call your attention to each word of the text.

Observe first, that the Lord says, "I will put *my Spirit* within you." Now it does not say, "the influences of the Spirit shall come within you,"—note that: but, "I will put *my Spirit* within you." It is literally the fact that God himself, the Eternal Spirit in *propria persona,* in his own person, resides and dwells within the renewed heart. I again remark that it is not said, "I will put the grace of my Spirit, I will put the work of my Spirit," but, "I will put *my Spirit* within you." It is the Holy Ghost himself who in very deed lives in every heart of flesh, every new heart and right spirit. Can you get that thought? Simple as it is, it is one of the greatest marvels under the sun. An incarnate God is a mystery,—the Word was made flesh and dwelt among us; but, here is another mystery, God dwells in every son of God. God dwelleth in us, and we in him. The mystery of the incarnation is not greater than that of the Holy Ghost's indwelling, nor does it appear to me to involve more condescension. I marvel at Christ's dwelling *with* sinners, and I marvel equally at the Holy Ghost's dwelling *in* sinners. God himself, for whom the universe is not too vast a temple, the ever blessed Spirit in whose presence the heavens are not clean, yet saith, "To this man will I look even to him that is poor, and of a contrite spirit, and that trembleth at my word." The indwelling of the Holy Ghost within us implies the exercise of his influences, the bestowal of his gifts, and the implantation of his graces; and, moreover, it involves the exercise of all his sacred offices, for where the Holy Ghost indwells he acts as a teacher, an illuminator, a Comforter, a Creator, a strengthener, a preserver: all that he is in all his offices he will be according to his own will to every man in whom he takes up his abode.

Note a little word also in the text worthy of your attention. "I will put *my* Spirit within you." It is not the spirit of angels, it is not the spirit of good men, it is God's own Spirit who takes up his residence in every sinner's heart when God renews it. "*My* Spirit." And, perhaps, this may allude to the fact that this is the self-same Spirit which abode without measure in our Lord Jesus Christ. We have a union of experience with Christ in the fact that the same oil which anointed him anoints us, the same dew which fell upon his branch refreshes ours, the same holy fire which burned in his breast is kindled in ours. "I will put *my* Spirit within you."

Observe also carefully the words, *"within you,"* "I will put my Spirit *within you."* We thank God that we come near to the Spirit of God when we devoutly read the Holy Scriptures, for he wrote them, and his mind is in them; but we have a greater privilege than this. We thank God when the Spirit acts upon us under a sermon, or under any form of Christian teaching, so that we feel the Spirit of God to be with us; but we have a richer privilege even than this. "I will put my Spirit," not with you, nor side by side with you, nor in a book, nor in an oracle, nor in a temple, nor in one of your fellow-men, but "I will put my Spirit *within* YOU," in your own souls, in your own renewed hearts. This is marvellous. Augustine, when reflecting upon the various glories which come to God, and the benefits which accrue to men through redemption, none of which could have been revealed without

the fall of Adam, exclaimed, *"O beata culpa!"* "Oh! happy
fault;" and I have the self-same expression trembling on my
lips. Where sin abounded grace has much more abounded.
Sin, which laid man in the dust, and made him like a devil,
has afforded an opportunity for mercy to step in, and lifted
humanity higher than before. What was man in Eden compared with man in Christ? In Paradise he was perfect in
beauty, but in Jesus he wears a radiance superlative, for the
Holy Ghost is within him. In Adam man was made a living
soul, but in Christ Jesus he has now risen to the dignity and
majesty of a quickening spirit.

My brethren, where the Holy Spirit enters he is able to
subdue all things unto himself. When the ark came unto the
Philistine temple, down went Dagon; and when the Holy
Ghost enters the soul, sin falls and is broken. If the Holy
Spirit be within, we may rest assured he will tolerate no
reigning sin. He is a spirit of burning, consuming our dross;
a spirit of light, chasing away our darkness. When he makes
a heart his temple, he will scourge out the buyers and sellers
who pollute it. He is not only the purifier within but the
protector too; from temptations that assail us from without
he is as an unconquerable garrison to our soul, making us
impregnable to all assaults. Treasonable sins lurk within us,
but the omniscient eye of God discerns each evil ambush,
and he lays his hand upon every sin which hides itself away
in the dark recesses of our nature. With such an indweller
we need not fear, but that this poor heart of ours will yet
become perfect as God is perfect; and our nature through his
indwelling shall rise into complete meetness for the inheritance of the saints in light. Oh, what blessings are here, and
in what royal language are they all promised! "I will put my
Spirit within you." How positive! How decisive! Suppose they
will not accept the Spirit? Suppose they strive against the
Spirit? Suppose their free-will should get the mastery?
Suppose nonsense! When the Lord says, "I will," nothing
remains to be supposed. If he speaks to chaos, it is order. Do
not say, "Suppose chaos refused to be arranged?" When
Jehovah speaks to darkness, it becomes light. Do not say,
"But, suppose the darkness resists?" What shall resist his
fiat? When the Lord comes forth in his omnipotence who
shall stay his hand, or say unto him, "What doest thou?"

When the Spirit comes to deal in sovereign grace with the hearts of men, without violating their wills he has the power to accomplish his divine purpose, and it shall be accomplished to the praise of the glory of his grace.

III. Lastly, we must ask you to give your thoughts a moment to THE BLESSED RESULTS which come from all this. The indwelling Spirit leads every man in whom he reigns into obedience to the ways of God. I said that the work of grace is commenced from within, but the work does not end there. Before we have considered the whole of the covenant promise we shall find that change of life is guaranteed, a change apparent in works and actions, "Ye shall keep my judgments and do them." We do not begin with works, but we go on to works. Faith first receives the blessing, and then produces holy work. We will not allow the effect to take the place of the cause, but we are equally sure that the effect follows after the cause.

Now, observe the promise of the text before us: "I will cause you to walk in my statutes." The soul that possesses the Spirit becomes active. It walks. It is not passive, as one carried by main force; it works because the Spirit works in it, "to will and to do of his own good pleasure." The man who has no active godliness may fear whether he has any grace at all. If I am only a receiver, and have never brought forth fruit, I may fear that I am the ground that is "nigh unto cursing," for if I were a field that the Lord has blessed, I should yield him a harvest. The Spirit *causes* us to walk, but yet *we* ourselves walk. He works in us to do, but the doing is actually our own. He does not repent, and he does not believe; he has nothing to repent of, and he has nothing to believe. Neither does the Spirit perform works for us—we are led to do these ourselves. We repent and we believe, and we do good works, because he causes us to do so. A willing walk with God is a sweet result of the Holy Spirit's indwelling.

The Holy Ghost leads us to holy habits, for, mark the phrase, "I will cause you to *walk* in my ways." The figure does not represent us as taking a run now and then, or as leaping a step or two and then lying down, but as walking on and on, steadily and continuously. Mere excitement may produce momentary zeal, and transient morality, but habitual holiness is the fruit of the Spirit.

Note, next, the delight it implies. "I will cause you to *walk* in my ways," not as a man who toils, but as one who walks at ease. The believer finds it as sweet to walk in God's ways as Isaac felt it sweet to walk in the fields at eventide. We are not slaves sweating in sore bondage, but children serving with delight. His commandments are not grievous. His yoke is easy and his burden is light.

It implies, too, holy perseverance; the words have the meaning of continuing to follow after holiness. It is a small matter to begin, but to hold out to the end is the testing point.

The text promises to us a complete obedience,—"I will cause you to walk in my statutes, and to keep my judgments." A Christian man is obedient to God,—he minds the first table; he is just to man,—he does not despise the second table. Statutes and judgments are equally dear to believers. We are not willing to give a lame, one-sided obedience to God. The Holy Ghost, when he makes us devout Godward, makes us honest manward.

And the Holy Ghost also works a holy care for righteousness in the soul. "I will cause you to *keep* my judgments;"—that is, to have an exactness of obedience, a precision, a deliberation, a willingness to find out God's will, and a care to attend to it in every jot and tittle. A man in whom dwells the Holy Ghost is careful not to yield himself to the traditions of men but to the commands of God. He pays no attention to the statutes of the great councils of the church, or the ordinances of popes, or the laws of priests, or the mandates of bishops; but he searches out the will of the Lord only. The knee of his conscience bows with lowly reverence before the Lord, but nowhere else. He who has bound us to his altar has loosed all other bonds, so that the traditions of men and the ordinances of priests are contemptible unto us. To God, and God alone, the renewed heart renders obedience, but that obedience he does render.

Now, to what a delightful consummation has our text conducted us. It began with a renewed heart, and it ends in a purified life. It commenced with taking away the stone and giving the flesh; now it gives us the life of Christ written out, in living characters in our daily practice. Glory be to God for this! O soul, if thou art a partaker of it, thou wilt join in this thanksgiving; and if thou art not renewed as yet, I beseech thee do not go about to find these good things anywhere but where they are. At the cross foot thou wilt find a change of heart; where fell the drops of blood from Jesus' nailed hands and feet there is salvation. The Spirit of God will give you a right spirit, and, consequently, a pure life. Look not to your own efforts; rake not the dunghill of your own heart; to the Holy Ghost look you through the blood of the precious Saviour.

Now, to close. All this glorifies God doubly. It glorifies God that a man should walk in his ways; it glorifies God yet more that such obedience should be the result of divine power. The outward life honours God, but the inward, spiritual, gracious work which produced that life, honours him yet more abundantly.

While this glorifies God doubly, it ennobles the soul supremely. To be made holy is to receive a patent of nobility; to be made holy by the indwelling of the Holy Ghost, oh, what shall we say to this! Bring hither the poorest peasant; let her if you will be an aged woman, wrinkled and haggard with labour and with years; let her be ignorant of all learning; but, let me know that in her there is faith in Christ, and that consequently the Holy Ghost dwells in her; I will reverence her above all emperors and kings, for she is above them. What are these crowned ones but men who, perhaps, have waded through slaughter to a throne, while she has been uplifted by the righteousness of Jesus. Their dynasty is, after all, of mushroom growth, but she is of the blood royal of the skies. She hath God within her; Christ is waiting to receive her into his bliss; heaven's inhabitants without her could not be perfected, nor God's purpose be fulfilled, therefore is she noblest of the noble. Judge not after the sight of the eyes, but judge ye after the mind of God, and let saved sinners be precious in your sight. Honour also the Holy Spirit. Speak of him with lowly awe. Never take his name in vain. Take heed lest ye blaspheme it. Reverently seek his company, rejoice in his gifts, love him, quench him not, strive not against him, bow beneath his power, and may he dwell in you, and make you meet to dwell with him for ever, for his name's sake. Amen.

9

The Leading Of The Spirit, The Secret Token Of The Sons Of God

"For as many as are led by the Spirit of God, they are the sons of God."   Romans 8:14

Children are expected to bear some likeness to their parent. Children of God, born of the grandest of all parents, regenerated by the almighty energy of the divine Spirit, are sure to bear a high degree of likeness to their heavenly Father. We cannot be like God in many of his divine attributes, for they are unique and incommunicable: it is not possible for us to wield his power, or to possess his infinite knowledge, neither can we be independent and self-existent, or possessors of sovereignty or worshipfulness. Man can never be so expressly the image of the Father as Jesus is, for he is in a mysterious sense the only begotten Son of God. We can imitate God, however, in many of his attributes; mainly those of a moral and spiritual kind. We must in these qualities be "imitators of God as dear children," or our heavenly pedigree cannot be made out. The point mentioned in the text must never be a matter of question, for if that be doubtful our filial relationship to God is unproved. We must be "led by the Spirit of God." That divine Spirit who is ever with the Father and the Son must be evermore with us so that we are guided, instructed, impelled, quickened, actuated, influenced by him, or else we must not dare to think ourselves the sons of God.

The idea of a divine fatherhood extending over all mankind

does not appear to have been recognised by the apostle Paul, in this text at any rate. Here the fatherhood is for some, not for all, and the text discriminates between the "as many as are led by the Spirit of God" and the rest of mankind who are under no such influence. In men who are devoid of the Holy Ghost there is another spirit, and that other spirit marks them out as sons of another father: "they are of their father the devil, for his works they do." There have been two seeds from the beginning, the seed of the woman and the seed of the serpent, and it is both untrue and immoral to believe God stands in the same relation to the two opposing families. No, my brethren, *our* Father who is in heaven is not to be claimed as father by the unbeliever, for to them Jesus expressly says, "If God were your Father, ye would love me."

The text furnishes us with a very simple but sharp and decisive test, which we shall do well to use upon ourselves. It should be employed to try every one of us. If it had said, "As many as have been baptized are the sons of God," we might have been content to sit very easily in our places. If it had said, "As many as eat and drink at the holy feast of Christian fellowship are the children of God," we might have remembered how short a time ago we were sitting with the saints around the communion table. If the doing of certain external acts, or the utterance of certain prayers, or the avowal of orthodox principles, or abstinence from the grosser vices, had been made the royal mark and heavenly seal of the children of God we might have taken our ease after ascertaining that we are correct as to these things. If being united with an earnest church, and being members of a faithful community had been divinely ordained to be an unquestionable certificate of sonship with the Lord Most High, we might have rested perfectly satisfied without putting ourselves into the crucible: but, since these things are not so arranged, I trust that none of us will be so unwise as to neglect the examination which the text suggests to every prudent mind. Come, my brethren, take nothing for granted on so weighty a business as your soul's eternal interests, but search for evidence and see to the matter as wise householders would do if their whole substance were at stake. Those who are "led by the Spirit of God" are the sons

of God; those who are not led by the Spirit of God are not his
sons: therefore search and see what spirit is in you, that ye
may know whose children ye are.

To help you in this matter I purpose that we should consider, first, where it is that the Spirit of God leads men, that
we may see whether he has ever led us there.

I. WHITHER DOES THE SPIRIT OF GOD LEAD THE SONS OF
GOD?

First of all, he leads them to *repentance*. One of the first
acts of the Holy Spirit is to guide the sons of God to the
mercy-seat with tears in their eyes. He leads us into the
abominable chambers of imagery concealed within our fallen
nature, unfastens door after door and sets open before our
enlightened eyes the secret places polluted with idols and
loathsome images portrayed upon the wall. He points out
with his hand of light the idol gods, the images of jealousy,
the unclean and abominable things within our nature, and
thus he astonishes us into humility. We could not have
believed that such evil things haunted our souls, but his
discoveries undeceive us and correct our boastful estimates
of ourselves. Then, with that same finger, he points to our
past life and shows us the blots, the errors, the wilful sins,
the sins of ignorance, the aggravated transgressions, the
offenses against light and knowledge, which have marred
our career from our youth up: and whereas, previously, we
looked upon the page of our life, and thought it fair, when
the Spirit has led us into light we see how black our history
has been, and, being filled with shame and sorrow, we cry
out for the ear of God, that we may there confess our sin, and
acknowledge that if he should smite us into hell it would be
no more than we deserve. Dear friend, did the Holy Spirit
ever lead you to the stool of repentance? Did he ever cause
you to see how basely you have treated your God, and how
shamefully you have neglected your Saviour? Did he ever
make you bemoan yourself for your iniquities? There is no
way to heaven but by Weeping-cross. He who never felt the
burden of his sin will yet be crushed beneath its enormous
weight when, like some tottering cliff, in judgment's dreadful
hour, it will fall upon him and grind him to powder. No man
ever goes to the chamber of true repentance till the Holy
Spirit leads him there, but every child of God knows what it

is to look on him whom he has pierced, and mourn for his
sin. Holy sorrow for sin is as indispensable as faith in the
atoning blood, and the same Spirit who gives us peace
through the great sacrifice also works in us a hearty grief for
having grieved the Lord. If you have from your youth up
never felt any special mourning for sin, then may God begin
the gracious work in your heart, for salvation is certainly not
wrought in you. You must have repentance, for repentance
is absolutely necessary to the divine life. "Except ye repent
ye shall all likewise perish." The prodigal must cry, "Father,
I have sinned;" the publican must smite on his breast and
pray, "God be merciful to me a sinner." As well destroy one
of the valves of the heart and yet hope to live as take away
repentance, which is the inseparable life-companion of faith.
A dry-eyed faith is no faith at all. When a man has his face
towards Jesus his back is necessarily turned on his sins. As
well look for spring in the garden without the snowdrop as
look for grace in the heart without penitence. That faith
which is not accompanied by repentance is a spurious faith,
and not the faith of God's elect; for no man ever trusts Christ
till he feels he needs a Saviour, and he cannot have felt that
he needs a Saviour unless he has been wearied with the
burden of his sin. The Holy Ghost leads men first to repentance.

He leads them at the same time, while they think little of
themselves, to *think much of Jesus*. Were you ever led to the
cross, beloved? Did you ever stand there, and feel the burden
fall from off your shoulders, and roll away into the Redeemer's sepulchre? When Dr. Neale, the eminent Ritualist, took
John Bunyan's "Pilgrim's Progress," and Romanized it, he
represented the pilgrim as coming to a certain bath, into
which he was plunged and washed, and then his burden was
washed away. He explains this to be the bath of baptism,
though I have never yet seen in any Ritualistic church a
baptistry large enough to wash a pilgrim in. However,
according to this doctored edition of the allegory, Christian
was washed in the laver of baptism, and all his sins were
thus removed. That is the High Church mode of getting rid
of sin: John Bunyan's way, and the true way, is to lose it at
the cross. Now, mark what happened. According to Dr.
Neale's "Pilgrim's Progress," that burden grew again on the

pilgrim's back, and I do not wonder that it did, for a burden which baptism can remove is sure to come again: but the burden which is lost at the cross never appears again for ever. There is no effectual cleansing for sin except by faith in that matchless atonement offered once for all on Calvary's bloody tree, and, as many as are led there by the Spirit of God are the sons of God. The Spirit of God never led a man to think little of Christ, and much of priests. The Spirit of God never led a man to think little of the atoning blood and of simple faith in it, and much of outward forms and ceremonies. The Spirit of God sinks the man and lifts up the Saviour, lowers flesh and blood into the grave, and gives to man new life in the risen Lord, who also hath ascended up on high. "He shall glorify me," said Christ of the Comforter; and that indeed is the Comforter's office.

Now, my dear friends, has the Spirit ever made the Lord Jesus glorious in your eyes? Brethren and sisters, this is the one point above all others. If the Holy Ghost has never made Christ precious to you, you know nothing about him. If he has not lifted Jesus up and sunk your own confidences, if he has not made you feel that Christ is all you want, and that more than all in him you find, then he has never wrought a divine change in your heart. Repentance and faith must stand gazing upon the bleeding Saviour, or else hope will never join them and bring peace as his companion.

When the Spirit has glorified Jesus he leads us to know *other truths*. The Holy Ghost leads the sons of God into all truth. Others go astray after this falsehood or that, but the sheep of God will not hear the voice of strange leaders, their ears are closed to their flatteries: "a stranger will they not follow, for they know not the voice of strangers." Beloved, no lie is of the truth, and no man who receives a lie has been led by the Spirit of God into it, let him say what he may. On the other hand, truth is like a closed chamber to the un-regenerate man; he may read the table of contents of the precious storehouse, but into that secret room he cannot enter: there is one that hath the key of David, who openeth and no man shutteth; and the key with which he openeth is the power of the Holy Ghost. When he opens up a doctrine to a man, the man learns it aright, but he never can know it else. You may go to college, and sit at the feet of the most learned Gamaliel of the day, but you can never know the truth in the heart unless the Holy Ghost shall teach you. We never know a truth in the power of it till it is burned into our soul, as with a hot iron, by an experience of its power, or engraved as upon brass by the mystic revelation of the Spirit. Only the Spirit of God can interweave the truth with the heart, and make it part and parcel of ourselves, so that it is in us and we are in it. Have you thus been led into the truth? If so, give God the glory, for thus the Spirit of God certifies your adoption.

The children of God are led not only into knowledge, but into *love*. They are brought to feel the warmth of love as well as to see the light of truth. The Spirit of God causes every true-born son of God to burn with love to the rest of the family. He who is a stranger to Christian love is a stranger to divine grace. Brethren, we have our disputes, for we dwell where it must needs be that offences come; but we would be slow to take offense and slower still to give it, for we are one in Christ Jesus, and our hearts are knit together by his Spirit. I take it that no honest man ought to hold his tongue concerning any of the errors of the day, it is a mean way of cultivating ease for yourself, and gaining a popularity not worth the having; we must speak the truth whether we offend or please, but this is to be done *in* love and *because* of love. God save from that suggestion of Satan which advises us to speak only those soft things which please men's ears, for he who gives way to this persuasion is a traitor to truth and to the souls of men. The true man of God must speak against every evil and false way; but there beats in his heart a strong affection to every child of God, whatever his errors and his faults may be. The knife of the surgeon is mercifully cruel to the cancer, not out of ill-will to his patient, but out of an honest desire to benefit him; such affectionate faithfulness we have need to cultivate. Love to the saints is the token of the saints. There is an inner church of God's own elect, within every one of the Christian denominations, and this church is made up of men spiritually enlightened, who know the marrow and mystery of the gospel, and whenever they meet, however diversified may be their views, they recognize one another by a sort of sacred freemasonry, the one Spirit which quickens them all alike leaps within them as it recognises the one life in the bosoms of others. Despite their mental divergences, ecclesiastical associations, and doctrinal differences, spiritual men no sooner hear the pass-word, and catch the mystic sign, than they cry, "Give me thy hand, my brother, for my heart is even as thy heart. The Spirit of God has led me and he has led thee, and in our way we tread step by step together; therefore let us have fellowship with each other." The outsiders of the camp, the mixed multitude that come up out of Egypt with our Israel, fall both into fighting and lusting; but the children of the living God, who make the central body-guard of the ark of the Lord, are one in heart with each other, and must be so. "We know that we have passed from death unto life, because we love the brethren."

The Holy Spirit leads us into *intense love for the souls of sinners*. If any man shall say, "It is no business of mine whether men are lost or saved," the Spirit of God never led him into such inhumanity. Bowels of iron have never felt the touch of the Spirit of Love. If ever a preacher's spirit and teaching legitimately lead you to the conclusion that you may view the damnation of your fellow men with com-placency or indifference, you may be sure that the Spirit of God never led him or you in that direction. The devil has more to do with some men's pitiless theology than they imagine. Christ's eyes wept over the sinner's doom, may the Lord save us from thinking of it in any other spirit. He who does not love his fellow man whom he has seen, how can he love God whom he has not seen? Does God look with complacency upon the ruin of our race? Did he not love men so well that he gave his only begotten Son for them? And will he have his own children cold, stoical, and indifferent to the loss of human souls? Beloved, if we dwell with Cain and cry, "Am I my brother's keeper?" the Spirit of God never led us there; he leads us into tenderness, sympathy, compassion, and tearful effort, if by any means we may save some.

Further, the Spirit of God leads the sons of God into *holiness*. I shall not attempt to define what holiness is. That is best seen in the lives of holy men. Can it be seen in your lives? Beloved, if you are of a fierce, unforgiving spirit, the Holy Ghost never led you there; if you are proud and hectoring, the Holy Ghost never led you there; if you are covetous, and lustful after worldly gain, the Holy Ghost never led you there; if you are false in your statements, and unjust in your actions, the Holy Ghost never led you there. If I hear of a professor of religion in the ball-room or the theatre, I know that the Holy Ghost never led him there; if I find a child of God mixing with the ungodly, using their speech, and doing their actions, I am persuaded the Holy Ghost never led him there. But if I see a man living as Christ would have lived, loving and tender, fearless, brave, honest, in all things minding to keep a good conscience before God and men, I hope that the Spirit of God has led him; if I see that man devout before his God, and full of integrity before his fellow men, then I hope and believe that the Spirit of God is his leader and influences his character. "The fruit of the Spirit is love, joy, peace, longsuffering, gentleness, goodness, faith, meekness, temperance: against such there is no law. And they that are Christ's have crucified the flesh with the affections and lusts." I do not wish to speak sharply, but I feel that I must speak plainly, and I feel bound to say that there is far too much hypocrisy among professing Christian people. Many wear the name of Christian, and have nothing else that is Christian about them. It is sorrowful that it should be so, but so it is: false professors have lowered the standard of Christian character, and made the church so like the world that it is hard to say where one begins and the other ends. We exercise church discipline as best we can, but for all that there is a seed of mischief which does not develope into open and overt sin which we cannot remove by discipline, for we are forbidden to root up the tares lest we root up the wheat with them. Men and brethren, we must be holy! It is of no use our talking about being orthodox in belief: we must be orthodox in life, and, if we are not, the soundest creed will only increase our damnation. I hear men boast that they are Nonconformists to the backbone, as if that were the essential matter: better far be Christians to the heart. What is the use of ecclesiastical Nonconformity if the heart is still conformed to the world? Another man will glory that he is a Conformist, but what is the good of that unless he is conformed to the image of Christ? Holiness is the main consideration, and if we are not led into it by the Spirit of holiness neither are we the sons of God.

Furthermore, the Holy Ghost leads those who are the children of God into *vital godliness*—the mystic essence of spiritual life. For instance, the Holy Ghost leads the saints to prayer, which is the vital breath of their souls. Whenever they get true access to the mercy-seat it is by his power. The Holy Spirit leads them to search the word, and opens their understandings to receive it; he leads them into meditation, and the chewing of the cud of truth; he leads them into fellowship with himself and with the Son of God. He lifts them right away from worldly cares into heavenly contemplations; he leads them away to the heavenly places, where Christ sitteth at the right hand of God, and where his saints reign with him. Beloved, have you ever felt these leadings? I am talking of them, but do *you* understand them? Are these things matters of constant experience with you? It is easy to say, "Yes, I know what you mean." Have you felt them? Are these every-day things with you, for, as the Lord liveth, if you have not been led into prayer, and into communion with God, the Spirit of God is not in you, and you are none of his?

The Spirit of God, moreover, leads the sons of God into *usefulness*, some in one path, and some in another, while a few are conducted into very eminent service, and into self-consecration of the highest order. We bless God for missionaries who have been led of the Spirit of God among the wildest tribes to preach Jesus Christ. We thank God for holy women who, at home, have been led into the darkest parts of this city to labour amongst the most fallen and depraved, to lift up Christ before them that he might lift them up to himself. Blessed are those men and women who are led by the Spirit of God into labours more abundant, for the more abundant shall be their joy. Methinks I ought to remind you all that if you are doing nothing for Jesus the Spirit of God has never led you into this idleness. If you eat the fat and drink the sweet in the house of God, but never do a hand's turn for the household, the Spirit of God cannot have taught you this abominable sloth. There is a something for everyone of us to do, a talent committed to the charge of every believer, and if we have the Spirit of God dwelling in us he will tell us what the Lord has appointed us to perform, he will strengthen us for the doing of it, and set his seal and blessing upon it when it is done. Those dead branches of the vine which yield no clusters for the Lord, either by patience in suffering or activity in working, have no evidence that they are of the household of faith. Those who take no part in labours for Jesus can hardly hope that they will ultimately be partakers in his glory with him.

Thus have I, in a plain manner, without diving too deep into the matter, given you an answer to the question, "Whither does the Spirit of God lead the sons of God?"

II. I shall now answer another question with still greater brevity—HOW DOES THE SPIRIT LEAD THE SONS OF GOD? The reply would be this: *the Spirit of God operates upon our spirits mysteriously.* We cannot explain his mode of operation, except that we shall probably be right if we conclude that he operates upon our spirits somewhat in the same way in which our spirits operate upon other men's spirits, only after a nobler sort. Now, how do I influence the spirit of my friend? I do it usually by imparting to him something which I know, which I hope will have power over his mind by suggesting motives to him, and so influencing his acts. I cannot operate upon my neighbour's mind mechanically; no tool can touch the heart, no hand can shape the mind. We act upon matter by machinery, but upon mind by argument, by reason, by instruction, and so we endeavour to fashion men as we desire. *One great instrument which the Holy Ghost uses upon the mind is the word of God.* The word, as we have it printed in the Bible, is the great instrument in the hand of the Spirit for leading the children of God in the right way. If you want to know what you ought to do, say as the old Scotchman used to say to his wife, "Reach down yon Bible." That is the map of the way, the heavenly pilgrim's knapsack guide; and if you are led by the word of God the Spirit of God is with the word, and works through it, and you are led by the Spirit of God. Quote chapter and verse for an action, and, unless you have wrested the passage, you may rest assured you have acted rightly. Be sure that such and such a thing is a command of God written in the book, inspired by the Holy Ghost, and you do not need a voice of thunder from heaven or an angelic whisper, you have a more sure word of prophecy, unto which you will do well if you take heed as unto a light that shineth in a dark place.

The Spirit of God also speaks through his ministers. The word preached is often blest, as well as the word written, but this can only be the case when the word preached is in conformity with the word written. At times God's ministers seem to give the written word its own voice, so that it sounds forth as if just spoken by the seer who originally received it. As they speak it drops into the ear like honey from the comb, it leaps forth like water from the wellhead; and at such times goes into the heart fresh and warm, with even a greater energy than when we read it alone in our chamber. How often do we feel when we read a truth in a book (even though that book is God's word) our sluggish condition prevents its having such power over us as it has when a man of God who has experienced it, and tasted it, and handled it, and speaks of it as the outpouring of his own soul. May God grant that the ministry which you usually attend may be to you the voice of God. May it be guidance to your feet, comfort to your heart, invigoration to your faith, and refreshment to your soul, and while you are sitting in the house of prayer may you feel, "That word is for me: I came here not knowing what to do, but I have received direction; I was faint and weary, but I have obtained consolation and strength. The voice of the pastor has been as the oracle of God to my soul, and now I go my way comforted as Hannah did when the Lord's servant had spoken peace to her soul."

Upon another point I would speak with great caution, and would have you think of it with more caution still, for it is a matter which has been sadly abused and turned to fanatical purposes. The Spirit of God does, I believe, *directly, even apart from the word, speak in the hearts of the saints.* There are inward monitions which are to be devoutly obeyed, guidances mysterious and secret, which must be implicitly followed. It is not a subject for common talk, but is meant for the ear of the intelligent believer who will not misunderstand us. There will come to you sometimes, you know not why, certain inward checks, such as Paul received when he assayed to go into Mysia, but the Spirit suffered him not. There is a certain act which you might do or might not do, but an impulse comes upon you which seems to say, "Not that, or not now." Do not violate that inward restraint.

"Quench not the Spirit." At another time a proper thing, a fit thing will have been forgotten by you for a time, but it comes upon you strongly that it is to be done at once, and for some reason you cannot shake off the impression. Do no violence to that impulse. It is not to every man that the Holy Ghost speaks in such a way; but he has his favoured ones, and these must jealously guard the privilege, for perhaps if they are deaf when he speaks he may never speak to them any more in that way. If we render reverent obedience to divine monitions they will become far more common with us. "Why," says one, "you run into Quakerism." I cannot help that. If this is Quakerism I am so far a Quaker: names do not concern me one way or another. You each one know whether your personal experience gives confirmation to what I have advanced or otherwise, and there let the question end; for, mark you, I advance this with caution, and do not set up such monitions as indispensable signs of a son of God. There is a story told (and many such some of us could tell almost as striking) of a certain friend who one night was influenced to take his horse from the stable, and ride some six or seven miles to a certain house where lived a person whom he had never seen. He arrived at dead of night, knocked at the door, and was answered by the master of the house, who seemed to be in great confusion of mind. The midnight visitor said, "Friend, I have been sent to thee, I know not why, but surely the Lord has some reason for having sent me to thee. Is there anything peculiar about thy circumstances?" The man, struck with amazement, asked him to come up stairs, and there showed him a halter tied to a beam. He was putting the rope about his neck to commit suicide when a knock sounded at the door, he resolved that he would go down and answer the call, and then return and destroy himself; but the friend whom God had sent talked to him, brought him to a cooler mind, and helped him in the pecuniary difficulty which embarrassed him, and the man lived to be an honourable Christian man. I solemnly declare that monitions equally powerful have guided me, and their results have been remarkable to me at any rate. For the most part these are secrets between God and my own soul, neither am I eager to break the seal and tell them to others. There are too many swine about for us to be very lavish with our pearls. If we were obedient to such impulses if we did not save suicides we might save souls, and might often be in the hands of God as angels sent from heaven: but we are like the horse and the mule, which have no understanding, whose mouth must be held in with bit and bridle; we are not tender enough to be sensitive to the divine influence when it comes, and so the Lord does not please to speak to many of us in this way so frequently as we could desire. Still, it is true that "as many as are led by the Spirit of God," however he may lead them, "they are the sons of God."

Let me here remark that being "*led* by the Spirit of God" is a remarkable expression. It does not say, "As many as are driven by the Spirit of God." No, the devil is a driver, and when he enters either into men or into hogs he drives them furiously. Remember how the whole herd ran violently down a steep place into the sea. Whenever you see a man fanatical and wild, whatever spirit is in him it is not the Spirit of Christ. The Spirit of Christ is forcible, it worketh mightily, but it is a quiet Spirit; it is not an eagle, but a dove. He comes as a rushing wind, and fills the house where the disciples are sitting, but at the same time he comes not as a whirlwind from the wilderness to smite the four corners of the habitation, or it would become a ruin. He comes as a flame of fire sitting upon each of the favoured ones, but it is not a flame of fire that burns the house and destroys Jerusalem. No, the Spirit of God is gentle; he does not drive, but lead. "As many as are led by the Spirit of God, they are the sons of God." The Spirit treats us honourably in thus working; he does not deal with us as with dumb, driven cattle, or soulless waves of the sea; he treats us as intelligent beings, made for thought and reflection. He leads us as a man guideth his child, or as one leadeth his fellow, and we are honoured by subjecting our minds and wills to so divine a Spirit. Never is the will truly free until the Holy Ghost sweetly subdues it to willing obedience.

Thus the Spirit of God works, though we cannot explain the method, for that is a thing too wonderful for us, and sooner may we know the path of an eagle in the air, or the way of a serpent upon a rock. As we cannot walk in search of the springs of the sea, so is this also hidden from all living. We have said somewhat upon the subject, and, as far as we can, have answered the question, "How does the Spirit of God lead the children of God?" but we are of yesterday, and know nothing, and, therefore, confessing our ignorance, we pass on.

III. The last question is, WHEN DOES THE SPIRIT LEAD THE SONS OF GOD? Ah, brethren, that question needs anxious answering.

The Spirit of God *would* always lead the sons of God, but, alas, there are times when even children of God will not be led. They are wilful and headstrong, and start aside. The healthy condition of a child of God is to be always led by the Spirit of God. Mark this—led by the Spirit every day; not on Sundays only, nor alone at periods set apart for prayer, but during every minute of every hour of every day. We ought to be led by the Spirit in little things as well as in great matters, for, observe, if we were led by the Spirit all our lives in all other matters, yet, if only one action apart from the Spirit were suffered to run to its full results, it would ruin us. The mercy is that the Lord restoreth our souls; but there is never a single hour when a Christian can afford to wander from the way of the Spirit. If you have a guide along an intricate pathway, and you allow him to conduct you for half an hour, and then say, "Now, I shall direct myself for the next five minutes," in that short space you will lose the benefit of having a guide at all. It is clear that a pilot who only occasionally directs the ship is very little better than none. If you were traversing an unknown and difficult pathway it would render all directions useless if you were to say, "They told me to turn to the right at this tower, but I mean to try the left." That one turning will affect the whole of your after journey. If we err, and are really sons of God, our divine leader will make us retrace our steps with bitter tears, and feel what an evil and bitter thing it is to have chosen our own delusions. If we use our divine leader wisely we shall always follow him. Child of God, the Spirit must lead you in everything. "Well, but," say you, "*will* he?" Ah, "Will he?" Yes, to your astonishment. When you are in difficulties, consult the Holy Spirit in the Word. Hear what God speaks in the inspired volume, and if no light comes from thence kneel down and pray. When you see a sign-post in a country road, and it tells you which way to go, you are glad to follow its directions; but if in your perplexities you see no sign-post, what are you to do? *Pray.* Cast yourself upon the divine guidance, and you shall make no mistake; for even if you happen to pick the roughest road it will be the right one if you have selected it with holy caution, and in the fear of God. Beloved, the Lord will never let a vessel be dashed upon the rocks whose tiller has been given into his hands. Give up the helm to God, and your barque will thread the narrow winding channel of life, avoid every sandbank and sunken rock, and arrive safely at the fair havens of eternal bliss.

The question—when are the sons of God led by the Spirit? is to be answered thus,—when they are as they should be they are always distinctly led by him; and though, owing to sin in them, they are not always obedient to the same degree, yet the power which usually influences their lives is the Spirit of God.

Now I close, using the text thus. First as a *test.* Am I a child of God? If so, I am led by the Spirit. Am I led by the Spirit? I am afraid some of you never think of that matter. By whom are you led? Hundreds of religious people are led by their minister or by a Christian friend, and so far so good for them; but their religion will be a failure unless they are led by the Spirit. Let me put the question again that you may not shirk it,—Are you led by the Spirit? If you are you are a child of God, and if not you are none of his.

That gives me a second use of the text, namely, the use of *consolation.* If you are a child of God you will be led by the Spirit. Now, are you in doubt to-night? Are you embarrassed? Are you in difficulties? Then the sons of God are led by the Spirit, and you will be led. Perhaps you are looking a long way ahead, and you are afraid of difficulties in your old age, or at the death of a relative. Now, God has not given us eyes to pry into the future, and what is the use of our peering where we cannot see? Leave it all to your heavenly Father; and you will be unerringly led by the Holy Ghost. When you come to the place where you thought there would be a difficulty, very likely there will be none. "Who shall roll away the stone from the door of the sepulchre?" said the holy women, but when they came to the sepulchre, lo, the stone was rolled away already. Go on as a child of God, walking by faith, with the full assurance that the path of faith, if not an easy one, will always be a safe one; and all will be well, and you will be led in a right way to a city of habitations.

The last word of all is, the text is an *assurance*. If you are led by the Spirit of God then you are most certainly a son of God. Can you say to-night, "I do yield myself up to the Lord's will. I am not perfect, I wish I were; I am burdened with a thousand infirmities, but yet if the Lord will teach me I am willing to learn, if he will have patience with me I will strive to follow him. Oh, what would I give to be perfectly holy! I long to be pure within. I wish above all things else in this world that I may never grieve my God, but walk with him in the light as he is in the light, and have fellowship with him, while the blood of Jesus Christ his Son cleanses me from all sin"? My brother, be well assured that none ever longed like that but a child of God. Flesh and blood hath not revealed this unto thee. No soul, except an heir of heaven, ever had such wishings, and aspirings, and groanings after holiness, and such sorrowings over failures and mistakes. The text does not say, "He who runs in the Spirit is a son of God," but he that is *led* by the Spirit of God. Now, we may stumble whilst we are being led; a man may go very slowly while he is being led; he may go on crutches he is being led; he may crawl on his hands and knees while he is being led: but none of these absolutely prevent his being truly led. With all your weaknesses and infirmities, the point is—Are you led by the Spirit of God? If you are, all your infirmities and failures are forgiven you for Christ's name's sake, and your being led is the mark of your being born from above. Go home and rejoice in your sonship, and pray God if you have been weak to make you strong, if you have been lame to heal you, and, if you have crept along on your hands and knees, to help you to walk uprightly; but, after all, bless him that his Spirit does lead you. If you can only walk, ask him to make you run; and if you can run, ask him to make you mount on wings as eagles. Do not be satisfied with anything short of the highest attainments; and, at the same time, if you have not reached them, do not despair. Remember that in most families there are babes as well as men and women: the little child in long clothes carried in the arms, and laid on the breast, is just as dear to the parent as the son who in the fulness of his manhood marches by his father's side, and takes his share in the battle of life. You are sons of God if you are led by the Spirit, however small your stature and feeble your grace. The age, strength, or education of the man are not essential to his sonship, but the trueness of his birth is the all-important matter. See ye to it that ye are led by the Spirit, or your parentage is not from above.

If you have been condemned by this sermon, then fly away to Jesus, and penitently and trustfully rest in him. May the Spirit of God lead you to do that, and you are then a child of God. May he bless you now. Amen.

10

The Sword Of The Spirit

"And take...the sword of the Spirit, which is the word of God."
                                        Ephesians 6:17

To be a Christian is to be a warrior. The good soldier of Jesus Christ must not expect to find ease in this world: it is a battle-field. Neither must he reckon upon the friendship of the world; for that would be enmity against God. His occupation is war. As he puts on piece by piece of the panoply provided for him, he may wisely say to himself, "This warns me of danger; this prepares me for warfare; this prophesies opposition."

Difficulties meet us even in standing our ground; for the apostle, two or three times, bids us— "Stand." In the rush of the fight, men are apt to be carried off their legs. If they can keep their footing, they will be victorious; but if they are borne down by the rush of their adversaries, everything is lost. You are to put on the heavenly armor in order that you may stand; and you will need it to maintain the position in which your Captain has placed you. If even to stand requires all this care, judge ye what the warfare must be! The apostle also speaks of *withstanding* as well as standing. We are not merely to defend, but also to assail. It is not enough that you are not conquered; you have to conquer: and hence we find, that we are to take, not only a helmet to protect the head, but also a sword, with which to annoy the foe. Ours, therefore, is a stern conflict, standing and withstanding; and

we shall want all the armour from the divine magazine, all
the strength from the mighty God of Jacob.

It is clear from our text that our defence and our conquest
must be obtained by sheer fighting. Many try compromise;
but if you are a true Christian, you can never do this business well. The language of deceit fits not a holy tongue. The
adversary is the father of lies, and those that are with him
understand the art of equivocation; but saints abhor it. If we
discuss terms of peace, and attempt to gain something by
policy, we have entered upon a course from which we shall
return in disgrace. We have no order from our Captain to
patch up a truce, and get as good terms as we can. We are
not sent out to offer concessions. It is said that if we yield a
little, perhaps the world will yield a little also, and good may
come of it. If we are not too strict and narrow, perhaps sin
will kindly consent to be more decent. Our association with
it will prevent its being so barefaced and atrocious. If we are
not narrow-minded, our broad doctrine will go down with
the world, and those on the other side will not be so greedy
of error as they now are. No such thing. Assuredly this is not
the order which our Captain has issued. When peace is to be
made, he will make it himself, or he will tell us how to
behave to that end; but at present our orders are very
different.

Neither may we hope to gain by being neutral, or granting
an occasional truce. We are not to cease from conflict, and
try to be as agreeable as we can with our Lord's foes, fre-
quenting their assemblies, and tasting their dainties. No
such orders are written here. You are to grasp your weapon,
and go forth to fight.

Neither may you so much as dream of winning the battle
by accident. No man was ever holy by a happy chance.
Infinite damage may be done by carelessness; but no man
ever won life's battle by it. To let things go on as they please,
is to let them bear us down to hell. We have no orders to be
quiet, and take matters easily. No; we are to pray always,
and watch constantly. The one note that rings out from the
text is this:—TAKE THE SWORD! TAKE THE SWORD! No longer
is it, talk and debate! No longer is it, parley and
compromise! The word of thunder is—*Take the sword*. The
Captain's voice is clear as a trumpet—*Take the sword!* No

Christian man here will have been obedient to our text unless with clear, sharp, and decisive firmness, courage, and resolve, he takes the sword. We must go to heaven sword in hand, all the way. "TAKE THE SWORD." On this command I would enlarge. May the Holy Spirit help me!

It is noteworthy that there is only one weapon of offence provided, although there are several pieces of armour. The Roman soldier usually carried a spear as well as a sword. We have seen frequent representations of the legionary standing upon guard as sentry, and he almost always stands with a spear in his right hand, while his sword hangs at his side. But Paul, for excellent reasons, concentrates our offensive weapon in one, because it answers for all. We are to use *the sword*, and that only. Therefore, if you are going to this fight, see well to your only weapon. If you are to have no other, take care that you have this always in your hand. Let the Captain's voice ring in your ear, *"Take the sword! Take the sword!"*, and so go forth to the field.

Notice, first, *the sword you are to take is the sword of the Spirit, which is the Word of God*. That is our first head; and the second is equally upon the surface of the text: *This sword is to be ours*. We are ordered to take the sword of the Spirit, and so make it our own sword.

I. First, the Word of God which is to be our one weapon is of noble origin; for it is "THE SWORD OF THE SPIRIT." It has the properties of a sword, and those were given it by the Spirit of God.

Here we note that *the Holy Spirit has a sword*. He is quiet as the dew, tender as the anointing oil, soft as the zephyr of eventide, and peaceful as a dove; and yet, under another aspect, he wields a deadly weapon. He is the Spirit of judgment and the Spirit of burning, and he beareth not the sword in vain. Of him it may be said, "The Lord is a man of war: Jehovah is his name."

The Word of God in the hand of the Spirit wounds very terribly, and makes the heart of man to bleed. Do you not remember, some of you, when you used to be gashed with this sword Sunday after Sunday? Were you not cut to the heart by it, so as to be angry with it? You almost made up your mind to turn away from hearing the gospel again. That sword pursued you, and pierced you in the secrets of your soul, and made you bleed in a thousand places. At last you were "pricked in the heart", which is a far better thing than being "cut to the heart"; and then execution was done, indeed. That wound was deadly, and none but he that killed could make you alive. Do you recollect how, after this, your sins were slain one after another? Their necks were laid on the block, and the Spirit acted as an executioner with his sword. After that, blessed be God, your fears, and doubts, and despair, and unbelief, were also hacked to pieces by this same sword. The Word gave you life; but it was at the first a great killer. Your soul was like a battle-field after a great fight, under the first operations of the divine Spirit, whose sword returneth not empty from the conflict.

Beloved, the Spirit of God has war with the Amalek of evil and error from generation to generation. He will spare none of the evils which now pollute the nations; his sword will never be quiet till all these Canaanites are destroyed. The Holy Spirit glorifies Christ not only by what he reveals, but also by what he overturns. The strife may be weary, but it will be carried on from age to age, till the Lord Jesus shall appear; for ever shall the Spirit of God espouse the cause of love against hate, of truth against error, of holiness against sin, of Christ against Satan. He will win the day, and those who are with him shall in his might be more than conquerors. The Holy Spirit has proclaimed war, and wields a two-edged sword.

The Holy Spirit wields no sword but the Word of God. This wonderful Book, which contains the utterances of God's mouth, is the one weapon which the Holy Ghost elects to use for his warlike purposes. It is a spiritual weapon, and so is suitable to the Holy Spirit. The weapons of his warfare are not carnal: he never uses either persecution or patronage, force or bribery, glitter of grandeur, or terror of power. He works upon men by the Word, which is suitable to his own spiritual nature, and to the spiritual work which is to be accomplished. While it is spiritual, this weapon is "mighty through God." A cut from the Word of God will cleave a man's spirit from head to foot; so sharp is this sword. Though by long practice in sin a man may have coated him- self as with mail impenetrable, yet the Word of the Lord will divide the northern iron and the steel. The Holy Ghost can make a man feel the divine power of the sacred Word in the very centre of his being. For battling with the spirits of man, or with spirits of an infernal kind, there is no weapon so keen, so piercing, so able to divide between the joints and marrow, so penetrating as to the thoughts and intents of the heart. The Word, in the Spirit's hand, gives no flesh-wound, but cuts into the man's heart, and so wounds him that there is no healing save by supernatural power. The wounded conscience will bleed; its pains will be upon it day and night; and though it seek out a thousand medicines, no salve but one can cure a gash which this terrible sword has made. This weapon is two-edged; indeed, it is all edge; and whichever way it strikes, it wounds and kills. There is no such a thing as the flat of the sword of the Spirit: it has a razor edge every way. Beware how you handle it, you critics; it may wound even you: it will cut you to your destruction, one of these days, except ye be converted. He that uses the Word in the Lord's battles may use it upon carnal hopes, and then strike back upon unbelieving fears; he may smite with one edge the love of sin, and then with the other the pride of self-righteousness. It is a conquering weapon in all ways, this wondrous sword of the Spirit of God.

The Word, we say, is the only sword which the Spirit uses. I know the Holy Ghost uses gracious sermons; but it is only in proportion as they have the Word of God in them. I know the Holy Ghost uses religious books; but only so far as they are the Word of God told out in other language. Conviction, conversion, and consolation still are wrought, and only by the Word of God. Learn, then, the wisdom of using the Word of God for holy purposes. The Spirit has abundant ability to speak of his own self, apart from the written Word. The Holy Ghost is God, and therefore he is the greatest spirit in the universe. All wisdom dwells in him. He thought out the laws which govern nature and direct providence. The Holy Spirit is the great teacher of human spirits: he taught Bezaleel and the artificers in the wilderness how to make the fine linen, and the gold and carved work for the tabernacle. All arts and sciences are perfectly known to him, and infinitely more than men can ever discover. Yet he will not use these things in this holy controversy. In the quarrel of his covenant he neither uses philosophy, nor science, nor rhetoric. In con-

tending against the powers of darkness, "The sword of the
Spirit is the Word of God." "It is written" is his master-
stroke. Words which God has spoken by holy men of old, and
has caused to be recorded on the sacred page—these are the
battle-axe and weapons of war of his Spirit. This Book
contains the Word of God, and is the Word of God; and this
it is which the Holy Ghost judges to be so effectual a weapon
against evil that he uses this, and this only, as his sword in
the great conflict with the powers of darkness.

*The Word is the sword of the Spirit because it is of his own
making.* He will not use a weapon of human workmanship,
lest the sword boast itself against the hand that wields it.
The Holy Ghost revealed the mind of God to the minds of
holy men; he spake the word into their hearts, and thus he
made them think as he would have them think and to write
what he willed them to write: so that what they spoke and
wrote was spoken and written as they were moved by the
Holy Ghost. Blessed be the Holy Spirit for deigning to use so
many writers, and yet himself to remain the veritable
Author of this collection of holy books. We are grateful for
Moses, for David, for Isaiah, for Paul, for Peter, for John, but
most of all for that superintending Editor, that innermost
Author of the whole sacred volume—even the Holy Ghost. A
warrior may well be careful as to the make of his sword. If a
man had made his own sword, had tempered the metal, had
himself passed the blade through many fires, and wrought it
to perfection, then, if he were a skilful workman, he would
feel confidence in his sword. When work is done nowadays,
it is, as a rule, badly done. Work done by contract is usually
scamped in some part or another; but when a man does a
work for himself he is likely to do it thoroughly, and produce
an article which he can depend upon. The Holy Ghost has
made this Book himself: every portion of it bears his initial
and impress; and thus he has a sword worthy of his own
hand, a true Jerusalem blade of heavenly fabric. He delights
to use a weapon so divinely made, and he does use it right
gloriously.

*The Word of God is also the sword of the Spirit because he
puts the edge upon it.* It is because he is in it that it is so
keen and cutting. I believe in the inspiration of Holy
Scripture, not only in the day when it was written, but

onward, and even to this day. It is still inspired; still doth
the Holy Ghost breathe through the chosen words. I told you
the sword was all edge; but I would add that the Holy Spirit
makes it so. It would have no edge at all if it were not for his
presence within it, and his perpetual working by it. How
many people read their Bibles, and yet derive no more
benefit therefrom than if they had read an old almanack! In
fact, they would more easily keep awake over an ancient
Bradshaw than over a chapter of Scripture. The ministers of
the gospel may preach God's Word in all sincerity and
purity, and yet, if the Spirit of God be not present, we might
as well have preached mere moral essays, for no good can
come of our testimony. The Holy Ghost rides in the chariot of
Scripture, and not in the waggon of modern thought.
Scripture is that ark of the covenant which contains the
golden pot of manna, and also bears above it the divine light
of God's shining. The Spirit of God worketh in, by, and
through, and with the Word; and if we keep to that Word, we
may rest assured that the Holy Ghost will keep with us, and
make our testimony to be a thing of power. Let us pray the
blessed Spirit to put an edge on our preaching, lest we say
much and accomplish little. Hear us in this thing, O blessed
One!

It is "the sword of the Spirit" because *he alone can instruct
us in the use of it.* You think, young man, that you can pick
up your Bible, and go and preach from it at once, properly
and successfully. You have made a presumptuous mistake. A
sword is a weapon which may do hurt to the man who
flourishes with it in mere wanton pride. No one can handle
the sword of the Spirit aright save the chosen man whom
God hath ordained from before the foundation of the world,
and trained in feats of arms. By this the elect of God are
known—that they love the Word of God, and they have a
reverence for it, and discern between it and the words of
man. Notice the lambs in the field, just now; and there may
be a thousand ewes and lambs; but every lamb finds out its
own mother. So does a true-born child of God know where to
go for the milk which is to nourish his soul. The sheep of
Christ know the Shepherd's voice in the Word, and a
stranger will they not follow, for they know not the voice of
strangers. God's own people have discernment to discover

and relish God's own Word. They will not be misled by the cunning craftiness of human devices. Saints know the Scriptures by inward instinct. The holy life, which God has infused into believers by his Spirit, loves the Scriptures, and learns how to use them for holy purposes. Young soldier, you must go to the training-ground of the Holy Spirit to be made a proficient swordsman. You will go in vain to the metaphysician or to the logician; for neither of these knows how to handle a spiritual weapon. In other arts they may be masters; but in the sacred use of diving theology they are mere fools. In the things of the Word we are dunces till we enter the school of the Holy Ghost. He must take of the things of Christ, and show them unto us. He must teach us how to grip this sword by faith, and how to hold it by watchfulness, so as to parry the adversary's thrust, and carry the war into the foeman's territory. He is well taught who can swing this great two-handed sword to and fro, and mow a lane through the midst of his opponents, and come out a conqueror at the end. It may take a long time to learn this art; but we have a right skilful Teacher. Those of us who have been in this warfare thirty or forty years feel that we have not yet reached the full use of this sword; nay, I know for one, that I need daily to be taught how to use this mysterious weapon, which is capable of so much more than I have yet supposed. It is the sword of the Spirit, adapted for the use of an Almighty arm, and therefore equal to the doing of far more than we think. Holy Spirit, teach us new feats of arms by this thy sword!

But, chiefly, it is the sword of the Spirit, because *he is the great Master in the use of it.* Oh, that he would come and show us this morning how he can thrust and cleave with it! In this house of prayer we have often seen him at his work. Here the slain of the Lord have been many. We have seen this sword take off the head of many a Goliath doubt, and slay a horde of cares and unbeliefs. We have seen the Spirit pile up heaps on heaps of the slain when the Word of conviction has gone forth, and men have seen sin to be sin, and fallen down as dead before the Lord and his law. We also know what the use of the sword by the Spirit of God means, for within our own being he has left marks of his prowess. He has killed our doubts and fears, and left no more mistrusts to worry us. There was a man of God who was frequently subject to doubts, even doubts upon the fundamentals of religion. He hated this state of mind; but still he could not get rid of the habit of evil questioning. In answer to prayer, the Spirit came, and convinced him of the pride of his intellect, and of the wickedness of setting up his judgment against the Word of the Lord; and from that day forward he was never the subject of another fit of unbelief. He saw things clearly in the light of the Holy Spirit; and that is to see them indeed. The great giant of doubt is sorely wounded by the sword of the Spirit—yea, he is slain outright; for the Spirit works in the believer such a conviction of the truth that assurance banishes suspicion. When the Holy Spirit deals with the lusts of the flesh, and the lusts of the eye and the pride of life, these also lie at his feet, trophies to the power of his mighty weapon, even the Word of God! The Holy Spirit is glorious in the use of this sword. He finds that this weapon suits his hand, and he seeks no other. Let us use it also, and be glad to do so. Though it is the sword of the Spirit, yet our feebler hand may grasp it; yea, and find in the grasping that somewhat of the divine power comes unto our arm.

Dear brethren, is it not a very high honour put upon you, as soldiers of the cross, that you should be allowed, nay, commanded to take the sword of the Spirit? The raw recruit is not trusted with the general's sword; but here are you armed with the weapon of God the Holy Ghost, and called upon to bear that sacred sword which is so gloriously wielded by the Lord God himself. This we are to bear, and no other. Does the timid heart enquire, "Wherewithal, my Master, shall I meet my adversaries"? "Here," saith the Holy Ghost, "take this! This is my own sword; I have done great marvels with it; take it, and nothing shall stand against you." When you remember the potency of this sword, when the Spirit tests it upon yourself, you may take it with confidence, and use it in your holy war with full assurance. That Word of God which could convert *you*, can convert anybody; if it could kill your despair, it can remove another man's despondency; if it has conquered your pride and self-will, it can subdue the like in your children and your neighbours. Having done what it has certainly done for you,

you may have a full persuasion that, before its power, no case is hopeless. Wherefore, see to it, that you use from this day forth no other weapon than the sword of the Spirit, which is the Word of God.

II. This fairly lands me in the second portion of my discourse. The Word of God is the sword of the Spirit; but IT IS ALSO TO BE OUR SWORD.

Here I must begin again, and go over much the same ground. *We shall need a sword.* Our warfare is not child's play: we mean business. We have to deal with fierce foes, who are only to be met with keen weapons. Buffets will not suffice in this contest; we must come to sword-cuts. You may be of a very quiet spirit, but your adversaries are not so. If you attempt to play at Christian warfare, they will not. To meet the powers of darkness is no sham battle. They mean mischief. Nothing but your eternal damnation will satisfy the fiendish hearts of Satan and his crew. You must take not so much a flag to unfurl, or a drum to beat, as a sword to use, and a specially sharp sword too. In this combat you will have to use a sword such as even evil spirits can feel, capable of dividing asunder of soul and spirit, and of the joints and marrow. If you are to live through this fight, and come off victorious, no form of conflict will suffice less sharp and cutting than sword-work. Depend upon it that in this struggle you will be forced to come to close quarters. The foe aims at your heart, and pushes home. A spear will not do, nor bow and arrow; the enemy is too near for anything but hand-to-hand fighting. Brethren, our foes are not only of our house, but of our heart. I find an enemy within which is always near, and I cannot get away from him. I find that my antagonist will get his hand on my throat if he can. If our foes were far away, and we could play upon them with artillery which would kill at six or seven miles' distance, we might lead a pretty easy life. But no; they are *here!* At our doors! Yea, within us; nearer than hands and feet. Now for the short sword: the claymore of Holy Scripture, to stab and cut, near and now. No sling and stone will avail us here, but we must take the sword. You have to slay your foe, or your foe will slay you. It is with us Christians as it was with the Highlanders in battle, when their leader called out to them, "Lads, there they are! If you dinna kill them they will kill you." There is no room for peace: it is war to the knife, not only now, but to life's end.

The use of the sword is needful for attack. I have reminded you several times already that it will not suffice for the Christian to guard against sin, and ward off temptation from himself; he has to assail the powers of evil. In our case, the best method of defence is an attack. I have heard of one who would bring an action in law to gain his ends, for he thought this better than being the defendant. That may be matter of question; but in war it is often safer to assail than defend. Carry the warfare into the enemy's territory. Be trying to win from the adversary, and he will not win so much from you. Do not merely be sober yourselves, but attack drunkenness. Do not be content with being free from superstition yourself, but expose it wherever it appears. Do not merely be devout when you feel obliged to be so, but pray for the growth of the kingdom; pray always. Do not merely say, "I will keep Satan out of my family by bringing up my children aright", but go to the Sunday-school, and teach other children, and so carry the war over the border. God forbid that we should ever go to war as a nation! But if we were at war with some nation on the Continent, I should certainly say, "Let the continentals have the battles on their own ground: we do not want a campaign over here." It is wise to keep the war in the enemy's own regions. If we had fought the devil more in the world, he might never have been able to invade the church so terribly as he has done. Attack with the sword, for it is your calling, and thus will you best defend yourself.

We need the sword for real fighting. Do you think that you can dream yourselves into heaven? or ride there in the chariot of ease? or fly on the wings of brass music? You make a great mistake if you so imagine. A real war is raging, your opponents are in deadly earnest, and you must take your sword.

And, further, *we need this sword: this sword of the Spirit, which is the Word of God.* We say with David, "There is none like that; give it me." It has wrought such wonders that we prefer it to all others. No other will match the enemy's weapon. If we fight the devil with human reason, the first time our wooden sword comes in contact with a Satanic temptation it will be cut in pieces. If you do not wield a true Jerusalem blade you are in grave peril; your weapon will break off at the hilt, and where will you be? Standing defenceless, with nothing but the handle of a broken sword in your hand, you will be the object of your adversary's ridicule. You must have this sword, for no other will penetrate the foe, and no other will last out the battle. After twenty years, what has become of the pious resolutions of your youth? What is the staying power of your consecration made in the hour of enthusiasm? Alas, how little trust can be placed in it! What would become of us after thirty years of fighting, if we had not the Word of God to rely upon? The Word of the Lord endureth for ever; but nothing else does. We may do well in early days, but we shall fail in old age if we have not eternal verities to fall back upon.

I can commend this sword to you all, my brethren, although you are so varied in character. This sword suits every hand. Youth or age may alike use this weapon. These dear girls from the Orphanage, and yonder lads from the Bible-class, may fight the battle of their youth with the Word of God; for Holy Scripture may impress and guide our freshest life. You that have grown grey, you that have passed seventy or eighty, you will value the Bible more than ever, and you will find that this sword is the best for veteran warriors. Young men and young women, here is a sword suited for all of you, and well does it become the hand of the feeblest and the gentlest. The Holy Ghost has in the sacred Word prepared an implement of warfare suited for great minds and small, for the cultured and the uneducated. A wonderful sword this is, which, in the hand of faith, reveals an adaptation marvellous to the last degree.

Whatever others may say, it is sufficient for us that this is the regulation sword. A soldier is not left to choose his own equipment; he must carry such arms as his sovereign appoints. This is the regulation sword in Christ's army. The sword of the Spirit, which is the Word of God, is what you are bidden to take; and if you in wilfulness resolve to exchange it for another, you commit an act of rebellion, and you make the change at your own risk and peril. Come, then, let us each one take the Word of God, and carry it nearer our hearts than ever; for such is the word of command, "Take the sword of the Spirit, which is the word of God."

Now, see what we are told to do. We need a sword; we need this sword; *we are to take this sword.* Note that we are not told that we may lay it down: the demand to take the sword is continuous, and there is no hint of its being suspended. There is a time, of course, when the soldier of her Majesty may remove his sword from his side, and put off his regimentals; there is never such a time with a Christian. One might have thought, from what we have seen of late, that orders had come from headquarters that the soldiers were to lay down the sword of the Spirit, the Word of God, and take to lighter weapons. Entertainments, amusements, farces, and sing-song are now used to do what the gospel has failed to achieve! Is it not sadly so? Well, if any will try these silly toys, I can only say that they have no command from their Lord to warrant them in their proceedings. Take all these things, and see what they will do; but you make the trial at your own risk, and on your own heads the result of failure will fall.

The standing-orders are to take the sword of the Spirit, and no new regulation has ever been issued by the great Captain of salvation. From the days of Paul till now, the word stands, "Take the sword of the Spirit." All other things will surely fail, and hence the one sole abiding command is, "Take the sword of the Spirit." We are not told to hang up this sword for exhibition. Certain people have a handsomely-bound Bible to lie upon the table of the best room; and a fine ornament it is. A Family Bible is a treasure. But I pray you do not let your love of the Bible end there. With a soldier in war, a sword is not meant to be hung up in the tent, nor even to be flourished in the air; but it is issued to be used. Nor are we to push this sword into a sheath, as many do who take the Bible, and add so much of criticism, or of their own opinion to it, that its edge is not felt. Many men use their low opinion of inspiration as a scabbard into which they push the Bible down. Their vast knowledge makes a beautiful scabbard, and they push down the sword, saying, "Keep still there! O sword of the Lord, rest and be quiet!" After we have preached our heart out, and men have felt the power of it, they make a desperate effort to imprison the Word in their unbelieving theory, or in their worldliness. They hold down

the Word all the week with a firm hand, for fear its edge or
point should wound them. It is the scabbard of culture, or
philosophy, or of progress, and in this they shut up the living
Word of God as in a coffin.

We are not to bury the Word under other matters; but we
are to take it as a sword: which means, as I understand it,
first, *believe it*. Believe every portion of it; believe it with a
true and real faith, not with a mere credal faith, which says,
"This is the orthodox thing." Believe it as a matter of fact for
every day, affecting your life. Believe it. And when you have
believed it, then *study it*. Oh, for a closer study of the Word
of God! Are there not some of you who have never even
heard or read all that the Lord has said? Are there not
passages of the Bible which have never been read by you? It
is a melancholy fact that there should be even a line of the
sacred Scriptures which has never once come under your
eye. Do read the Bible right through, from beginning to end.
Begin tomorrow: nay, begin to-day, and go steadily through
the whole of the sacred books, with prayer and meditation.
Never let it be suspected by you that God has recorded
truths in his Word which you have never even once read.
Study the Word, and work out its meaning. Go deep into the
spirit of inspiration. He gets most gold who digs the deepest
in this mine. They used to say of certain mines in Cornwall
that the deeper you went the richer was the ore; assuredly is
it so with the mines of inspired Scripture. The deeper you go
under the Spirit's guidance the larger is the reward for your
toil. Take the sword with the grip of sincere faith; hold it fast
by a fuller knowledge, and then exercise yourself daily in its
use. The sword is to be taken for earnest fight. You will not
be long before occasion arises in such a world as this. You
will have to parry with it, to pierce with it, to cut with it, and
to kill with it. "Where shall I begin?" says one. Begin at
home, and, for many a day, you will have your hands full.
When you have slain all the rebels at home, and long before
that, you may take a turn at those around you in the world,
and in the professing church. Inside your own heart you will
find a band of bandits which should be exterminated. There
will always be need to keep the sword going within your own
territory. End this civil war before you go into foreign parts.
When the war within the city of Mansoul has been

victoriously carried through, besiege the heart of your friend, your child, your neighbour. Behold, the world lieth in the wicked one! Errors abound, and colossal systems of falsehood still stand aloft. Men are still dragged down by the arch-deceiver. Surely, we feel our swords flying out of their sheaths when we think of the millions who are being ruined by sin and error. Oh, for a mighty onslaught upon the powers of darkness!

Once more, *we are to take this sword with a purpose.* We are to use it that we may be able to stand and to withstand. If you want to stand, draw the sword, and smite your doubts. How fiercely unbelief assails! Here comes a doubt as to your election. Pierce it through with the Word. Anon comes a doubt as to the precious blood. Cleave it from head to foot with the assurance of the Word that the blood of Jesus cleanseth us from all sin. Here comes another doubt, and yet another. As quick as arm can move, drive texts of Scripture through every new fallacy, every new denial of truth, and spit the whole of them upon the rapier of the Word. It will be for your good to kill these doubts outright. Do not play with them, but fight them in real earnest. You will find that temptations also will come in hordes. Meet them with the precepts of sacred Writ, and slay even the desire of evil by the Spirit's application of the Holy Word. The washing of water by the Word is a glorious cleanser. Discouragements will arise like mists of the morning. Oh, that God's Word may shine them away with the beams of the promises! Your afflictions multiply, and you will never be able to overcome impatience and distrust except by the infallible Word of God. You can bear trial, and bear it patiently, if you use this weapon to kill anxiety. You will "stand fast in the evil day", and having done all, you will still stand, if this sword be in your hand.

You have not only to stand fast yourselves, but you have to win souls for Christ. Do not try to conquer sin in others, or capture a heart for Jesus, except with the sword of the Spirit. How the devil laughs when we try to make converts apart from Holy Scripture and the Holy Spirit! He laughs, I say; for he derides our folly. What can you do, you children, playing with your little wooden swords—what can you do against men covered from head to foot with the steel mail of

the habit of sin? Sunday-school teachers, teach your children
more and more the pure Word of God; and preachers, do not
try to be original, but be content to take of the things of
Christ, and show them to the people; for that is what the
Holy Ghost himself does; and you will be wise to use his
method and his sword. No sinner around you will be saved
except by the knowledge of the great truths contained in the
Word of God. No man will ever be brought to repentance, to
faith, and to life in Christ, apart from the constant application of the truth through the Spirit. I hear great shouting,
great noises everywhere, about great things that are going
to be done: let us see them. The whole world is going to be
embraced within the church; so they say. I fear the world
will not be much the better for inclusion in such a church.
Big boasters should heed the word of the wise man, "Let not
him that girdeth on his harness boast himself as he that
putteth it off." If the champion goeth forth with any other
sword than the Word of God, he had better not boast at all;
for he will come back with his sword broken, his shield cast
away, and himself grimy with dishonour. Defeat awaits that
man who forsakes the Word of the Lord.

I have done when I have asked you to remember that the
text is in the present tense: *Take unto you the sword of the
Spirit even now*. What varieties of people there are here this
morning! Believers have come hither in all sorts of perils; let
them each one take the sword of the Spirit, and they will
overcome every foe. Here, too, are seekers who wish to be
Christians; but they cannot compass it. What is the matter
this morning? "Oh," says one, "I have been in the habit of
sinning, and the habit is very strong upon me." Fight with
sinful habits with the Word of God, as the sword of the
Spirit: so only will you conquer your evil self. Find a text of
Scripture that will cleave your sin down to the chine, or stab
it to the heart. "Alas! Satan tempts me horribly," cries one;
"I have been lately assailed in many ways." Have you? You
are not the first. Our divine Lord in the wilderness was
tempted of the devil. He might have fought Satan with a
thousand weapons; but he chose to defeat him with this one
only. He said, "It is written; it is written; it is written." He
pricked the foeman so sorely with this sharp point, that the
arch-adversary thought to try the same sword; and he also

began to say, "It is written." But he cut himself with this sword, for he did not quote the passages correctly, nor give the whole of them; and the Master soon found the way to knock aside his sword, and wound him still more. Follow your Lord's example. "Oh, but," says one, "I am so low in spirits." Very well; fight lowness of spirits with the Word of God. "The doctor recommended me," says one, "to take a little spirits to raise my spirits." Those doctors are always having this sin laid to their charge. I am not so sure that they are not often maligned. You like the dose, and that is why you take it. Try the Word of God for lowness of spirits, and you will have found a sure remedy. I find, if I can lay a promise under my tongue, like a sweet lozenge, and keep it in my mouth or mind all the day long, I am happy enough. If I cannot find a Scripture to comfort me, then my inward troubles are multiplied. Fight despondency and despair with the sword of the Spirit. I cannot tell what your particular difficulty may be at this moment; but I give you this direction for all holy warfare—"Take the sword of the Spirit, which is the word of God." You must overcome every enemy; and this weapon is all you need. If you, my hearer, would overcome sin and conquer unbelief, take such a word as this, "Look unto me, and be ye saved, all the ends of the earth;" and as you look you shall be saved, and doubt shall die, and sin be slain. God grant you his Spirit's aid, for Christ's sake! Amen.

11

The Holy Ghost-The Great Teacher

"Howbeit when he, the Spirit of truth, is come, he will guide you into all truth: for he shall not speak of himself; but whatsoever he shall hear, that shall he speak: and he will shew you things to come."   John 16:13

This generation hath gradually, and almost imperceptibly, become to a great extent a godless generation. One of the diseases of the present generation of mankind is their secret but deep-seated godlessness, by which they have so far departed from the knowledge of God. Science has discovered to us second causes; and hence, many have too much forgotten the first Great Cause, the Author of all: they have been able so far to pry into secrets, that the great axiom of the existence of a God, has been too much neglected. Even among professing Christians, while there is a great amount of religion, there is too little godliness: there is much external formalism, but too little inward acknowledgment of God, too little living on God, living with God, and relying upon God. Hence arises the sad fact that when you enter many of our places of worship you will certainly hear the name of God mentioned; but except in the benediction, you would scarcely know there was a Trinity. In many places dedicated to Jehovah the name of Jesus is too often kept in the background; the Holy Spirit is almost entirely neglected; and very little is said concerning his sacred influence. Even religious men have become to a large degree godless in this age. We sadly require more preaching regarding God; more preaching of those things which look not so much at the creature to be saved, as at God the Great One to be extolled. My firm conviction is, that in proportion as we have more regard for the sacred godhead, the wondrous Trinity in Unity, shall we see a greater display of God's power, and a more glorious manifestation of his might in our churches. May God send us a Christ-exalting, Spirit-loving ministry— men who shall proclaim God the Holy Ghost in all his offices, and shall extol God the Saviour as the author and finisher of our faith; not neglecting that Great God, the Father of his people, who, before all worlds, elected us in Christ his Son, justified us through his righteousness, and will inevitably preserve us and gather us together in one, in the consummation of all things at the last great day.

Our text has regard to God the Holy Spirit; of Him we shall speak and Him only, if His sweet influence shall rest upon us.

The disciples had been instructed by Christ concerning certain elementary doctrines, but Jesus did not teach his disciples more than what we should call the A B C of religion. He gives his reasons for this in the 12th verse: "I have yet many things to say unto you, but you cannot bear them now." His disciples were not possessors of the Spirit. They had the Spirit so far as the work of conversion was concerned, but not as to the matters of bright illumination, profound instruction, prophecy, and inspiration. He says, "I am now about to depart, and when I go from you I will send the Comforter unto you. Ye cannot bear these things now, howbeit, when he, the Spirit of truth is come, he will guide you into all truth." The same promise that he made to his apostles, stands good to all his children; and in reviewing it, we shall take it as *our* portion and heritage, and shall not consider ourselves intruders upon the manor of the apostles, or upon their exclusive rights and prerogatives; for we conceive that Jesus says even to us, "When he, the Spirit of truth is come, he will guide you into all truth."

Dwelling exclusively upon our text, we have five things. First of all, here is *an attainment mentioned*—a knowledge of all truth; secondly, here is *a difficulty suggested*—which is, that we need guidance into all truth; thirdly, here is *a person provided*—"when he, the Spirit shall come, he shall guide you into all truth;" fourthly, here is *a manner hinted at*—"he shall guide you into all truth;" fifthly here is *a sign given as to the working of the Spirit*—we may know whether he works, by his "guiding us into *all* truth,"—into all of one thing; not *truths*, but *truth*.

I. Here is AN ATTAINMENT MENTIONED, which is a knowledge of all truth. We know that some conceive doctrinal knowledge to be of very little importance, and of no practical use. We do not think so. We believe the science of Christ crucified and a judgment of the teachings of Scripture to be exceedingly valuable; we think it is right, that the Christian ministry should not only be arousing but instructing; not merely awakening, but enlightening; that it should appeal not only to the passions but to the understanding. We are far from thinking doctrinal knowledge to be of secondary importance; we believe it to be one of the first things in the Christian life, to know the truth, and then to practice it. We scarcely need this morning tell you how desirable it is for us to be well taught in things of the kingdom.

First of all, *nature itself*, (when it has been sanctified by grace), *gives us a strong desire to know all truth*. The natural man separateth himself and intermeddleth with all knowledge. God has put an instinct in him by which he is rendered unsatisfied if he cannot probe mystery to its bottom; he can never be content until he can unriddle secrets. What we call curiosity is something given us of God impelling us to search into the knowledge of natural things; that curiosity, sanctified by the Spirit, is also brought to bear in matters of heavenly science and celestial wisdom. "Bless the Lord," said David, "O my soul, and *all that is within me* bless his holy name!" If there is a curiosity within us, it ought to be employed and developed in a search after truth. "All that is within me," sanctified by the Spirit should be developed. And, verily, the Christian man feels an intense longing to bury his ignorance and receive wisdom. If he, when in his natural estate panted for terrestrial knowledge, how much more ardent is the wish to unravel, if possible, the sacred mysteries of God's Word! A true Christian is always intently reading and searching the Scripture that he may be able to certify himself as to its main and cardinal truths. I do not think much of that man who does not wish to understand doctrines; I cannot conceive him to be in a right position when he thinks it is no matter whether he believes a lie or truth, whether he is heretic or orthodox, whether he received the Word of God as it is written, or as it is diluted and misconstrued by man. God's Word will ever be to a Christian a source of great anxiety; a sacred instinct within will lead him to pry into it; he will seek to understand it. Oh! there are some who forget this, men who purposely abstain from mentioning what are called high doctrines, because they think if they should mention high doctrines they would be dangerous; so they keep them back. Foolish men! they do not know anything of human nature; for if they did understand a grain's worth of humanity, they would know that the hiding of these things impels men to search them out. From the fact that they do not mention them, they drive men to places where these and these only, are preached. They say, "If I preach election, and predestination, and these dark things, people will all go straight away, and become Antinomians." I am not so sure if they were to be called Antinomians it would hurt them much; but hear me, oh, ye ministers that conceal these truths, that is the way to make them Antinomians, by silencing these doctrines. Curiosity is strong; if you tell them they must not pluck the truth, they will be sure to do it; but if you give it to them as you find it in God's Word, they will not seek to "wrest" it. Enlightened men *will* have the truth, and if they see election in Scripture they will say, "*it is there*, and I will find it out. If I cannot get it in one place, I will get it in another." The true Christian has an inward longing and anxiety after it; he is hungry and thirsty after the word of righteousness, and he must and will feed on this bread of heaven, or at all hazards he will leave the husks which unsound divines would offer him.

Not only is this attainment to be desired because nature teaches us so, but a knowledge of all truth is *very essential for our comfort*. I do believe that many persons have been distressed half their lives from the fact that they had not clear views of truth. Many poor souls, for instance, under conviction, abide three or four times as long in sorrow of mind as they would require to do if they had some one to instruct them in the great matter of justification. So there are believers who are often troubling themselves about falling away; but if they knew in their soul the great consolation that we are kept by the grace of God through faith unto salvation, they would be no more troubled about it. So have I found some distressed about the unpardonable sin; but if God instructs us in that doctrine, and shows us that no conscience that is really awakened ever can commit that sin, but that when it is committed God gives us up to a seared conscience, so that we never fear or tremble afterwards, all that distress would be alleviated. Depend on this, the more you know of God's truth—all things else being equal—the more comfortable you will be as a Christian. Nothing can give a greater light on your path than a clear understanding of divine things. It is a mingle-mangled gospel too commonly preached, which causes the downcast faces of Christians. Give me the congregation whose faces are bright with joy, let their eyes glisten at the sound of the gospel, then will I believe that it is God's own words they are receiving. Instead thereof you will often see melancholy congregations whose visages are not much different from the bitter countenance of poor creatures swallowing medicine, because the word spoken terrifies them by its legality, instead of comforting them by its grace. We love a cheerful gospel, and we think "all the truth" will tend to comfort the Christian.

"Comfort again?" says another, "always comfort." Ah, but there is another reason why we prize truth, because we believe that a true knowledge of all the truth *will keep us very much out of danger.* No doctrine is so calculated to preserve a man from sin as the doctrine of the grace of God. Those who have called it a licentious doctrine did not know anything at all about it. Poor ignorant things, they little knew that their own vile stuff was the most licentious doctrine under heaven. If they knew the grace of God in truth, they would soon see that there was no preservative from lying like a knowledge that we are elect of God from the foundation of the world. There is nothing like a belief in my eternal perseverance, and the immutability of my Father's affection, which can keep me near to him from a motive of simple gratitude. Nothing makes a man so virtuous as belief of truth. A lying doctrine will soon beget a lying practice. A man cannot have an erroneous belief without by-and-bye having an erroneous life. I believe the one thing naturally begets the other. Keep near God's truth; keep near his word; keep the head right, and especially keep your heart right with regard to truth, and your feet will not go far astray.

Again, I hold also that this attainment to the knowledge of all truth is very desirable for *the usefulness which it will give us in the world at large.* We should not be selfish: we should always consider whether a thing will be beneficial to others. A knowledge of all truth will make us very serviceable in this world. We shall be skilful physicians who know how to take the poor distressed soul aside, to put the finger on his eye, and take the scale off for him, that heaven's light may comfort him. There will be no character, however perplexing may be its peculiar phase, but we shall be able to speak to it and comfort it. He who holds the truth, is usually the most useful man. As a good Presbyterian brother said to me the other day: "I know God has blessed you exceedingly in gathering in souls, but it is an extraordinary fact that nearly all the men I know—with scarcely an exception—who have been made useful in gathering in souls, have held the great doctrines of the grace of God." Almost every man whom God has blessed to the building up of the church in prosperity, and around whom the people have rallied, has been a man who has held firmly free grace from first to last, through the finished salvation of Christ. Do not you think you need have errors in your doctrine to make you useful. We have some who preach Calvinism all the first part of the sermon, and finish up with Arminianism, because they think that will make them useful. Useful nonsense!—That is all it is. A man, if he cannot be useful with the truth, cannot be useful with an error. There is enough in the pure doctrine of God, without introducing heresies to preach to sinners. As far as I know, I never felt hampered or cramped in addressing the ungodly in my life. I can speak with as much fervency, and yet not in the same style as those who hold the contrary views of God's truth. Those who hold God's word, never need add something untrue in speaking to men. The sturdy truth of God touches every chord in every man's heart. If we can, by God's grace, put our hand inside man's heart, we want nothing but that whole truth to move him thoroughly, and to stir him up. There is nothing like the real truth and the whole truth, to make a man useful.

II. Now, again, here is a DIFFICULTY SUGGESTED, and that is—that we require a guide to conduct us into all truth. The difficulty is that truth is not so easy to discover. There is no man born in this world by nature who has the truth in his heart. There is no creature that ever was fashioned, since the fall, who has a knowledge of truth innate and natural. It has been disputed by many philosophers whether there are such things as innate ideas at all. But is of no use disputing as to whether there are any innate ideas of truth. There are none such. There are ideas of everything that is wrong and evil; but in us—that is our flesh—there dwelleth no *good* thing; we are born in sin, and shapened in iniquity; in sin did our mother conceive us. There is nothing in us good, and no tendency to righteousness. Then, since we are not born with the truth, we have the task of searching for it. If we are to be blest by being eminently useful as Christian men, we must be well instructed in matters of revelation; but here is the difficulty—that we cannot follow without a guide the winding paths of truth. Why this?

First, because of *the very great intricacy of truth itself.* Truth itself is no easy thing to discover. Those who fancy they know everything and constantly dogmatise with the spirit of "We are the men, and wisdom will die with us," of course see no difficulties whatever in the system they hold; but I believe, the most earnest student of Scripture will find things in the Bible which puzzle him; however earnestly he reads it, he will see some mysteries too deep for him to understand. He will cry out "Truth! I cannot find thee; I know not where thou art, thou art beyond me; I cannot fully view thee." Truth is a path so narrow that two can scarce walk together in it; we usually tread the narrow way in single file; two men can seldom walk arm in arm in the truth. We believe the same truth in the main but we cannot walk together in the path, it is too narrow. The way of truth is very difficult. If you step an inch aside on the right you are in a dangerous error, and if you swerve a little to the left you are equally in the mire. On the one hand there is a huge precipice, and on the other a deep morass; and unless you keep to the true line, to the breadth of a hair, you will go astray. Truth is a narrow path indeed. It is a path the eagle's eye hath not seen, and a depth the diver hath not visited. It is like the veins of metal in a mine, it is often of excessive thinness, and moreover it runneth not in one continued layer. Lose it once, and you may dig for miles and not discover it again; the eye must watch perpetually the direction of the lode. Grains of truth are like the grains of gold in the rivers of Australia—they must be shaken by the hand of patience, and washed in the stream of honesty, or the fine gold will be mingled with sand. Truth is often mingled with error, and it is hard to distinguish it; but we bless God it is said, "When the Spirit of truth is come, he will guide you into all truth."

Another reason why we need a guide is, *the insidiousness of error*. It easily steals upon us, and, if I may so describe our position, we are often like we were on Thursday night in that tremendous fog. Most of us were feeling for ourselves, and wondering where on earth we were. We could scarcely see an inch before us. We came to a place where there were three turnings. We thought we knew the old spot. There was the lamp-post, and now we must take a sharp turn to the left. But not so. We ought to have gone a little to the right. We have been so often to the same place, that we think we know every flag-stone;—and there's our friend's shop over the way. It is dark, but we think we must be quite right, and all the while we are quite wrong, and find ourselves half-a-mile out of the way. So it is with matters of truth. We think, surely this is the right path; and the voice of the evil one whispers, "that is the way, walk ye in it." You do so, and you find to your great dismay, that instead of the path of truth, you have been walking in the paths of unrighteous-ness and erroneous doctrines. The way of life is a labyrinth; the grassiest paths and the most bewitching, are the farthest away from right; the most enticing, are those which are garnished with wrested truths. I believe there is not a counterfeit coin in the world so much like a genuine one, as some errors are like the truth. One is base metal, the other is true gold; still in externals they differ very little.

We also need a guide, because *we are so prone to go astray*. Why, if the path of heaven were as straight as Bunyan pictures it, with no turning to the right hand or left—and no doubt it is,—we are so prone to go astray, that we should go to the right hand to the Mountains of Destruction, or to the left in the dark Wood of Desolation. David says, "I have gone astray like a lost sheep." That means very often: for if a sheep is put into a field twenty times, if it does not get out twenty-one times, it will be because it cannot; because the place is hurdled up, and it cannot find a hole in the hedge. If grace did not guide a man, he would go astray, though there were hand-posts all the way to heaven. Let it be written, "Miklat, Miklat, the way to refuge," he would turn aside, and the avenger of blood would overtake him, if some guide did not, like the angels in Sodom, put his hand on his shoulders, and cry, "Escape, escape, for thy life! look not behind thee; stay not in all the plain." These, then, are the reasons why we need a guide.

III. In the third place, here is A PERSON PROVIDED. This is none other than God, and this God is none other than a person. This person is "he, the Spirit," the "Spirit of truth;" not an influence or an emanation, but actually a person. "When the Spirit of truth is come, he shall guide you into all truth." Now, we wish you to look at this guide to consider how adapted he is to us.

In the first place, he is *infallible*; he knows everything and cannot lead us astray. If I pin my sleeve to another man's coat, he may lead me part of the way rightly, but by-and-bye he will go wrong himself, and I shall be led astray with him; but if I give myself to the Holy Ghost and ask his guidance, there is no fear of my wandering.

Again, we rejoice in this Spirit because he is *ever-present*. We fall into a difficulty sometimes; we say, "Oh, if I could take this to my minister, he would explain it; but I live so far off, and am not able to see him." That perplexes us, and we turn the text round and round and cannot make anything out of it. We look at the commentators. We take down pious Thomas Scott, and, as usual, he says nothing about it if it be a dark passage. Then we go to holy Matthew Henry, and if it is an easy Scripture, he is sure to explain it; but if it is a text hard to be understood, it is likely enough, of course, left in his own gloom. And even Dr. Gill himself, the most con- sistent of commentators, when he comes to a hard passage, manifestly avoids it in some degree. But when we have no commentator or minister, we have still the Holy Spirit. And let me tell you a little secret: whenever you cannot understand a text, open your Bible, bend your knee, and pray over that text; and if it does not split into atoms and open itself, try again. If prayer does not explain it, it is one of the things God did not intend you to know, and you may be content to be ignorant of it. Prayer is the key that openeth the cabinets of mystery. Prayer and faith are sacred pick-locks that can open secrets, and obtain great treasures. There is no college for holy education like that of the blessed Spirit, for he is an ever-present tutor, to whom we have only to bend the knee, and he is at our side, the great expositor of truth.

But there is one thing about the suitability of this guide which is remarkable. I do not know whether it has struck you—the Holy Spirit can "guide us *into* a truth." Now, man can guide us *to* a truth, but it is only the Holy Spirit who can "guide us *into* a truth." "When he, the Spirit of truth, shall come, he shall guide you *into*"—mark that word—"all truth." Now, for instance, it is a long while before you can lead some people to election; but when you have made them see its correctness, you have not led them "into" it. You may show them that it is plainly stated in Scripture, but they will turn away and hate it. You take them to another great truth, but they have been brought up in a different fashion, and though they cannot answer your arguments, they say, "The man is right, perhaps," and they whisper—but so low that conscience itself cannot hear—"but it is so contrary to my prejudices, that I cannot receive it." After you have led them *to* the truth, and they see it is true, how hard it is to lead them *into* it! There are many of my hearers who are brought *to* the truth of their depravity, but they are not brought *into* it, and made to feel it. Some of you are brought to know the truth that God keeps us from day to day; but you rarely get into it, so as to live in continual dependence upon God the Holy Ghost, and draw fresh supplies from him. The thing is—to get inside it. A Christian should do with truth as a snail does with his shell—live inside it, as well as carry it on his back, and bear it perpetually about with him. The Holy Ghost, it is said, shall lead us into all truth. You may be brought to a chamber where there is an abundance of gold and silver, but you will be no richer unless you effect an entrance. It is the Spirit's work to unbar the two leaved gates, and bring us into a truth, so that we may get inside it, and, as dear old Rowland Hill said, "Not only hold the truth, but have the truth hold us."

IV. Fourthly, here is A METHOD SUGGESTED: "He shall guide you into all truth." Now I must have an illustration. I must compare truth to some cave or grotto that you have heard of, with wondrous stalactites hanging from the roof, and others starting from the floor; a cavern, glittering with spar and abounding in marvels. Before entering the cavern you inquire for a guide, who comes with his lighted flambeau. He conducts you down to a considerable depth, and you find yourself in the midst of the cave. He leads you through different chambers. Here he points to a little stream rushing from amid the rocks, and indicates its rise and progress; there he points to some peculiar rock and tells you its name; then takes you into a large natural hall, tells you how many persons once feasted in it; and so on. Truth is a grand series of caverns, it is our glory to have so great and wise a conductor. Imagine that we are coming to the darkness of it. He is a light shining in the midst of us to guide us. And by the light he shows us wondrous things. In three ways the Holy Ghost teaches us: by suggestion, direction, and illumination.

First, he guides us into all truth *by suggesting it*. There are thoughts that dwell in our minds that were not born there, but which were exotics brought from heaven and put there by the spirit. It is not a fancy that angels whisper into our ears, and that devils do the same: both good and evil spirits hold converse with men; and some of us have known it. We have had strange thoughts which were not the offspring of our souls, but which came from angelic visitants; and direct temptations and evil insinuations have we had which were not brewed in our own souls, but which came from the pestilential cauldron of hell. So the Spirit doth speak in men's ears, sometimes in the darkness of the night. In ages gone by he spoke in dreams and visions, but now he speaketh by his Word. Have you not at times had unaccountably in the middle of your business a thought concerning God and heavenly things, and could not tell whence it came? Have you not been reading or studying the Scripture, but a text came across your mind, and you could not help it;

though you even put it down it was like cork in water, and
would swim up again to the top of your mind. Well, that good
thought was put there by the Spirit; he often guides his
people into all truth by suggesting, just as the guide in the
grotto does with his flambeau. He does not say a word,
perhaps, but he walks into a passage himself, and you follow
him; so the Spirit suggests a thought, and your heart follows
it up. Well can I remember the manner in which I learned
the doctrines of grace in a single instant. Born, as all of us
are by nature, an Arminian, I still believed the old things I
had heard continually from the pulpit, and did not see the
grace of God. I remember sitting one day in the house of God
and hearing a sermon as dry as possible, and as worthless as
all such sermons are, when a thought struck my mind—how
came I to be converted? I prayed, thought I. Then I thought,
how came I to pray? I was induced to pray by reading the
Scriptures. How came I to read the Scriptures? Why—I did
read them; and what led me to that? And then, in a moment,
I saw that God was at the bottom of all, and that he was the
author of faith. And then the whole doctrine opened up to
me, from which I have not departed.

But sometimes he leads us *by direction*. The guide points
and says—"There, gentlemen, go along that particular path;
that is the way." So the Spirit gives a direction and tendency
to our thoughts; not suggesting a new one but letting a
particular thought when it starts take such-and-such a
direction; not so much putting a boat on the stream as steer-
ing it when it is there. When our thoughts are considering
sacred things he leads us into a more excellent channel from
that in which we started. Time after time have you commenced a meditation on a certain doctrine and, unaccountably, you were gradually led away into another, and you saw
how one doctrine leaned on another, as is the case with the
stones in the arch of a bridge, all hanging on the keystone of
Jesus Christ crucified. You were brought to see these things
not by a new idea suggested, but by direction given to your
thoughts.

But perhaps the best way in which the Holy Ghost leads us
into all truth is by *illumination*. He illuminates the Bible.
Now, have any of you an illuminated Bible at home? "No,"
says one, "I have a morocco Bible; I have a Polyglot Bible; I

have a marginal reference Bible." Ah! that is all very well
but have you an illuminated Bible? "Yes, I have a large
family Bible with pictures in it." There is a picture of John
the Baptist baptizing Christ by pouring water on his head
and many other nonsensical things; but that is not what I
mean: have you an illuminated Bible? "Yes; I have a Bible
with splendid engravings in it." Yes; I know you may have;
but have you an illuminated Bible? "I don't understand what
you mean by an illuminated Bible." Well, it is the Christian
man who has an illuminated Bible. He does not buy it
illuminated originally, but when he reads it

> "A glory gilds the sacred page,
>   Majestic like the sun;
> Which gives a light to every age,
>   It gives, but borrows none."

There is nothing like reading an illuminated Bible, beloved.
You may read to all eternity, and never learn anything by it,
unless it is illuminated by the Spirit; and then the words
shine forth like stars. The book seems made of gold leaf;
every single letter glitters like a diamond. Oh! it is a blessed
thing to read an illuminated Bible lit up by the radiance of
the Holy Ghost. Hast thou read the Bible and studied it, my
brother, and yet have thine eyes been unenlightened? Go
and say, "O Lord, gild the Bible for me. I want an expounded
Bible. Illuminate it; shine upon it; for I cannot read it to
profit, unless thou enlightenest me." Blind men may read
the Bible with their fingers, but blind souls cannot. We want
a light to read the Bible by; there is no reading it in the dark.
Thus the Holy Spirit leads us into all truth, by suggesting
ideas, by directing our thoughts, and by illuminating the
Scriptures when we read them.

V. The last thing is AN EVIDENCE. The question arises,
How may I know whether I am enlightened by the Spirit's
influence, and led into all truth? First, you may know the
Spirit's influence by its *unity*—he guides us into all *truth*:
secondly, by its *universality*—he guides us into *all* truth.

First, if you are judging a minister, whether he has the
Holy Ghost in him or not, you may know him in the first
place, by *the constant unity of his testimony*. A man cannot
be enlightened by the Holy Spirit, who preaches yea and

nay. The Spirit never says one thing at one time and another thing at another time. There are indeed many good men who say both yea and nay; but still their contrary testimonies are not both from God the Spirit, for God the Spirit cannot witness to black and white, to a falsehood and truth. It has been always held as a first principle, that truth is one thing. But some persons say, "I find one thing in one part of the Bible and another thing in another and though it contradicts itself I must believe it." All quite right, brother, if it did contradict itself; but the fault is not in the wood but in the carpenter. Many carpenters do not understand dove-tailing; so there are many preachers who do not understand dove-tailing. It is very nice work, and it is not easily learnt; it takes some apprenticeship to make all doctrines square together. Some preachers preach very good Calvinism for half-an-hour, and the next quarter-of-an hour Arminianism. If they are Calvinists, let them stick to it; if they are Arminians, let them stick to it; let their preaching be all of a piece. Don't let them pile up things only to kick them all down again; let us have one thing woven from the top throughout, and let us not rend it. How did Solomon know the true mother of the child? "Cut it in halves," said he. The woman who was not the mother, did not care so long as the other did not get the whole, and she consented. "Ah!" said the true mother, "give her the living child. Let her have it, rather than cut it in halves." So the true child of God would say "I give it up, let my opponent conquer; I do not want to have the truth cut in halves. I would rather be all wrong, than have the word altered to my taste." We do not want to have a divided Bible. No, we claim the whole living child or none at all. We may rest assured of this, that until we get rid of our linsey-wolsey doctrine, and cease to sow mingled seed, we shall not have a blessing. An enlightened mind cannot believe a gospel which denies itself; it must be one thing or the other. One thing cannot contradict another, and yet it and its opposite be equally true. You may know the Spirit's influence then, by the unity of its testimony.

And you may know it by its *universality*. The true child of God will not be led into some truth but into all truth. When first he starts he will not know half the truth, he will believe it but not understand it; he will have the germ of it but not the sum total in all its breadth and length. There is nothing like learning by experience. A man cannot set up for a theologian in a week. Certain doctrines take years to develop themselves. Like the aloe that taketh a hundred years to be dressed, there be some truths that must lie long in the heart before they really come out and make themselves appear so that we can speak of them as that we do know; and testify of that which we have seen. The Spirit will gradually lead us into all truth. For instance, if it be true that Jesus Christ is to reign upon the earth personally for a thousand years, as I am inclined to believe it is, if I be under the Spirit, that will be more and more opened to me, until I with confidence declare it. Some men begin very timidly. A man says, at first, "I know we are justified by faith, and have peace with God, but so many have cried out against eternal justification, that I am afraid of it." But he is gradually enlightened, and led to see that in the same hour when all his debts were paid, a full discharge was given; that in the moment when its sin was cancelled, every elect soul was justified in God's mind, though they were not justified in their own minds till afterwards. The Spirit shall lead you into all truth.

Now, what are the practical inferences from this great doctrine? The first is with reference to the Christian who is afraid of his own ignorance. How many are there who are just enlightened and have tasted of heavenly things, who are afraid they are too ignorant to be saved! Beloved, God the Holy Spirit can teach any one, however illiterate, however uninstructed. I have known some men who were almost idiots before conversion, but they afterwards had their faculties wonderfully developed. Some time ago there was a man who was so ignorant that he could not read, and he never spoke anything like grammar in his life, unless by mistake; and moreover, he was considered to be what the people in his neighborhood called "daft." But when he was converted, the first thing he did was to pray. He stammered out a few words, and in a little time his powers of speaking began to develop themselves. Then he thought he would like to read the Scriptures, and after long, long months of labour, he learned to read. And what was the next thing? He thought he could preach; and he did preach a little in his own homely way, in his house. Then he thought "I must read a few more books." And so his mind expanded, until, I believe he is at the present day, a useful minister, settled in a country village, labouring for God. It needs but little intellect to be taught of God. If you feel your ignorance do not despair. Go to the Spirit—the great Teacher—and ask his sacred influence; and it shall come to pass that he "shall guide you into all truth."

Another inference is this: whenever any of our brethren do not understand the truth let us take a hint as to the best way of dealing with them. Do not let us controvert with them. I have heard many controversies, but never heard of any good from one of them. We have had controversies with certain men called Secularists, and very strong arguments have been brought against them; but I believe that the day of judgment shall declare that a very small amount of good was ever done by contending with these men. Better let them alone; where no fuel is the fire goeth out; and he that debateth with them puts wood upon the fire. So with regard to Baptism. It is of no avail to quarrel with our Pædo-baptist friends. If we simply pray for them that the God of truth may lead them to see the true doctrine, they will come to it far more easily than by discussions. Few men are taught by controversy, for

"A man convinced against his will, is of the same opinion still."

Pray for them that the Spirit of truth may lead them "into all truth." Do not be angry with your brother, but pray for him; cry, "Lord! open thou his eyes that he may behold wondrous things out of thy law."

Lastly, we speak to some of you who know nothing about the Spirit of truth, nor about the truth itself. It may be that some of you are saying, "We care not much which of you are right, we are happily indifferent to it." Ah! but, poor sinner, if thou knewest the gift of God, and who it was that spake the truth, thou wouldst not say, "I care not for it;" if thou didst know how essential the truth is to thy salvation, thou wouldst not talk so; if thou didst know that the truth of God is—that thou art a worthless sinner, but if thou believest, then God from all eternity, apart from all thy merits, loved thee, and bought thee with the Redeemer's blood, and justified thee in the forum of heaven, and will by-and-bye justify thee in the forum of thy conscience through the Holy Ghost by faith; if thou didst know that there is a heaven for thee beyond the chance of a failure, a crown for thee, the lustre of which can never be dimmed;—then thou wouldst say, "Indeed the truth is precious to my soul!" Why, my ungodly hearers, these men of error want to take away the truth, which alone can save you, the only gospel that can deliver you from hell; they deny the great truths of free-grace, those fundamental doctrines which alone can snatch a sinner from hell; and even though you do not feel interest in them now, I still would say, you ought to desire to see them promoted. May God give you to know the truth in your hearts! May the Spirit "guide you into all truth!" For if you do not know the truth here, recollect there will be a sorrowful learning of it in the dark chambers of the pit, where the only light shall be the flames of hell! May you here know the truth! And the truth shall make you free: and if the Son shall make you free, you shall be free indeed, for he says, "I am the way, the truth, the life." Believe on Jesus, thou chief of sinners; trust his love and mercy, and thou art saved, for God the Spirit giveth faith and eternal life.

12

The Oil Of Gladness

"Thou lovest righteousness, and hatest wickedness: therefore God, thy God, hath anointed thee with the oil of gladness above thy fellows."   Psalm 45:7

We know that the anointing received by our Lord Jesus Christ was the resting of the Spirit of God upon him without measure. We are not left to any guesswork about this, for in Isaiah lxi. 1 we are told, "The Spirit of the Lord is upon me, because the Lord hath anointed me." Our Lord appropriated these very words to himself when he went into the synagogue at Nazareth and opened the book at the place wherein these words are written, and said, "This day is this Scripture fulfilled in your ears." The Apostle Peter also, in Acts x. 38, speaks of "How God anointed Jesus of Nazareth with the Holy Ghost and with power": so that we know both on Old and New Testament authority that the anointing which rested upon the Lord Jesus Christ was the unction of the Holy Ghost. Therefore, by the "oil of gladness" which we have before us in the text is intended the Holy Spirit himself, or one of the gracious results of his sacred presence. The divine Spirit has many attributes, and his benign influences operate in divers ways, bestowing upon us benefits of various kinds, too numerous for us to attempt to catalogue them. Amongst these is his comforting and cheering influence. "The fruit of the Spirit is joy." In Acts xiii. 52 we read, "The disciples were filled with joy and with the Holy Ghost." Wherever he comes as an anointing, whether upon the Lord or upon his people, upon the Christ or the Christians, upon the Anointed or upon those whom he anoints, in every case the ultimate result is joy and peace. On the head of our great High Priest he is joy, and this oil of gladness flows down to the skirts of his garments. To the Comforter, therefore, we ascribe "the oil of gladness."

From this great truth we learn another, namely, the perfect co-operation of the three persons of the blessed Trinity in the work of our redemption. The Father sends the Son, the Son with alacrity comes to redeem us, and the Spirit of God is upon him; so that Father, Son, and Spirit have each a part in the saving work, and the one God of heaven and earth is the God of salvation. A very interesting subject is the work of the Spirit upon the person of our Lord Jesus Christ. We see the Holy Ghost mysteriously operating in the formation and birth of the holy child Jesus, for by the overshadowing of the Holy Ghost was he born of a woman. This work of the Holy Spirit was manifested to all believing eyes when the Lord Jesus came out of the waters of the Jordan after his baptism, and the Holy Spirit descended like a dove and rested upon him. Before he was said to "wax strong in spirit," but afterwards he is described as "full of the Holy Ghost." Then was he led of the Spirit and inspired by his divine energy, and this was shown throughout the whole of his life, for the Spirit was with him in innumerable miracles and in the demonstration and power which followed his words, so that he spoke as one having authority, and not as the Scribes. In him was abundantly fulfilled the prophecy which saith, "And the spirit of the Lord shall rest upon him, the spirit of wisdom and understanding, the spirit of counsel and might, the spirit of knowledge and of the fear of the Lord; And shall make him of quick understanding in the fear of the Lord; and he shall not judge after the sight of his eyes, neither reprove after the hearing of his ears: But with righteousness shall he judge the poor, and reprove with equity for the meek of the earth." The Holy Spirit had also a peculiar interest in his resurrection, for he was "declared to be the Son of God with power, according to the spirit of holiness by the resurrection from the dead." He was "put to death in the flesh, but quickened by the Spirit." That same Spirit wrought even more fully when the Lord ascended up

on high, and led captivity captive; then, succeeding his
ascension, the gifts of the cloven tongues of fire and the
rushing mighty wind were witnessed by his disciples, for the
Spirit of God was given abundantly to the church in
connection with the ascension of the Redeemer. Oh, how
sweetly doth the Spirit co-operate with Christ at this very
day, for it is he that takes of the things of Christ and reveals
them unto us. He is the abiding witness in the church to the
truth of the gospel, and the worker of all our gifts and
graces. Jesus gives repentance, but the Spirit works it; faith
fixes upon Christ, but the Spirit of God first creates faith
and opens the eye which looks to Jesus. The whole of this
dispensation through it is the peculiar office of the Spirit of
God to be revealing Christ to his people, and Christ in his
people, and Christ in the midst of an ungodly and gainsaying
generation, for a testimony against them. Blessed be the
name of the Holy Spirit, that he is the divine anointing, and
so proves his hearty assent to the great plan of redemption.

We now come, however, more closely to the text. The Spirit
of God is here considered in one of his influences or
operations as "the oil of gladness": we shall speak of this in
the following way. First, *the saviour's anointing with gladness;* secondly, *the reason for the bestowal of this oil of joy
upon him;* and, thirdly, *the manner of the operation of this
sacred anointing upon ourselves.*

I. Let us carefully consider THE SAVIOUR'S ANOINTING WITH
GLADNESS. We are, perhaps, surprised to read of our Lord in
connection with gladness. Truly he was the Man of Sorrows
and acquainted with grief, yet this sorrowful aspect was that
which he presented to the superficial outside observer; and
those who look within the veil of his flesh know well that a
mystic glory shone within his soul. Did not David say of him
as the King of Israel—"His glory is great in thy salvation:
honour and majesty hast thou laid upon him. For thou hast
made him most blessed for ever: thou hast made him
exceeding glad with thy countenance."? I fully believe that
there was never on the face of the earth a man who knew so
profound and true a gladness as our blessed Lord. Did he not
desire that his joy might be in his people that their joy might
be full? Does not benevolence beget joy, and who so kind as
he? Is it not a great joy to suffer self-sacrifice for beloved

ones? And who so disinterested as he? Is there not sure to be
happiness in the heart where the noblest motives are para-
mount and the sweetest graces bear sway? And was not this
pre-eminently the case with our Lord? Let us see.

The gladness of our Lord Jesus may be viewed, first, as *the
gladness which he had* IN *his work*. The Son of God delighted
in the work which his Father had given him to do. This
delight he declared as God, in the old eternity! "Lo I come; in
the volume of the book it is written of me, I delight to do thy
will, O God." This delight he had shown as man even before
his great public anointing, for when he was yet a child he
said, "Wist ye not that I must be about my Father's business?" Evidently, even while yet a youth, he anticipated with
delight the great business which he had to do for his Father,
and commencing in a measure to do it amongst the doctors
in the temple at Jerusalem. But the day came in which he
had reached the appointed age, and he at once went forth to
John to be baptised by him in Jordan, being eager to fulfill
all righteousness. Then the Spirit of God came down upon
him, and he was openly and visibly anointed, and you see
from the moment when he began to stand before the public
eye, with what alacrity he pursued his life work. We find
him fasting, but he has been speaking to a woman by the
well's brink, and the joy which he has felt while blessing her
has made him quite forget the necessity for food, and he tells
his disciples "I have meat to eat that ye know not of." He felt
great gladness in that woman's joy, as she believed in him,
and in the expectation of yet more numerous converts from
those who were flocking from Samaria, of whom he said "Lift
up now your eyes, for behold the fields are white already
unto the harvest." That joy in his work made him abhor all
idea of turning from its awful consummation, and led him to
say to Peter's suggestion "Get thee behind me, Satan." We
see it also in such expressions as this, "I have a baptism to
be baptised with, and how am I straitened till it be
accomplished." We read that when the time came that he
should be received up, he stedfastly set his face to go to
Jerusalem. His frequent allusions to his own decease by a
shameful death, all showed that he viewed with intense
satisfaction the great object after which he was reaching.
Once, indeed, his joy flowed over so that others could see it,

when he said, "I thank thee, O Father, Lord of heaven and earth, because thou hast hid these things from the wise and prudent, and hast revealed them unto babes." "At that hour Jesus rejoiced in spirit." Let it never be forgotten that we must not expect to see in the life of Christ great ebullitions of manifest exultation, because he was sent on purpose to bear our sicknesses, and to be "stricken of God and afflicted." His deep joy was concealed by his many griefs, even as the inner glory of the tabernacle of old was hidden beneath coverings of badgers' skins. He was the sun under a cloud, but he was the sun still. If you have a small burden to carry, you may have an excess of strength which you can display in leaping or running, but if you have an enormous load to sustain, your steady bearing of it may be an equally sure proof of your strength: so also, if your trials are light, your joyous spirits may vent themselves in smiles and songs, but if you are severely afflicted it will need all your joyfulness to keep you from sinking. Our blessed Lord had a load upon him infinitely transcending any weight of sorrow ever borne by the most burdened of his people, and it needed the wonderful joy which I feel sure we are justified in ascribing to him to balance the marvellous grief which he had to endure. The uplifting influence of this joy sufficed to bring him into a condition of calm, quiet, serene majesty of spirit. Nothing strikes you more in the Saviour than the quiet peacefulness with which he pursues the even tenor of his way. Now, if he had not possessed great stores of secret joy his spirit would have been famished for want of sustenance. You would have found him constantly sighing and weeping; his words and tones would have become a terror to those around him, and his whole appearance would have appeared melancholy and depressing to the last degree, whereas his manner was cheerful and attractive—let the little children who thronged around him bear witness to that. He was a man of sorrows, but he was not a preacher of sorrows, neither do his life or his discourses leave an unhappy impression upon the mind. The fact, probably is, that he was both the greatest rejoicer and the greatest mourner that ever lived, and between these two there was an equilibrium of mind kept up, so that wherever you meet him, with the exception of his agony in the garden, he is peaceful and

serene. You neither see him dancing like David before the
ark, nor yet like David bewailing the loss of one he loved
with a "Would God I had died for thee." He does not, like
Elijah, run before the king's chariot, nor lie down under the
juniper to die. He neither strives nor cries, nor causes his
voice to be heard in the streets; his peace is like a river, and
his heart abides in the Sabbath of God.

We see, then, that *in* his work our great High Priest was
anointed with the oil of gladness above his fellows, but we
also note that those who are his fellows do in their degree
partake in this oil of gladness, and are enabled to feel joy in
the work which is appointed them of the Lord. While our
King is anointed with the oil of gladness it is also written of
the virgin souls who wait upon his church, "With gladness
and rejoicing shall they be brought, they shall enter into the
King's palace." If any professing Christian man here is
engaged in a work which he does not feel glad to do, I
question if he is in his right place. Occasional fits of depression there may be, but these are not because we do not love
the work, but because we cannot do it so well as we would
desire. We are tired in the work, but not tired of it. The Lord
loves to employ willing workmen. His army is not made up
of pressed men, but of those whom grace has made volun-
teers. "Serve the Lord with gladness." Our Lord does not set
us task work, and treat us like prisoners in gaol, or slaves
under the lash. I sometimes hear our life-work called a task.
Well, the expression may be tolerated, but I confess I do not
like it to be applied to Christian men. It is no task to me at
any rate to preach my Master's gospel, or to serve him in
any way. I thank God every day that "to me, who am less
than the least of all saints, is this grace given, that I should
preach among the Gentiles the unsearchable riches of
Christ." You teachers in the school, I hope your labour of
love is not a bondage to you! An unwilling teacher will soon
make unwilling scholars. Yea, I know that those of you who
serve the Lord find a reward in the work itself, and gladly
pursue it. I am sure you will not prosper in it if it be not so.
If you follow your work unwillingly, and regret that you ever
undertook it, and feel encumbered by it, you will do no good.
No man wins a race who has no heart in the running. In this
respect the joy of the Lord is your strength, and as your

Master was anointed with the oil of gladness in his work, so must you be. Yet, beloved fellow labourer, you will never be so glad in your work as *he* was in his, nor will you ever be able to prove that gladness by such self-denials, by such agonies, and such a death. He has proved how glad he was to save sinners, because "for the joy that was set before him, he endured the cross, despising the shame." Blessed Emmanuel, thou art justly anointed with the oil of gladness above thy fellows.

We further note that our Lord had this oil of gladness FROM *his work*. Even while he was engaged in it he derived some joy from it, though it was but as the gleanings of the vintage compared with the after results. He did reap in joy as well as sow in tears, for many became his disciples, and over each one of these he rejoiced. It was impossible that the Good Shepherd should have saved so many sheep as he did without rejoicing when he threw them on his shoulders to bear them to the fold. Assuredly he rejoiced that he had found the sheep which he had lost. But the fulness of his joy was left till after he had ascended on high, then indeed was he anointed with the oil of gladness, and the voice was heard, "Go forth, O ye daughters of Zion, and behold king Solomon with the crown wherewith his mother crowned him in the day of his espousals, and in the day of the gladness of his heart." My brethren, the joy of our Lord Jesus Christ now that he knows his beloved are securely his, and no longer the slaves of sin and heirs of wrath, is too great to be measured. He has redeemed unto himself a people in whom his soul delights. For them the price is fully paid, for them the penalty has been completely endured, for them all chains are broken, and for them the prison house is razed to its foundation: for them hath he bruised the serpent's head, for them hath he by death destroyed death, and led captive him that had the power of death, even the devil.

> "All his work and warfare done,
> He into his heaven is gone,
> And before his Father's throne,
> Now is pleading for his own."

He now continues to receive into his joy the multitudes whom the Spirit brings to him, for whom of old he shed his precious blood. You cannot conceive the gladness of Christ. If you have ever brought one soul to Christ you have had a drop of it, but his gladness lies not only in receiving them, but in actually being the author of salvation to every one of them. The Saviour looks upon the redeemed with an unspeakable delight, thinks of what they used to be, thinks of what they would have been but for his interposition, thinks of what they now are, thinks of what he means to make them in that great day when they shall rise from the dead; and as his heart is full of love to them he joys in their joy, and exults in their exultation. Their heavens swell their Mediator's heaven, and in their myriad embodiments of bliss, each one reflects his own felicity, and so (speaking after the manner of men) increases it, for he lives ten thousand lives by living in them, and enjoys unnumbered joys in their joys. I speak with humblest fear lest in any word I should speak amiss, for he is God as well as man, but this is certain, that there is a joy of our Lord into which he will give his faithful ones to enter, a joy which he has won by passing through the shame and grief by which he has redeemed mankind. The oil of gladness is abundantly poured on that head which once was crowned with thorns.

Now, brethren, you, also, can be partakers in this joy. When he makes you in your little measure to be instrumentally saviours of others, then you also partake of his gladness; but as I have said before, you cannot know its fulness, for he is in this respect anointed with the oil of gladness above his fellows. "Who is this that cometh from Edom, with dyed garments from Bozrah? this that is glorious in his apparel, travelling in the greatness of his strength? I that speak in righteousness, mighty to save. I have trodden the winepress alone; and of the people there was none with me." Returning from the battle and the spoil he has a joy with which none can intermeddle, for his own right hand and his holy arm hath gotten unto him the victory.

Again, our Lord Jesus has the oil of gladness poured upon him in another sense, namely, because *his person and his work are the cause of ineffable gladness in others.* Oh, I wish I had a week in which to talk upon this point—a week —one could scarcely enter upon the theme in that time! We sang just now—

> "Jesus, *the very thought* of thee,
> With sweetness fills my breast."

The oil of gladness upon him is so sweet that we have only to think upon it and it fills us with delight. There is gladness in his very name.

> "Exult all hearts with gladness,
> At sound of Jesus' name;
> What other hath such sweetness,
> Or such delight can claim?"

What gladness he created when here below. His birth set the skies ringing with heavenly music, and made the hearts of expectant saints to leap for joy. In after days a touch of the hem of his garment made a woman's heart glad when she felt the issue of her blood staunched, and a word from his lips made the tongue of the dumb to sing. For him to lay his hand upon the sick was to raise them from their beds of sickness, and deliver them from pain and disease. His touch was gladness then, and a spiritual touch is the same now. To-day to preach of him is gladness, to sing of him is gladness, to trust him is gladness, to work for him is gladness, to have communion with him is gladness. To come to his table, and there to feast with him, is gladness; to see his image in the eyes of his saints is gladness; to see that image only as yet begun to form in the heart of a young convert is gladness. Everything about him is gladness. All his garments smell of myrrh, and aloes, and cassia. Nothing comes within a mile of him but what it makes you glad to think that he has been so near it. The very print of his foot has comfort in it, and the wounds in his hands are windows of hope. I have known some who have had to carry a cross for his dear sake, and they have kissed and hugged that cross, and gloried in their tribulations because they were borne for him. Fellowship with him has turned the bitterest potion into generous wine. Beloved, if these distant glimpses are so precious, what must it be to see him face to face? I have tried to conceive it, and I protest that even in attempting the conception my spirit seems to swoon at the prospect of such supreme delight. Only to hear the music of his footfall on the

other side the partition wall raises longings in my heart too
strong, too eager to be long endured. What, death, art thou
all that divides me from seeing my Lord? I would gladly die
a million deaths to see him as he is and to be like him. What,
a slumber in the grave for this poor body! Is that all I have
to dread? Then let it slumber, and let the worms consume it,
for "I know that my Redeemer liveth, and that he shall stand
at the latter day upon the earth: and though after my skin
worms destroy this body, yet in my flesh shall I see God."
Oh, what will it be to see him? To see HIM that loved us so,
to mark the wounds with which he purchased our redemption, to behold his glory, to listen to that dear voice of his,
and to hear him say, "Well done, good and faithful servant."
To lie in his bosom for ever, truly neither eye hath not seen,
nor ear heard the like of this bliss. More than the bride longs
for the marriage day do we expect the bridal feast of heaven,
but of all the dainties on that royal table there will not be
one that will be equal to himself, for to see him will be all the
heaven we desire. He is better than heaven's harp or angels,
and the cause of greater gladness than streets of gold or
walls of jasper.

Brethren, can we share this power to distribute joy?
Assuredly we can. If the Lord Jesus be with us we can give
joy to others. I know some whose very presence comforts
their fellows; their words are so full of consolation, and their
hearts so overflowing with sympathy that they make gladness wherever they go. Ay, but the best of you, ye sons of
consolation, are not anointed with the oil of gladness to the
same extent as he was. Above his fellows, even above
Barnabas the son of consolation; above the best and the
tenderest sympathizers is he thus anointed, and from him
there pours forth a continual stream of effectual consolation
which becomes the oil of joy to those who wear the garments
of heaviness. Thus much upon the first point, the Saviour's
anointing of gladness.

II. Let us now consider THE REASON FOR THE BESTOWAL OF
THIS ANOINTING UPON HIM. It is given in the text. He is
anointed above his fellows, because it is said of him, *"Thou
lovest righteousness, and hatest wickedness."* The perfect
righteousness of Christ has brought to him this gladness,
because perfect holiness there must be before there can be

perfect happiness. Sin is the enemy of joy. Let the sinner say what he likes, sin can no more dwell with real joy than the lion will lie down with the lamb. To be perfectly glad you must be perfectly cleansed from sin, for until you are so cleansed you cannot possess the oil of gladness to the measure that Christ possessed it. As the believer is delivered from the power of sin he is brought into a condition in which the joy of the Lord can more and more abide in him. Now, every way Jesus loved righteousness intensely and hated wickedness intensely. He died that he might establish righteousness; and that he might destroy wickedness from off the face of the earth; therefore it is that he has greater gladness, because he had greater holiness. Moreover, you know that in any holy enterprise if the business succeeds, the joy of the worker is proportionate to the trial it has cost him. In the great battle of righteousness our Lord has led the van, in the great fight against wickedness our Saviour has borne the brunt of the battle; therefore, because he to the death loved righteousness and to the agony and bloody sweat strove against sin, the accomplished conquest brings him the greatest joy. He has done the most for the good cause, and therefore he is anointed with the oil of gladness above his fellows.

Now, note there is another reason why he is anointed, and there is another view of the anointing. He is anointed above his fellows, which shows that those who are in fellowship with him are anointed too. You observed in our reading that the high priest had the oil poured on his head, but the sons of Aaron who were minor priests were sprinkled with this same oil mixed with the blood of the sacrifice. On Christ this anointing is poured above his fellows, and then upon his fellows in communion with himself there comes the sprinkling of the oil. We have our measure; he has it without measure. Now, beloved, Christ is anointed above his fellows that his fellows may be anointed with him. Even as he ascended above all things that he might fill all things, so is he anointed above his fellows that he may anoint his fellows; and through the power of the anointing we are told that his people come into the same condition of righteousness as himself. Turn to Isaiah lxi., which passage we have already had before us, and you find as follows—"To appoint unto them that mourn in Zion, to give unto them beauty for ashes, the oil of joy for mourning, the garment of praise for the spirit of heaviness; that"—mark this!—*"that they might be called trees of righteousness."* Now, observe, that we first read, "Thou lovest righteousness and hatest wickedness, therefore God hath anointed thee with the oil of gladness," and then we meet with the parallel with reference to ourselves, "The oil of joy for mourning, that they may be called trees of righteousness." He is anointed because he is righteous; we are anointed that we may be righteous, and thus in Christ we come into the condition in which it is safe for us to be glad, and possible for joy to dwell in us. To the unrighteous the oil of gladness cannot come, but to the righteous there ariseth light even in darkness. "There is no peace saith my God, unto the wicked." The holy oil was forbidden to be placed upon a stranger to God's holy house; and upon man's flesh it could not be poured, because man's flesh is a corrupt, polluted thing. This oil of gladness comes only on those who are born into God's Israel by regeneration, and are delivered from walking after the flesh; these the Lord makes to be as "trees of righteousness, the planting of the Lord, that he may be glorified." See then the two reasons why Christ has received the anointing, first because he is righteous himself; and secondly, that he may make others righteous. Therefore is the Spirit of the Lord God upon him that he may give the oil of joy to his own chosen, and make them righteous, even as he is righteous, glad as he is glad.

III. We will now meditate upon THE MANNER OF THE OPERATION OF THIS OIL OF GLADNESS UPON US. Jesus is anointed with the oil of gladness above his fellows. Now, we have to show that his fellows are anointed with the oil of gladness too. Did not David say, "Thou anointest mine head with oil; my cup runneth over"? so that we can say of ourselves what we say of our Lord, we are anointed, for he was anointed. Now, in what respects does the anointing of the Holy Spirit give us gladness? I shall notice eight things, and touch but very briefly on each.

First, we too, through Jesus Christ, are *anointed to an office*, "for he hath made us"—whisper it to one another in the joy of delight—"He hath made us kings and priests unto God, and we shall reign for ever and ever." When the oil went on Aaron's head, you know how it ran down his beard, even Aaron's beard, unto the skirts of his garments, and now this day this anointing oil, which made the king and the priest, has fallen upon us too. Blessed be his name, shall we not be glad? It is very inconsistent with our position if we are not. Are you a king and do you not rejoice?

> "Why should the children of our King
> Go mourning all their days?
> Sweet Comforter, descend and bring
> Some unction of thy grace."

May the gladness now come to you. You are priests to God. Shall the anointed priests serve their Lord with gloomy countenances? No: rejoice in the Lord always, all ye priests of his that are anointed to this blessed work. "Bless the Lord, O house of Israel: bless the Lord, O house of Aaron."

We, too, are *consecrated to the Lord*, for the oil poured upon the priest was the oil of consecration. From that time forward he was a dedicated man; he could not serve anyone but God; he, above all the rest of the congregation, was the man of God for ever as long as ever he lived. So beloved, we have been consecrated: the Spirit of God has sanctified us and set us apart unto the Lord, as it is written, "Ye are not your own; ye are bought with a price." Our Lord said in his matchless prayer, "They are not of the world, even as I am not of the world." "Sanctify them," said he, "by thy truth, thy word is truth." Yes, blessed be God, we are consecrated men and women: we belong to the Lord, and are vessels for the Master's use, hallowed from all other uses to be the Lord's. "For I will be to them a God, they shall be to me a people." Does not this make you glad? Are you really set apart to be the Lord's own sons and daughters, and hallowed to be used by him in his service both here and hereafter, and do you not rejoice? O my soul, dost thou not feel the trickling of the consecrating oil adown thy brow even now, and does it not make thy face to shine and make thy heart happy, because thou art now the Lord's?

Thirdly, by this oil we are also *qualified for our office*. You see the Spirit descended upon Christ that he might have the spirit of wisdom, and power, and so be strengthened and qualified to discharge his sacred work. Now, the Spirit of

God is upon every believer in this sense. Remember how in his First Epistle, second chapter, and twentieth verse, John says, "Ye have an unction from the Holy One, and ye know all things," or "ye are able to discern all things." And further on, in that same chapter, he says, "This anointing teacheth you all things." Well, if we are to serve the Lord a main gift is knowledge, for how can we instruct the ignorant, or guide the perplexed, except we know ourselves? And it is this anointing which teaches us, and makes us fit for the service to which the Master has called us. Oh, does the Holy Spirit then lead us into all truth, and give us knowledge, and shall we not rejoice? Ignorance means sorrow, but the light of the knowledge of God in the face of Jesus Christ means joy. O brethren, will ye not bless God to-day for what the Spirit of God has taught you? If you do not, what must you be made of? for he has taught you such wonderful lessons so full of joy. Even if he has never taught you more than this, that whereas you were once blind and now you see, he has taught you enough to make your heart rejoice as long as you live. Is he not the oil of gladness?

Fourthly, the Spirit of God *heals us of our diseases.* The Eastern mode of medicine was generally the application of oil, and I should not wonder if in the course of years it should be discovered that the modern pharmacy, with all its drugs, is not worth so much as the old-fashioned method. Certainly, when the Holy Spirit spake concerning sick men, and advised that medicines should be used, and prayer for their restoration, he prescribed anointing with oil. I suppose that anointing with oil was mentioned because it was the current medicine of the times, but it could not have been injurious or altogether absurd, or the Holy Spirit would not in any measure have sanctioned it. I will not raise the question, however. But a frequent medicine of the olden time was, undoubtedly, anointing with oil, and it is well known that olive oil does possess very remarkable healing qualities. I have read in books of one or two instances of the bites of serpents having the venom effectually removed by the use of olive oil. It is more commonly used in countries where it grows than here, and it is in many ways a very useful medicine. Certainly the Holy Spirit is that to us. What wounds and bruises have been healed with this oil.

Before the Spirit came they were putrefying, they had not
been bound up nor mollified with ointment, but now this
ointment, mixed after the art of the apothecary, with the
costliest spices, has effectually healed us, and what remains
of the old sores and wounds it continues still to heal; and so
wonderful is its power it will ultimately take out every scar,
and we shall be without spot or wrinkle or any such thing
through its healing power. Shall we not, therefore, be glad
and rejoice in the Lord, for if restoration to health makes us
happy surely the renewal of our spiritual youth should make
our hearts bound for joy?

Thus also we are *suppled and softened*. Oil applied to the
body supples and softens, and, believe me, brethren, nothing
is more akin to joy than softness and tenderness of heart. If
ever you meet with a hard-hearted proud man, he is not a
happy man and if he should seem to be happy in his pride it
is a dangerous and deadly happiness, and the sooner it is
taken away the better. Where God dwells is heaven, and
where does he dwell? With the humble and the contrite
heart. That is a beautiful expression of David's, I have drank
joy out of it, "Make me to hear joy and gladness that the
bones which thou hast broken may rejoice." Oh, there is
never a bone in manhood's system that knows how to rejoice
till God has broken it, and when it is broken then comes the
mighty Physician and applies the oil and restores the bone to
infinitely more than its former strength, and then the bones
which had been broken become each one so many new
arguments for gratitude, and all our healed wounds become
mouths of praise unto the Most High. We are thus softened
and gladdened.

By the oil of the Holy Spirit we are also *strengthened*. Oil
well rubbed into the system was anciently assumed to be a
great strengthener, and I suppose it was. Certainly the Holy
Spirit is the strength of Christians, and where he is the
strength there is sure to be joy. "The joy of the Lord is your
strength."

Oil, too, is a *beautifier*. The Easterns did not think themselves fit for their banquets till they had washed their face
and anointed themselves with perfumed oil. They were very
fond of locks dripping with oil and faces bright therewith.
Certainly there is a beauty which the Spirit gives to men,

which they can never obtain in any other way. Oh, the
excellence of the character that is formed by the hand of the
Spirit of God! It is a beautiful thing which even God himself
delights to look upon; it is a thing of beauty, and in the most
emphatic sense a joy for ever. He that is made comely with
the comeliness which the Holy Spirit gives must be a happy
man. Other beauty may bring sorrow, but the beauty of
holiness makes us akin to angels.

Once more, it becomes a *perfume*. When oil was poured on
a man his presence scented the air around him, and when
the Spirit of God is given to us it is perceived by other
spiritual minds. Cannot you detect in a brother's prayer that
he has been with Jesus? Do you not know by the lives of
some of Christ's dear saints that he is very familiar with
them? Do you not perceive that they have had a special
anointing? The ungodly world cannot tell it, but saints
discern it. The nostril of the wicked is only pleased by the
leeks, and the garlic, and the onions of Egypt, but the
believing nostril has been sanctified, and it perceives the
delicate myrrh and cinnamon, and sweet calamus and
cassia, which make up the anointing oil. The rare combination of sacred qualities which make up a holy character
will be seen in the believer in whom the Holy Spirit displays
his power, and as a consequence he will be glad at heart.

Furthermore, I have many things to say unto you, but ye
cannot hear them now, for the time is spent. Therefore I will
only say, I pray, brethren, that the anointing may be ours in
all the various senses I have mentioned. I should like all of
you to go away happy. You children of God, be as glad as
ever you can be. I would to God that a sacred gladness rang
through this house like a marriage peal: yet for all that, do
not forget that Jesus has joy above you all. You may be very
glad, but *he* is gladder still. You may sing his praises, but he
leads the sacred orchestra of heaven. "In the midst of the
congregation will I praise thee," saith he. Rejoice in his joy.
I have often thought it did not matter any more what
became of me so long as *he* is victorious. A soldier in battle,
sorely wounded, lies bleeding in a ditch, but he hears the
sound of the trumpets, and they tell him the commander is
coming along, the King for whom his loyal heart is willing to
bleed, and he enquires, "Have they won the day?" "Oh, yes,"

they say, "he has won the day, and the enemy are flying before him." The soldier exclaims, "Thank God, I can die." It is the soldier's joy to die with victory ringing in his ears. Our Lord is glad, and therefore we are glad.

> "Let him be crowned with majesty
> Who bowed his head to death,
> And be his honour sounded high
> By all things that have breath."

If it be so we will be content to say, like David, "The prayers of David, the son of Jesse, are ended." We have no more to pray for: we have done with the world, done with wishing, done with everything, if Christ reigns, and all things are under his foot. May this joy be yours. Amen.

13

Praying In The Holy Ghost

"...praying in the Holy Ghost."   Jude 20

These words occur in a passage where the apostle is indicating the contrast between the ungodly and the godly. The ungodly are mocking, speaking great swelling words, and walking after their ungodly lusts, while the righteous are building up themselves in their most holy faith, and keeping themselves in the love of God. The ungodly are showing the venom of their hearts by mourning and complaining, while the righteous are manifesting the new principle within them by "praying in the Holy Ghost." The ungodly man bears wormwood in his mouth, while the Christian's lips drop with the virgin honey of devotion. As the spider is said to find poison in the very flowers from which the bees suck honey, so do the wicked abuse to sin the selfsame mercies which the godly use to the glory of God. As far as light is removed from darkness, and life from death, so far does a believer differ from the ungodly. Let us keep this contrast very vivid. While the wicked grow yet more wicked, let us become more holy, more prayerful, and more devout, saying with good old Joshua, "Let others do as they will, but as for me and my house, we will serve the Lord."

Observe, that the text comes in a certain order in the context. The righteous are described, first of all, as building themselves up in their most holy faith. Faith is the first grace, the root of piety, the foundation of holiness, the dawn of godliness; to this must the first care be given. But we must not tarry at the first principles. Onward is our course. What then follows at the heels of faith? What is faith's firstborn child? When the vine of faith becomes vigorous and produces fruit unto holiness, which is the first ripe cluster? Is it not prayer—"praying in the Holy Ghost"? That man has no faith who has no prayer, and the man who abounds in faith will soon abound in supplication. Faith the mother and prayer the child are seldom apart from one another; faith carries prayer in her arms, and prayer draws life from the breast of faith. Edification in faith leads to fervency in supplication. Elijah first manifests his faith before the priests of Baal, and then retires to wrestle with God upon Carmel. Remark our text carefully, and see what follows after "praying in the Holy Ghost." "Keep yourselves in the love of God." Next to prayer comes an abiding sense of the love of God to us and the flowing up of our love towards God. Prayer builds an altar and lays the sacrifice and the wood in order, and then love, like the priest, brings holy fire from heaven and sets the offering in a blaze. Faith is, as we have said, the root of grace, prayer is the lily's stalk, and love is the spotless flower. Faith sees the Saviour, prayer follows him into the house, but love breaks the alabaster box of precious ointment and pours it on his head. There is, however, a step beyond even the hallowed enjoyments of love, there remains a topstone to complete the edifice; it is believing expectancy—"Looking for the mercy of our Lord Jesus Christ unto eternal life." Farseeing hope climbs the staircase which hope has builded, and bowing upon the knees of prayer looks through the window which love has opened, and sees the Lord Jesus Christ coming in his glory and endowing all his people with the eternal life which is to be their portion. See then the value of prayer as indicating the possession of faith, and as foreshadowing and support-ing the strength and growth of love.

Coming directly to the text, we remark that the apostle speaks of prayer, but he mentions only one kind of praying. Viewed from a certain point, prayers are of many sorts. I suppose that no two genuine prayers from different men could be precisely alike. Master-artists do not often multiply

the same painting; they prefer to give expression to fresh
ideas as often as they grasp the pencil, and so the Master-
Artist, the Holy Spirit, who is the author of prayer, does not
often produce two prayers that shall be precisely the same
upon the tablets of his people's hearts. Prayers may be
divided into several different orders. There is *deprecatory*
prayer, in which we deprecate the wrath of God, and entreat
him to turn away his fierce anger, to withdraw his rod, to
sheath his sword. Deprecatory prayers are to be offered in
all times when calamity is to be feared, and when sin has
provoked the Lord to jealousy. Then there are *supplicatory*
prayers, in which we supplicate blessings and implore mercies from the liberal hand of God, and entreat our heavenly
Father to supply our wants out of his riches in glory by
Christ Jesus. There are prayers which are personal, in
which the suppliant pleads mainly concerning himself, and
there are pleadings which are intercessory, in which like
Abraham, the petitioner intercedes for Sodom, or entreats
that Ishmael might live before God. These prayers for others
are to be multiplied as much as prayers for ourselves, lest
we make the mercy-seat to become a place for the exhibition
of spiritual selfishness. The prayer may be public or private,
vocal or mental, protracted or ejaculatory. Prayer may be
salted with confession, or perfumed with thanksgiving; it
may be sung to music, or wept out with groanings. As many
as are the flowers of summer, so many are the varieties of
prayer.

But while prayers are of these various orders, there is one
respect in which they are all one if they be acceptable with
God;—they must be every one of them "in the Holy Ghost."
That prayer which is not in the Holy Ghost is in the flesh;
that which is born of the flesh is flesh, and we are told that
they which are in the flesh cannot please God. All that
cometh of our corrupt nature is defiled and marred, and
cannot be acceptable with the most holy God. If the heavens
are not pure in his sight, how shall those prayers which are
born of the earth be acceptable with him? The seed of
acceptable devotion must come from heaven's storehouse.
Only the prayer which comes from God can go to God. The
dove will only bear a letter to the cote from which it came,
and so will prayer go back to heaven if it came from heaven.

We must shoot the Lord's arrows back to him. That desire which he writes upon our heart will move his heart and bring down a blessing, but the desires of the flesh have no power with him.

Desirous to press this great truth upon the minds of my brethren this morning, I shall use the few words of the text in five ways.

I. First we shall use the text as A CRUCIBLE to try our prayers in. I beseech you examine yourselves with rigorous care. Use the text as a fining pot, a furnace, a touchstone, or a crucible by which to discern whether your prayers have been true or not, for this is the test, have they been in very deed "praying in the Holy Ghost"?

Brethren and sisters, we need not judge those who pray unintelligible prayers, prayers in a foreign tongue, prayers which they do not understand: we know without a moment's discussion of the question that the prayer which is not even understood cannot be a prayer in the Spirit, for even the man's own spirit does not enter into it, how then can the Spirit of God be there? The mysterious words or Latin jargon of the priests cannot come up before God with acceptance. Let us, therefore, keep our judgment for ourselves. There may be those present who have been in the habit of using from their infancy *a form of prayer*. You perhaps would not dare to go out to your day's business without having repeated that form at the bedside; you would be afraid to fall asleep at night without going through the words which you have set yourselves to repeat. My dear friends, may I put the question to you, will you try to answer it honestly, Have you prayed in the Holy Ghost? Has the Holy Spirit had anything to do with that form? Has he really made you to feel it in your heart? Is it not possible that you have mocked God with a solemn sound upon a thoughtless tongue? Is it not probable that from the random manner in which one comes to repeat a well-known form that there may be no heart whatever in it, and not an atom of sincerity? Does not God abhor the sacrifice where the heart is not found? It would be a melancholy thing if we had increased our sins by our prayers. It would be a very unhappy fact if it should turn out that when we have bowed the knee in what we thought to be the service of God, we were actually insulting the God of

heaven by uttering words which could not but be disgusting
to him because our hearts did not go with our lips. Let us
rest assured that if for seventy years we have punctually
performed our devotions by the use of the book, or of the
form which we have learnt, we may the whole seventy years
never once have prayed at all, and the whole of that period
we may have been living in God's esteem an ungodly,
prayerless life, because we have never worshipped God, who
is a spirit, in spirit and in truth, and have never prayed in
the Holy Ghost. Judge yourselves, brethren, that ye be not
judged.

But are there not others of us who never did use a written
prayer, who from our earliest childhood have eschewed and
even abhorred forms of prayer, who nevertheless have good
reason to try our prayer just as much as others? We have
given forth *extemporaneous utterances,* and those extemporaneous utterances necessarily required some little
exercise of the mind, some little attention, but still we may
have been heartless in them. I suppose we are well aware
that we can get into such a habit of extemporaneous prayer
that it is really very little or no better than if we repeated
what we had learnt. There may be such a fluency acquired
by practice that one's speech may ripple on for five or ten
minutes, or a quarter of an hour, and yet the heart may be
wandering in vanity or stagnant in indifference. The body
may be on its knees, and the soul on its wings far away from
the mercy seat.

Let us examine how far our public prayers have been in
the Holy Ghost. The preacher standing here begs God to
search him in that matter. If he has merely discharged the
business of public prayer because it is his official duty to
conduct the devotions of the congregation, he has much to
account for before God; to lead the devotions of this vast
throng without seeking the aid of the Holy Ghost is no light
sin. And what shall be said of the prayers at prayer meetings? Are not many of them mere words? It were better if our
friends would not speak at all rather than speak in the flesh.
I am sure that the only prayer in which the devout hearer
can unite, and which is acceptable with God, is that which
really is a heart-prayer, a soul-prayer, in fact, a prayer
which the Holy Ghost moves us to pray. All else is beating

the air, and occupying time in vain. My brethren, I thank
God that there are so many of you in connection with this
church who are gifted in prayer, and I wish that every
member of every Christian church could pray in public. You
should all try to do so, and none of you should give it up
unless it becomes an absolute impossibility; but oh! my
brethren who pray in public, may it not be sometimes with
you as with others of us—the exercise of gift and not the
outflow of grace? and if so, ask the Lord to forgive you such
praying, and enable you to wait upon him in the power of the
Holy Ghost.

We may not forget to scrutinise our more private prayers,
our supplications at the family altar, and above all, our
prayers in that little room which we have dedicated to
communion with God. O brethren, we might well be sick of
our prayers, if we did but see what poor things they are!
There are times when it is a sweet and blessed thing to lay
hold of the horns of the altar, and to feel that the blood
which sprinkles the altar has sprinkled you, that you have
spoken to God and prevailed. Oh, it is a blessed thing to
grasp the Angel of the covenant, and to wrestle with him
even hour after hour, saying, "I will not let thee go except
thou bless me;" but I fear me these are not constant things;
we may say of them that they are angels' visits, few and far
between. Come, my brethren, put your prayers into this
crucible of "praying in the Holy Ghost;" you will cast in much
metal, but there will come out little of fine gold. Come
hither, and lay your prayers upon this threshingfloor, and
thresh them with this text, "praying in the Holy Ghost;" and
oh, how much of straw and of chaff will there be, and how
little of the well-winnowed grain! Come hither and look
through this window at the fields of our devotions, overgrown with nettles, and briars, and thistles, a wilderness of
merely outward performances; and how small that little
spot, enclosed by grace, which God the Holy Spirit himself
has cleared, and digged, and planted, from which the fruit of
prayer has been brought forth unto perfection! May our
heavenly Father teach us to be humble in his presence, as
we reflect how little even of our best things will stand the
test of his searching eye, and may those of us who are his
saints come to him afresh, and ask him to fill us with his

Spirit, and to accept us in his Son.

II. We shall next use the text as A CORDIAL. It is a very
delightful reflection to the Christian mind that God observes
his people, and does not sit as an indifferent spectator of
their conflicts and difficulties. For instance, he closely observes us in our prayers. He knows that prayer while it
should be the easiest thing in the world is not so; he knows
that we erring ones find it not always easy to approach him
in the true spirit of supplication, and he observes this with
condescending compassion. That is a precious verse for those
hearts which are very weak and broken, "He knoweth our
frame: he remembereth that we are dust;" and that other,
"Like as a father pitieth his children, so the Lord pitieth
them that fear him." He takes notice of our frailties and of
our failures in the work of supplication, he sees his child fall
as it tries to walk, and marks the tears with which it be-
moans its weakness. "The eyes of the Lord are upon the
righteous, and his ears are open unto their cry."

A sweeter thought remains in the text, namely, that
having considered these failures of ours, which are many of
them sinful, our Lord is not angry with us on account of
them, but instead of being turned to wrath he is moved to
pity for us and love towards us. Instead of saying, "If you
cannot pray, you shall not have; if you have not grace
enough even to ask aright, I will shut the gates of mercy
against you;" he deviseth means by which to bring the lame
and the banished into his presence; he teacheth the ignorant
how to pray, and strengthens the weak with his own
strength. Herein also he doeth wonders, for the means
whereby he helpeth our infirmity are exceedingly to be
marvelled at. That help is not to be found in a book or in the
dictation of certain words in certain consecrated places, but
in the condescending assistance of God himself, for who is he
that is spoken of in the text but God? The Holy Ghost, the
third person of the adorable Trinity, helpeth our infirmities,
making intercession for us with groanings that cannot be
uttered. It is a mark of wondrous condescension that God
should not only answer our prayers when they are made, but
should make our prayers for us. That the King should say to
the petitioner, "Bring your case before me, and I will grant
your desire," is kindness, but for him to say, "I will be your

secretary, I will write out your petition for you, I will put it
into proper words and use fitting phrases so that your petition shall be framed acceptably," this is goodness at its
utmost stretch; but this is precisely what the Holy Ghost
does for us poor, ignorant, wavering, weak sons of men. I am
to understand from the expression, "praying in the Holy
Ghost," that the Holy Ghost is actually willing to help me to
pray, that he will tell me how to pray, and that when I get to
a point where I am at a pause and cannot express my
desires, he will appear in my extremity and make intercession in me with groanings which cannot be uttered. Jesus
in his agony was strengthened by an angel, you are to be
succoured by God himself. Aaron and Hur stayed up the
hands of Moses, but the Holy Ghost himself helpeth your
infirmities. My beloved brethren in Christ, the thought
needs no garnishing of oratorical expressions; take it as a
wedge of gold of Ophir and value it, it is priceless, beyond all
price. God himself the Holy Ghost condescends to assist you
when you are on your knees, and if you cannot put two
words together in common speech to men, yet he will help
you to speak with God; ah! and if at the mercy seat you fail
in words, you shall not fail in reality, for your heart shall
conquer. God wants not words. He never reads our petitions
according to the outward utterance, but according to the
inward groaning. He notices the longing, the desiring, the
sighing, the crying. Remember that the outward of prayer is
but the shell, the inward of prayer is its true kernel and
essence. If prayer be wafted to heaven in the song of the
multitude, with the swell of glorious music, it is not one whit
more acceptable to God than when it is wailed forth in the
bitter cry of anguish from a desolate spirit. That cry so
discordant to human ear is music to the ear of God.

> "To him there's music in a sigh,
> And beauty in a tear."

Notice this then, and be comforted.

III. The text may further serve as A CHART to direct us in
the way of prayer. Here I shall need to speak at greater
length. Praying how? By the book? Without book? In public?
In private? By the way? In the house? On your knees?
Standing? Sitting? Kneeling? Nothing is said about these;

posture, place, and time are all left open. There is no rubric
except one—"*in the Holy Ghost.*" That is indispensable. That
granted, nothing else signifies one whit. If it be praying in
the Holy Ghost, all else may be as you will. What does praying in the Holy Ghost mean? The word may be translated,
"*by* the Holy Ghost," or "*through* the Holy Ghost," as well as
"*in* the Holy Ghost;" and the phrase means, first, *praying in
the Holy Ghost's power.* The carnal mind knows nothing
about this. I might as well express myself in high Dutch as
in English upon this point to an unregenerate man; but
regenerate men, who are born of the Spirit, and live in the
Spirit-world are cognisant of communications between their
spirits and the Holy Spirit who is now resident in the midst
of the church of God. We know that the Divine Spirit,
without the use of sounds, speaks in our hearts, that without
an utterance which the ear can hear he can make our soul
know his presence and understand his meaning. He casteth
the spiritual shadow of his influence over us, colouring our
thoughts and feelings according to his own design and will.
It is a great spiritual fact which the Christian knoweth for
certain that the Holy Ghost, the Divine Spirit, has frequent
dealings with spiritual minds, and imparts to them of his
power. Our new-born spirit has a certain degree of power in
it, but the power is never fully manifested or drawn out
except when the Spirit of God quickeneth our spirit and
excites it to activity. Our spirit prays, but it is because it is
overshadowed and filled with the power of the Holy Ghost. I
cannot just now explain myself, but I mean this, that if I, as
a man, could go to the throne of grace and only pray as my
fleshly nature would pray, that prayer would be unaccept-
able; but when I go to the mercy seat and my new nature
prays as the Holy Ghost enables me to pray, then my prayer
will succeed with God. If I do before God at the throne what
flesh and blood can do and no more, I have done nothing, for
that which is of the flesh still mounts no higher than flesh;
but if, in coming before the throne of the heavenly grace,
God's eternal Spirit speaks to my soul and lifts it out of the
dead level of fallen humanity, and brings it up to be filled
with divine force, if that Spirit is in me a well of water
springing up unto everlasting life, if I receive that divine
light and power of the Holy Ghost, and if in his power I

fervently draw near to God, my prayer must be prevalent
with God. This power may be possessed by every Christian.
May God grant it to all of his people now, that they may all
pray in the Spirit! That, I think, is one meaning of the text
—praying in the power of the Spirit.

No doubt the principal sense of the text is praying in the
Spirit *as to matter.* We do not know always what to pray for,
and, brethren, if we were to refrain from prayer for a few
minutes till we did know it would be a good and wise rule.
The habit into which we have fallen in extemporaneous
praying of always praying directly when we are asked,
without an instant's pause in which to think of what we are
going to ask, is very prejudicial to the spirit of prayer. I
would like when I am alone, to take a few minutes to
consider what I am going to ask of God, for otherwise it
seems to me to be like seeking an interview with one of the
officers of state, to ask for something which might occur to
us at the moment. How would you like to have an audience
with Lord Derby, and then consider all of a sudden what it
was you had come about? Surely common sense would say,
Tarry awhile till you have your case mapped out in your own
mind, and then when you clearly know yourself what it is
you want, you will be able to ask for what you need. Should
we not wait upon God in prayer, asking him to reveal to us
what those matters are concerning which we should plead
with him? Beware of hit-or-miss prayers. Never make hap-
hazard work of supplication. Come to the throne of grace
intelligently understanding what it is that you require. It is
well with us in prayer when the Holy Ghost guides the mind.
Are not all spiritual men conscious of this, that they feel
themselves shut up us to certain matters, and only free in
another direction; then let them obey the Holy Spirit and
pray as he directs, for he knows what should be our petition.
Well, what then? My dear brother, pray for that which God
the Spirit moves you to pray for, and be very sensitive of the
Holy Spirit's influence. I like a metaphor used by Thomas
Shillitoe in his "Life," when he says, he wished his own mind
to be like a cork upon the water, conscious of every motion of
the Spirit of God. It were well to be so sensitive of the Spirit
of God, that his faintest breath should cause a ripple upon
the sea of our soul, and make it move as the Spirit would

have it. We have reached a high state of sanctification when
God the Spirit and our own inward spirit are perfectly in
accord. May we be led into that unspeakably blessed state!
We do not pray aright if we think what it is *we* want and *we*
wish for, and then ask for it in selfish wilfulness; but we
pray aright when we consent to that which is the mind of the
Spirit, and speak as he moveth us to speak. We shall be
surely enriched with good things when we wait for the very
matter of our supplications to have it all from him. Lord,
teach us to pray. Put thou the thoughts into our minds, the
desires into our hearts, and the very words into our lips, if it
be thy will, that so all through it we may be praying in the
Spirit and not in the flesh.

The main part of praying in the Spirit must lie not merely
in the Spirit's power, or in the Spirit's teaching us the
matter, but in the Spirit's assisting us *in the manner.* Observe, brethren, the many ways there are of praying which
are obnoxious to God; observe them and avoid them. There is
but one manner of praying which the Lord accepts. You
know what it is; I will briefly describe its attributes. He that
cometh to God must remember that he is "a Spirit, and that
they who worship him must worship him in spirit and in
truth, for the Father seeketh such to worship him." The very
first essential of prayer is to pray *in truth,* and we do not
pray in truth unless the Spirit of God leads our vain minds
into the sincerity and reality of devotion. To pray in truth, is
this—it is not to use the empty expression of prayer, but to
mean what we say; it is for the heart to agonize with God
and heave with strong desires, and where will you obtain
such a manner of prayer except in the spiritual man, when
moved by the Holy Ghost? The carnal man, if he be foolish
enough, can intone a prayer; the carnal man can "read the
office," and "do duty" as well as anybody else who can read in
a book, but he is not praying; no prayer can come from him.
Only the spiritual man can sigh and long, and cry in his
inmost heart, and in the chamber of his soul before God, and
he will not do it except as the Spirit of truth leadeth him in
sincerity into the secret of heart-prayer.

Praying in the Holy Ghost is praying in *fervency.* Cold
prayers, my brethren, ask the Lord not to hear them. Those
who do not plead with fervency, plead not at all. As well

speak of lukewarm fire as of lukewarm prayer; it is essential that it be red-hot. Real prayer is burnt as with hot iron into a man's soul, and then comes forth from the man's soul like coals of juniper which have a most vehement heat. Such prayers none but the Holy Ghost can give. I have heard from this spot prayers which I never can forget, nor will you ever forget them either. Last January and February there were times when certain of our brethren were helped to pray with such power that we were bowed down in humiliation, and anon upborne as on the wings of eagles in the power of supplication. There is a way of praying with power in which a man seems to get hold of the posts of heaven's gate, as Samson grasped the pillars of the temple, and appears as though he would pull all down upon himself sooner than miss the blessing. It is a brave thing for the heart to vow, "I will not let thee go except thou bless me." That is praying in the Holy Ghost. May we be tutored in the art of offering effectual fervent prayer!

Next to that, it is essential in prayer that we should pray *perseveringly.* Any man can run fast at a spurt, but to keep it up mile after mile, there is the battle. And so, certain hot spirits can pray very fervently once now and then, but to continue in prayer—who shall do this except the Spirit of God sustaineth him? Mortal spirits flag and tire. The course of mere fleshly devotion is as the course of a snail which melts as it crawls. Carnal minds go onward and their devotion grows small by degrees and miserably less, as they cry out, "What a weariness it is!" But when the Holy Ghost fills a man and leads him into prayer, he gathers force as he proceeds, and grows more fervent even when God delays to answer. The longer the gate is closed the more vehemently does he use the knocker, till he thunders in his prayer; and the longer the Angel lingers the more resolved is he that if he grasps him with a death-grip he will never let him go without the blessing. Beautiful in God's sight is tearful and yet unconquerable importunity. Jesus delights to be laid hold of by one who says, "I cannot take 'No' for an answer, this blessing I must have, for thou hast promised it and thou hast taught me to ask for it, and I will not believe that thou canst belie thyself." Surely we must have the Holy Spirit to help us thus to pray.

Praying in the Spirit we shall be sure to pray in a *holy* frame of mind. Brethren and sisters, do you ever get distracted in your minds? "Ah," say you, "I wonder when I am not." I will venture to say that you have come into this house burdened, and yet on the road you were saying, "This is a blessed Sabbath day, I feel I have God's presence;" some silly gossip met you on the steps, and told you an idle tale which distracted you. You may even get quietly seated here, and then the recollection of a child at home, or the remembrance of what somebody said about six weeks ago will perplex your mind, so that you cannot pray. But when the Holy Spirit cometh, he takes a scourge of small cords and drives these buyers and sellers out of the temple and leaves it clear for God, and then you can come with a holy, devout frame of mind, fixed and settled in your great object of approach to God. This is to approach him in the Spirit. Oh for more of this blessed, undisturbed devotion!

I could not, however, finish the description of praying in the Spirit if I did not say that it means praying *humbly,* for the Holy Spirit never puffs us up with pride. He is the Spirit that convinces of sin, and so bows us down in contrition and brokenness of spirit. We must pray before God like the humble publican, or we shall never go forth justified as he was. We shall never sing *Gloria in excelsis* except we pray to God *De profundis;* out of the depths must we cry, or we shall never see the glory in the highest.

True prayer must be *loving* prayer, if it be praying in the Holy Ghost. Prayer should be perfumed with love, saturated with love; love to our fellow saints, and love to Christ. Moreover, it must be a prayer full of *faith.* The effectual fervent prayer of a man prevails only as he believes in God, and the Holy Spirit is the author of faith in us, and nurtures and strengthens it so that we pray believing God's promise. Oh that this blessed combination of excellent graces, priceless and sweet as the spices of the merchant, might be fragrant within us because the Holy Ghost's power is shed abroad in our hearts! Time fails me, therefore I must dispense with a full description of what praying in the Holy Ghost is, but I hope you will possess it and so understand it.

IV. Fourthly, I shall use the text as A CHERUB to proclaim our success in prayer. Praying in the Spirit—blessed word!

—then with such prayer it is an absolute certainty that I must succeed with God in prayer. If my prayer were my own prayer, I might not be so sure of it, but if the prayer which I utter be God's own prayer written on my soul, God is always one with himself, and what he writes on the heart is only written there because it is written in his purposes. It is said by an old divine, that prayer is the shadow of Omnipotence. Our will, when God the Holy Spirit influences it, is the indicator of God's will. When God's people pray, it is because the blessing is coming, and their prayers are the shadow of the coming blessing. Rest assured of this, brethren, God never did belie himself, he never contradicted in one place what he said in another. You and I may contradict ourselves, not only through untruthfulness, but even through infirmity; we may not be able to stand to our word, and we may forget what we did say, and so in another place may say something that contradicts it, but God is neither infirm as to memory, nor yet changeable as to will; what he promised yesterday he fulfils to-day, and what he said in one place, he declares in another. Then if God saith in my heart, "Pray for So-and-so," it is because he has said it in the book of his decrees. The Spirit of God's writing in the heart always tallies with the writing of destiny in the book of God's eternal purpose. Rest assured that you cannot but succeed when you have laid your soul like a sheet of paper before the Lord, and asked him to write upon it; then it is no more your own prayer merely, but the Spirit making intercession in you according to the will of God. At such time you need not say, "I hope God will answer the prayer;" he will do it—he is pledged to do it. It is a kind of infidelity to say, "I do not know whether the Lord is true to his promise or no, but I hope he is." He is true; let God be true and every man a liar. Oh! if more of you tried him as some of us have been compelled to do, you would have to hold up your hands in astonishment, and say, "Verily, whatever else is not a fact, it is a fact that God who sitteth in the highest heavens listens to the cries of his people, and gives them according to the desire of their hearts." If the Spirit teaches you to pray, it is as certain as that twice two make four, that God will give you what you are seeking for.

V. Then I will use the text in conclusion as A CHARIOT in

which to convey our own souls onward in the delightful exercise of prayer. The exercise allotted to us to-day and to-morrow is that of praying in the Spirit. Brethren and sisters, it is delightful to some of us to believe that the Spirit of God is the author of the great wave of prayer now breaking over the churches to which we belong. It was not of our devising or planning, but it was the motion of God's Holy Spirit upon a few brethren who desired to spend a day in solemn prayer, and found such blessing in it that they could not but tell others of it; that then others spontaneously moved, and without a word of demur or difference of opinion all said, "Amen; let us meet together for prayer also." The spirit of brotherly kindness, unanimity and love was given to our denomination, and then a spirit of earnest desire to bring down a blessing from God. We have known the time when it was not so. We have known the time when a day of fasting and prayer if not despised, at any rate would not have been appreciated as it will be now. We are of one heart in this matter, and I know from communications with many Christian men, that many of God's people already feel as if they were peculiarly in prayer, as if it were no effort now to pray, but as if it were their very breath now to breathe out longing desires for the revival of saints and the ingathering of sinners.

Brethren of this church, you have had God's presence for many years, you have been favoured with much of "praying in the Holy Ghost," and seen with your eyes the great things God has done in answer to supplication. Will one of you draw back now? Will there be one man to-day or to-morrow who will not be earnest in prayer? Will one man, or even one child, in union with this church, be lukewarm in prayer? I would say, Sin not against the Lord by abstaining from going up to the mercy-seat with your brethren. Offend not the Lord so that he deprive you of the blessing, because you deprive yourself of joining in the exercise. My dear friends, it was when they were all met together with one accord in one place, that suddenly they heard the sound as of a rushing, mighty wind. We cannot be all in one place, but, at any rate, let us be all with one accord. What, do you say you have nothing to pray for? What! no children unconverted, no friends unsaved, no neighbours who are still in darkness?

What! Live in London and not pray for sinners! Where do
you live! Is it in some vast wilderness, amidst "some
boundless contiguity of shade," where rumour of sin and of
ignorance has never reached your ear? No, you are living in
the midst of millions, of ungodly millions, of millions that
despise the God who made them, that despise the gospel of
Christ—of millions, not thousands—hear that word, and see
if you can tell its meaning; *millions* who are living without
God and without hope, and are going down to hell. We have
throughout the realm, too, dangerous mischiefs spreading;
need I so continually remind you of them; Infidelity wearing
the mitre, and Popery usurping the place of Protestantism.
You are assailed by the wolf and the lion, the serpent and
the bear; all forms of mischief are coming forth to attack the
church. Not pray! If you pray not, shall I say, May you smart
for your negligence? Nay I dare not in the slightest shade
speak as though I imprecated a woe upon you, but the woe
will come upon you, depend upon it. If I say it not, yet will
God say it at this present hour, "Curse ye Meroz, saith the
Lord, because they came not up to the help of the Lord, to
the help of the Lord against the mighty." We are not asking
you to contribute of your wealth in this case. If we did the
Lord Jesus has a right to it, and you should freely give it;
neither are we asking you all this day to preach, if we did
some of you might be excused for want of ability; but we
claim your prayer, and must not be denied. Not able to pray!
then are you graceless, Christless, hopeless, lost, and I will
not ask you to join with us, but ask you first to go to God for
yourselves. But if you are a Christian you can pray. Poverty
does not make you poor in prayer, want of education need
not hinder you upon your knees, want of position and rank
in society will be no incumbrance to you when you deal with
God, who hears the poor man when he cries and answers
him with a largess of grace.

Brethren and sisters, if you love Christ, if you ever felt his
love shed abroad in your heart, if you have been washed in
his blood, if you have been saved from wrath through him, if
you are new creatures in him, if you hope to see his face with
acceptance at the last, I might put it to you as a demand, but
I press it upon you as a brotherly entreaty, join with us in
praying in the Holy Ghost. Shall one start back? Take heed

then, if you refuse to unite with your brethren in prayer, lest when you choose to cry you should find yourself straitened and shut up in prison. Beware, lest by refusing to pray now that the Spirit of God has come, you afterwards feel yourself deprived of the comfortable presence of the Holy Ghost, and find the sweetness of devotion to have departed from you. The Lord send a blessing. He must send it, our hearts will break if he does not; we feel that it is coming; we have grasped the promise, we have pleaded with Jehovah; we have pleaded the blood of Jesus; we are pleading it now; we mean to continue in such pleading till the blessing comes, and we may rely upon it that the heavenly shower will soon descend. He has not said to the seed of Jacob, "Seek ye my face in vain." Brethren, be hopeful, but do let us unanimously join in praying in the Holy Ghost.

May the Lord bless you, dear friends, in this respect for Jesus' sake.

14

Adoption-The Spirit And The Cry

"And because ye are sons, God hath sent forth the Spirit of his Son into your hearts, crying, Abba, Father."   Galatians 4:6

We do not find the doctrine of the Trinity in Unity set forth in Scripture in formal terms, such as those which are employed in the Athanasian creed; but the truth is continually taken for granted, as if it were a fact well known in the church of God. If not laid down very often, in so many words, it is everywhere held in solution, and it is mentioned incidentally, in connection with other truths in a way which renders it quite as distinct as if it were expressed in a set formula. In many passages it is brought before us so prominently that we must be wilfully blind if we do not note it. In the present chapter, for instance, we have distinct mention of each of the three divine Persons. "God," that is the Father, "sent forth the Spirit," that is the Holy Spirit; and he is here called "the Spirit *of his Son.*" Nor have we the names alone, for each sacred person is mentioned as acting in the work of our salvation: see the fourth verse, "God *sent forth* his Son"; then note the fifth verse, which speaks of the Son as *redeeming* them that were under the law; and then the text itself reveals the Spirit as coming into the hearts of believers, and *crying* Abba, Father. Now, inasmuch as you have not only the mention of the separate names, but also certain special operations ascribed to each, it is plain that you have here the distinct personality of each. Neither the Father, the Son, nor the Spirit can be an influence, or a mere form of existence, for each one acts in a divine manner, but with a special sphere and a distinct mode of operation. The error of regarding a certain divine person as a mere influence, or emanation, mainly assails the Holy Ghost; but its falseness is seen in the words—"crying, Abba, Father": an influence could not cry; the act requires a person to perform it. Though we may not understand the wonderful truth of the undivided Unity, and the distinct personality of the Triune Godhead, yet, nevertheless, we see the truth revealed in the Holy Scriptures: and, therefore, we accept it as a matter of faith.

The divinity of each of these sacred persons is also to be gathered from the text and its connection. We do not doubt the divinity of the Father, for he is here distinctly mentioned as "God": twice is the Father evidently intended when the word "God" is used. That the Son is God is implied, for though made of a woman, as to his human nature, he is described as "sent forth" and, therefore, he was pre-existent before he was sent forth and made of a woman; this, together with his being called the Son of God, and his being spoken of as able to redeem, are to our minds sufficient proofs of deity. The Spirit is said to do what only God can do, namely, to dwell in the hearts of all believers. It were not possible for any being to cry in the hearts of a multitude of men if he were not omnipresent and therefore divine. So that we have the name of each divine Person, the working of each, the personality of each, and in some degree the deity of each, within the compass of a few lines. As for believers in the Lord Jesus Christ, they know how needful is the co-operation of the entire Trinity to our salvation, and they are charmed to see the loving union of all in the work of deliverance. We reverence the Father, without whom we had not been chosen or adopted: the Father who hath begotten us again unto a lively hope by the resurrection of Jesus Christ from the dead. We love and reverence the Son by whose most precious blood we have been redeemed, and with whom we are one in a mystic and everlasting union: and we adore and love the divine Spirit, for it is by him that we have been regenerated, illuminated, quickened, preserved, and sanctified; and it is through him that we receive the seal and witness within our hearts, by which we are assured that we are indeed the sons of God. As God said of old, "Let us make man in our image, after our likeness," even so do the divine Persons take counsel together, and all unite in the new creation of the believer. We must not fail to bless, adore, and love each one of the exalted Persons, but we must diligently bow in lowliest reverence before the one God— Father, Son, and Holy Ghost. "Glory be to the Father, and to the Son, and to the Holy Ghost; as it was in the beginning, is now, and ever shall be, world without end. Amen."

Having noted this most important fact, let us come to the text itself, hoping to enjoy the doctrine of the Trinity while we are discoursing upon our adoption, in which wonder of grace they each have a share. Under the teaching of the divine Spirit may we be drawn into sweet communion with the Father through his Son Jesus Christ, to his glory and to our benefit.

Three things are very clearly set forth in my text: the first is *the dignity of believers*—"ye are sons;" the second is *the consequent indwelling of the Holy Ghost*—"because ye are sons, God hath sent forth the Spirit of his Son into your hearts;" and the third is *the filial cry*—crying, "Abba, Father."

I. First, then, THE DIGNITY OF BELIEVERS. Adoption gives us the rights of children, regeneration gives us the nature of children: we are partakers of both of these, for we are sons.

And let us here observe that *this sonship is a gift of grace received by faith.* We are not the sons of God by nature in the sense here meant. We are in a sense "the offspring of God" by nature, but this is very different from the sonship here described, which is the peculiar privilege of those who are born again. The Jews claimed to be of the family of God, but as their privileges came to them by the way of their fleshly birth, they are likened to Ishmael, who was born after the flesh, but who was cast out as the son of the bondwoman, and compelled to give way to the son of the promise. We have a sonship which does not come to us by nature, for we are "born not of blood, nor of the will of the flesh, nor of the will of man, but of God." Our sonship comes by promise, by the operation of God as a special gift to a peculiar seed, set apart unto the Lord by his own sovereign grace, as Isaac was. This honour and privilege come to us, according to the connection of our text, by faith. Note well the twenty-sixth

verse of the preceding chapter (Gal. iii. 26): "For ye are all
the children of God by faith in Christ Jesus." As unbelievers
we know nothing of adoption. While we are under the law as
self-righteous we know something of servitude, but we know
nothing of sonship. It is only after that faith has come that
we cease to be under the schoolmaster, and rise out of our
minority to take the privileges of the sons of God.

Faith worketh in us the spirit of adoption, and our
consciousness of sonship, in this wise: first, *it brings us
justification.* Verse twenty-four of the previous chapter says,
"The law was our schoolmaster to bring us unto Christ, that
we might be justified by faith." An unjustified man stands in
the condition of a criminal, not of a child: his sin is laid to his
charge, he is reckoned as unjust and unrighteous, as indeed
he really is, and he is therefore a rebel against his king, and
not a child enjoying his father's love. But when faith realizes
the cleansing power of the blood of atonement, and lays hold
upon the righteousness of God in Christ Jesus, then the
justified man becomes a son and a child. Justification and
adoption always go together. "Whom he called them he also
justified," and the calling is a call to the Father's house, and
to a recognition of sonship. Believing brings forgiveness and
justification through our Lord Jesus; it also brings adoption,
for it is written, "But as many as received him, to them gave
he power to become the sons of God, even to them that
believe on his name."

Faith brings us into the realization of our adoption in the
next place by *setting us free from the bondage of the law.*
"After that faith is come, we are no longer under a
schoolmaster." When we groaned under a sense of sin, and
were shut up by it as in a prison, we feared that the law
would punish us for our iniquity, and our life was made
bitter with fear. Moreover, we strove in our own blind
self-sufficient manner to keep that law, and this brought us
into yet another bondage, which became harder and harder
as failure succeeded to failure: we sinned and stumbled
more and more to our soul's confusion. But now that faith
has come we see the law fulfilled in Christ, and ourselves
justified and accepted in him: this changes the slave into a
child, and duty into choice. Now we delight in the law, and
by the power of the Spirit we walk in holiness to the glory of

God. Thus it is that by believing in Christ Jesus we escape
from Moses, the taskmaster, and come to Jesus, the Saviour;
we cease to regard God as an angry Judge and view him as
our loving Father. The system of merit and command, and
punishment and fear, has given way to the rule of grace,
gratitude, and love, and this new principle of government is
one of the grand privileges of the children of God.

Now, *faith is the mark of sonship in all who have it,*
whoever they may be, for "ye are all the children of God by
faith in Christ Jesus" (Gal. iii. 26). If you are believing in
Jesus, whether you are Jew or Gentile, bond or free, you are
a son of God. If you have only believed in Christ of late, and
have but for the past few weeks been able to rest in his great
salvation, yet, beloved, now are you a child of God. It is not
an after privilege, granted to assurance or growth in grace;
it is an early blessing, and belongs to him who has the
smallest degree of faith, and is no more than a babe in grace.
If a man be a believer in Jesus Christ his name is in the
register-book of the great family above, "for ye are all the
children of God by faith in Christ Jesus." But if you have no
faith, no matter what zeal, no matter what works, no matter
what knowledge, no matter what pretensions to holiness you
may possess, you are nothing, and your religion is vain.
Without faith in Christ you are as sounding brass and a
tinkling cymbal, for without faith it is impossible to please
God. Faith then, wherever it is found, is the infallible token
of a child of God, and its absence is fatal to the claim.

This according to the apostle is further illustrated by our
baptism, for in baptism, if there be faith in the soul, there is
an open putting on of the Lord Jesus Christ. Read the
twenty-seventh verse: "For as many of you as have been
baptized into Christ have put on Christ." In baptism you
professed to be dead to the world and you were therefore
buried into the name of Jesus: and the meaning of that
burial, if it had any right meaning to you, was that you
professed yourself henceforth to be dead to everything but
Christ, and henceforth your life was to be in him, and you
were to be as one raised from the dead to newness of life. Of
course the outward form avails nothing to the unbeliever,
but to the man who is in Christ it is a most instructive
ordinance. The spirit and essence of the ordinance lie in the

soul's entering into the symbol, in the man's knowing not alone the baptism into water, but the baptism into the Holy Ghost and into fire: and as many of you as know that inward mystic baptism into Christ know also that henceforth you have put on Christ and are covered by him as a man is by his garment. Henceforth you are one in Christ, you wear his name, you live in him, you are saved by him, you are altogether his. Now, if you are one with Christ, since he is a son, you are sons also. If you have put on Christ, God seeth you not in yourself but in Christ, and that which belongeth unto Christ belongeth also unto you, for if you be Christ's then are you Abraham's seed and heirs according to the promise. As the Roman youth when he came of age put on the *toga,* and was admitted to the rights of citizenship, so the putting on of Christ is the token of our admission into the position of sons of God. Thus are we actually admitted to the enjoyment of our glorious heritage. Every blessing of the covenant of grace belongs to those who are Christ's, and every believer is in that list. Thus, then, according to the teaching of the passage, we receive adoption by faith as the gift of grace.

Again, *adoption comes to us by redemption.* Read the passage which precedes the text: "But when the fulness of the time was come, God sent forth his Son, made of a woman, made under the law, to redeem them that were under the law, that we might receive the adoption of sons." Beloved, prize redemption, and never listen to teaching which would destroy its meaning or lower its importance. Remember that ye were not redeemed with silver and gold, but with the precious blood of Christ, as of a lamb without blemish. You were under the law, and subject to its curse, for you had broken it most grievously, and you were subject to its penalty, for it is written, "the soul that sinneth, it shall die"; and yet again, "cursed is everyone that continueth not in all things that are written in the book of the law to do them." You were also under the terror of the law, for you feared its wrath; and you were under its irritating power, for often when the commandment came, sin within you revived and you died. But now you are redeemed from all; as the Holy Ghost saith, "Christ hath redeemed us from the curse of the law, being made a curse for us: for it is written, Cursed is

every one that hangeth on a tree." Now ye are not under the
law, but under grace, and this because Christ came under
the law and kept it both by his active and his passive
obedience, fulfilling all its commands and bearing all its
penalty on your behalf and in your room and stead.
Henceforth you are the redeemed of the Lord, and enjoy a
liberty which comes by no other way but that of the eternal
ransom. Remember this; and whenever you feel most
assured that you are a child of God, praise the redeeming
blood; whenever your heart beats highest with love to your
great Father, bless the "firstborn among many brethren,"
who for your sakes came under the law, was circumcised,
kept the law in his life, and bowed his head to it in his death,
honouring, and magnifying the law, and making the justice
and righteousness of God to be more conspicuous by his life
than it would have been by the holiness of all mankind, and
his justice to be more fully vindicated by his death than it
would have been if all the world of sinners had been cast into
hell. Glory be to our redeeming Lord, by whom we have
received the adoption!

Again, we further learn from the passage that *we now
enjoy the privilege of sonship.* According to the run of the
passage the apostle means not only that we are children, but
that we are full-grown sons. "Because ye are sons," means,—
because the time appointed of the Father is come, and you
are of age, and no longer under tutors and governors. In our
minority we are under the schoolmaster, under the regimen
of ceremonies, under types, figures, shadows, learning our A
B C by being convinced of sin; but when faith is come we are
no longer under the schoolmaster, but come to a more free
condition. Till faith comes we are under tutors and
governors, like mere boys, but after faith we take our rights
as sons of God. The Jewish church of old was under the yoke
of the law; its sacrifices were continual and its ceremonies
endless; new moons and feasts must be kept; jubilees must
be observed and pilgrimages made: in fact, the yoke was too
heavy for feeble flesh to bear. The law followed the Israelite
into every corner, and dealt with him upon every point: it
had to do with his garments, his meat, his drink, his bed, his
board, and everything about him: it treated him like a boy at
school who has a rule for everything. Now that faith has

come we are full grown sons, and therefore we are free from
the rules which govern the school of the child. We are under
law to Christ, even as the full-grown son is still under the
discipline of his father's house; but this is a law of love and
not of fear, of grace and not of bondage. "Stand fast therefore
in the liberty wherewith Christ hath made us free, and be
not entangled again with the yoke of bondage." Return not to
the beggarly elements of a merely outward religion, but keep
close to the worship of God in spirit and in truth, for this is
the liberty of the children of God.

Now, by faith *we are no more like to bond-servants*. The
apostle says that "the heir, as long as he is a child, differeth
nothing from a servant, though he be lord of all; but is under
tutors and governors till the time appointed of the father."
But beloved, now are ye the sons of God, and ye have come
to your majority: now are ye free to enjoy the honours and
blessings of the Father's house. Rejoice that the free spirit
dwells within you, and prompts you to holiness; this is a far
superior power to the merely external command and the
whip of threatening. Now no more are you in bondage to
outward forms, and rites, and ceremonies; but the Spirit of
God teacheth you all things, and leads you into the inner
meaning and substance of the truth.

Now, also, saith the apostle, *we are heirs*—"Wherefore
thou art no more a servant, but a son; and if a son, then an
heir of God through Christ." No man living has ever realised
to the full what this means. Believers are at this moment
heirs, but what is the estate? It is God himself! We are heirs
of God! Not only of the promises, of the covenant engage-
ments, and of all the blessings which belong to the chosen
seed, but heirs of God himself. "The Lord is my portion, saith
my soul." "This God is our God for ever and ever." We are not
only heirs to God, to all that he gives to his firstborn, but
heirs of God himself. David said, "The Lord is the portion of
mine inheritance and of my cup." As he said to Abraham,
"Fear not Abraham, I am thy shield and thine exceeding
great reward," so saith he to every man that is born of the
Spirit. These are his own words—"I will be to them a God,
and they shall be to me a people." Why, then, O believer, are
you poor? All riches are yours. Why then are you sorrowful?
The ever-blessed God is yours. Why do you tremble?

Omnipotence waits to help you. Why do you distrust? His immutability will abide with you even to the end, and make his promise steadfast. All things are yours, for Christ is yours, and Christ is God's; and though there be some things which at present you cannot actually grasp in your hand, nor even see with your eye, to wit, the things which are laid up for you in heaven, yet still by faith you can enjoy even these, for "he hath raised us up together, and made us sit together in the heavenlies in Christ," "in whom also we have obtained an inheritance," so that "our citizenship is in heaven." We enjoy even now the pledge and earnest of heaven in the indwelling of the Holy Ghost. Oh what privileges belong to those who are the sons of God!

Once more upon this point of the believer's dignity, *we are already tasting one of the inevitable consequences of being the sons of God.* What are they? One of them is the opposition of the children of the bondwoman. No sooner had the apostle Paul preached the liberty of the saints, than straightway there arose certain teachers who said, "This will never do; you must be circumcised, you must come under the law." Their opposition was to Paul a token that he was of the free woman, for behold, the children of the bondwoman singled him out for their virulent opposition. You shall find, dear brother, that if you enjoy fellowship with God, if you live in the spirit of adoption, if you are brought near to the Most High, so as to be a member of the divine family, straightway all those who are under bondage to the law will quarrel with you. Thus saith the apostle, "As then he that was born after the flesh persecuted him that was born after the Spirit, even so it is now." The child of Hagar was found by Sarah mocking Isaac, the child of promise. Ishmael would have been glad to have shown his enmity to the hated heir by blows and personal assault, but there was a superior power to check him, so that he could get no further than "mocking." So it is just now. There have been periods in which the enemies of the gospel have gone a great deal further than mocking, for they have been able to imprison and burn alive the lovers of the gospel; but now, thank God, we are under his special protection as to life and limb and liberty, and are as safe as Isaac was in Abraham's house. They can mock us, but they cannot go any further, or else some of us would be

publicly gibbeted. But trials of cruel mockings are still to be
endured, our words are twisted, our sentiments are misrepresented, and all sorts of horrible things are imputed to
us, things which we know not, to all which we would reply
with Paul, "Am I therefore become your enemy because I tell
you the truth?" This is the old way of the Hagarenes, the
child after the flesh is still doing his best to mock him that is
born after the Spirit. Do not be astonished, neither be
grieved in the least degree when this happens to any of you,
but let this also turn to the establishment of your confidence
and to the confirmation of your faith in Christ Jesus, for he
told you of old, "If ye were of the world, the world would love
his own: but because ye are not of the world, but I have
chosen you out of the world, therefore the world hateth you."

II. Our second head is THE CONSEQUENT INDWELLING OF
THE HOLY GHOST IN BELIEVERS;—"God hath sent forth the
Spirit of his Son into your hearts." *Here is a divine act of the
Father.* The Holy Ghost proceedeth from the Father and the
Son: and God hath sent him forth into your hearts. If he had
only come knocking at your hearts and asked your leave to
enter, he had never entered, but when Jehovah sent him he
made his way, without violating your will, but yet with
irresistible power. Where Jehovah sent him there he will
abide, and go no more out for ever. Beloved, I have no time
to dwell upon the words, but I want you to turn them over in
your thoughts, for they contain a great depth. As surely as
God sent his Son into the world to dwell among men, so that
his saints beheld his glory, the "glory as of the only begotten
of the Father, full of grace and truth," so surely hath God
sent forth the Spirit to enter into men's hearts, there to take
up his residence that in him also the glory of God may be
revealed. Bless and adore the Lord who hath sent you such
a visitor as this.

Now, note the style and title under which the Holy Spirit
comes to us: *he comes as the Spirit of Jesus.* The words are
"the Spirit of his Son," by which is not meant the character
and disposition of Christ, though that were quite true, for
God sends this unto his people, but it means the Holy Ghost.
Why, then, is he called the Spirit of his Son, or the Spirit of
Jesus? May we not give these reasons? It was by the Holy
Ghost that the human nature of Christ was born of the

Virgin. By the Spirit our Lord was attested at his baptism, when the Holy Spirit descended upon him like a dove, and abode upon him. In him the Holy Spirit dwelt without measure, anointing him for his great work, and by the Spirit he was anointed with the oil of gladness above his fellows. The Spirit was also with him, attesting his ministry by signs and wonders. The Holy Ghost is our Lord's great gift to the church; it was after his ascension that he bestowed the gifts of Pentecost, and the Holy Spirit descended upon the church to abide with the people of God for ever. The Holy Ghost is the Spirit of Christ, because, also, he is Christ's witness here below; for "there are three that bear witness on earth, the Spirit, and the water, and the blood." For these and many other reasons he is called "the Spirit of his Son," and it is he who comes to dwell in believers. I would urge you very solemnly and gratefully to consider the wondrous con-descension which is here displayed. God himself the Holy Ghost, takes up his residence in believers. I never know which is the more wonderful, the incarnation of Christ or the indwelling of the Holy Ghost. Jesus dwelt here for awhile in human flesh untainted by sin, holy, harmless, undefiled, and separate from sinners; but the Holy Ghost dwells continually in the hearts of all believers, though as yet they are imperfect and prone to evil. Year after year, century after century, he still abideth in the saints, and will do so till the elect are all in glory. While we adore the incarnate Son, let us adore also the indwelling Spirit whom the Father hath sent.

Now notice *the place wherein he takes up his residence—* "God hath sent forth the Spirit of his Son *into your hearts.*" Note, that it does not say into your heads or your brains. The Spirit of God doubtless illuminates the intellect and guides the judgment, but this is not the commencement nor the main part of his work. He comes chiefly to the affections, he dwells with the heart, for with the heart man believeth unto righteousness, and "God hath sent forth the Spirit of his Son into your hearts." Now, the heart is the centre of our being, and therefore doth the Holy Ghost occupy this place of vantage, He comes into the central fortress and universal citadel of our nature, and thus takes possession of the whole. The heart is the vital part; we speak of it as the chief residence of life, and therefore the Holy Ghost enters it, and as the living God dwells in the living heart, taking possession of the very core and marrow of our being. It is from the heart and through the heart that life is diffused. The blood is sent even to the extremities of the body by the pulsings of the heart, and when the Spirit of God takes possession of the affections, he operates upon every power, and faculty, and member of our entire manhood. Out of the heart are the issues of life, and from the affections sanctified by the Holy Ghost all other faculties and powers receive renewal, illumination, sanctification, strengthening, and ultimate perfection.

This wonderful blessing is ours "because we are sons;" and *it is fraught with marvellous results.* Sonship sealed by the indwelling Spirit brings us peace and joy; it leads to nearness to God and fellowship with him; it excites trust, love, and vehement desire, and creates in us reverence, obedience, and actual likeness to God. All this, and much more, because the Holy Ghost has come to dwell in us. Oh, matchless mystery! Had it not been revealed it had never been imagined, and now that it is revealed it would never have been believed if it had not become matter of actual experience to those who are in Christ Jesus. There are many professors who know nothing of this; they listen to us with bewilderment as if we told them an idle tale, for the carnal mind knoweth not the things that be of God; they are spiritual, and can only be spiritually discerned. Those who are not sons, or who only come in as sons under the law of nature, like Ishmael, know nothing of this indwelling Spirit, and are up in arms at us for daring to claim so great a blessing: yet it is ours, and none can deprive us of it.

III. Now I come to the third portion of our text—THE FILIAL CRY. This is deeply interesting. I think it will be profitable if your minds enter into it. Where the Holy Ghost enters there is a cry. "God hath sent forth the Spirit of his Son, crying, 'Abba, Father.'" Now notice, *it is the Spirit of God that cries*—a most remarkable fact. Some are inclined to view the expression as a Hebraism, and read it, he "makes us to cry;" but, beloved, the text saith not so, and we are not at liberty to alter it upon such a pretence. We are always right in keeping to what God says, and here we plainly read

of the Spirit in our hearts that he is crying "Abba, Father."
The apostle in Romans viii. 15 says, "Ye have received the
Spirit of adoption, whereby *we* cry, Abba, Father," but here
he describes the Spirit himself as crying "Abba, Father." We
are certain that when he ascribed the cry of "Abba, Father"
to us, he did not wish to exclude the Spirit's cry, because in
the twenty-sixth verse of the famous eighth of Romans he
says, "Likewise the Spirit also helpeth our infirmities: for we
know not what we should pray for as we ought: but the
Spirit itself maketh intercession for us with groanings which
cannot be uttered." Thus he represents the Spirit himself as
groaning with unutterable groanings within the child of God,
so that when he wrote to the Romans he had on his mind the
same thought which he here expressed to the Galatians,—
that it is the Spirit itself which cries and groans in us "Abba,
Father." How is this? Is it not ourselves that cry? Yes,
assuredly; and yet the Spirit cries also. The expressions are
both correct. The Holy Spirit prompts and inspires the cry.
He puts the cry into the heart and mouth of the believer. It
is his cry because he suggests it, approves of it, and educates
us to it. We should never have cried thus if he had not first
taught us the way. As a mother teaches her child to speak,
so he puts this cry of "Abba, Father" into our mouths; yea, it
is he who forms in our hearts the desire after our Father,
God, and keeps it there. He is the Spirit of adoption, and the
author of adoption's special and significant cry.

Not only does he prompt us to cry but he works in us a
sense of need which compels us to cry, and also that spirit of
confidence which emboldens us to claim such relationship to
the great God. Nor is this all, for he assists us in some
mysterious manner so that we are able to pray aright; he
puts his divine energy into us so that we cry "Abba, Father"
in an acceptable manner. There are times when *we* cannot
cry at all, and then he cries in us. There are seasons when
doubts and fears abound, and so suffocate us with their
fumes that we cannot even raise a cry, and then the
indwelling Spirit represents us, and speaks for us, and
makes intercession for us, crying in our name, and making
intercession for us according to the will of God. Thus does
the cry "Abba, Father" rise up in our hearts even when we
feel as if we could not pray, and dare not think ourselves

children. Then we may each say, "I live, yet not I, but the Spirit that dwelleth in me." On the other hand, at times our soul gives such a sweet assent to the Spirit's cry that it becometh ours also, but then we more than ever own the work of the Spirit, and still ascribe to him the blessed cry, "Abba, Father."

I want you now to notice a very sweet fact about this cry; namely, that *it is literally the cry of the Son.* God hath sent the Spirit of his Son into our hearts, and that Spirit cries in us exactly according to the cry of the Son. If you turn to the gospel of Mark, at the fourteenth chapter, thirty-sixth verse, you will find there what you will not discover in any other evangelist (for Mark is always the man for the striking points, and the memorable words), he records that our Lord prayed in the garden, "Abba, Father, all things are possible unto thee; take away this cup from me: nevertheless not what I will, but what thou wilt." So that this cry in us copies the cry of our Lord to the letter—"Abba, Father." Now, I dare say you have heard these words "Abba, Father" explained at considerable length at other times, and if so, you know that the first word is Syrian or Aramaic; or, roughly speaking, Abba is the Hebrew word for "father." The second word is in Greek, and is the Gentile word, "πατηρ," or *pater,* which also signifies father. It is said that these two words are used to remind us that Jews and Gentiles are one before God. They do remind us of this, but this cannot have been the principal reason for their use. Do you think that when our Lord was in his agony in the garden that he said, "Abba, Father" because Jews and Gentiles are one? Why should he have thought of that doctrine, and why need he mention it in prayer to his Father? Some other reason must have suggested it to him. It seems to me that our Lord said "Abba" because it was his native tongue. When a Frenchman prays, if he has learned English he may ordinarily pray in English, but if ever he falls into an agony he will pray in French, as surely as he prays at all. Our Welsh brethren tell us that there is no language like Welsh—I suppose it is so *to them:* now they will talk English when about their ordinary business, and they can pray in English when everything goes comfortably with them, but I am sure that if a Welshman is in a great fervency of prayer, he flies to his Welsh tongue to find full expression. Our Lord in his agony used his native language, and as born of the seed of Abraham he cries in his own tongue, "Abba." Even thus, my brethren, we are prompted by the spirit of adoption to use our own language, the language of the heart, and to speak to the Lord freely in our own tongue. Besides, to my mind, the word "Abba" is of all words in all languages the most natural word for father. I must try and pronounce it so that you see the natural childishness of it, "Ab-ba," "Ab-ba." Is it not just what your children say, ab, ab, ba, ba, as soon as they try to talk? It is the sort of word which any child would say, whether Hebrew, or Greek, or French, or English. Therefore, Abba is a word worthy of introduction into all languages. It is truly a child's word, and our Master felt, I have no doubt, in his agony, a love for child's words. Dr. Guthrie, when he was dying, said, "Sing a hymn," but he added, *"Sing me one of the bairns' hymns."* When a man comes to die he wants to be a child again, and longs for bairns' hymns and bairns' words. Our blessed Master in his agony used the bairns' word, "Abba," and it is equally becoming in the mouth of each one of us. I think this sweet word "Abba" was chosen to show us that we are to be very natural with God, and not stilted and formal. We are to be very affectionate, and come close to him, and not merely say "Pater," which is a cold Greek word, but say "Abba," which is a warm, natural, loving word, fit for one who is a little child with God, and makes bold to lie in his bosom, and look up into his face and talk with holy boldness. "Abba" is not a word, somehow, but a babe's lisping. Oh, how near we are to God when we can use such a speech! How dear he is to us and dear we are to him when we may thus address him, saying, like the great Son himself, "Abba, Father."

This leads me to observe that *this cry in our hearts is exceedingly near and familiar.* In the sound of it I have shown you that it is childlike, but the tone and manner of the utterance are equally so. Note that it is *a cry.* If we obtain audience with a king we do not cry, we speak then in measured tones and set phrases; but the Spirit of God breaks down our measured tones, and takes away the formality which some hold in great admiration, and he leads us to *cry,* which is the very reverse of formality and stiffness.

When we cry, we cry, "Abba": even our very cries are full of the spirit of adoption. A cry is a sound which we are not anxious that every passer-by should hear; yet what child minds his father hearing him cry? So when our heart is broken and subdued we do not feel as if we could talk fine language at all, but the Spirit in us sends forth cries and groans, and of these we are not ashamed, nor are we afraid to cry before God. I know some of you think that God will not hear your prayers, because you cannot pray grandly like such-and-such a minister. Oh, but the Spirit of his Son cries, and you cannot do better than cry too. Be satisfied to offer to God broken language, words salted with your griefs, wetted with your tears. Go to him with holy familiarity, and be not afraid to cry in his presence, "Abba, Father."

But then *how earnest it is:* for a cry is an intense thing. The word implies fervency. A cry is not a flippant utterance, nor a mere thing of the lips, it comes up from the soul. Hath not the Lord taught us to cry to him in prayer with fervent importunity that will not take a denial? Hath he not brought us so near to him that sometimes we say, "I will not let thee go except thou bless me"? Hath he not taught us so to pray that his disciples might almost say of us as they did of one of old, "Send her away, for she crieth after us." We do cry after him, our heart and our flesh crieth out for God, for the living God, and this is the cry, "Abba, Father, I must know thee, I must taste thy love, I must dwell under thy wing, I must behold thy face, I must feel thy great fatherly heart overflowing and filling my heart with peace." We cry, "Abba, Father."

I shall close when I notice this, that *the most of this crying is kept within the heart,* and does not come out at the lips. Like Moses, we cry when we say not a word. God hath sent forth the Spirit of his Son *into our hearts,* whereby we cry, "Abba, Father." You know what I mean: it is not alone in your little room, by the old arm-chair, that you cry to God, but you call him "Abba, Father," as you go about the streets or work in the shop. The Spirit of his Son is crying, "Abba, Father," when you are in the crowd or at your table among the family. I see it is alleged as a very grave charge against me that I speak as if I were familiar with God. If it be so, I make bold to say that I speak only as I feel. Blessed be my

heavenly Father's name, I know I am his child, and with
whom should a child be familiar but with his father? O ye
strangers to the living God, be it known unto you that if this
be vile, I purpose to be viler still, as he shall help me to walk
more closely with him. We feel a deep reverence for our
Father in heaven, which bows us to the very dust, but for all
that we can say, "Truly our fellowship is with the Father and
with his Son, Jesus Christ." No stranger can understand the
nearness of the believer's soul to God in Christ Jesus, and
because the world cannot understand it, it finds it convenient to sneer, but what of that? Abraham's tenderness to
Isaac made Ishmael jealous, and caused him to laugh, but
Isaac had no cause to be ashamed of being ridiculed, since
the mocker could not rob him of the covenant blessing. Yes,
beloved, the Spirit of God makes you cry "Abba, Father," but
the cry is mainly within your heart, and there it is so
commonly uttered that it becomes the habit of your soul to
be crying to your heavenly Father. The text does not say that
he had cried, but the expression is *"crying"*—it is a present
participle, indicating that he cries every day "Abba, Father."
Go home, my brethren, and live in the spirit of sonship.
Wake up in the morning, and let your first thought be "My
Father, my Father, be with me this day." Go out into
business, and when things perplex you let that be your
resort—"My Father, help me in this hour of need." When you
go to your home, and there meet with domestic anxieties, let
your cry still be, "Help me, my Father." When alone you are
not alone, because the Father is with you: and in the midst
of the crowd you are not in danger, because the Father
himself loveth you. What a blessed word is that,—"The
Father himself loveth you"! Go, and live as his children.
Take heed that ye reverence him, for if he be a father where
is his fear? Go and obey him, for this is right. Be ye imitators
of God as dear children. Honour him wherever you are, by
adorning his doctrine in all things. Go and live upon him, for
you shall soon live with him. Go and rejoice in him. Go and
cast all your cares upon him. Go henceforth, and whatever
men may see in you may they be compelled to own that you
are the children of the Highest. "Blessed are the
peacemakers, for they shall be called the children of God."
May you be such henceforth and evermore. Amen and amen.

15

The Holy Spirit Glorifying Christ

"He shall glorify me: for he shall receive of mine, and shall shew it unto you." John 16:14

We always need the Spirit of God in our preaching; but I think we more especially require his divine direction and instruction when the subject is *himself*: for the Holy Spirit is so mysterious in his varied attributes and operations, that unless He himself shall reveal himself to us, and give us the words in which to speak of Him, we shall surely fail either to understand for ourselves, or to enlighten others. In *his* light we see light, but without him we grope like blind men in the dark.

Certain sins against the Holy Ghost continually exist in a degree in the Christian Church. *Unholiness of life* grieves the Holy Spirit. When Christian men walk not according to the gospel; when their conversation is not ordered according to the pattern of Christ, then the Holy Spirit who hath no fellowship with unholiness, withdraweth himself in a measure from the Church. *Discord*, too, strife among brethren, forgetfulness of the new commandment, that we love one another, grieveth the sacred Dove: for as his nature is peaceable, as his office is to be the peace-giver, so he tarrieth not where there is the din and noise of contending parties. So, also, when he perceiveth his saints to be diseased with *worldliness*, when we prefer the treasures of Egypt to the reproach of Christ, and seek rather the things which are

seen, which are temporal, than the things which are not
seen, which are eternal, then again is the Holy Ghost
quenched, and departeth from our midst. Above all, pride,
and that *murmuring, rebellion, unbelief, obstinacy,* and self-
seeking which pride leads to—all this grieveth the Holy
Ghost, for he dwelleth with those who are "humble and of a
contrite spirit;" and where there is the voice of murmuring,
where one man seeketh to lift himself above another, and all
to exalt themselves above their despised Lord, the Holy
Ghost hideth himself and suffereth barrenness to take the
place of plenty, and death to reign where once life tri-
umphed. These are a few of the common and the constant
infirmities of the Church, by which the Holy Ghost is much
hindered in those marvellous manifestations which otherwise would be common and usual in the midst of our Israel.

But there are two faults of the Church which appear to me
periodically to manifest themselves. The one is when men
ascribe wrong things to the Holy Ghost, and maketh him the
author of human novelties and delusions. In seasons when
the minds of good men were anxiously alive to spiritual
operations, certain weak-headed or designing persons have
grown fanatical, and being bewildered by their own confused
feelings, and puffed up by their fleshly mind, have forsaken
the true light which is in the Word, to follow after the
will-o'-the-wisps of their own fancies, the ignis-fatuui of
their own brains. Such vain-glorious fools aspiring to be
leaders, masters of sects, will boldly tell to men of itching
ears that fresh doctrines have been specially revealed to
them. They prate much of what they call the inner light
(which is often an inner darkness), which dim candle they
exalt above the light of the word of God, and tell you that
marvellous things have been taught to them in dreams and
visions. Ah! this is a high and crying crime. What, will you
lay at the door of the Holy Ghost a deed which God hath
solemnly cursed? Do you not start back at such a thought? Is
it not almost blasphemy to imagine it? And yet remember,
he that adds a single word to the canon of inspiration is
cursed. Give ear to the very words of the Lord our God, "If
any man shall add unto these things, God shall add unto
him the plagues that are written in this book: and if any
man shall take away from the words of the book of this

prophecy, God shall take away his part out of the book of life, and out of the holy city, and from the things which are written in this book." And do you think the Holy Ghost would do that which involves a curse upon man? If I venture to add to God's word, or to take from it, I do it with this as my penalty, that God shall blot my name out of the Book of Life and out of the holy city; and yet these base pretenders, who would lay their foolish notions at the door of God the Holy Ghost, will have it that he has taught them more than is in the Book, that he has removed that which God laid down as the grand land-mark, and added to the finished testimony of God. Let none of you have any sort of patience with men who talk thus. Deny their very first principle, tell them—whether it be the deceiver of Western America, or the false prophet of Arabia—tell them that they are all impostors, for they ascribe to the Holy Ghost that which is impossible for him to commit, a violation of the revealed will of God in which it is declared that the canon of inspiration is shut up once for all. A little of this evil I detect among godly people. I find that sometimes even gracious men think they have had revelations. Texts of Scripture are no doubt laid home by the Holy Ghost to the souls of men as much to-day as in Paul's time, and there can be no doubt whatever that the Spirit bringeth all things to our remembrance whatsoever Christ hath taught, and that he leadeth us into all truth; but when a man tells me that the Holy Ghost has revealed to him something that is not in the Bible, he lies! Is that a hard word? It doth but express the truth. The man may have dreamed his revelation, he may have fancied it, but the Holy Spirit never goeth beyond the written word. "He shall take of mine, and shall show it unto you." And beyond what Christ hath spoken and what Christ hath taught, the Holy Spirit goeth in no sense and in no respect. You understand what Christ has taught through the Spirit's teaching; but anything beyond the teaching of Christ and his apostles must be not of God but of man. This is a most important principle to be held fast by all godly people, for the day may come when false prophets shall arise, and delude the people, and by this shall we be able to discover them; if they claim ought beyond what Christ hath revealed, put them aside, for they be false prophets, wolves in sheep's

clothing. The Spirit only teacheth us that which Christ hath
taught beforehand either by himself or by the inspired
apostles. "He shall take of mine and shall show it unto you."
Just now we are in little danger from the excesses of fevered
brains, for, as a rule, our sin is in being far too cold and dead
to spiritual influences. I fear me we are liable to another
evil, and are apt to forget the person and work of the Comforter altogether. We fear some congregations might say,
"We have not so much as heard whether there be any Holy
Ghost." From many modern sermons would you know that
there was a Holy Spirit? If it were not for the benediction or
the doxology you might go in and out many churches and
meeting-houses by the year together, and scarcely know that
there was such a person as that blessed, blessed giver of all
good, the Holy Ghost. Sometimes we hear a little about his
influences, as if the Holy Spirit were not as truly a person as
even Jesus Christ himself, who in flesh and blood trod this
earth. Oh, dear friends, I fear the first danger, that of
running wild with whimsies and fancies about inner lights
and new revelations; but I equally dread this last, this
putting the revelation above the revealer, this taking the
book without the author, this preaching of the truth without
the great truth-applier, this going forth to work with the
sword, forgetting that it is the sword of the Spirit, and only
mighty as the Holy Ghost maketh it "mighty to the pulling
down of strongholds." May this Church ever continue to
reverence the Holy Spirit without exaggerating his work!
May we prize him, love him, and adore him, because he so
wondrously glorifies our blessed Lord.

With this, by way of preface, I shall now come at once to
our text, using it three ways—first, *as a test to try various
things by*; secondly, *as a direction how to honour Jesus*, and
thirdly, *as a stimulus, stirring us up to glorify Christ*.

I. First, then, we shall use our text AS A TEST.

There are a thousand things that claim to be of the Holy
Ghost; how can we know whether they are or not? Here is a
simple mode of discovering, "He shall glorify me."

1. Let us, first of all, apply this test to *ministries*. There
are crowds of preachers and reverend divines now-a-days in
the world; but all are not ministers of God who are so called.
A true minister is a creation of the God of heaven. It is no

more in the power of the Church than it is in the power of the bishops to make ministers. Independency is as weak as Episcopacy on this point. God alone ordains ministers; all that the Church can do is to recognise them. We cannot make them at our colleges; we cannot make them by the laying on of hands, nor even by the choice of the Church. God must make them; God must ordain them; it is only for the Church to perceive God's work and cheerfully to submit to his choice. Now, there are some ministries which clearly are not of the Holy Ghost, because they glorify ceremonies. We could take you into certain places of worship where the general strain of ministry is a glorification of baptism, the blessed Eucharist, confirmation, priesthood, and so on. There you hear much of the childish millinery with which they deck the altar, and much is said of those grotesque garments in which their priests disguise themselves. We could point to many places where the main object of teaching seems to be to exalt a rubric, to magnify a liturgy, to hold up a hierarchy, or to extol a ritual. Now all such ministries we may at once sweepingly and unerringly condemn. They are not of the Holy Ghost, for the Holy Spirit teacheth us not to magnify outward rites, but Christ; and that teaching is not of the Holy Ghost which doth not glorify the Lord Jesus.

Into other places we might take you where very clearly the object is the extolling of doctrine. From the first of January to the last of December the brother bitterly contends for the favourite corners of his faith. Doctrine, with certain friends, is everything, and their rigid orthodoxy is the one care of their life. Now, against a sound creed and the doctrines of grace we have not a word to say. God be thanked that we love these things as much as those who exalt them above measure; and are not a whit behind the chiefest of these champions in our zeal for orthodoxy; but still our Lord is, and must be, the leading theme of our ministry, and we must continue to exalt him rather than Calvinism, or any other system of theology. We are bold to say it, much as we love the Master's throne, we love the Master better still; and dearly as we love battling for the walls of his vineyard, yet the clusters of his Eshcol are sweeter to our taste. We love Christ better than creed, and we think we would rather magnify our Master than any set of truths, however important they may be.

There are certain doctrinal brethren, good enough in their way, but still you can evidently see that the doctrine of election is a thing that they contend more for than the doctrine of the redemption of Christ, or if it be redemption, it is rather the *speciality* of redemption than the divine sacrifice itself. I love to preach the distinguishing grace of God but I am far from thinking that some four or five points comprise all the truths which God has revealed. Be it ours to preach the doctrines as Dr. Hawker preached them, with Christ as their sum and substance; "a full Christ for empty sinners," be this our theme. To a great extent it is true of a ministry that seeketh only to exalt doctrines, that it hath not the fulness of the Holy Ghost in it, for of the Holy Spirit it is written "He shall glorify *me*."

Another class of brethren are well known to those of us who have looked upon the Church of God at large, whose ministry tends mainly to magnify a certain experience—If you have felt thus and thus, and so and so, no words of praise can be too strong for you; but if you have been led in another way, in a different path, then depend on it, according to the judgment of these divines, you never knew vital godliness at all. They are as intimate with the secrets of heaven as the Pope himself, and are quite as infallible as he, in their small dominions. Some of these brethren have no doubt gone through a very deep and awful experience: they have lived so much in sin, and have been so untrue to their Lord, that it is little marvel if they have to walk in darkness and see no light. But these brethren hold up that experience as a model, and tell us that unless we know all they have learned, we are not Christ's. Now, I say not a word against experimental preaching; I believe it to be the most soul-fattening preaching in the world, but it must be experience about Christ, it must be an experience that leads me out of self to Jesus, and if any ministry be experimental, yet if it do not exalt Christ, I have cause to suspect whether the Holy Ghost is with it, for this standeth as an unchanging rule— "He shall glorify *me*."

And, dear brethren, once again, we are cursed with some few men—would God they were fewer—whose teaching constantly is, "morality;" if we will do this, and that, and the other, we shall be saved—the old law of Moses is toned down, and then held up as the road to heaven. Now, at once, ye may forsake the synagogues where such men are in the chief places; for if any man exalt the works of flesh, and not the finished work of Christ; if the doings, the willings, the prayings, the feelings of man, be put in the place of the blood and righteousness of our Lord Jesus Christ, his ministry is not of the Holy Ghost. And what might I say of many who produce on the Sabbath-day their pretty little essays, their elaborate disquisitions, their high-sounding periods?—what shall I say of all these but that they are as "sounding brass, and a tinkling cymbal," inasmuch as they forget Christ, the person of Christ—God and man; the work of Christ—his atonement and righteousness; the resurrection of Christ— the life and joy of the saints; the intercession of Christ—our hope and our strength; and the second advent of Christ, which is as the bright morning-star to every weary watcher in this world's darkness. That ministry, and that ministry only, is of the Holy Ghost which magnifies Christ Jesus.

And here, dear brethren in the ministry—and there are some such present—how bitterly may you and I lament much of our ministry because it hath not glorified Christ! When we shall lie stretched upon our dying beds, we shall look back with satisfaction to that poor stammering sermon in which we magnified the Master; we shall look with intense regret to that well-delivered oration in which we glorified a sect, or lifted up an ordinance at the expense of our Lord. Oh, what joy it shall be to remember that we did lift *him* up, that however feebly, yet we did extol *him*; that though sometimes utterance would not come as our heart would have it, yet we did point to his flowing wounds and say, "Behold the way to God." Oh! the sweet bliss of a Whitfield when he retires to his last couch, to feel that he did preach Jesus, whether it was at the market cross, or on the hill side, or in the Church, or in the barn; what a consolation to feel that he did cry faithfully, "Other foundation can no man lay than that which is laid!" Oh! the curse on the other hand, that shall rest on a man who, in his last moments, shall have to reflect—"I preached other men's sermons, and talked of anything but Christ; I lifted up anything but the Lord!" Oh! how shall the howlings of his eternal doom

commence in his ear, how shall the judgments of God get
hold upon him even before he passes to the dread tribunal of
the Most High. We must, as preachers, come back more and
more to this rule, to feel that if the Holy Ghost be in us he
will make us glorify Christ.

2. Having thus tried ministries, let us now take the same
test with regard to *doctrine;* and very briefly here lay it
down as a self-evident truth that any teaching, whatever
authority it may claim, which does not glorify Christ, is most
assuredly false; and on the other hand, I think we shall
seldom be wrong if we believe that when a teaching lifts
Christ up and puts many crowns upon his head, it must be a
doctrine according to godliness.

Dear friends, Socinianism must be utterly abhorred of us,
for it strikes at once at the Deity of our blessed Lord and
Master. We cannot give to such persons even the name of
Christians. Mahometans they may be—it were well if they
would join with those men—they may be good men, they
may be moral men, they may be excellent citizens, but
Christians they cannot be, if they deny our Lord to be very
God of very God, and worthy to be worshipped even as is the
Father. I marvel much that sundry Dissenters should have
fraternized with Arians and Socinians in attacking the
Church of England, in the present sorrowfully mistaken
onslaught called the Bicentenary, and I can only pray that
the Lord may not visit them for this shameful confederacy
with his enemies. In Arminianism, which is a mixture of
truth and error, there is the doctrine of the saints falling
from grace—a doctrine which is more dishonourable to
Christ than I can tell you—which to my mind, seems to put
its black and sooty finger right adown the escutcheon of my
Lord and Master, setting him as a laughing-stock to the
whole world, as one who begins to build and is not able to
finish, there is a blot upon his power; he loves and yet he
loves not to the end, there is a blot upon his faithfulness; he
says, "I give unto my sheep eternal life and they shall never
perish, neither shall any pluck them out of my hand," and
yet they do perish, according to that doctrine which is a
stain upon his veracity. In fact, the doctrine of final falling
impugns the whole character of Christ so much, that it
would render him unworthy of our faith. When they shall

prove that one who was once in Christ hath fallen away and hath been lost, I know not Christ, for he hath violated his word. He can no more be "the truth," when he hath thus put his own promises into the background, and suffered his darlings to fall into the power of the dog. If there be anything in Scripture as plain as noon-day, it is the doctrine that "He that believeth in him *hath* everlasting life and shall never perish, neither shall he come into condemnation;" and if the child of God can be disinherited, if Christ can divorce his spouse, if the good shepherd shall lose his sheep; if the limbs of Christ's mystical body can be cut off; or can be allowed to rot, then I know not what Scripture teacheth, nor do I understand how Christ can be worthy of the believer's trust. That doctrine, I think, must be reprobated, because it staineth the honour and glory of Christ. Without alluding to others, let that suffice as an instance. Examine well all doctrines; look not at them with complacency because they are put in cunning language, or asserted in vigorous declamation; but if you perceive that any teaching dishonours Christ and maketh much of human ability, if it exalts man and derogates from the grace of God, it is false and dangerous; and if, on the other hand, it layeth man in the dust and lifteth up Christ as a Saviour, the Alpha and Omega, the beginning and the end of salvation, you may safely say that is the Holy Ghost's doctrine, for He shall glorify Christ.

3. Again, we may use our text as a means by which to try much of the *conviction*, through which a sinner passes. In the first dawn of our spiritual life, a mighty tempest of spiritual influence sweeps over the heart. The Holy Ghost is active, and the prince of the power of the air is active too. There is more of God and more of devil in a new convert, than perhaps in any other stage of human existence; for just then Satan rageth with extraordinary fury to drag back the soul to destruction, and the Holy Ghost worketh in him mightily, with a power which only omnipotence can wield. How, in this confusion, can a man know what part of his conviction is of God, and what part of the devil? Young man, hearken to me, you have a thought in your head that you are too great a sinner to be saved. That is not of the Holy Ghost, clearly, because it detracts from the power of Christ as a

Saviour; that cannot be of the Holy Spirit, for the Holy Spirit glorifies Christ. "Yes, sir, but I feel myself to be a great sinner, utterly lost and ruined." That is of the Holy Spirit, because it lays you low in order that the greatness of Christ's salvation may be the mere apparent. "Oh, but," you say, "I am not fit to come to Christ." Surely this feeling is not of the Holy Ghost, but of the devil, for it does not glorify Christ. What, are you to make yourself *fit* to come to Christ? Why, that is making you a Christ; yes, it is making you an Antichrist, which is no work of heaven, but a foul design of hell. "But I heard old Mr. So-and-So say the other day, sir, that when he was converted, he seemed to be dragged by the hair of his head to the very depths of hell, and his soul was full of blasphemy, and his heart was in such an awful state that he cursed the day of his birth, because he thought he was shut out of the covenant, and was utterly lost beyond the reach of mercy." Very well, no doubt what he has told you was his veritable experience; but do you want to experience every piece of devilry that a good man has known? Because a good man trips and falls into the gutter, must you trip and fall there too? Because Jonah descends into the whale's belly, must we all dive into the sea? I tell you, soul, that much of what your friend felt was not of God, but of his own corrupt heart, and of the devil, and he knows it, and he will confess the same to you. Why, therefore, should you pant after that which is sinful and satanic? Why should you desire to drink the poison of asps, and snuff the fumes of Tophet? Nay, but if the Lord brings thee, this morning, to put thy soul just as it is into the hands of the Redeemer, honouring him by a childlike trust, thou hast an experience infinitely more precious than the howling of fiends, and the ravings of thy proud heart could ever yield thee. To be nothing, and to accept Christ as everything, is worked in us of the Holy Ghost; but all the rest, those horrible insinuations, that terrible hell-shaking, may be well dispensed with; good men have felt these, but they are not good things; they come from Satan, and are to be avoided and prayed against, but not to be sought after. I pray you, therefore, let the Holy Spirit lead you in his own way, and ask not to be led in a way of your own choice. Why long for darkness when the Master wills to let thee walk in the light?

Into these balances, then, put all your convictions, and
discover how far they are of God, and how far of Satan. That
which glorifies Christ is of the Holy Ghost; all the rest is of
flesh, or of hell.

4. Thus, also, we may test what is called *experience.* Very
much of the experience of a Christian is not Christian experience. If any person should mount the platform and say,
"I will tell you the experience of a man," and then inform us
that he had been five times tried at the Old Bailey, you
would say, "Well, *you* may have experienced that disgrace,
but it is not fair to call it human experience." So, a Christian
man may fall into great darkness, and into sin too; let us
mournfully confess it. But then, if he shall set up his
darkness and his sin as being Christian experience, we say,
"No; we do not judge *you, you* may be a Christian and know
all this, but we cannot allow *you* to judge *us,* and decide our
spiritual state according to your peculiar method of feeling. I
fear that many biographies have done as much mischief as
service; because while no doubt they comfort many who fall
into the same state, yet a sufficient discrimination is not
made between the man stirred by the powers of evil, and the
same man when filled with the Holy Ghost. Where we get to
that which cometh from beneath we ought to write always in
the spirit of our apostle who cannot describe himself without
an agony. "Oh! wretched man that I am! Who shall deliver
me from the body of this death? I thank God through Jesus
Christ my Lord." That which glorifies Christ is true
Christian experience, and that which does aught but this, a
Christian may experience, but it is not Christian experience.

5. Let us lift the scales of judgment once more. I think our
text gives us an excellent test by which to *try ourselves.* My
hearer, art thou saved or not, this morning? If thou be saved,
the bent, the tenour, the bias of thy life is to glorify Christ.
What sayest thou in looking back? Does the past glorify
Christ? Can you say now with all your heart, "Yes, glory be
to his name; when I think of the love that cleansed me from
such sin; of the grace that broke a heart so hard as mine; of
the faithfulness that has kept me to this day, I can only
glorify Christ." And what about the present? "Oh," can you
say, "when I think of what I now am by the grace of God, and
what I should have been now if the grace had not prevented;

when I look within and see so much blackness, I must
magnify the grace that keeps me; and when I look without
and see so many temptations, I must and will speak well of
his dear name; I must glorify my Lord Jesus." And what dost
thou say about the future? Wilt thou glorify him *then*? I
think I see even the timid ones with their eyes a little
brightening up when they say "Ay! if he will but once bring
me across the river, if I ever get beyond gunshot of the devil,
and behold the face of Christ in glory, I will sing loudest of
all the crowd. I will magnify him with all my powers, for I
shall owe more to him than any one else before the throne; I
will never cease to sing with all the blood-washed throng,

> "Bring forth the royal diadem,
> And crown him Lord of all."

Oh! if your heart is not so that Christ is all to you, and if
your soul is not desiring this morning to honour him, him
only, then indeed I fear me the Holy Ghost has had no
dealing with your spirit, for where he has been at work, he
must, he shall glorify Christ.

II. We are now to use our text as A DIRECTION. How are we
to glorify Christ?

The text tells us that we must have the Holy Spirit. Let
our text, then, be sanctified to our *humiliation*. Here are we
saved, by the rich love of Christ, delivered from our sins, and
made alive unto God, and yet we are such weak things that
we cannot glorify Christ without the indwelling of the Holy
Ghost. We may pant, and long, and pray that we may have
helped to honour our Master, but we shall only dishonour
him and disgrace his cause, unless the Holy Spirit hold us
up and strengthen us. Dost thou hear that, Christian man?
Thou hast ten talents, but those ten talents shall make thee
ten times a worse defaulter to thy Master unless the Holy
Ghost help thee. Thou hast eloquence, thou hast wit, thou
hast wealth; with none of these canst thou glorify Christ,
unless the Holy Ghost be with thee; for "*He* shall glorify me."
Man cannot, except as the Holy Ghost be with him. Bow
your heads, then, O ye saints of God, and ascribe ye glory
unto the Holy Spirit, but unto yourselves be shame and
confusion of face. Let us employ this text as an excitement to
earnest prayer. We as a Church, and I may speak freely for

my own flock, we long to see Christ glorified. It is to this end
we seek to train up our sons, young men in our much-loved
college, that they may go forth as preachers of the Word. We
have agencies by which we hope to do something in our
generation for our Master, but what is everything we can do
without the Holy Ghost? Let us, therefore, pray without
ceasing. Oh, without prayer what are the Church's agencies,
but the stretching out of a dead man's arm, or the lifting up
of the lid of a blind man's eye? Only when the Holy Spirit
comes, is there any life and force and power. Cry then
mightily unto God, O ye who seek to glorify Christ, for
without the Holy Spirit ye utterly fail. And here what a
lesson our text reads us of *entire dependence* upon the Holy
Spirit. Nothing can ye do ye ministers of God, nothing ye
faithful watchmen of Jerusalem, nothing can ye do ye
teachers of youth, nothing ye heralds of the cross in foreign
fields, nothing ye ten thousands who are willing to give all
your substance, your time, and your talents, absolutely
nothing can ye accomplish until God the Holy Spirit comes.
We are by the sea-side; there are a number of ships left high
and dry by the ebb of the tide. A long tract of mud stretches
out before us. What is to be done? Call the king's horses,
bring the king's men, gather together the wise and the
mighty; what can they all do? Nothing; their learning can
only avail to prove most clearly that they can do nothing.
But see the tide rolls in, wave after wave rises from the
deep, and lo every ship floats, and all the mud and sand is
covered with the fulness of the sea. So is it with the
Churches, we all lie high and dry upon the beach, and there
is nothing but the rock and mud of our own inability that is
visible, and we can do nothing, absolutely nothing, till lo! the
holy tide comes; the blessed spirit of revival, the Holy Ghost,
is poured out, and now the heaviest Church is floating out to
sea, and that which was most inactive begins to move! Oh!
what can we not do if we have the Holy Spirit? What can we
do if we have him not? See our utter and entire dependence
upon him. When we, as a Church, first came out into broader
light and more public notice, I bear my witness, we had an
entire dependence upon the Holy Ghost. What prayers have
I heard, what strivings and what groanings. We are reaping
now the ripe fruits of the early sowing. Lo, your minister,

but a stripling from the country all untrained in academic
lore, knowing nothing but just the doctrine of the cross,
came forth before the multitudes to tell out simply the Word.
How he felt his nothingness then, and how often he told you
so! You cried to God, and the child, the lad was helped. What
mighty deeds were done in the conversion of hundreds! And
now we have a name, and there is a great temptation to rest
upon our success, and for men to think there is something in
the preacher, that he can gather the crowd, can preach the
Word, and it is sure to be blessed when he preaches it.
Brethren, again I say we are nothing, we are less than
nothing. Your minister a fool, and nought beyond, except the
Holy Ghost be with him; able to do nothing except mischief;
nothing that shall be profitable to you, or make any heart
glad but the heart of the evil one, unless the Holy Ghost be
with us still. Joyously would I receive again the jeer, the
sneer, the constant slander that was heaped upon my devoted head, if I might have back again your entire
dependence upon the Holy Ghost. Oh, members of this
Church, you who have been quickened under our word, let
not your faith stand in the wisdom of man, but still in the
demonstration of the Spirit; and let us one and all feel that
we are still as weak as water, and as vain as the whistling
wind, unless he that was first with us be with us still. "He
shall glorify me." The Holy Ghost shall do it. None can do it
if he be absent.

I know I am addressing some this morning who have seen
the goings forth of the Holy One of Israel. In fact we as a
Church have had to rejoice these nearly nine years in a
blessed revival, but how diligent should we be while we have
that revival, in order that we may retain it! All the farmers
in England cannot make it leave off raining, but when it
does leave off, and the sun shines, I know what they can
do—get their wheat in as quick as they can. All the sailors
on the ocean cannot make a capful of wind; when the sail
flaps to and fro they cannot make it swell out as in the gale,
but what can they do when the wind does blow? They can
crowd on every yard of canvas. So all the Christians in the
world cannot make the Holy Spirit work. "The wind bloweth
where it listeth, and thou hearest the sound thereof, but
canst not tell whence it cometh nor whither it goeth;" but

what we can do is this, when we have the Holy Spirit, we can use him; when He is with us we can work. We must make hay while the sun shines; we must grind while the wind blows, we must be active and diligent for God when the visitation of the Holy Spirit is with us. The revival has to a great extent ceased in many places. I fear me it is because they did not diligently use its influence. In Ireland how much of revival there was, but the Holy Spirit withdrew necessarily because it was held up as a curiosity. Every newspaper reeked with the news of the revival; people went from England to see it; it could not last then. God never does His great works to be stared at, to be held up as curiosities. The thing was ruined the moment men began curiously to talk of it and spread abroad the news thereof as of a phenomenon worthy of philosophical investigation. These good things should never be made a subject of "Come, see my zeal for the Lord of Hosts;" while the good work goes on we should be so hard at work for the Master, that we have not time to put into every penny newspaper the tale of what God is doing. Let us then be up while the Master is with us and doing His work, doing it in the Spirit's own way, seeking to glorify Jesus, and seeking to retain the Spirit in our midst.

III. And now, lastly, I am to take my text by way of A STIMULUS. Does the Holy Ghost glorify Christ? Ah, then, how should we aim to do it! Let us make, then, beloved brothers and sisters in Christ, let us make this the one object of our life, to glorify Christ. You have been a man in a large way of business. Could you say while you were doing business so largely that your object was to honour Christ in it? Well you have come down in the world; you have a smaller shop now. Yes, but suppose you can glorify God more. Then you are in a better position than you used to be. I have seen many a man who prospered in his soul and honoured his Master much, who has made a wrong step, and has injured his usefulness and happiness; wanting to get more business, he has launched into wide speculations, and has had less time for serving his Lord, and has thus really been in a worse position, for spirituals were under a decay. You may have seen in the newspapers an instance of what sometimes comes through getting wealthy. A man and his wife were prospering in a little way of business, as hard-

working people, near Birmingham. A friend died and left the
wife some £1,300, no great sum, but quite enough to ruin a
man. They at once took a public-house, and you will
remember that he now lies in prison on a charge of murder-
ing his wife. Little marvel that when, tempted by what little
they had to seek after more, they entered upon an ill
occupation in order to increase their wealth; that evil trade
soon led to vicious habits and to death. Now I have seen
believers mournfully impoverish their souls by seeking after
carnal wealth instead of seeking Christ; but let a man's only
object be to glorify Christ, and he will feel very little concern
where providence places him, so long as he may still
promote his one object, and put crowns on the Redeemer's
head.

This brings me to say, brethren, while we make this our
aim, let us take every opportunity of glorifying Christ. We
throw thousands of opportunities away. Where we might do
good we neglect it. I chide my own self here very bitterly and
very often, but I fear me I might chide many of you too. You
had an opportunity yesterday, but you lost it; you might
have spoken for Christ but you did not. No one can tell the
good you might have done, but you did not do it. You were
backward. Oh! as the Holy Ghost glorifies Christ everywhere, so do you! I pray you do this always, not merely at
particular times, but make your whole life a glorifying of
Christ. As I sat on an omnibus yesterday, I heard a man
saying behind me, how greatly he admired the continental
way of keeping Sundays—going to the church in the
morning, and going to the theatre at night. "Don't you see,"
he said, "it is irrational to think that the Almighty expects
us to spend the whole day in praying. There is no man living
who can pray for six hours together, let alone twelve." That
was just putting in broad language what most ungodly
people feel, but then I wonder what they would make of the
Apostle Paul's admonition, "Pray without ceasing." Here was
a man who thought that nobody could pray for six hours
together, while the saints of God are to continue always in
prayer. No man comes up to the stature of the Christian, or
such a man as he should be, unless he cannot only pray for
six hours together, but his whole life long. It was said of
good old Rowland Hill, that people did not so much notice

his particular times of retirement, for he was a man who was always praying, wherever he might be. You would often find him alone talking to himself, and ever in company his heart would be going away to the object of his best love, he would still be in communion with Christ. Be ye always glorifying Christ, Christians, from the rising of the sun unto the going down thereof. Whether ye work at a lapstone, or drive a plough, or lay the stones in a building; serve the Master in all these things; whether ye are diligent with the pen, or whether ye buy and sell, or plough the sea, do all even to your eating or your drinking in the name of the Lord Jesus, and so like the Holy Spirit let it be said of you, "He shall glorify me."

We conclude by endeavouring to magnify our Master ourselves. I want to say just two or three things to glorify him, and they shall be just these. I shall say this to the poor troubled doubting sinner, "Sinner, my Master is able to save you." "Oh, but I am the biggest sinner out of hell." Yes, but he is the greatest of all Saviours. "Yes, but I have gone over head and ears in iniquity." Yes, but he was baptised also in his agonies that he might save you. "Oh, but he *cannot* save me!" Ay! but he can; and if I am now addressing the scum of the earth, one of the devil's sweepings, one who is hardly fit for decent company, my Master is able to save you. Unto the uttermost he saveth, and your sin, though black, he can cleanse, and make you whiter than snow.

I would say something else to glorify *him*. He is willing to save you; his generous heart desireth you. Your perishing will not make him glad, but he will weep over you as he did over Jerusalem; but your being saved will give him to see of the travail of his soul. "Do you know who you are speaking to, sir?" No I don't, but my Master does; for now he fixes his poor tearful eyes on thee. Where is the sinner? Behind that pillar is he, or in yonder corner? The Master looketh at him, and he saith, "Come unto me all ye that labour and are heavy laden, and I will give you rest. Take my yoke upon you, and learn of me, for I am meek and lowly of heart, and ye shall find rest unto your souls." What, are ye so far away? How loudly doth he call you, "Come, sinner, repent and come." Art thou willing to come? Lo! he meets thee, in the road he meets thee; embracing thee, he falls upon thy neck to kiss thee. He saith, even this morning he saith it, "Take off his rags and clothe him in fine apparel; wash him and make him clean, for I have put away his sins like a cloud, and like a thick cloud his iniquities." That which glorifies Christ the most of all is the preaching of the Gospel to sinners, and therefore have I glorified him now, and would do so as long as I live. Believe in the Lord Jesus Christ and thou shalt be saved, for he that believeth and is baptized shall be saved; he that believeth not shall be damned. God give us to glorify Christ by trusting in Him! Amen.

16

The Personality Of The Holy Ghost

"And I will pray the Father, and he shall give you another Comforter, that he may abide with you for ever; even the Spirit of truth; whom the world cannot receive, because it seeth him not, neither knoweth him: but ye know him; for he dwelleth with you, and shall be in you."   John 14:16-17

You will be surprised to hear me announce that I do not intend this morning to say anything about the Holy Spirit as the Comforter. I propose to reserve that for a special sermon this evening. In this discourse I shall endeavour to explain and enforce certain other doctrines which I believe are plainly taught in this text and which I hope God the Holy Ghost may make profitable to our souls. Old John Newton once said that there were some books which he could not read; they were good and sound enough; but, said he, "they are books of halfpence;—you have to take so much in quantity before you have any value; there are other books of silver, and others of gold, but I have one book that is a book of bank notes; and every leaf is a bank note of immense value." So I found with this text: that I had a bank note of so large a sum, that I could not tell it out all this morning. I should have to keep you several hours, before I could unfold to you the whole value of this precious promise—one of the last which Christ gave to his people.

I invite your attention to this passage, because we shall find in it some instruction on four points; first, concerning *the true and proper personality of the Holy Ghost;* secondly, concerning *the united agency of the glorious Three Persons in the work of our salvation;* thirdly, we shall find *something to establish the doctrine of the indwelling of the Holy Ghost in the souls of all believers;* and fourthly, we shall find out *the reason why the carnal mind rejects the Holy Ghost.*

I. First of all, we shall have some little instruction concerning the proper PERSONALITY OF THE HOLY SPIRIT. We are so much accustomed to talk about the influence of the Holy Ghost, and his sacred operations and graces, that we are apt to forget that the Holy Spirit is truly and actually a person—that he is a subsistence—an existence; or as we Trinitarians usually say, one person in the essence of the Godhead. I am afraid that, though we do not know it, we have acquired the habit of regarding the Holy Ghost as an emanation flowing from the Father and the Son, but not as being actually a person himself. I know it is not easy to carry about in our mind the idea of the Holy Spirit as a person. I can think of the Father as a person, because his acts are such as I can understand. I see him hang the world in ether; I behold him swaddling a new-born sea in bands of darkness; I know it is he who formed the drops of hail, who leadeth forth the stars by their hosts, and calleth them by their name; I can conceive of Him as a person, because I behold his operations. I can realize Jesus, the Son of Man, as a real person, because he is bone of my bone and flesh of my flesh. It takes no great stretch of my imagination to picture the babe in Bethlehem, or to behold the "Man of sorrows and acquainted with grief;" or the King of martyrs, as he was persecuted in Pilate's hall, or nailed to the accursed tree for our sins. Nor do I find it difficult at times to realize the person of my Jesus sitting on his throne in heaven; or girt with clouds and wearing the diadem of all creation, calling the earth to judgment, and summoning us to hear our final sentence. But when I come to deal with the Holy Ghost, his operations are so mysterious, his doings are so secret, his acts are so removed from everything that is of sense, and of the body, that I cannot so easily get the idea of his being a person; but a person he is. God the Holy Ghost is not an influence, an emanation, a stream of something flowing from the Father; but he is as much an actual person as either God the Son, or God the Father. I shall attempt this morning a little to establish the doctrine, and to show you the truth of it—that God the Holy Spirit is actually a person.

The first proof we shall gather from the pool of holy baptism. Let me take you down, as I have taken others, into the pool, now concealed, but which I wish were always open to your view. Let me take you to the baptismal font, where believers put on the name of the Lord Jesus; and you shall hear me pronounce the solemn words, "I baptize thee in the name,"—mark, "in the name," not names,—"of the Father, and of the Son, and of the Holy Ghost." Every one who is baptized according to the true form laid down in Scripture must be a Trinitarian: otherwise his baptism is a farce and a lie, and he himself is found a deceiver and a hypocrite before God. As the Father is mentioned, and as the Son is mentioned, so is the Holy Ghost; and the whole is summed up as being a Trinity in unity, by its being said, not the names, but the "name" the glorious name, the Jehovah name, "of the Father and of the Son and of the Holy Ghost." Let me remind you that the same thing occurs each time you are dismissed from this house of prayer. In pronouncing the solemn closing benediction, we invoke on your behalf the love of Jesus Christ, the grace of the Father, and the fellowship of the Holy Spirit, and thus, according to the apostolick manner, we make a manifest distinction between the persons, showing that we believe the Father to be a person, the Son to be a person, and the Holy Ghost to be a person. Were there no other proofs in Scripture, I think these would be sufficient for every sensible man. He would see that if the Holy Spirit were a mere influence, he would not be mentioned in conjunction with two whom we all confess to be actual and proper persons.

A second argument arises from the fact that the Holy Ghost has actually made different appearances on earth. The Great Spirit has manifested himself to man; he has put on a form, so that whilst he has not been beheld by mortal men, he has been so veiled in appearance that he was seen, so far as that appearance was concerned, by the eyes of all beholders. See you Jesus Christ our Saviour? There is the river Jordan, with its shelving banks, and its willows weeping at its side. Jesus Christ, the Son of God, descends into the stream, and the holy Baptist, John, plunges him into the waves. The doors of heaven are opened; a miraculous appearance presents itself; a bright light shineth from

the sky, brighter than the sun in all its grandeur, and down
in a flood of glory descends something which you recognize
to be a dove. It rests on Jesus—it sits upon his sacred head,
and as the old painters put a halo round the brow of Jesus,
so did the Holy Ghost shed a resplendence around the face of
him who came to fulfill all righteousness, and therefore
commenced with the ordinances of baptism. The Holy Ghost
was seen as a dove, to mark his purity and his gentleness,
and he came down like a dove *from heaven* to show that it is
from heaven alone that he descendeth. Nor is this the only
time when the Holy Ghost has been manifest in a visible
shape. You notice that company of disciples gath-ered
together in an upper room; they are waiting for some
promised blessing, by-and-by it shall come. Hark! there is a
sound as of a rushing mighty wind, it fills all the house
where they are sitting; and astonished, they look around
them, wondering what will come next. Soon a bright light
appears, shining upon the heads of each: cloven tongues of
fire sat upon them. What were these marvellous appearances of wind and flame but a display of the Holy Ghost in
his proper person? I say the fact of an appearance manifests
that he must be a person. An influence could not appear—an
attribute could not appear: we cannot see attributes—we
cannot behold influences. The Holy Ghost must then have
been a person; since he was beheld by mortal eyes, and came
under the cognizance of mortal sense.

Another proof is from the fact, that personal qualities are,
in Scripture, ascribed to the Holy Ghost. First, let me read to
you a text in which the Holy Ghost is spoken of as having
understanding. In the First Epistle to the Corinthians,
chapter ii., you will read, "But as it is written, eye hath not
seen, nor ear heard, neither hath it entered into the heart of
man, the things which God hath prepared for them that love
him. But God hath revealed them unto us by his Spirit: for
the Spirit searcheth all things, yea, the deep things of God.
For what man knoweth the things of a man, save the spirit
of man which is in him? Even so the things of God knoweth
no man, but the Spirit of God." Here you see an understanding—a power of knowledge is ascribed to the Holy
Ghost. Now, if there be any persons here whose minds are of
so preposterous a complexion that they would ascribe one

attribute to another, and would speak of a mere influence having understanding, then I give up all the argument. But I believe every rational man will admit, that when anything is spoken of as having an understanding it must be an existence—it must, in fact, be a person. In the 12th chapter, 11th verse of the same Epistle, you will find a *will* ascribed to the Holy Spirit. "But all these worketh that one and the self-same Spirit, dividing to every man severally as he will." So it is plain the Spirit has a will. He does not come from God simply at God's will, but he has a will of his own, which is always in keeping with the will of the infinite Jehovah, but is, nevertheless, distinct and separate; therefore, I say he is a person. In another text *power* is ascribed to the Holy Ghost, and power is a thing which can only be ascribed to an existence. In Romans xv. 13, it is written, "Now the God of hope fill you with all joy and peace in believing, that ye may abound in hope through the power of the Holy Ghost." I need not insist upon it, because it is self-evident, that wherever you find understanding, will, and power, you must also find an existence; it cannot be a mere attribute, it cannot be a metaphor, it cannot be a personified influence; but it must be a person.

But I have a proof which, perhaps, will be more telling upon you than any other. Acts and deeds are ascribed to the Holy Ghost; therefore he must be a person. You read in the first chapter of the Book of Genesis, that the Spirit brooded over the surface of the earth, when it was as yet all disorder and confusion. This world was once a mass of chaotic matter; there was no order; it was like the valley of darkness and of the shadow of death. God the Holy Ghost spread his wings over it; he sowed the seeds of life in it; the germs from which all beings sprang were implanted by him; he impregnated the earth so that it became capable of life. Now it must have been a person who brought order out of confusion: it must have been an existence who hovered over this world and made it what it now is. But do we not read in Scripture something more of the Holy Ghost? Yes, we are told that "holy men of old spake as they were moved by the Holy Ghost." When Moses penned the Pentateuch, the Holy Ghost moved his hand; when David wrote the Psalms, and discoursed sweet music on his harp, it was the Holy Spirit that

gave his fingers their Seraphic motion; when Solomon
dropped from his lips the words of the Proverbs of wisdom,
or when he hymned the Canticles of love, it was the Holy
Ghost who gave him words of knowledge and hymns of rapture. Ah! and what fire was that which touched the lips of
the eloquent Isaiah? What hand was that which came upon
Daniel? What might was that which made Jeremiah so
plaintive in his grief? or what was that which winged
Ezekiel, and made him like an eagle, soar into mysteries
aloft, and see the mighty unknown beyond our reach? Who
was it that made Amos, the herdsman, a prophet? Who
taught the rough Haggai to pronounce his thundering
sentences? Who showed Habbakuk the horses of Jehovah
marching through the waters? or who kindled the burning
eloquence of Nahum? Who caused Malachi to close up the
book with the muttering of the word curse? Who was in each
of these, save the Holy Ghost? And must it not have been a
person who spake in and through these ancient witnesses?
We must believe it. We cannot avoid believing it, when we
recall that "holy men of old spake as they were moved by the
Holy Ghost."

And when has the Holy Ghost ceased to have an influence
upon men? We find that still he deals with his ministers and
with all his saints. Turn to the Acts, and you will find that
the Holy Ghost said, "Separate me Paul and Barnabas for
the work." I never heard of an attribute saying such a thing.
The Holy Spirit said to Peter, "Go to the centurion, and what
I have cleansed, that call not thou common." The Holy Ghost
caught away Philip after he had baptised the eunuch, and
carried him to another place; and the Holy Ghost said to
Paul, "Thou shalt not go into that city, but shalt turn into
another." And we know that the Holy Ghost was lied unto by
Ananias and Sapphira, when it was said, "Thou hast not lied
unto man, but unto God." Again, that power which we feel
every day who are called to preach—that wondrous spell
which makes our lips so potent—that power which gives us
thoughts which are like birds from a far-off region, not the
natives of our soul—that influence which I sometimes
strangely feel, which, if it does not give me poetry and
eloquence, gives me a might I never felt before, and lifts me
above my fellow-man—that majesty with which he clothes

his ministers, till in the midst of the battle they cry, aha! like
the war-horse of Job, and move themselves like leviathans in
the water—that power which gives us might over men, and
causes them to sit and listen as if their ears were chained, as
if they were entranced by the power of some magician's
wand—that power must come from a person, it must come
from the Holy Ghost.

But is it not said in Scripture, and do we not feel it, dear
brethren, that it is the Holy Ghost who regenerates the soul?
It is the Holy Ghost who quickens us. "You hath he quickened who were dead in trespasses and sins." It is the Holy
Spirit who imparts the first germ of life, convincing us of sin,
of righteousness, and of judgment to come. And is it not the
Holy Spirit who after that flame is kindled, still fans it with
the breath of his mouth and keeps it alive? Its author is its
preserver. Oh! can it be said that it is the Holy Ghost who
strives in men's souls, that it is the Holy Ghost who brings
them to the foot of Sinai, and then guides them into the
sweet place that is called Calvary—can it be said that he
does all these things, and yet is not a person? It may be said,
but it must be said by fools; for he never can be a wise man
who can consider that these things can be done by any other
than a glorious person—a divine existence.

Allow me to give you one more proof, and I shall have
done. Certain feelings are ascribed to the Holy Ghost, which
can only be understood upon the supposition that he is
actually a person. In the 4th chapter of Ephesians, verse 30,
it is said that the Holy Ghost can be grieved: "Grieve not the
Holy Spirit of God, whereby ye are sealed unto the day of
redemption." In Isaiah, chapter lxiii. v. 10 it is said that the
Holy Ghost can be vexed: "But they rebelled, and vexed his
Holy Spirit, therefore he was turned to be their enemy, and
he fought against them." In Acts, chapter vii. v. 51, you read
that the Holy Ghost can be resisted: "Ye stiff-necked and
uncircumcised in heart and ears, ye do always resist the
Holy Ghost; as your fathers did, so do ye." And in the 5th
chapter, 9th verse, of the same book, you will find that the
Holy Ghost may be tempted. We are there informed that
Peter said to Ananias and Sapphira, "How is it that ye have
agreed together to tempt the Spirit of the Lord?" Now, these
things could not be emotions which might be ascribed to a

quality or an emanation; they must be understood to relate to a person; an influence could not be grieved; it must be a person who can be grieved, vexed, or resisted.

And now, dear brethren, I think I have fully established the point of the personality of the Holy Ghost; allow me now, most earnestly, to impress upon you the absolute necessity of being sound upon the doctrine of the Trinity. I knew a man, a good minister of Jesus Christ he is now, and I believe he was before he turned aside unto heresy—he began to doubt the glorious divinity of our blessed Lord, and for years did he preach the heterodox doctrine, until one day he happened to hear a very eccentric old minister preaching from the text, "But there the *glorious Lord* shall be unto us a place of broad rivers and streams, wherein shall go no galley with oars, neither shall gallant ship pass thereby. Thy tacklings are loosed: they could not well strengthen their mast, they could not spread the sail." "Now," said the old minister, "you give up the Trinity, and your tacklings are loosed, you cannot strengthen your masts. Once give up the doctrine of three persons, and your tacklings are all gone; your mast, which ought to be a support to your vessel, is a rickety one, and shakes." A gospel without a Trinity!—it is a pyramid built upon its apex. A gospel without the Trinity!— it is a rope of sand that cannot hold together. A gospel without the Trinity!—then, indeed, Satan can overturn it. But, give me a gospel with the Trinity, and the might of hell cannot prevail against it; no man can any more overthrow it, than a bubble could split a rock, or a feather break in halves a mountain. Get the thought of the three persons, and you have the marrow of all divinity. Only know the Father, and know the Son, and know the Holy Ghost to be One, and all things will appear clear. This is the golden key to the secrets of nature; this is the silken clue of the labyrinths of mystery, and he who understands this, will soon understand as much as mortals e'er can know.

II. Now for the second point—the UNITED AGENCY of the three persons in the work of our salvation. Look at the text, and you will find all the three persons mentioned. "I,"—that is the Son—"will pray the Father, and he shall give you another Comforter." There are the three persons mentioned, all of them doing something for our salvation. "I will pray," says the Son. "I will send," says the Father. "I will comfort," says the Holy Ghost. Now, let us for a few moments discourse upon this wonderous theme—the unity of the Three Persons with regard to the great purpose of the salvation of the elect. When God first made man, he said, "Let *us* make man," not let *me*, but "Let us make man in our own image." The covenant Elohim said to each other, "Let us unitedly become the Creator of man." So, when in ages far gone by, in eternity, they said, "Let us save man." It was not the Father who said, "Let *me* save man," but the three persons conjointly said with one consent, "Let *us* save man." It is to me a source of sweet comfort, to think that it is not one person of the Trinity that is engaged for my salvation; it is not simply one person of the Godhead who vows that he will redeem me; but it is a glorious trio of Godlike ones, and the three declare, unitedly, "*We* will save man."

Now, observe here, that each person is spoken of as performing a separate office. "I will pray," says the Son—that is intercession. "I will send," says the Father—that is donation. "I will comfort," says the Holy Spirit—that is supernatural influence. Oh! if it were possible for us to see the three persons of the Godhead, we should behold one of them standing before the throne with outstretched hands crying day and night, "O Lord, how long?" We should see one girt with Urim and Thummim, precious stones, on which are written the twelve names of the tribes of Israel; we should behold him crying unto his Father, "Forget not thy promises, forget not thy covenant," we should hear him make mention of our sorrows, and tell forth our griefs on our behalf, for he is our intercessor. And could we behold the Father, we should not see him a listless and idle spectator of the intercession of the Son, but we should see him with attentive ear listening to every word of Jesus, and granting every petition. Where is the Holy Spirit all the while? Is he lying idle? Oh, no; he is floating over the earth, and when he sees a weary soul, he says, "Come to Jesus, he will give you rest." When he beholds an eye filled with tears, he wipes away the tears, and bids the mourner look for comfort on the cross. When he sees the tempest-tossed believer, he takes the helm of his soul and speaks the word of consolation; he helpeth the broken in heart, and bindeth up their wounds; and ever

on his mission of mercy, he flies around the world, being
everywhere present. Behold how the three persons work
together. Do not then say, "I am grateful to the Son,"—so
you ought to be, but God the Son no more saves you than
God the Father. Do not imagine that God the Father is a
great tyrant, and that God the Son had to die to make him
merciful. It was not to make the Father's love flow towards
his people. Oh, no. One loves as much as the other; the three
are conjoined in the great purpose of rescuing the elect from
damnation.

But you must notice another thing in my text, which will
show the blessed unity of the three—the one person promises to the other. The Son says, "I will pray the Father."
"Very well," the disciples may have said, "We can trust you
for that." "And he will send you." You see here is the Son
signing a bond on behalf of the Father. "He will send you
another Comforter." There is a bond on behalf of the Holy
Spirit, too. "And he will abide with you forever." One person
speaks for the other, and how could they if there were any
disagreement between them? If one wished to save, and the
other did not, they could not promise on one another's
behalf. But whatever the Son says, the Father listens to;
whatever the Father promises, the Holy Ghost works; and
whatever the Holy Ghost injects into the soul, that God the
Father fulfils. So the three together mutually promise on
one another's behalf. There is a bond with three names
appended,—Father, Son, and Holy Ghost. By three immu-
table things, as well as by two, the Christian is secured
beyond the reach of death and hell. A Trinity of Securities,
because there is a trinity of God.

III. Our third point is the INDWELLING of the Holy Ghost
in believers. Now beloved, these first two things have been
matters of pure doctrine; this is the subject of experience.
The indwelling of the Holy Ghost is a subject so profound,
and so having to do with the inner man, that no soul will be
able truly and really to comprehend what I say, unless it has
been taught of God. I have heard of an old minister, who told
a Fellow of one of the Cambridge Colleges, that he understood a language that he never learnt in all his life. "I have
not," he said, "even a smattering of Greek, and I know no
Latin, but thank God I can talk the language of Canaan, and

that is more than you can." So, beloved, I shall now have to talk a little of the language of Canaan. If you cannot comprehend me, I am much afraid it is because you are not of Israelitish extraction; you are not a child of God nor an inheritor of the kingdom of heaven.

We are told in the text, that Jesus would send the Comforter, who would abide in the saints for ever; who would dwell with them and be in them. Old Ignatius, the martyr, used to call himself Theophorus, or the God-bearer, "because," said he, "I bear about with me the Holy Ghost." And truly every Christian is a God-bearer. Know ye not that ye are temples of the Holy Ghost? for he dwelleth in you. That man is no Christian who is not the subject of the indwelling of the Holy Spirit; he may talk well, he may understand theology and be a sound Calvinist; he will be the child of nature finely dressed, but not the living child. He may be a man of so profound an intellect, so gigantic a soul, so comprehensive a mind, and so lofty an imagination, that he may dive into all the secrets of nature; may know the path which the eagle's eye hath not seen, and go into depths where the ken of mortals reacheth not; but he shall not be a Christian with all his knowledge; he shall not be a son of God with all his researches; unless he understands what it is to have the Holy Ghost dwelling in him, and abiding in him, yea, and that for ever.

Some people call this fanaticism, and they say, "You are a Quaker; why not follow George Fox?" Well, we would not mind that much; we would follow any one who followed the Holy Ghost. Even he, with all his eccentricities, I doubt not, was, in many cases, actually inspired by the Holy Spirit; and whenever I find a man in whom there rests the Spirit of God, the Spirit within me leaps to hear the Spirit within him, and he feels that we are one. The Spirit of God in one Christian soul recognizes the Spirit in another. I recollect talking with a good man, as I believe he was, who was insisting that it was impossible for us to know whether we had the Holy Spirit within us or not. I should like him to be here this morning, because I would read this verse to him: "But ye know him, for he dwelleth with you, and shall be in you." Ah! you think you cannot tell whether you have the Holy Spirit or not. Can I tell whether I am alive or not? If I were touched

by electricity, could I tell whether I was or not? I suppose I
should; the shock would be strong enough to make me know
where I stood. So, if I have God within me—if I have Deity
tabernacling in my breast—if I have God the Holy Ghost
resting in my heart, and making a temple of my body, do you
think I shall know it? Call ye it fanaticism if ye will; but I
trust that there are some of us who know what it is to be
always, or generally, under the influence of the Holy Spirit
—always in one sense, generally in another. When we have
difficulties we ask the direction of the Holy Ghost. When we
do not understand a portion of Holy Scripture, we ask God
the Holy Ghost to shine upon us. When we are depressed,
the Holy Ghost comforts us. You cannot tell what the
wondrous power of the indwelling of the Holy Ghost is: how
it pulls back the hand of the saint when he would touch the
forbidden thing; how it prompts him to make a covenant
with his eyes; how it binds his feet, lest they should fall in a
slippery way; how it restrains his heart, and keeps him from
temptation. O ye who know nothing of the indwelling of the
Holy Ghost, despise it not. O despise not the Holy Ghost, for
it is the unpardonable sin. "He that speaketh a word against
the Son of Man, it shall be forgiven him, but he that
speaketh against the Holy Ghost, it shall never be forgiven
him, either in this life, or that which is to come." So saith the
Word of God. Therefore, tremble, lest in anything ye despise
the influences of the Holy Spirit.

But before closing this point, there is one little word which
pleases me very much, that is, "for ever." You knew I should
not miss that; you were certain I could not let it go without
observation. "Abide with you for ever." I wish I could get an
Arminian here to finish my sermon. I fancy I see him taking
that word, "for ever." He would say, "for—for ever;" he would
have to stammer and stutter; for he never could get it out all
at once. He might stand and pull it about, and at last he
would have to say, "the translation is wrong." And then I
suppose the poor man would have to prove that the original
was wrong too. Ah! but blessed be God, we can read it—"He
shall abide with you for ever." Once give me the Holy Ghost,
and I shall never lose him till "for ever" has run out; till
eternity has spun its everlasting rounds.

   IV. Now we have to close up with a brief remark on the

reason why the world rejects the Holy Ghost. It is said, "Whom the world cannot receive, because it seeth him not, neither knoweth him." You know what is sometimes meant by "the world,"—those whom God, in his wondrous sovereignty, passed over when he chose his people: the preterite ones; those passed over in God's wondrous preterition—not the reprobates who were condemned to damnation by some awful decree; but those passed over by God, when he chose out his elect. These cannot receive the Spirit. Again, it means all in a carnal state are not able to procure themselves this divine influence; and thus it is true, "Whom the world cannot receive."

The unregenerate world of sinners despises the Holy Ghost, "because it seeth him not." Yes, I believe this is the great secret why many laugh at the idea of the existence of the Holy Ghost—because they see him not. You tell the worldling, "I have the Holy Ghost within me." He says, "I cannot see it." He wants it to be something tangible: a thing he can recognize with his senses. Have you ever heard the argument used by a good old Christian against an infidel doctor? The doctor said there was no soul, and he asked, "Did you ever see a soul?" "No," said the Christian. "Did you ever hear a soul?" "No." "Did you ever smell a soul?" "No." "Did you ever taste a soul?" "No." "Did you ever feel a soul?" "Yes," said the man—"I feel I have one within me." "Well," said the doctor, "there are four senses against one: you have only one on your side." "Very well," said the Christian, "Did you ever see a pain?" "No." "Did you ever hear a pain?" "No." "Did you ever smell a pain?" "No." "Did you ever taste a pain?" "No." "Did you ever feel a pain?" "Yes." "And that is quite enough, I suppose, to prove there is a pain?" "Yes." So the worldling says there is no Holy Ghost, because he cannot see it. Well, but we feel it. You say that is fanaticism, and that we never felt it. Suppose you tell me that honey is bitter, I reply, "No, I am sure you cannot have tasted it; taste it, and try." So with the Holy Ghost; if you did but feel his influence, you would no longer say there is no Holy Spirit, because you cannot see it. Are there not many things, even in nature, which we cannot see? Did you ever see the wind? No; but ye know there is wind, when ye behold the hurricane tossing the waves about and rending down the habitations of men; or when in the soft evening zephyr it kisses the flowers, and maketh dewdrops hang in pearly coronets around the rose. Did ye ever see electricity? No, but ye know there is such a thing, for it travels along the wires for thousands of miles, and carries our messages, though you cannot see the thing itself, you know there is such a thing. So you must believe there is a Holy Ghost working in us, both to will and to do, even though it is beyond our senses.

But the last reason why worldly men laugh at the doctrine of the Holy Spirit is because they do not know it. If they knew it by heart-felt experience, and if they recognised its agency in the soul; if they had ever been touched by it; if they had been made to tremble under a sense of sin; if they had had their hearts melted; they would never have doubted the existence of the Holy Ghost.

And now, beloved, it says, "He dwelleth with you, and shall be in you." We will close up with that sweet recollection—the Holy Ghost dwells in all believers, and shall be with them.

One word of comment and advice to the saints of God, and to sinners, and I have done. Saints of the Lord! ye have this morning heard that God the Holy Ghost is a person; ye have had it proved to your souls. What follows from this? Why, it followeth how earnest ye should be in prayer to the Holy Spirit, as well as *for* the Holy Spirit. Let me say that this is an inference that you should lift up your prayers to the Holy Ghost; that you should cry earnestly unto him; for he is able to do exceeding abundantly above all you can ask or think. See this mass of people; what is to convert it? See this crowd; who is to make my influence permeate through the mass? You know this place has now a mighty influence, and God blessing us, it will have an influence, not only upon this city but upon England at large; for we now enjoy the press as well as the pulpit; and certainly, I should say before the close of the year, more than two hundred thousand of my productions will be scattered through the land—words uttered by my lips, or written by my pen. But how can this influence be rendered for good? How shall God's glory be promoted by it? Only by incessant prayer for the Holy Spirit; by constantly calling down the influence of the Holy Ghost upon us; we want him to rest upon every page that is printed, and upon every word that is uttered. Let us then be doubly earnest in pleading with the Holy Ghost, that he would come and own our labours, that the whole church at large may be revived thereby, and not ourselves only, but the whole world share in the benefit.

Then to the ungodly, I have this one closing word to say. Ever be careful how you speak of the Holy Ghost. I do not know what the unpardonable sin is, and I do not think any man understands it; but it is something like this: "He that speaketh a word against the Holy Ghost, it shall never be forgiven him." I do not know what that means: but tread carefully! There is danger; there is a pit which our ignorance has covered by sand; tread carefully! you may be in it before the next hour. If there is any strife in your heart to-day, perhaps you will go to the ale-house and forget it. Perhaps there is some voice speaking in your soul, and you will put it away. I do not tell you you will be resisting the Holy Ghost and committing the unpardonable sin; but it is somewhere there. Be very careful. Oh! there is no crime on earth so black as the crime against the Holy Spirit. Ye may blaspheme the Father, and ye shall be damned for it, unless ye repent, ye may blaspheme the Son, and hell shall be your portion, unless ye are forgiven; but blaspheme the Holy Ghost, and thus saith the Lord, "There is no forgiveness, neither in this world, nor in the world which is to come." I cannot tell you what it is, I do not profess to understand it; but there it is. It is the danger signal; stop! man, stop! If thou hast despised the Holy Spirit; if thou hast laughed at his revelations, and scorned what Christians call his influence, I beseech thee, stop! This morning seriously deliberate. Perhaps some of you have actually committed the unpardonable sin; stop! Let fear stop you; sit down. Do not drive on so rashly as you have done, Jehu! Oh! slacken your reins! Thou who art such a profligate in sin; thou who hast uttered such hard words against the Trinity; stop! Ah, it makes us all stop. It makes us all draw up and say, "Have I not perhaps so done?" Let us think of this; and let us not at any time trifle either with the words, or the acts, of God the Holy Ghost.

17

The Fruit Of The Spirit: Joy

"But the fruit of the Spirit is love, joy..."   Galatians 5:22

Observe, "the *fruit* of the Spirit," for the product of the Spirit of God is one. As some fruits are easily divisible into several parts, so you perceive that the fruit of the Spirit, though it be but one, is threefold, nay, it makes three times three,—"love, joy, peace; longsuffering, gentleness, goodness; faith, meekness, temperance,"—all one. Perhaps "love" is put first not only because it is a right royal virtue, nearest akin to the divine perfection, but because it is a comprehensive grace, and contains all the rest. All the commandments are fulfilled in one word, and that word is "love"; and all the fruits of the Spirit are contained in that one most sweet, most blessed, most heavenly, most God-like grace of love. See that ye abound in love to the great Father and all his family, for if you fail in the first point how can you succeed in the second? Above all things, put on love, which is the bond of perfectness. As for joy, if it be not the first product of the Spirit of God, it is next to the first, and we may be sure that the order in which it is placed by the inspired apostle is meant to be instructive. The fruit of the Spirit is love first, as comprehensive of the rest; then joy arising out of it. It is remarkable that joy should take so eminent a place; it attaineth unto the first three, and is but one place lower than the first. Look at it in its high position, and if you have missed it, or if you have depreciated it, revise your judgment, and endeavour with all your heart to attain to it, for depend upon it, this fruit of the Spirit is of the utmost value. This morning, as I can only speak upon one theme, I leave *love* for another occasion, and treat only of joy. May its divine author, the Holy Ghost, teach us how to speak of it to our profit and his own glory.

It is quite true that the Spirit of God produces sorrow, for one of his first effects upon the soul is holy grief. He enlightens us as to our lost condition, convincing us of sin, of righteousness, and of judgment, and the first result upon our hearts is astonishment and lamentation. Even when we look to Christ by the work of the Spirit one of the first fruits is sorrow: "They shall look on him whom they have pierced, and they shall mourn for him, and be in bitterness for him as one that is in bitterness for his first-born." But this sorrow is not the ultimate object of the Spirit's work, it is a means to an end. Even as the travail of the mother leadeth up to the joy of birth, so do the pangs of repentance lead up to the joy of pardon and acceptance. The sorrow is, to use a scriptural figure, the blade, but the full corn in the ear is joy; sorrow helps on the fruit, but the fruit itself is joy. The tears of godly grief for sin are all meant to sparkle into the diamonds of joy in pardoning love.

This teaches us, then, that we are not to look upon bondage as being the object of the work of the Spirit of God, or the design of the Lord in a work of grace. Many are under bondage to the law: they attempt to keep the commands of God, not out of love, but from slavish fear. They dread the lash of punishment, and tremble like slaves; but to believers it is said, "Ye are not under the law, but under grace," and "Ye have not received the spirit of bondage again to fear; but ye have received the Spirit of adoption, whereby we cry, Abba, Father." To be in bondage under the law, to be afraid of being cast away by God, and visited with destruction on account of sin after we have trusted in Jesus,—this is not the work of the Spirit of God in believers, but the black offspring of unbelief or ignorance of the grace of God which is in Christ Jesus our Lord.

Neither is a painful dread or a servile terror a fruit of the Spirit. Many worship even the Lord Jesus himself at a distance: they know not that believers are "a people near unto him." They are afraid of God, but they never delight in him; they attend to worship, not because they rejoice in it, but because they think it must be done. Their secret feeling is—"What a weariness it is," but necessity compels. They know nothing of a child's joy in sure and full forgiveness, spoken by the Father's own lips as he pressed them to his bosom. His kiss was never warm upon their cheek, the ring was never on their finger, nor the best robe upon their shoulder; the music and the dancing of the joyous family, who are in harmony with the father's joy over the lost son, have never charmed their ears. They are still under dread, which is the fruit of superstition rather than "the fruit of the Spirit." Many things they do and suffer, and all in vain: if the Son did but make them free they would be free indeed.

I know some whom I am very far from despising, but whom on the contrary I greatly value, whose religion, sincere as I know it is, is sadly tinged with gloomy colours. They are afraid of assurance, for they dread presumption: they dare not speak of their own salvation with the certainty with which the Bible saints were wont to speak of it; they always say "I hope" and "I trust." They would seem to be total abstainers from joy; they are suspicious of it lest it should be carnal excitement or visionary hope. They hang their heads like bulrushes, and go mourning all their days, as if the religion of Christ knew no higher festival than a funeral, and all its robes were the garments of despair. Brethren, despondency is not the fruit of the Spirit. Make no mistake: depression is frequently the fruit of indigestion, or of satanic temptation, or of unbelief, or of some harboured sin, but "the fruit of the Spirit is joy." Constantly looking within your own self instead of looking alone to Christ is enough to breed misery in any heart. I have also known gloomy expressions to be the fruit of affectation, the fruit of the unwise imitation of some undoubtedly good person who was of a downcast spirit. Some of the best of men have had a melancholy turn, but they would have been better men if this had been overcome. Imitate their many virtues: take the pot of ointment and pick out the dead fly. O my brethren, look well to it that ye bring forth the genuine, holy, sacred, delicious fruit of the Spirit, which in one of its forms is "joy." Do not

covet the counterfeit of earthly joy, but seek to the good
Spirit to bear the true fruit in you.

I. In speaking upon this joy I shall notice, first, the fact
that IT IS BROUGHT FORTH. Brethren, the Spirit of God is not
barren: if he be in you he must and will inevitably produce
his own legitimate fruit, and "the fruit of the Spirit is joy."

We know this to be the fact because *we ourselves are
witnesses of it.* Joy is our portion, and we are cheered and
comforted in the Saviour. "What!" say you, "are we not
depressed and sorrowful at times?" Yea, verily; and yet what
Christian man or woman among us would make an exchange with the gayest of all worldlings? Your lot is somewhat hard, my brother, and sometimes your spirit sinks
within you; but do you not count yourself to be, even at your
worst, happier than the worldling at his best? Come, would
you not take your poverty, even with your mourning, rather
than accept his wealth with all his hilarity, and give up your
hope in God? I am persuaded you would: you would not
change your blest estate for a monarch's crown. Well, then,
that which you would not change is a good thing, and full of
joy to your heart.

Brethren, we experience extraordinary joys at times. Some
are of an equable temperament, and they are almost to be
envied, for a stream of gentle joy always glides through their
spirit. Others of us are of a more excitable character, and
consequently we fall very flat at times. Ay, but then we have
our high days and holidays, and mounting times, and then
we outsoar the wings of eagles. Heaven itself can hardly
know more ecstatic joy than we have occasionally felt; we
shall be vessels of greater capacity there, but even here we
are at times full to the brim of joy—I mean the same joy
which makes heaven so glad. At times God is pleased to
inundate the spirit with a flood of joy, and we are witnesses
that "happy is the people whose God is the Lord." We do not
dance before the ark every day, but when we do, our joy is
such as no worldling can understand: it is far above and out
of his sight.

Besides our own witness, *the whole history of the church
goes to show that God's people are a joyful people.* I am sure
that if in reading the history of the first Christian centuries
you are asked to point out the men to be envied for their joy,

you would point to the believers in Jesus. There is a room in
Rome which is filled with the busts of the emperors. I have
looked at their heads: they look like a collection of prize-
fighters and murderers, and scarcely could I discover on any
countenance a trace of joy. Brutal passions and cruel
thoughts deprived the lords of Rome of all chance of joy.
There were honourable exceptions to their rule, but taking
them all round you would look in vain for moral excellence
among the Cæsars, and lacking this thing of beauty they
missed that which is a joy. Turn now to the poor, hunted
Christians, and read the inscriptions left by them in the
catacombs; they are so calm and peaceful that you say
instinctively—a joyous people were wont to gather here.
Those who have been most eminent in service and in
suffering for Christ's sake have been of a triumphant spirit,
dauntless because supported by an inner joy: their calm
courage made them the wonder of the age. The true
Christian is a different type of manhood from the self-
indulgent tyrant; there is almost as much advance from the
coarseness of vice to holiness as there is from the
chimpanzee to the man. I do not know how much Tiberias
and Caligula and Nero used to sing; happy men they certainly were not. I can hardly imagine them singing, except at
their drunken orgies, and then in the same tone as tigers
growl; but I do know that Paul and Silas sang praises unto
God with their feet in the stocks, and the prisoners heard
them; and I know also that this was the mark of the
Christians of the first age, that, when they assembled on the
Lord's-day, it was not to groan, but to sing praise to the
name of one Christos, whom they worshipped as a God. High
joys were common then, when the bridegroom comforted his
bride in the dens and caves of the earth. Those pioneers of
our holy faith were destitute, afflicted, tormented, yet were
they men of whom the world was not worthy, and men who
counted it all joy to suffer persecution for Christ's sake. Now,
if in the very worst times God's people have been a happy
people, I am sure they are so now. I would appeal to the
biographies of men of our own day, and challenge questioning as to the statement that their lives have been among the
most desirable of human existences for they possessed a joy
which cheered their sorrows, blessed their labours, sweet-

ened their trials, and sustained them in the hour of death. *With some Christians this fruit of the Spirit is perpetual, or almost so.* I do not doubt that many walk with God as Enoch did throughout the whole day of their life, always peaceful and joyful in the Lord. I have met with some, dear brethren and sisters, of that kind, whose breath has been praise, whose life has been song. How I envy them, and chide my own heart that I cannot always abide in their choice condition. It is to be accomplished, and we will press forward till we are "always rejoicing." But with others joy is not constant, and yet it is frequent. David had his mourning times, when tears were his meat day and night, and yet God was his exceeding joy. How thankful we ought to be for the portrait of David's inner self, which is presented to us in the Book of Psalms. With all his down-castings, what joys he had: David was, on the whole, a joyous man. His Book of Psalms has in it lyrics of delight; the gladdest hymns that ever leaped from human tongues. David is, I believe, the type of a great majority of the people of God, who if not "always rejoicing" are yet often so. Please to recollect that the utmost fulness of joy could hardly be enjoyed always in this mortal life. I believe that the human frame is not in this world capable of perpetual ecstasy. Look at the sun, but look not too long lest you be blinded by excess of light. Taste of honey, but eat not much of it, or it will no longer please the palate. Let your ear be charmed with the Hallelujah chorus, but do not dream that you could endure its harmonies all the hours of the day; before long you would cry out for eloquent pauses, and sweet reliefs of silence. Too much even of delight will weary our feeble hearts, and we shall need to come down from the mount. Our bodies require a portion of sleep, and that which is inevitable to the flesh has its likeness in the spirit; it must be quiet and still. I believe it is inevitable also, more or less, that the loftiest joy should be balanced by a sinking of heart. I do not say that depression is certain to follow delight, but usually some kind of faintness comes over the finite spirit after it has been lifted up into communion with the infinite. Do not, therefore, set too much store by your own feelings as evidences of grace. "The fruit of the Spirit is joy," but you may not at this moment be conscious of joy· trees are not always bearing fruit, and yet "their substance is in them when they lose their leaves." Some young people say, "Oh, we know we are saved, because we are so happy." It is by no means a sure evidence, for joy may be carnal, unfounded, unspiritual. Certain Christians are afraid that they cannot be in a saved state because they are not joyous, but we are saved by faith and not by joy. I was struck with the remark of Ebenezer Erskine when he was dying, and some one said to him, "I hope you have now and then a *blink* to bear up your spirit under affliction"; he promptly replied, "I know more of *words* than of *blinks";* that is to say, he had rather trust a promise of God than his own glimpses of heaven; and so would I. The word of God is a more sure testimony to the soul than all the raptures a man can feel. I would sooner walk in the dark, and hold hard to a promise of my God, than trust in the light of the brightest day that ever dawned. Precious as the fruit is, do not put the fruit where the root should be. Please to recollect that. Joy is not the root of grace in the soul, it is the fruit, and must not be put out of its proper position. "The fruit of the Spirit is joy," and it is brought forth in believers: not alike in all, but to all believers there is a measure of joy.

II. Secondly, THIS JOY IS OF A SINGULAR CHARACTER. It is singular for this reason, that *it often ripens under the most remarkable circumstances.* As I have already said, the highest joy of Christians has often been experienced in their times of greatest distress. Tried believers have been happy when smarting under pain, or wasting away with disease. Sick beds have been thrones to many saints; they have almost feared to come out of the furnace, because the presence of the Lord in the midst of the fire has made it none other than the gate of heaven to their souls. Saints in poverty have been made exceeding rich, and when they have eaten a dry crust they have found a flavour with it which they never discovered in the dainties of their abundance. Many children of God, even when driven away from the outward means of grace, have nevertheless enjoyed such visits of God, such inlets of divine love, that they have wondered whence such joy could come. In the wilderness waters leap forth, and streams in the desert. Believers are not dependent upon circumstances. Their joy comes not from what they have, but from what they are; not from where they are, but from whose they are; not from what they enjoy, but from that which was suffered for them by their Lord. It is a singular joy, then, because it often buds, blossoms, and ripens in winter time, and when the fig tree does not blossom, and there is no herd in the stall, God's Habakkuks rejoice in the God of their salvation.

It is a singular joy, too, because *it is quite consistent with spiritual conflict.* He that is an heir of heaven may cry, "O wretched man that I am, who shall deliver me from the body of this death?" and yet, ere the sigh is over, he may sing, "I thank God, through Jesus Christ our Lord." Sorrowful, yet always rejoicing; struggling, yet always victorious; cast down, but not destroyed; persecuted, but not forsaken; troubled, and yet all the while triumphant; such is the mingled experience of the saints. Oh, this is the wondrous grace, this joy which can live side by side with conflict of the sorest sort.

This joy is special because *at times it is altogether beyond description.* One who was of a sober disposition called it "joy unspeakable and full of glory." "Full of glory!" That is a wonderful expression. A drop of glory is sweet, but, oh, to taste a joy that is full of glory—is that possible here? Ay, and some of us bear witness that it is so: we have felt joy that we dare not tell, and could not tell if we dared: men would turn again and rend us, condemning us as utterly fanatical or out of our minds if we were to cast these pearls before them; but, oh, if they could guess what delicious draughts are held within the jewelled chalice of divine communion they would be ready to wade through hell itself to drink from it. Our joy is altogether unspeakable joy at times.

One more singularity there is in it, for *it is all the while solid, thoughtful, rational joy.* The joy of the ungodly is like the crackling of thorns under a pot, noisy, flashy, but soon over. The ungodly man feels merry, but really if you come to look into his mirth there is nothing in it but flame without fuel, sparkle without solidity; but the Christian's joy is such that he has as much reason for it as if it were a deduction from mathematics. He has as just a right to be joyful as he has to eat his own bread: he is certain of his pardon, for God has told him that a believer in Christ is not condemned; and he is sure of his acceptance, for he is justified by faith. He knows that he is secure, for Christ has given him eternal life, and said that his sheep shall never perish. He is happy, not for causes at which he guesses, but by infallible reasons plainly revealed in God's word. This makes him joyful in the Lord when others wonder that he is so, for he perceives arguments for happiness which are unknown to the thoughtless crowd.

That word "joyful" is a very sweet and clear one. "Happiness" is a very dainty word, but yet it is somewhat insecure because it begins with a "hap," and seems to depend on a chance which may *happen* to the soul. We say "happy-go-lucky," and that is very much the world's happiness, it is a kind of thing that may hap and may not hap; but there is no hap in the fruit of the Spirit which is joy. When we are joyful or full of joy, and that of the best kind, we are favoured indeed. No man taketh this joy from us, and a stranger intermeddleth not with it; it is a celestial fruit, and earth cannot produce its like.

III. Thirdly, I would now refresh your memories, and by the help of the Spirit of God bring back former joys to you: THIS JOY IS EXPERIENCED BY THE CHRISTIAN UNDER VARIOUS FORMS. Sometimes he experiences it in *hearing the word:* it is written concerning Samaria there was great joy in that city because Philip went down and preached the gospel to them. Blessed are the people that know the joyful sound. However, joy of hearing lies in *believing* what you hear. We get joy and peace in believing. When you get a grip of the word, when the glad tidings become a message to your own soul, and the Spirit speaks it to your own heart, then you say, "Go on, man of God. Your sermon will not be too long to-day, for the Lord is laying it home to my soul." The reason why people grumble at long sermons often is because they do not feed on them. Very seldom the hungry man murmurs at having too big a meal. It is a delightful thing to hear the word faithfully preached. Have you not sometimes exclaimed, "How beautiful upon the mountains are the feet of him that bringeth glad tidings"? That is one occasion of joy.

But what joy there is, dear friends, in *the salvation of God* when we heartily receive it. Oh, how we bless the God of our salvation, and how we praise him that he hath saved us from our sins and from the wrath to come, by giving us ever-

lasting consolation and good hope through grace, by the
sacrifice of his dear Son. Frequently we revel in *the privileges of the covenant.* The joy of my heart when I think of the
doctrine of *election* is quite inexpressible. That hymn which
begins—

> "In songs of sublime adoration and praise,
>   Ye pilgrims to Zion who press,
> Break forth, and extol the great Ancient of days,
>   His rich and distinguishing grace,"

is often with me, and makes my heart merry.

Then the doctrine of *redemption,* of which I tried to speak
last Sabbath-day: how joyous it is! What bliss to know that
the Redeemer liveth. "Unto you that believe he is precious,"
and a fulness of joy flows forth at every remembrance of
him. Then that doctrine of *justification* is the marrow of joy.
Oh, to think that we are just in the sight of God through
Jesus Christ. All the doctrines of grace, especially that of
final perseverance, are joyful truths. I protest that, if you
take final perseverance from me, you have robbed the Bible
of one of its crowning attractions. Jesus has not given us a
transient salvation, but his salvation shall be for ever. I will
quote again those matchless words of his: "I give unto my
sheep eternal life, and they shall never perish, neither shall
any pluck them out of my hand." Honey flows here as in the
wood of Jonathan; put it to your mouth and your eyes shall
be enlightened. The joy of God's people when they can get
half-an-hour alone, and sit down and crack a dish of those
nuts called the doctrines of grace, is such as philosophical
worldlings might well desire: the modern gospel has no such
wines on the lees well refined.

But, brethren, our grandest joy is in *God* himself. Paul
says, "and not only so, but we joy in God through our Lord
Jesus Christ." Oh, to think of the great Father! What a
melting of spirit comes over the child of God if at midnight
he looks up at the stars, and considers the heavens and
cries, "What is man, that thou art mindful of him!" To think
that he is not only mindful of us, but that he has taken us to
be his Sons and daughters! To feel the Spirit within our
hearts crying, "Abba, Father! Abba, Father!" Oh, this is joy
in the profoundest sense,

How sweet to think of Jesus Christ the Son, the glorious incarnate God, the surety, the satisfaction, the representative, the all in all of his people. We joy in God through our Lord Jesus Christ. Nor do we miss the joy of the Spirit, when we know that he dwells in us. He sanctifies us, comforts us, and guides us in the road to heaven. Oh brethren, this is a sea of bliss, the infinite deeps of the eternal godhead! Leap from all your miseries into this sea of glory. Plunge into the joy of your Lord.

This being so, we have a joy in all God's *ordinances:* "with joy do we draw water out of the wells of salvation." What a joy prayer is: I hope you find it so. The Lord hath said, "I will make them joyful in my house of prayer." And what a joy it is to get answers to our petitions, even as our Lord says, "Ask and ye shall receive, that your joy may be full." Has not your joy been full, till your eyes have been dim with tears and you have not hardly dared to tell how wondrously God has answered you? The mercy-seat is lit up with joy. What a joyous ordinance is that of praise! We come up to the sanctuary and bring our offering to God, and present him our oblation, just as the Jew of old brought his bullock or his lamb; and we joyfully present our gift unto the Most High. Then we begin to sing his praises, and our joy is the chief musician upon our stringed instruments. How our spirits rise as we adore the Lord! The amount of happiness felt in this Tabernacle when we have been singing unto the Lord can never be measured. For my own part, I have seemed to stand just outside the wall of the New Jerusalem joining in the hymns which are sung within the gates of the eternal city. One joy note has helped another, and the volume of sound has affected every part of our being and stirred us up to vehemence of joy.

And oh, what joy there is in coming to the Lord's table! May we experience it to-night, as we have often done before. The Lord is known to us in the breaking of bread, and that knowledge is blissful.

But I have scarcely begun the list yet, for we have a great joy in *the salvation of other people.* Perhaps one of the choicest delights we know is when we partake in the joy of the good Shepherd over his lost sheep, when he calls us together, for we also are his friends and his neighbours, and bids us rejoice that he has found the sheep which was lost. Especially do we joy and rejoice if the poor wanderer has been brought back by our means. The jewels of an emperor are nothing compared with the riches we possess in winning a soul for Christ. "They that sow in tears shall reap in joy." The joy of harvest is great, the joy of the man who comes again rejoicing, bringing his sheaves with him. Do you know this joy, brothers and sisters? If you do not, rouse yourselves, and may this sweet fruit of the Spirit yet be yours.

Oh, the joy of seeing Christ exalted! John the Baptist said, "He must increase, but I must decrease." He called himself the Bridegroom's friend, and rejoiced greatly in the Bridegroom's joy. We can sympathise with him when we can bring about a marriage between Christ, and any poor soul, and help to put the ring on the finger. The joy we feel is of the purest and loveliest order, for it is unselfish and refined. Let Jesus be exalted, and we ask no more. If he reigns we reign; if he is lifted up our hearts are more than satisfied.

Brethren, if we ever become perfect in heart, we shall joy in *all the divine will,* whatever it may bring us. I am trying, if I can, to find a joy in rheumatism, but I cannot get up to it yet. I have found a joy when it is over,—I can reach that length,—and I can and do bless God for any good result that may come of it; but when the pain is on me, it is difficult to be joyous about it, and so I conclude that my sanctification is very incomplete, and my conformity to the divine will is sadly imperfect. Oh, the splendour of God's will! If a man were as he ought to be, God's will would charm him, and he would not wish for the smallest change in it. Poverty, sickness, bereavement, death, are all to be rejoiced in when our will is merged in the will of God. What! Would you alter God's infinitely wise appointment? Would you wish to change the purpose of unerring love? Then you are not wholly reconciled to God; for when the head gets quite right the heart climbs where Paul was when he said, "We glory in tribulations also, knowing that tribulation worketh patience, and patience experience." It needs a Samson to kill the lion of affliction, and you cannot get honey out of it until it is conquered; but we might all be Samsons if we would but lay hold on the strength of God by faith.

Dear brethren and sisters, tho list of joys, which I am even now only commencing, contains the joy of *an easy conscience,* the joy of feeling you have done right before God, the joy of knowing that your object, though misunderstood and misrepresented, was God's glory. This is a jewel to wear on one's breast—a quiet conscience. Then there is the joy of communion with Christ, the joy of fellowship with his saints, the joy of drinking deep into Christ's spirit of self-sacrifice. There, too, is the joy of expecting his glorious advent, when he and his saints shall reign upon the earth, and the joy of being *with him for ever.* The joy of *heaven,* the joy of which we have been singing just now. These joys are countless, but I will pause here and leave you to make a fuller catalogue when you are at home. May the Holy Spirit not only refresh your memories concerning old joys, but bring forth out of his treasury new delights that your joy may be full.

IV. I must notice, in the fourth place, that THIS FRUIT OF THE SPIRIT MAY BE CHECKED IN ITS GROWTH. Some of you may have muttered while I have been speaking of this joy, "I do not know much about it." Perhaps not, friend—shall I tell you why? Some people are too full of the joy of the world, the joy of getting on in business, the joy of a numerous family, the joy of health, the joy of wealth, the joy of human love, or the joy which comes of the pride of life. These joys may be your idols, any you know the joy of the Lord will not stand side by side with an idolatrous delight in the things of this world. See to that. Dagon must fall if the ark of the Lord is present: the world must lose its charms if you are to joy in Christ Jesus.

Our joy is sadly diminished by our unbelief. If ye will not believe neither shall ye be established. Ignorance will do the same to a very large extent. Many a Christian has a thousand reasons for joy which he knows nothing of. Study the Word and ask for the teaching of the Spirit of God that you may understand it; so shall you discover wells of delight. Joy is diminished, also, by walking at a distance from God. If you get away from the fire you will grow cold: the warmest place is right in front of it, and the warmest place for a believing heart is close to Christ in daily fellowship with him.

It may be that sin indulged is spoiling our joy. "This little hand of mine," as Mr. Whitfield once said, "can cover up the sun as far as my eyes are concerned." You have only to lift a

naughty, rebellious hand, and you can shut out the light of
God himself: any known sin will do it. Trifling with sin will
prove a kill-joy to the heart.

I believe that many lose the joy of the Lord because they
do not put it in the right place. See where it lives. Look at
my text: "The fruit of the Spirit is love, joy, and peace."
There joy stands in the centre; "love" is on one side and
"peace" on the other. Find a man who never loved anybody
and you have found a joyless man. This man's religion
begins and ends with looking to his own safety. The only
point he longs to know is,—is he himself saved? He never
knows joy, poor creature; how can he? As to peace, where is
it? He has none, because wherever he goes he growls, and
grumbles, and snarls, and barks at everybody. There is no
peace where he is, he is always quarrelling, and then he
says, "I have little joy." He does not live in the right house
for joy. Joy dwells at No. 2. "Love" is No. 1: "joy" is No. 2;
"peace" is No. 3; and if you pull down either of the houses on
the side, No. 2 in the middle will tumble down. Joy is the
centre of a triplet, and you must have it so or not at
all:—"Love, joy, peace." Thus have I shown how the growth
of joy can be checked. I pray you do not allow such an evil
thing to be wrought in your heart.

V. But, lastly, IT OUGHT TO BE CAREFULLY CULTIVATED.
There is an obligation upon a Christian to be happy. Let me
say it again: there is a responsibility laid upon a Christian to
be cheerful. It is not merely an invitation, but it is a
command—"Be glad in the Lord and rejoice, ye righteous."
"Rejoice in the Lord alway; and again I say, Rejoice." Gloomy
Christians, who do not resist despondency and strive against
it, but who go about as if midnight had taken up its abode in
their eyes, and an everlasting frost had settled on their
souls, are not obeying the commands of God. The command
to rejoice is as undoubted a precept of God as to love the
Lord with all your heart. The vows of God are upon you, O
believer, and they bind you to be joyful.

In this joyfulness you shall find many great advantages.
First, it is a great advantage in itself to be happy. Who
would not rejoice if he could? Who would not rejoice when
God commands him? Rejoicing will nerve you for life's
duties. "The joy of the Lord is your strength." A man who

goes about Christ's work in an unwilling, miserable spirit will do it badly and feebly. He may do it earnestly, but there will be no life or energy about him. Hear how the sailors when they pull the rope will shout and sing, and work all the better for their cheery notes. I do not believe our soldiers would march to battle with half their present courage if they tramped along in silence. Beat the drums! Let the trumpet sound forth its martial note! Every man is eager for the fray while soul-stirring music excites him. Let your heart make music unto God, and you will fight valiantly for the kingdom of your Lord.

Holy joy will also be a great preventive. The man who feels the joy of the Lord will not covet worldly joy. He will not be tempted to make a God of his possessions or of his talents, or of anything else. He will say, "I have joy in God; these things I am very thankful for, but they are not my joy." He will not crave the aesthetic in worship, for his joy will be in God and his truth, and not in external forms. Some people's idea of joy in religion lies in fine singing, charming music, pretty dresses, splendid architecture, or showy eloquence. They need this because they do not know the secret joy of the Lord, for when that holy passion reigns within, you may sit inside four whitewashed walls, and not hear a soul speak for a whole hour and a half, and yet you may have as intense a joy as if you listened to the most earnest oratory or the sweetest song.

Joy in God is suitable to our condition!

> "Why should the children of a king
> Go mourning all their days?"

What are we at now, some of us? We have been hanging our harps on the willows: let us take them down; the willow boughs will bend. Thank God, we did not break the harps, though we did hang them there. Let us get into our right position; children of the happy God should themselves be happy.

Joy is certainly the best preparation for the future. We are going where, if we learn to groan never so deeply, our education will be lost, for melancholy utterances are unknown up there. We are going where, if we learn to sing with sacred joy, our education will be useful; for the first thing we shall hear when we get into heaven will undoubtedly be, "Hallelujah to God and the Lamb;" and if we have been joyful on earth we shall say, "Ah, I am at home here." To enter heaven with a joyful soul is only to rise from downstairs to the upper chamber where the music knows no discord. It is the same song in both places, "Unto him that loved us and washed us from our sins in his blood."

Joy in the Lord will be very helpful to you as to usefulness. I am sure a Christian man's usefulness is abridged by dreariness of spirit. What nice Sunday-school teachers some Christians I know of would make! "Come ye children, hearken unto me, I will teach you the miseries of religion;" and the dear brother begins by telling the children about the Slough of Despond, and Giant Despair, and the Valley of the Shadow of Death. He wonders when he gets home that the dear children are not attracted to the ways of godliness. Are they likely to be? A member of a church who has no joy of the Lord is little likely to encourage or influence others: they edge off from him. Even those who try to comfort him find it is to no purpose, and so they give him a wide berth. You hear him stand up to address an assembly of believers, to tell his experience, and after a very little of it you feel you have had enough. Those who drink wine will tell you that half a dozen drops of vinegar are more than they want in a glass of wine, and those who carry the cruet about wherever they go are not choice company. I do not find fault with gloomy souls, but they might be more useful if they could live more in the sunlight.

The joy of the Lord is the most injurious to Satan's empire of anything. I am of the same mind as Luther, who, when he heard any very bad news, used to say, "Come, let us sing a psalm, and spite the devil." There is nothing like it: whenever anything happens that is rough and ugly, and seems to injure the kingdom of Christ, say to yourself, "Bless the Lord, glory be to his name." If the Lord has been dishonoured by the falling away of a false professor, or the failure of the ministry in any place, let us give him all the more honour ourselves, and in some measure make up for all that has happened amiss.

And, lastly, holy joy is very pleasing to God. God delights in the joy of his creatures. He made them to be happy. His first and original design in the creation of all beings is his own glory in their happiness. When his people rejoice he rejoices. Some of you spent Christmas day in the bosom of your families. Possibly you have a large family; ten or twelve were at home on that day, with a grandchild or two. I will tell you what was your greatest joy on that day: it was to see the happiness of your children, and to mark how they enjoyed what you had provided for them. They are only little children, some of them, creeping about on the floor, but they pleased you because they were so pleased themselves. The cry of a little child delights your heart to hear it, for it gives us joy to behold joy in those we love. Suppose your sons and daughters had all come marching in on Christmas day in a very gloomy state of mind, cold, loveless, joyless; suppose that they did not enjoy anything, but grumbled at you and at one another, you would be quite sad, and wish the day to be soon over, and never come again for the next seven years. Thus in a figure we see that our heavenly Father delights in the delight of his children, and is glad to see them grateful and happy, and acting as children should do towards such a Parent. Now, brethren, rise as one man, and sing—

> "Then let our songs abound,
> And every tear be dry:
> We're marching thro' Immanuel's ground
> To fairer worlds on high."

18

The Pentecostal Wind And Fire

"And suddenly there came a sound from heaven as of a rushing mighty wind, and it filled all the house where they were sitting. And there appeared unto them cloven tongues like as of fire, and it sat upon each of them. And they were all filled with the Holy Ghost, and began to speak with other tongues, as the Spirit gave them utterance."   Acts 2:2-4

From the descent of the Holy Ghost at the beginning we may learn something concerning his operations at the present time. Remember at the outset that whatever the Holy Spirit was at the first, that he is now, for as God he remaineth for ever the same: whatsoever he then did he is able to do still, for his power is by no means diminished. As saith the prophet Micah, "O thou that art named the house of Jacob, is the spirit of the Lord straitened?" We should greatly grieve the Holy Spirit if we supposed that his might was less to-day than in the beginning. Although we may not expect, and need not desire the miracles which came with the gift of the Holy Spirit, so far as they were physical, yet we may both desire and expect that which was intended and symbolized by them, and we may reckon to see the like spiritual wonders performed among us at this day.

Pentecost, according to the belief of the Jews, was the time of the giving of the law; and if when the law was given there was a marvellous display of power on Sinai, it was to be expected that when the gospel was given, whose ministration is far more glorious, there should be some special unveiling of the divine presence. If at the commencement of the gospel we behold the Holy Spirit working great signs and wonders may we not expect a continuance—nay, if anything, an increased display of his power as the ages roll on? The law vanished away, but the gospel will never vanish; it shineth more and more to the perfect millennial day; therefore, I reckon that, with the sole exception of physical miracles, whatever was wrought by the Holy Ghost at the first we may look to be wrought continually while the dispensation lasts. It ought not to be forgotten that Pentecost was the feast of first fruits; it was the time when the first ears of ripe corn were offered unto God. If, then, at the commencement of the gospel harvest we see so plainly the power of the Holy Spirit, may we not most properly expect infinitely more as the harvest advances, and most of all when the most numerous sheaves shall be ingathered? May we not conclude that if the Pentecost was thus marvellous the actual harvest will be more wonderful still?

This morning my object is not to talk of the descent of the Holy Spirit as a piece of history, but to view it as a fact bearing upon us at this hour, even upon us who are called in these latter days to bear our testimony for the truth. The Father hath sent us the Comforter that he may dwell in us till the coming of the Lord. The Holy Ghost has never returned, for he came in accordance with the Saviour's prayer, to abide with us for ever. The gift of the Comforter was not temporary, and the display of his power was not to be once seen and no more. The Holy Ghost is here, and we ought to expect his divine working among us: and if he does not so work we should search ourselves to see what it is that hindereth, and whether there may not be somewhat in ourselves which vexes him, so that he restrains his sacred energy, and doth not work among us as he did aforetime. May God grant that the meditation of this morning may increase our faith in the Holy Ghost, and inflame our desires towards him, so that we may look to see him fulfilling his mission among men as at the beginning.

I. First, I shall call your attention to THE INSTRUCTIVE SYMBOLS of the Holy Spirit, which were made prominent at Pentecost. They were two. There was a sound as of a rushing mighty wind, and there were cloven tongues as it were of fire.

Take the symbols separately. The first is *wind*—an emblem of Deity, and therefore a proper symbol of the Holy

Spirit. Often under the Old Testament God revealed himself under the emblem of breath or wind: indeed, as most of you know, the Hebrew word for "wind" and "spirit" is the same. So, with the Greek word, when Christ talked to Nicodemus; it is not very easy for translators to tell us when he said "spirit" and when he said "wind;" indeed, some most correctly render the original all the way through by the word "wind," while others with much reason have also used the word "spirit" in their translation. The original word signified either the one or the other, or both. Wind is, of all material things, one of the most spiritual in appearance; it is invisible, ethereal, mysterious; hence, men have fixed upon it as being nearest akin to spirit. In Ezekiel's famous vision, when he saw the valley full of dry bones, we all know that the Spirit of God was intended by that vivifying wind which came when the prophet prophesied and blew upon the withered relics till they were quickened into life. "The Lord hath his way in the whirlwind," thus he displays himself when he works: "The Lord answered Job out of the whirlwind," thus he reveals himself when he teaches his servants.

Observe that this wind was on the day of Pentecost accompanied with a sound—a sound as of a rushing mighty wind; for albeit the Spirit of God can work in silence, yet in saving operations he frequently uses sound. I would be the last to depreciate meetings in which there is nothing but holy silence, for I could wish that we had more reverence for silence, and it is in stillness that the inner life is nourished; yet the Holy Ghost does not work for the advancement of the kingdom of God by silence alone, for faith cometh by hearing. There is a sound as of a rushing, mighty wind, when the word is sounded forth throughout whole nations by the publishing of the gospel. If the Lord had not given men ears or tongues silent worship would have been not only appropriate but necessary; but inasmuch as we have ears the Lord must have intended us to hear something, and as we have tongues he must have meant us to speak. Some of us would be glad to be quiet, but where the gospel has free course, there is sure to be a measure of noise and stir. The sound came on this occasion, no doubt, to call the attention of the assembly to what was about to occur, to arouse them, and to fill them with awe! There is something indescribably

solemn about the rush of a rising tempest; it bows the soul
before the sublime mystery of divine power. What more
fitting as an attendant upon divine working than the deeply
solemn rush of a mighty wind.

With this awe-inspiring sound as of a mighty wind, there
was clear indication of its coming from heaven. Ordinary
winds blow from this or that quarter of the skies, but this
descended from heaven itself: it was distinctly like a down-
draught from above. This sets forth the fact that the true
Spirit, the Spirit of God, neither comes from this place nor
that, neither can his power be controlled or directed by
human authority, but his working is ever from above, from
God himself. The work of the Holy Spirit is, so to speak, the
breath of God, and his power is evermore in a special sense
the immediate power of God. Coming downward, therefore,
this mysterious wind passed into the chamber where the
disciples were assembled, and filled the room. An ordinary
rushing mighty wind would have been felt outside the room,
and would probably have destroyed the house or injured the
inmates, if it had been aimed at any one building; but this
heavenly gust filled but did not destroy the room, it blessed
but did not overthrow the waiting company.

The meaning of the symbol is that as breath, air, wind, is
the very life of man, so is the Spirit of God the life of the
spiritual man. By him are we quickened at the first; by him
are we kept alive afterwards; by him is the inner life
nurtured, and increased, and perfected. The breath of the
nostrils of the man of God is the Spirit of God.

This holy breath was not only intended to quicken them,
but to invigorate them. What a blessing would a breeze be
just now to us who sit in this heavy atmosphere! How gladly
would we hail a gust from the breezy down, or a gale from
the open sea! If the winds of earth are so refreshing what
must a wind from heaven be! That rushing mighty wind
soon cleared away all earth-engendered damps and vapours;
it aroused the disciples and left them braced up for the
further work of the Lord. They took in great draughts of
heavenly life; they felt animated, aroused, and bestirred. A
sacred enthusiasm came upon them, because they were
filled with the Holy Ghost; and, girt with that strength, they
rose into a nobler form of life than they had known before.

No doubt this wind was intended to show the irresistible power of the Holy Ghost; for simple as the air is, and mobile and apparently feeble, yet set it in motion, and you feel that a thing of life is among you; make that motion more rapid, and who knows the power of the restless giant who has been awakened. See, it becomes a storm, a tempest, a hurricane, a tornado, a cyclone. Nothing can be more potent than the wind when it is thoroughly roused, and so, though the Spirit of God be despised among men, so much so that they do not even believe in his existence, yet let him work with the fulness of his power, and you will see what he can do. He comes softly, breathing like a gentle zephyr, which fans the flowers, but does not dislodge the insect of most gauzy wing, and our hearts are comforted. He comes like a stirring breeze, and we are quickened to a livelier diligence: our sails are hoisted and we fly before the gale. He comes with yet greater strength, and we prostrate ourselves in the dust as we hear the thunder of his power, bringing down with a crash false confidences and refuges of lies! How the firm reliances of carnal men, which seemed to stand like rocks, are utterly cast down! How men's hopes, which appeared to be rooted like oaks, are torn up by the roots before the breath of the convincing Spirit! What can stand against him? Oh! that we did but see in these latter days something of that mighty rushing wind which breaketh the cedars of Lebanon, and sweeps before it all things that would resist its power.

The second Pentecostal symbol was *fire*. Fire, again, is a frequent symbol of Deity. Abraham saw a burning lamp, and Moses beheld a burning bush. When Solomon had builded his holy and beautiful house, its consecration lay in the fire of God descending upon the sacrifice to mark that the Lord was there; for when the Lord had dwelt aforetime in the tabernacle, which was superseded by the temple, he revealed himself in a pillar of cloud by day and a pillar of fire by night. "Our God is a consuming fire." Hence the symbol of fire is a fit emblem of God the Holy Spirit. Let us adore and worship him. Tongues of flame sitting on each man's head betoken a personal visitation to the mind and heart of each one of the chosen company. Not to consume them came the fires, for no one was injured by the flaming tongue; to men whom the Lord has prepared for his approach there is no danger in his visitations. They see God, and their lives are preserved; they feel his fires, and are not consumed. This is the privilege of those alone who have been prepared and purified for such fellowship with God.

The intention of the symbol was to show them that the Holy Spirit would illuminate them, as fire gives light. "He shall lead you into all truth." Henceforth they were to be no more children untrained, but to be teachers in Israel, instructors of the nations whom they were to disciple unto Christ: hence the Spirit of light was upon them. But fire doth more than give light: it inflames; and the flames which sat upon each showed them that they were to be ablaze with love, intense with zeal, burning with self-sacrifice; and that they were to go forth among men to speak not with the chill tongue of deliberate logic, but with burning tongues of passionate pleading; persuading and entreating men to come unto Christ that they might live. The fire signified inspiration. God was about to make them speak under a divine influence, to speak as the Spirit of God should give them utterance. Oh! blessed symbol, would God that all of us experienced its meaning to the full and that the tongue of fire did sit upon every servant of the Lord. May a fire burn steadily within to destroy our sin, a holy sacrificial flame to make us whole burnt offerings unto God, a never-dying flame of zeal for God, and devotion to the cross.

Note that the emblem was not only fire, but a tongue of fire; for God meant to have a speaking church: not a church that would fight with the sword—with that weapon we have nought to do—but a church that should have a sword proceeding out of its mouth, whose one weapon should be the proclamation of the gospel of Jesus Christ. I should think from what I know of some preachers that when they had their Pentecost the influence sat upon them in the form of tongues of flowers; but the apostolic Pentecost knew not flowers, but flames. What fine preaching we have nowadays! What new thoughts, and poetical turns! This is not the style of the Holy Ghost. Soft and gentle is the flow of smooth speech which tells of the dignity of man, the grandeur of the century, the toning down of all punishment for sin, and the probable restoration of all lost spirits, including the archfiend himself. This is the Satanic ministry, subtle as the serpent, bland as his seducing words to Eve. The Holy Ghost calls us not to this mode of speech. Fire, intensity, zeal, passion as much as you will, but as for aiming at effect by polished phrases and brilliant periods—these are fitter for those who would deceive men than for those who would tell them the message of the Most High. The style of the Holy Ghost is one which conveys the truth to the mind in the most forcible manner,—it is plain but flaming, simple but consuming. The Holy Spirit has never written a cold period throughout the whole Bible, and never did he speak by a man a lifeless word, but evermore he gives and blesses the tongue of fire.

These, then, are the two symbols; and I should like you carefully to observe how the Holy Spirit teaches us by them. When he came from the Father to his Son, Jesus, it was as a dove. Let peace rest on that dear sufferer's soul through all his days of labour and through the passion which would close them. His anointing is that of peace: he needed no tongue of flame, for he was already all on fire with love. When the Holy Spirit was bestowed by the Son of God upon his disciples it was as breath—"He breathed on them and said, Receive the Holy Ghost." To have life more abundantly is a chief necessity of servants of the Lord Jesus, and therefore thus the Holy Ghost visits us. Now that we have the Holy Spirit from Christ as our inner life and quickening he also comes upon us with the intent to use us in blessing others, and this is the manner of his visitation,—he comes as the wind, which wafts the words we speak, and as fire which burns a way for the truth we utter. Our words are now full of life and flame; they are borne by the breath of the Spirit, and they fall like fire-flakes, and set the souls of men blazing with desire after God. If the Holy Spirit shall rest upon me or upon you, or upon any of us, to qualify us for service, it shall be after this fashion—not merely of life for ourselves, but of fiery energy in dealing with others. Come on us even now, O rushing mighty wind and tongue of fire, for the world hath great need. It lies stagnant in the malaria of sin and needs a healing wind; it is shrouded in dreadful night, and needs the flaming torch of truth. There is neither health nor light for it but from thee, O blessed Spirit; come, then, upon it through thy people.

Now put these two symbols together; only mind what you are at. Wind and fire together! I have kept them separate in my discourse hitherto; and you have seen power in each one; what are they together? Rushing mighty wind alone how terrible! Who shall stand against it? See how the gallant ships dash together, and the monarchs of the forest bow their heads. And fire alone! Who shall stand against it when it devours its prey? But set wind and fire to work in hearty union! Remember the old city of London. When first the flames began it was utterly impossible to quench them because the wind fanned the flame, and the buildings gave way before the fire-torrent. Set the prairie on fire. If a rain-shower falls, and the air is still, the grass may perhaps cease to burn, but let the wind encourage the flame, and see how the devourer sweeps along while the tall grass is licked up by tongues of fire. We have lately read of forests on fire. What a sight! Hear how the mighty trees are crashing in the flame! What can stand against it! The fire setteth the mountains on a blaze. What a smoke blackens the skies; it grows dark at noon. As hill after hill offers up its sacrifice, the timid imagine that the great day of the Lord has come. If we could see a spiritual conflagration of equal grandeur it were a consummation devoutly to be wished. O God, send us the Holy Ghost in this fashion: give us both the breath of spiritual life and the fire of unconquerable zeal, till nation after nation shall yield to the sway of Jesus. O thou who art our God, answer us by fire, we pray thee. Answer us both by wind and fire, and then shall we see thee to be God indeed. The kingdom comes not, and the work is flagging. O that thou wouldest send the wind and the fire! Thou wilt do this when we are all of one accord, all believing, all expecting, all prepared by prayer. Lord, bring us to this waiting state.

II. Secondly, my brethren, follow me while I call your attention to THE IMMEDIATE EFFECTS of this descent of the Holy Spirit, for these symbols were not sent in vain. There were two immediate effects: the first was *filling,* and the second was *the gift of utterance.* I call special attention to the first, namely, filling: "It filled all the house where they were sitting": and it did not merely fill the house, but the men— "They were all filled with the Holy Ghost." When they stood up to speak even the ribald mockers in the crowd noticed this, for they said, "These men are full," and though they added "with new wine," yet they evidently detected a singular fulness about them. We are poor, empty things by nature, and useless while we remain so: we need to be filled with the Holy Ghost. Some people seem to believe in the Spirit of God giving utterance only, and they look upon instruction in divine things as of secondary importance. Dear, dear me, what trouble comes when we act upon that theory! How the empty vessels clatter, and rattle, and sound! Men in such case utter a wonderful amount of nothing, and even when that nothing is set on fire it does not come to much. I dread a revival of that sort, where the first thing and the last thing is everlasting talk. Those who set up for teachers ought to be themselves taught of the Lord; how can they communicate that which they have not received? Where the Spirit of God is truly at work he first fills and then gives utterance: that is his way. Oh, that you and I were at this moment filled with the Holy Ghost. "Full!" Then they were not cold, and dead, and empty of life as we sometimes are. "Full." Then there was no room for anything else in any one of them! They were too completely occupied by the heavenly power to have room for the desires of the flesh. Fear was banished, every minor motive was expelled: the Spirit of God as it flooded their very being drove out of them everything that was extraneous. They had many faults and many infirmities before, but that day, when they were filled with the Spirit of God, faults and infirmities were no more perceptible. They became different men from what they had ever been before: men full of God are the reverse of men full of self. The difference between an empty man and a full man is something very wonderful. Let a thirsty person have an empty vessel handed to him. There may be much noise in the handing, but what a mockery it is as it touches his lips; but fill it with refreshing water, and perhaps there may be all the more silence in the passing it, for a full cup needs careful handling; but oh, what a blessing when it reaches the man's lips! Out of a full vessel he may drink his fill. Out of a full church the world shall receive salvation, but never out of an empty one. The first thing we want as a church is to be filled with the Holy Ghost: the gift of utterance will then come as a matter of course. They ask me, "May the sisters speak anywhere? If not in the assembly, may they not speak in smaller meetings?" I answer, yes, if they are full of the Holy Ghost. Shall this brother or that be allowed to speak? Certainly, if he be filled, he may flow. May a layman preach? I know nothing about laymen except that I am no cleric myself; but let all speak who are full of the Holy Ghost. "Spring up, O well." If it be a fountain of living water who would restrain it, who could restrain it? Let him overflow who is full, but mind he does not set up to pour out when there is nothing in him; for if he counts it his official duty to go pouring out, pouring out, pouring out, at unreasonable length, and yet nothing comes of it, I am sure he acts, not by the Holy Spirit, but according to his own vanity.

The next Pentecostal symbol was *utterance*. As soon as the Spirit of God filled them they began to speak at once. It seems to me that they began to speak before the people had come together. They could not help it; the inner forces demanded expression, and they must speak. So when the Spirit of God really comes upon a man, he does not wait till he has gathered an audience of the size which he desires, but he seizes the next opportunity. He speaks to one person, he speaks to two, he speaks to three, to anybody: he must speak, for he is full, and must have vent.

When the Spirit of God fills a man he speaks so as to be understood. The crowd spake different languages, and these Spirit-taught men spoke to them in the language of the country in which they were born. This is one of the signs of the Spirit's utterance. If my friend over yonder talks in a Latinized style to a company of costermongers, I will warrant you the Holy Ghost has nothing to do with him. If a learned brother fires over the heads of his congregation with a grand oration, he may trace his elocution, if he likes, to Cicero and Demosthenes, but do not let him ascribe it to the Holy Spirit, for that is not after his manner. The Spirit of God speaks so that his words may be understood, and if there be any obscurity it lies in the language used by the Lord himself. The crowd not only understood, but they felt. There were lancets in this Pentecostal preaching, and the hearers "were pricked in the heart." The truth wounded men, and the slain of the Lord were many, for the wounds

were in the most vital part. They could not make it out: they
had heard speakers before, but this was quite a different
thing. The men spake fire-flakes, and one hearer cried to his
fellow, "What is this?" The preachers were speaking flame,
and the fire dropped into the hearts of men till they were
amazed and confounded.

Those are the two effects of the Holy Spirit,—a fulness of
the Spirit in the ministry and the church, and next, a fire
ministry, and a church on fire, speaking so as to be felt and
understood by those around. Causes produce effects like
themselves, and this wind and fire ministry soon did its
work. We read that this "was noised abroad." Of course it
was, because there had been a noise as of a rushing mighty
wind. Next to that we read that all the people came together,
and were confounded. There was naturally a stir, for a great
wind from heaven was rushing. All were amazed and
astonished, and while some enquired believingly, others
began to mock. Of course they did: there was a fire burning,
and fire is a dividing thing, and this fire began to separate
between the precious and the vile, as it always will do when
it comes into operation. We may expect at the beginning of a
true revival to observe a movement among the people, a
noise, and a stir. These things are not done in a corner.
Cities will know of the presence of God, and crowds will be
attracted by the event.

This was the immediate effect of the Pentecostal marvel,
and I shall now ask you to follow me to my third point, which
is this:—

III. The Holy Spirit being thus at work, what was THE
MOST PROMINENT SUBJECT which these full men began to
preach about with words of fire? Suppose that the Holy
Spirit should work mightily in the church, what would our
ministers preach about? We should have a revival, should
we not, of the old discussions about predestination and free
agency? I do not think so: these are happily ended, for they
tended towards bitterness, and for the most part the dis-
putants were not equal to their task. We should hear a great
deal about the pre-millennial and the post-millennial advent, should we not? I do not think so. I never saw much of
the Spirit of God in discussions or dreamings upon times and
seasons which are not clearly revealed. Should we not hear

learned essays upon advanced theology? No, sir; when the
devil inspires the church we have modern theology; but
when the Spirit of God is among us that rubbish is shot out
with loathing. What did these men preach about? Their
hearers said, "We do hear them speak in our own tongues
the wonderful works of God." Their subject was the
wonderful works of God. Oh, that this might be to my dying
day my sole and only topic,—"The wonderful works of God."
For, first, they spoke of *redemption,* that wonderful work of
God. Peter's sermon was a specimen of how they spoke of it.
He told the people that Jesus was the Son of God, that they
had crucified and slain him, but that he had come to redeem
men, and that there was salvation through his precious
blood. He preached redemption. Oh, how this land will echo
again and again with "Redemption, redemption, redemption,
redemption by the precious blood," when the Holy Ghost is
with us. This is fit fuel for the tongue of flame: this is
something worthy to be wafted by the divine wind. "God was
in Christ, reconciling the world unto himself, not imputing
their trespasses unto them." "The blood of Jesus Christ his
Son cleanseth us from all sin." This is one of the wonderful
works of God of which we can never make too frequent
mention.

They certainly spoke of the next wonderful work of God,
namely, *regeneration.* There was no concealing of the work
of the Holy Spirit in that primitive ministry. It was brought
to the front. Peter said, "Ye shall receive the Holy Ghost."
The preachers of Pentecost told of the Spirit's work by the
Spirit's power: conversion, repentance, renewal, faith, holiness, and such things were freely spoken of and ascribed to
their real author, the divine Spirit. If the Spirit of God shall
give us once again a full and fiery ministry we shall hear it
clearly proclaimed, "Ye must be born again," and we shall
see a people forthcoming which are born, not of blood, nor of
the will of the flesh, but of the will of God, and by the energy
which cometh from heaven. A Holy Ghost ministry cannot be
silent about the Holy Ghost and his sacred operations upon
the heart.

And very plainly they spoke on a third wonderful work of
God, namely, *remission* of sin. This was the point that Peter
pushed home to them, that on repentance they should

receive remission of sins. What a blessed message is this;—
Pardon for crimes of deepest dye, a pardon bought with
Jesus' blood, free pardon, full pardon, irreversible pardon
given to the vilest of the vile when they ground their weapons of rebellion, and bow at the feet that once were nailed to
the tree. If we would prove ourselves to be under divine
influence, we must keep to the divine message of fatherly
forgiveness to returning prodigals. What happier word can
we deliver?

These are the doctrines which the Holy Ghost will revive
in the midst of the land when he worketh mightily—
redemption, regeneration, remission. If you would have the
Spirit of God resting on your labours, dear brothers and
sisters, keep these three things ever to the front, and make
all men hear in their own tongue the wonderful works of
God.

IV. I shall close by noticing, in the fourth place, what were
the GLORIOUS RESULTS of all this. Have patience with me, if
you find the details somewhat long. The result of the Spirit
coming as wind and fire, filling and giving utterance, was,
first, in the hearers' *deep feeling*. There was never, perhaps,
in the world such a feeling excited by the language of mortal
man as that which was aroused in the crowds in Jerusalem
on that day. You might have seen a group here, and a group
there, all listening to the same story of the wondrous works
of God, and all stirred and affected; for the heavenly wind
and fire went with the preaching, and they could not help
feeling its power. We are told that they were pricked in the
heart. They had painful emotions, they felt wounds which
killed their enmity. The word struck at the centre of their
being: it pierced the vital point. Alas, people come into our
places of worship nowadays to hear the preacher, and their
friends ask them on their return, "How did you like him?"
Was that your errand, to see how you liked him? What
practical benefit is there in such a mode of using the servants of God? Are we sent among you to give opportunities
for criticism? Yet the mass of men seem to think that we are
nothing better than fiddlers or play-actors, who come upon
the stage to help you while away an hour. O my hearers, if
we are true to our God, and true to you, ours is a more
solemn business than most men dream. The object of all true

preaching is the heart: we aim at divorcing the heart from sin, and wedding it to Christ. Our ministry has failed, and has not the divine seal set upon it, unless it makes men tremble, makes them sad, and then anon brings them to Christ, and causes them to rejoice. Sermons are to be heard in thousands, and yet how little comes of them all, because the heart is not aimed at, or else the archers miss the mark. Alas, our hearers do not present their hearts as our target, but leave them at home, and bring us only their ears, or their heads. Here we need the divine aid. Pray mightily that the Spirit of God may rest upon all who speak in God's name, for then they will create deep feeling in their hearers!

Then followed an *earnest enquiry*. "They were pricked in their heart, and they said to Peter and the rest of the apostles, Men and brethren, what shall we do?" Emotion is of itself but a poor result unless it leads to practical action. To make men feel is well enough, but it must be a feeling which impels them to immediate movement, or at least to earnest enquiry as to what they shall do. O Spirit of God, if thou wilt rest on me, even me, men shall not hear and go their way and forget what they have heard! They will arise and seek the Father, and taste his love. If thou wouldst rest on all the brotherhood that publish thy word men would not merely weep while they hear, and be affected while the discourse lasts, but they would go their way to ask, "What must we do to be saved?" This is what we need. We do not require new preachers, but we need a new anointing of the Spirit. We do not require novel forms of service, but we want the fire Spirit, the wind Spirit to work by us till everywhere men cry, "What must we do to be saved?"

Then came *a grand reception of the word*. We are told that they gladly received the word, and they received it in two senses: first, Peter bade them repent, and so they did. They were pricked to the heart from compunction on account of what they had done to Jesus, and they sorrowed after a godly sort, and quitted their sins. They also believed in him whom they had slain, and accepted him as their Saviour there and then, without longer hesitancy. They trusted in him whom God had set forth to be a propitiation, and thus they fully received the word. Repentance and faith make up a complete reception of Christ, and they had both of these.

Why should we not see this divine result to-day? We shall
see it in proportion to our faith.

But what next? Why, they were *baptized* directly. Having
repented and believed, the next step was to make confession
of their faith; and they did not postpone that act for a single
day; why should they? Willing hands were there, the whole
company of the faithful were all glad to engage in the holy
service, and that same day were they baptized into the name
of the Father, and of the Son, and of the Holy Spirit. If the
Holy Ghost were fully with us, we should never have to
complain that many believers never confess their faith, for
they would be eager to confess the Saviour's name in his own
appointed way. Backwardness to be baptized comes too often
of fear of persecution, indecision, love of ease, pride, or
disobedience; but all these vanish when the heavenly wind
and fire are doing their sacred work. Sinful diffidence soon
disappears, sinful shame of Jesus is no more seen, and
hesitancy and delay are banished for ever when the Holy
Spirit works with power.

Furthermore, there was not merely this immediate confession, but as a result of the Spirit of God there was *great
steadfastness.* "They continued steadfastly in the apostles'
doctrine." We have had plenty of revivals of the human sort,
and their results have been sadly disappointing. Under
excitement nominal converts have been multiplied: but
where are they after a little testing? I am sadly compelled to
own that, so far as I can observe, there has been much sown,
and very little reaped that was worth reaping, from much of
that which has been called revival. Our hopes were
flattering as a dream; but the apparent result has vanished
like a vision of the night. But where the Spirit of God is
really at work the converts stand: they are well-rooted and
grounded, and hence they are not carried about by every
wind of doctrine, but they continue steadfast in the apostolic
truth.

We see next that there was *abundant worship of God,* for
they were steadfast not only in the doctrine, but in breaking
of bread, and in prayer, and in fellowship. There was no
difficulty in getting a prayer meeting then, no difficulty in
maintaining daily communion then, no want of holy fellowship then; for the Spirit of God was among them, and the

ordinances were precious in their eyes. "Oh," say some, "if we could get this minister or that evangelist we should do well." Brothers, if you had the Holy Spirit you would have everything else growing out of his presence, for all good things are summed up in him.

Next to this there came *striking generosity*. Funds were not hard to raise: liberality overflowed its banks, for believers poured all that they had into the common fund. Then was it indeed seen to be true that the silver and the gold are the Lord's. When the Spirit of God operates powerfully there is little need to issue telling appeals for widows and orphans, or to go down on your knees and plead for missionary fields which cannot be occupied for want of money. At this moment our village churches can scarcely support their pastors at a starvation rate; but I believe that if the Spirit of God will visit all the churches, means will be forthcoming to keep all going right vigorously. If this does not happen, I tremble for our Nonconformist churches, for the means of their existence will be absent; both as to spiritual and temporal supplies they will utterly fail. There will be no lack of money when there is no lack of grace. When the Spirit of God comes, those who have substance yield it to their Lord: those who have but little grow rich by giving of that little, and those who are already rich become happy by consecrating what they have. There is no need to rattle the box when the rushing mighty wind is heard, and the fire is dissolving all hearts in love.

Then came *continual gladness*. "They did eat their meat with gladness." They were not merely glad at prayer-meetings and sermons, but glad at breakfast and at supper. Whatever they had to eat they were for singing over it. Jerusalem was the happiest city that ever was when the Spirit of God was there. The disciples were singing from morning to night, and I have no doubt the outsiders asked, "What is it all about?" The temple was never so frequented as then; there was never such singing before; the very streets of Jerusalem, and the Hill of Zion, rang with the songs of the once despised Galileans.

They were full of gladness, and that gladness showed itself in *praising God*. I have no doubt they broke out now and then in the services with shouts of, "Glory! Hallelujah!" I should not wonder but what all propriety was scattered to the winds. They were so glad, so exhilarated that they were ready to leap for joy. Of course we never say "Amen," or "Glory!" now. We have grown to be so frozenly proper that we never interrupt a service in any way, because, to tell the truth, we are not so particularly glad, we are not so specially full of praise that we want to do anything of the sort. Alas, we have lost very much of the Spirit of God, and much of the joy and gladness which attend his presence, and so we have settled into a decorous apathy! We gather the pinks of propriety instead of the palm branches of praise. God send us a season of glorious disorder. Oh for a sweep of wind that will set the seas in motion, and make our ironclad brethren now lying so quietly at anchor to roll from stem to stern. As for us, who are as the little ships, we will fly before the gale if it will but speed us to our desired haven. Oh for fire to fall again,—fire which shall affect the most stolid! This is a sure remedy for indifference. When a flake of fire falls into a man's bosom he knows it, and when the word of God comes home to a man's soul he knows it too. Oh that such fire might first sit upon the disciples, and then fall on all around!

For, to close, there was then a *daily increase* of the church—"The Lord added to the church daily such as should be saved." Conversion was going on perpetually; additions to the church were not events which happened once a year, but they were everyday matters, "so mightily grew the word of God and prevailed." O Spirit of God, thou art ready to work with us to-day even as thou didst then! Stay not, we beseech thee, but work at once. Break down every barrier that hinders the incomings of thy might. Overturn, overturn, O sacred wind! Consume all obstacles, O heavenly fire, and give us now both hearts of flame and tongues of fire to preach thy reconciling word, for Jesus' sake. Amen.

19

The Great Teacher And Remembrancer

"But the Comforter, which is the Holy Ghost, whom the Father will send in my name, he shall teach you all things, and bring all things to your remembrance, whatsoever I have said unto you."
John 14:26

The Saviour, when he departed from this world, provided for all the wants of his people, not so much by giving them divers benefits, as by promising them the presence of a gracious Person who should supply to them all that their spiritual needs might demand. I trust there are many of us who know in some degree the value of the promise, "I will send the Comforter unto you"; and that we know that when that Comforter comes, he brings us all good things. We have not to look in one place for quickening, and in another place for comfort, in another for instruction, and in a fourth for illumination; but when we receive the Spirit, we have all things in one. I may say of him, as of Jesus Christ, "In him dwelleth all the fulness of the Godhead bodily." In Jesus it dwelt in a real human nature, physical as well as spiritual, but in the Holy Spirit we have the same fulness of Deity, but he comes in and dwells, and resides in his people.

Our Saviour here directs us to one particular blessing, which the coming of the Holy Spirit would bring us, namely, that of divine instruction. In endeavouring to enter in some measure into the text to-night—too briefly to enter into it fully—we shall, first of all, remark, that the text suggests to us:—

I. THE VALUE OF ALL THAT JESUS CHRIST HAS SPOKEN,

For he tells us, that the Holy Spirit shall "bring to our remembrance all things whatsoever he has said unto us." When the Saviour was with his disciples, it is very possible that many of his choice sayings fell to the ground *for want of attention on their part.* They did not, perhaps, know that every word of his had a fulness in it, that should have been treasured up by them as of priceless worth. But now he tells them that it shall be the Holy Spirit's office to teach them all such truth, and to bring all their meanings to their remembrance. Brethren and sisters, there is a great danger nowadays in not attaching sufficient importance to the teaching of Scripture. You will sometimes hear persons speak very disparagingly of doctrinal truth, and others will smile at anything like dispensational truth. Some are inclined to throw experimental teaching in the background, and some few speak very sadly about practical truth. But our Lord here speaks of "all things whatsoever I have said unto you," and he also speaks of the Spirit teaching us "all things." We may, therefore, believe that every truth that is revealed in Scripture has its proper place and its importance, and we may gather this from the fact *that Christ has taken the trouble to speak it.* We do not believe that he has uttered one foolish word, nay more, not one useless word, for in the whole compass of his teaching there is not to be found a single passage which should have been left unsaid. There may be repetitions, but there are no redundancies. He may have taught the same truth in several shapes, but he has never taught it once too often. He has never revealed a truth which it were better to conceal, just as he has never concealed a truth which it would have been better to reveal. If my Lord has taught anything, it must be worth my while to learn it. If Christ lifts the veil, it is my privilege to look, and what he manifests to me I ought not to be slow to gaze upon.

Moreover, brethren, in addition to the importance which must attach to these things, because Christ has spoken them, there is this, that he now *sends the Holy Spirit to teach them to us.* If you say that any one part of the truth is unimportant, you do as good as say that to that extent the Holy Spirit has come upon an unimportant or valueless mission. You perceive it is declared that he is to teach us "all things"; but if some of those "all things" are really of such

minor importance and so quite non-essential, then surely it
is not worth while disturbing our minds with them. And so
to that degree, at any rate, we accuse the Holy Spirit of
having come to do what is not necessary to be done; and I
trust that our minds recoil with holy repulsion from such a
half-blasphemy as that. Brethren and sisters beloved, he
teaches us "all things," because it is needful for us to learn
all things, and so he comes to bring to our remembrance not
part, but, in turn, the whole of our Lord's wondrous teaching. That teaching is essential to our knowledge of divine
things, to our comfort and progress in spiritual things: that
remembrance is part of our soul's discipline and advance.

I wish that some of my friends would get this very simple
and very trite truth into the depths of their minds and
hearts; for then they would surely study a great many things
that they overlook now, and I think they would not be so apt
to excuse their own want of diligence in the school of Christ,
by saying, "Well, there are some all-important doctrines; we
have studied them, and that is enough." Brethren, when a
boy goes to school, he may say, "If I learn arithmetic, I shall
be able to be a tradesman, and that is what I shall be; I do
not want to read that dry Latin book; I do not care to read
that book of poetry; it does not matter about my writing such
a very elegant round hand." But the schoolmaster says, "My
boy, you are put under my teaching to learn all things, and it
is not for you to pick and choose what class you will attend."
Now, we are scholars under the tuition of the blessed Spirit,
and it is not for us to say, "I will learn the doctrine of justification by faith, and when I know that, I shall not trouble my
mind about election, I shall not raise any question about
final perseverance, I shall not enquire into the ordinances,
whether believer's baptism or infant baptism is right; I take
no interest in these things; I have learned the essential
matter, and I will neglect the rest." Thou will not say this if
thou art an obedient disciple, for dost thou not know that the
ministers of Christ have received a commission to teach all
things that Christ has taught them, and dost thou think that
our commission is frivolous and vexatious? Dost thou think
that Christ would bid us teach thee what it is no need of thee
to learn, or, especially, that the Holy Ghost would himself
come to dwell in the midst of his church and to teach them

all things, when out of those "all things" there are, according
to thy vain supposition, some things that were quite as well,
if not better, left alone? Brethren, whatever the Lord has
spoken as a master, concerns his servants: whatsoever he
has delivered as a prophet, concerns his disciples: whatsoever he has spoken as a friend, concerns us, his friends,
and whatsoever he has taught us as Lord, concerns everyone
of us as members of his body, of his flesh and his bones.

I must again reiterate this truth. I do not think I can leave
it without trying still further to impress it upon your minds.
There is a tendency, among us all, I suppose, to choose some
part of the truth, and attach undue importance to that, to
the neglect of other truths.

It is a grave question if this is not the origin of various
divisions which are to be found in the Church of Christ—not
so much heresy, as the attaching of disproportionate
importance to some truth, to the disparaging or neglecting of
others equally necessary. Some brother speaking to me the
other day, declared of a certain truth, "You cannot have too
much of a good thing." Whereupon I remarked, that a nose
was a good thing, but it might be possible so to exaggerate it
that you would spoil the beauty of the face; a mouth is a good
thing, and yet it may be very possible to have such a mouth
that there would be no particular beauty about the visage,
for the beauty of the man consists in proportion, and the
beauty of divine truth consists in the proportion in which
every part of it is brought into view. Now, there be some who
exaggerate one feature, and some another. There are some
brethren who are fond of what is called "the high side" of
doctrine. I am fond of it, too, very fond of it, but there is a
temptation to bring that out, and to neglect, perhaps, the
practical part of the gospel, and to cast into the background,
possibly, the invitations of the gospel, and those truths
which concern our usefulness in the world. Then, on the
other hand, there are some who are so enamoured of
experience that nothing but experimental truth will suit
them; they must be always harping upon that one string,
and they look down with contempt upon those who hold fast
doctrinal truth, which is very wrong, and shows that they
have not yet been led into all truth. Alas! how many are so
taken up with practical teaching that they grow legal for

want of having the salt of the doctrines of grace to keep them right. But oh! if it were possible for our minds to hold all truth, as far as a finite mind could grasp it! If we could but cast aside the prejudices of education, and, perhaps, of constitution, too, and say to the Holy Spirit, "My Lord, I will bind myself neither to this party nor to that; I will subscribe neither to this formula nor to that. I am prepared to receive thy mind into my mind; I am prepared to give up much that I hold dear, if thou wilt show me that it is not according to thy will, and I am prepared to receive the gospel from thee, as thou shalt be pleased to show it to me!" It is all truth, and not some truth, that the Holy Spirit comes to teach. To teach his children truth in all its harmony, truth in all its parts, truth indeed, as a whole.

But it may be said, "There must be some truths which are not so essential as others!" That is granted. There are some truths that are so vital to salvation and peace with God, and there are some others that do not vitally concern the regeneration and conversion of the soul, and upon these men may be in error, and yet not risk their souls for all eternity. But still, even these truths are part of the whole body of truth, and the body cannot do without its head and its heart, though it might lose a limb. Yet is that a reason why I should chop off a limb, or consent to have it maimed, because I could still exist without it? I could exist without an eye; shall I not, therefore, mind being blinded? There may be a bone in my body, possibly there are several, the use of which even the anatomist does not know. There are some nerves, especially nerves in connection with the organs of secretion, the use of which are not known to the best physiologists, but nobody, I suppose, would like to dispense with them.

Because each man who thinks must feel that that God who made the man knew best how to make him perfect, and how to adapt him to the position in which he would be placed. There may be bones or nerves in the human system which will never be used but once in our lives; and yet if they were not there we might not be able to get through that particular juncture. So is it with the truths of Scripture. There may be a truth which I shall never want to use, and which may never have a practical turn to serve in my life but once, and then if I do not happen to know that truth just at that time, I may entail on myself a host of sorrows through my own ignorance, but which I ought to have prevented.

The Holy Spirit comes to teach all truth, and I beg yet again for the fourth time to reiterate that all truth must be necessary for you and for me, or else the Spirit of God would not have come to teach it to us, and that while we may give more prominent importance to the greater and more vital truths, yet there is not one truth in Scripture to which we are allowed to say, "Be still; be quiet; we do not want you." Brethren, how many of you might be happy if you did but study doctrinal truth! You go lean and starved through the world, because your minister does not preach the doctrines of grace, does not give you the full weight of the truths of the sovereign grace of God.

Still, if you but studied them for yourselves, you might yet have a bright eye, and an elastic, bounding footstep, and rejoice in the everlasting love of God, which never leaves his people, but preserves and glorifies them in the end.

And some, too, are always groaning from a sense of inward corruption, and very properly studying their own hearts, but they might live gladsome, triumphant lives if they did but learn a little more of the liberty wherewith Christ makes his people free, and seek to drink in the precious truths of our standing in Christ, and our perfection in him. It is the wilful neglect or refusal to believe some majestic truth, that is the cause of nearly all our doubts and fears, and a great many other pieces of mischief that keep us from serving and honouring our Lord as he deserves to be served and honoured by those who are not their own, but are bought with a price.

This first point we may now leave, if the Holy Spirit will but bring it home with power to our souls, for this truth, among others, must be taught us by him. We now come to a second point, which is clearly in the text, namely, not only the value of all truth that our Lord Jesus Christ has spoken, but:—

II. THE NEED OF THE HOLY SPIRIT TO TEACH US ALL THE TRUTH.

But cannot an honest and a willing mind learn all the truth that is in Scripture, without the teaching of the Holy Spirit? I infer that it cannot, from the fact that the *Holy*

Spirit is provided. There is nothing that is unnecessary in the covenant of grace, and the divine Power is never unnecessarily exerted. It is constantly remarked of the miracles that there is not one of them that can be dispensed with, and God never interferes to do out of the course of nature what might be done according to the ordinary laws of nature. If the Christian were fully equipped to know and understand the divine mind without the teaching of the Holy Spirit, then the Holy Spirit would not have been given. We should not find the Holy Spirit here unless it were necessary that he should be here. Even with Christ for a teacher, mark—so that there was no fault in the teacher—with Christ for a teacher, the disciples did not learn these truths without the teaching of the Holy Spirit. I infer, therefore, that much more is that teaching now necessary, and that the Spirit of God should abide with us, to teach us truth, and to bring the things which we have learned to our remembrance. And why? Is it not because *there is a radical defect in us as disciples?* Are we not frequently inattentive? Do we not sometimes feel a want of interest in the truths which we receive from the Word, which I may now call the lips of Christ? A child may be very plainly taught, but if you cannot get its attention, if you cannot catch its will, and interest it, it will not learn much, but that which you teach it will glide like oil over a slab of marble; it does not penetrate and permeate, and consequently is not properly and thoroughly learned. And often on the Lord's Day you will hear most delightful truth, but if you are not interested in it, it does not catch your mind.

And in reading Scripture, how seldom do we show as much interest as we do in reading a letter from a friend? With what glistening eyes will some persons read the will of their relatives, and they never forget what they read there, because mind and heart are deeply interested.

But, alas! how often do we turn from these sacred pages without enough interest to learn what is in them!

We are not so roused as eagerly to drink in their spirit. We do not bring our souls up to the truth, and it is not any wonder, therefore, if we do not learn those truths which are so spiritual, that they cannot only be grasped by a soul in active, alert exercise.

Besides this, we do not learn, because of *our ready prejudice against the special truth we ought to learn.* A great part of God's truth is very unpalatable to human nature: to learn it is something like taking bitter medicine: people do not choose it with enthusiasm.

There are some truths which would always be unpalatable, even to Christians, Christians as they are, if it were not for the sugar which sometimes goes with the truth, and but for this it would be very nauseous to them. There are some minds which seem more than others to kick against certain points of divine truth, either from their prejudices, their education, or the nature and force of their constitution; and it is only the Spirit of God who can come and irresistibly convince the understanding. Ah! friends, when the scholar does not want to know, it needs a God to teach him; and sometimes our minds do not wish to know the truth. I should not like to say a hard thing of God's people, but I believe there are many of them who do not want to know too much. I have thought often that it has been the case with myself, and I believe it is the case with others. There is an awkward truth which, if it were learned, would throw us out of our present comfortable position, and might even necessitate a change of our ecclesiastical connections if we were to know it, and so we do not want to know it. We do not read any book that might make us know it. We try to look at things on our own side if we can, and do not look fairly at the subject, nor enquire into it. It must, therefore, need the Spirit of God to teach us when truth is so unpalatable, and we are so unwilling to learn it. Then, besides this, beloved, when we recollect *the intense spirituality of truth,* and how our carnal natures are always prone to adulterate it with our own predilections and the notions of the flesh; when all things around us bring down the truth from its high spiritual atmosphere, where alone it can flourish, into the smoky, cloudy region of our materialism, bring down food worthy of angels, to become poor bread even for mortals, then we see how desperately we need the Holy Spirit to help us as learners in the school of Christ.

We seize the fair fruit of divine truth with a careless, hasty hand, mar its heavenly bloom, never knowing its richest beauty and essence, and then we feel how true of us are Paul's words, inspired of the Holy Spirit, written to certain Christians, "Not as unto spiritual, but as unto carnal, and babes in Christ Jesus."

These, then, are a few of the reasons why the Spirit of God is needed. There are plenty more, of which we will speak another day, but I think every Christian knows experimentally that he never does learn the truth fully, and hold it tenaciously, except by the teaching and sustaining grace of God the Holy Spirit. I like our young people to learn the *Westminster Assembly's Confession of Faith.* It is a "form of sound words" that is well worth committing to memory; but even Christian people when they know them will find that, unless those truths are one by one brought home to the soul, they have only the shell of truth, but do not know the life and inner essence of it. We must have everything we truly learn burnt into us by the Holy Ghost. It must be taught us sometimes by painful experience, at other times by blissful enjoyment; sometimes by a marvelous illumination, a light shining upon a passage in such a way that we see it as we never saw it before, and though we may have read it twenty times, we now for the first time in our lives see its true meaning, and rejoice therein. Why, dear friends, what is the ministry without the Spirit of God? Do you not often come and go, and find no comfort in attending a place of worship? And even the Bible itself without the Spirit of God is but a lantern without a light, and what is even the mercy-seat, except the Holy Spirit be there, enabling us to drink into the very life and soul of the divine teaching. It is not that Book as it is there on the paper; it is that Book as it must be written on the fleshy tablets of our heart, which becomes to us the Word of God, the word of our salvation in which we rejoice, and upon which we often feed.

This second truth you know, and will never doubt, that we need the Holy Spirit to teach us truth. The third thing that is in the text is this—the Holy Spirit is said not only to teach us, but:—

III. TO BRING TO OUR REMEMBRANCE THE TRUTH WHICH WE HAVE RECEIVED.

Mark! The Holy Spirit does not now reveal fresh truth, beyond what is already in the Word of God. There is a special curse pronounced upon any who shall add to this Book; and you may rest assured that the Holy Spirit will not so transgress in a matter which he has peremptorily forbidden all his children to commit. When persons start up as prophets, or prophetesses, and tell us that they have had special visions from the Lord, and they know what is going to happen next year, we always understand that their proper destination is Bethlehem Hospital, and we begin directly to shun them and their books. We are persuaded that the Holy Spirit makes no such fresh revelations to men now, but teaches us what Christ taught, bringing all these things to our remembrance. What Christ has taught, and only that, it is his joyous work to make plain and clear, and powerful, to us.

Why do we need to have the truths thus spoken brought to our remembrance? Is it not that *we often trust our memories* not to forget these truths, but, "he who trusts his own heart is a fool," and so is he who relies absolutely on his own memory. For anything bad, alas! we may trust it only too well: we are sure to recollect the thing far better forgotten. But if it be anything very good and soul-inspiring, memory has a paralysis in the fingers, and cannot retain it in their grasp. You may remember a great many things in business; these are sure to write themselves deeply on the memory, but divine things, which concern the future state, are often written so illegibly that they are very readily blurred, blotted out, and we need the Holy Spirit to bring these things to our remembrance.

And then, again, *we are so constantly beset with cares* that it is little marvelous that the things of God should slip away from us. You have but one day in the week, as it were, devoted to these things; one day of building, and six of pulling down. With many it is one day's storing, and six days' scattering. It is but a slight advance that we make towards heaven. Believe me, it is one of the greatest joys of my heart to see you here so constantly at prayer meetings and on lecture nights, and it always seems to me to be one of the best signs of vital godliness that can well be exhibited, except a holy life, to see people willing to come out to the weeknight services; any hypocrite will come on Sundays, but to come on weekdays seems to me to be a favourable sign, and a proof of sincerity. But even then how little do we get! Perhaps there is trouble in the family; from the first thing in the morning till the last thing at night it is nothing but hard work, and there is the looking for the wherewithal we shall be clothed, and we do not always cast our care on him who careth for us. So, the thorns too often choke up the seed, and did not the Holy Spirit bring these things to our remembrance, they might quickly slip away altogether.

There is, again, brethren, another reason for needing to be reminded of these truths, namely, because *we forget what we do not thoroughly apprehend.* I have a notion that, as a rule, what a man thoroughly understands, through and through, he does not forget. When you have mastered a fact or truth, seen it from all points, grown familiar with it, it is not easy to let it slip. You may hold a joint of meat in your hand, and be very hungry all the while. But cook your joint, eat of it, and properly digest what you eat, and it is yours, and hunger goes. The man who receives truth in the mere letter of it may quickly forget it, but he who has received it in the spirit, understood it, digested it, assimilated it, will never altogether lose its nourishing and upbuilding power. When truth is understood, it is somewhat like it was with the boy from whom the priest took away his New Testament. "Ah!" said the boy, "but what will you do with the ten chapters that I have learned by heart. You cannot take those away."

Memory does not readily lose the things she really understands, and when the heart has penetrated into the marrow of truth, and truth into the marrow of the heart, it abides. But, alas! with the most of divine things, we do not seek to enter into them as we should. We hear them, and that is all; we hear, but we do not understand, and hence the Spirit of God is needed to ring the bells of heaven again and again in our ears, and to make us hear the same truth over and over again, bringing to remembrance what Christ has told us.

If it be asked how he does this, the answer is, that he does it by instrumentality, as well as by his own immediate action. He does it through the preaching of the Word. The Word of God brings to your mind the old truth that you have heard ever since you were a boy, or girl, and, thank God, it has not lost its preciousness, but is just as sweet to your ears now as it was when you heard it from old Dr. So-and-so, who has now gone home to heaven. Thank God you love that truth still, whenever it is brought to your remembrance. I like to use the same Bible always in my study, and to mark it, so that I may afterwards know the places which once filled me with delight and comfort, and sometimes the good old book which we have studied so long will thus bring things to our remembrance. Then there is communion with Christian brethren. Sometimes even an illiterate Christian brother may set a truth in such a light as you never saw it in before, just like some of those fine old pieces of architecture which are very fine from one point of view, but some day you are taken to another point, and you say, "Well, I think it is even more beautiful from this place of revealing than from the other." So my intercourse with Christian brethren often sheds for me a new light upon long-known and precious truth. But over and above all this, I believe that the Holy Spirit does actually come into contact with our spirits, apart from human instrumentality, and that when we are walking by the way, sitting in the house, or in our chamber of prayer, flashes sudden light upon the truth, and so we learn what we knew not before, and turning to God's Word we perceive it to be blest truth that was always there, but which we had not seen until the Holy Spirit opened our eyes. Brethren and sisters, if we do not know experimentally what it is to have the truth as it is in Jesus brought to our remembrance by the Holy Spirit, we must not rest satisfied until we do, for this is one of the marks and evidences, as well as one of the privileges of the child of God, that the Holy Spirit is his personal teacher. "All thy children shall be taught of the Lord," and again and again does the adorable Third Person of the Divine Trinity teach us the things of Christ, and bring them constantly to our remembrance.

I am sorry that I cannot enter more fully into this point for want of time, but we must new close with the last point, which is a question for us all:—

IV. HOW FAR HAS THIS OFFICE OF THE HOLY GHOST BEEN PERFORMED IN US?

I will first ask those of you who profess to be *the people of God:* Has the Holy Ghost taught you anything? Is that a hard question? It is one that was asked of old: "Have ye received the Holy Ghost since ye believed?" I am solemnly

afraid that there are some professors who are content to
have been convinced of sin, to have been led to trust in
Christ, but who, after that, are utterly indifferent to the
Holy Spirit as their teacher. They sit in the house of God, but
they do not apply their minds to learn the truth. They pin
their faith to somebody's sleeve, and are content to believe
according to the last speaker they hear, so that they will one
day believe one thing, and another day another thing, and so
are carried about with every wind of doctrine. Brethren,
these things ought not to be. Receiving Christ as a priest, we
ought also to receive him as a prophet, and if we be
quickened by the Holy Ghost, we ought also to seek to be
illuminated and instructed by him. Have you and I felt the
Holy Spirit at work with us, endearing doctrine, and making
it more precious to us? Have we, indeed, ever sought his
influence, or have we, though professing Christians, lived
thoughtlessly in this respect? Do you not think that if we
have done so, we have grieved the Holy Spirit? What grieves
a man more than to deny the importance of the office and
work for which he lives? What should grieve the Holy Spirit
more than this, among other things, to forget his office as
our instructor, and to ignore altogether the great purpose for
which he is to be found in the midst of the Christian Church
at all times? Surely we should be seeking with all our
prayers to pray, "Teach me, O God! and lead me in the plain
truth!" and we should long to sit with Mary at the Master's
feet. Do you really study your Bibles, my dear brothers and
sisters? Why you can scarcely bring out a magazine or a
newspaper nowadays, and make it pay, even with religious
people, without a tale! It is one of the signs of the times that
feeble fiction reading is as common among Christians as
among others, and that our young disciples, young men and
women both, must have a sensational novel in a religious
form, or they will not read at all. Time was when Christian
women, as well as men, read history, studied the fasci-
nations of science, and cultivated their best qualities of mind
and heart. And Christian men in days past, in the Puritanic
and later ages, sought to be acquainted with solid literature,
as well as with the Word of God. But it seems to be the last
mark of the degeneracy of God's people that they must have
their ears tickled with a straw, and cannot read solid truth.

You need not wonder that we cannot breed men on chaff, or
that they are blown about with every wind of doctrine, when
this is the food on which they live. There are certain
silkworms which grow the colour of the leaves they feed on,
and you may depend upon it that those who live on this
frivolous literature will lead frivolous lives, and those who
take nothing but these milk-and-water tales will not be
likely to have about them anything solid or robust, or
anything vigorously real. Do not talk to me of reading such
things! Brethren, when you and I have read our Bibles
through so as to find nothing there to interest us, it is high
time that we asked God to teach us how to read them. It is a
sign of a want of grace if the Bible is a dry book. It is a dry
book, a very dry book, to a graceless soul, but it has more in
it than all the rest of the volumes in the world put together;
and the more it is studied the more will the interest of the
student in it increase. Besides, we have such an abundance
of other Christian literature that no Christian ought to say
he is obliged to read the other poor stuff. We have no time to
spare for this, when the soul is starving and dying for lack of
knowledge. Let us pray the Holy Spirit to lead us into the
Word of God, and then give ourselves to its earnest and
loving study.

But this question will scarcely refer at all to some now
present. My dear hearers, are you *among those who have no
interest in these things?*

It is not likely that you should desire the Holy Spirit to
instruct you. There are, I fear, some here who have no hope,
and are without God in the world. The mere statement of the
fact ought to excite us all to prayer for such. But, alas! it is
so commonly known that there are many out of Christ, and
without hope, that we do not feel distressed about it as we
should. If there were fewer unregenerate sinners than there
are, we should probably be more concerned about them. If
there were only a dozen unconverted persons in the world,
all the Church of God would be praying for their conversion,
but because there are many millions of them, they are so
common, that we do not look upon them with the awe, the
tenderness, and the yearning sympathy which we ought to
feel.

There are some here to whom the Holy Spirit is an

unknown person, who have never been made alive unto God by him, and consequently cannot desire that they may be instructed by him. Oh! that the blessed Spirit would come and convince them of their sin in not believing, which is the greatest of all sins, and the very sin of which the Spirit comes to convince men. "He shall convince them of sin because they believe not on me." Oh! may he convince them of this sin, and then may they understand that there is nothing for them to do, but that Christ has done it for them, and that all they have to do is to receive the finished work, to wear the finished robe, to look to Jesus Christ, and to find life in the look. Pray for them, brethren, that the Holy Ghost may help their infirmities, that they may know Christ, and may come to him. May God bless the gospel to them whenever it is preached, and when they are told that "the Son of Man came into the world to seek and to save that which was lost," may they cry unto him, and trust him, for this is the vital part of the business, and, trusting in him, they shall enter into eternal life through Jesus Christ our Lord.

20

The Holy Spirit's Intercession

"Likewise the Spirit also helpeth our infirmities: for we know not what we should pray for as we ought: but the Spirit itself maketh intercession for us with groanings which cannot be uttered. And he that searcheth the hearts knoweth what is the mind of the Spirit, because he maketh intercession for the saints according to the will of God."   Romans 8:26-27

The Apostle Paul was writing to a tried and afflicted people, and one of his objects was to remind them of the rivers of comfort which were flowing near at hand. He first of all stirred up their pure minds by way of remembrance as to their sonship,—for, saith he, "as many as are led by the Spirit of God, they are the sons of God." They were, therefore, encouraged to take part and lot with Christ, the elder brother, with whom they had become joint heirs; and they were exhorted to suffer with him, that they might afterwards be glorified with him. All that they endured came from a Father's hand, and this should comfort them. A thousand sources of joy are opened in that one blessing of adoption. Blessed be the God and Father of our Lord Jesus Christ, by whom we have been begotten into the family of grace.

When Paul had alluded to that consoling subject he turned to the next ground of comfort—namely, that we are to be sustained under present trial by hope. There is an amazing glory in reserve for us, and though as yet we cannot enter upon it, but in harmony with the whole creation must continue to groan and travail, yet the hope itself should minister strength to us, and enable us patiently to bear "these light afflictions, which are but for a moment." This

also is a truth full of sacred refreshment: hope sees a crown
in reserve, mansions in readiness, and Jesus himself preparing a place for us, and by the rapturous sight she
sustains the soul under the sorrows of the hour. Hope is the
grand anchor by whose means we ride out the present
storm.

The apostle then turns to a third source of comfort,
namely, the abiding of the Holy Spirit in and with the Lord's
people. He uses the word "likewise" to intimate that in the
same manner as hope sustains the soul, so does the Holy
Spirit strengthen us under trial. Hope operates spiritually
upon our spiritual faculties, and so does the Holy Spirit, in
some mysterious way, divinely operate upon the new-born
faculties of the believer, so that he is sustained under his
infirmities. In his light shall we see light: I pray, therefore,
that we may be helped of the Spirit while we consider his
mysterious operations, that we may not fall into error or
miss precious truth through blindness of heart.

The text speaks of "our infirmities," or as many translators
put it in the singular—of "our infirmity." By this is intended
our affliction, and the weakness which trouble discovers in
us. The Holy Spirit helps us to bear the infirmity of our body
and of our mind; he helps us to bear our cross, whether it be
physical pain, or mental depression, or spiritual conflict, or
slander, or poverty, or persecution. He helps our infirmity;
and with a helper so divinely strong we need not fear for the
result. God's grace will be sufficient for us; his strength will
be made perfect in weakness.

I think, dear friends, you will all admit that if a man can
pray, his trouble is at once lightened. When we feel that we
have power with God and can obtain anything we ask for at
his hands, then our difficulties cease to oppress us. We take
our burden to our heavenly Father and tell it out in the
accents of childlike confidence, and we come away quite
content to bear whatever his holy will may lay upon us.
Prayer is a great outlet for grief; it draws up the sluices, and
abates the swelling flood, which else might be too strong for
us. We bathe our wound in the lotion of prayer, and the pain
is lulled, the fever is removed. But the worst of it is that in
certain conditions of heart we cannot pray. We may be
brought into such perturbation of mind, and perplexity of

heart, that we do not know how to pray. We see the mercy-seat, and we perceive that God will hear us: we have no doubt about that, for we know that we are his own favoured children, and yet we hardly know what to desire. We fall into such heaviness of spirit, and entanglement of thought, that the one remedy of prayer, which we have always found to be unfailing, appears to be taken from us. Here, then, in the nick of time, as a very present help in time of trouble, comes in the Holy Spirit. He draws near to teach us how to pray, and in this way he helps our infirmity, relieves our suffering, and enables us to bear the heavy burden without fainting under the load.

At this time our subjects for consideration shall be, firstly, *the help which the Holy Spirit gives:* secondly, *the prayers which he inspires;* and thirdly, *the success which such prayers are certain to obtain.*

I. First, then, let us consider THE HELP WHICH THE HOLY GHOST GIVES.

The help which the Holy Ghost renders to us meets the weakness which we deplore. As I have already said, if in time of trouble a man can pray, his burden loses its weight. If the believer can take anything and everything to God, then he learns to glory in infirmity, and to rejoice in tribulation; but sometimes we are in such confusion of mind that we know not what we should pray for as we ought. In a measure, through our ignorance, we never know what we should pray for until we are taught of the Spirit of God, but there are times when this beclouding of the soul is dense indeed, and we do not even know what would help us out of our trouble if we could obtain it. We see the disease, but the name of the medicine is not known to us. We look over the many things which we might ask for of the Lord, and we feel that each of them would be helpful, but that none of them would precisely meet our case. For spiritual blessings which we know to be according to the divine will we could ask with confidence, but perhaps these would not meet our peculiar circumstances. There are other things for which we are allowed to ask, but we scarcely know whether, if we had them, they would really serve our turn, and we also feel a diffidence as to praying for them. In praying for temporal things we plead with measured voices, ever referring our petition for revision to the will of the Lord. Moses prayed that he might enter Canaan, but God denied him; and the man that was healed asked our Lord that he might be with him, but he received for an answer, "Go home to thy friends." We pray evermore on such matters with this reserve, "Nevertheless, not as I will, but as thou wilt." At times this very spirit of resignation appears to increase our mental difficulty, for we do not wish to ask for anything that would be contrary to the mind of God, and yet we must ask for something. We are reduced to such straits that we must pray, but what shall be the particular subject of prayer we cannot for a while make out. Even when ignorance and perplexity are removed, we know not what we should pray for "as we ought." When we know the matter of prayer, we yet fail to pray in a right manner. We ask, but we are afraid that we shall not have, because we do not exercise the thought, or the faith, which we judge to be essential to prayer. We cannot at times command even the earnestness which is the life of supplication: a torpor steals over us, our heart is chilled, our hand is numbed, and we cannot wrestle with the angel. We know what to pray for as to objects, but we do not know what to pray for "as we ought." It is the manner of the prayer which perplexes us, even when the matter is decided upon. How can I pray? My mind wanders: I chatter like a crane; I roar like a beast in pain; I moan in the brokenness of my heart, but oh, my God, I know not what it is my inmost spirit needs; or if I know it, I know not how to frame my petition aright before thee. I know not how to open my lips in thy majestic presence: I am so troubled that I cannot speak. My spiritual distress robs me of the power to pour out my heart before my God. Now, beloved, it is in such a plight as this that the Holy Ghost aids us with his divine help, and hence he is "a very present help in time of trouble."

Coming to our aid in our bewilderment *he instructs us.* This is one of his frequent operations upon the mind of the believer: "He shall teach you all things." He instructs us as to our need, and as to the promises of God which refer to that need. He shows us where our deficiencies are, what our sins are, and what our necessities are; he sheds a light upon our condition, and makes us feel deeply our helplessness, sinfulness, and dire poverty; and then he casts the same light upon the promises of the Word, and lays home to the heart that very text which was intended to meet the occasion—the precise promise which was framed with foresight of our present distress. In that light he makes the promise shine in all its truthfulness, certainty, sweetness, and suitability, so that we, poor trembling sons of men, dare take that word into our mouth which first came out of God's mouth, and then come with it as an argument, and plead it before the throne of the heavenly grace. Our prevalence in prayer lies in the plea, "Lord, do as thou hast said." How greatly we ought to value the Holy Spirit, because when we are in the dark he gives us light, and when our perplexed spirit is so befogged and beclouded that it cannot see its own need, and cannot find out the appropriate promise in the Scriptures, the Spirit of God comes in and teaches us all things, and brings all things to our remembrance, whatsoever our Lord has told us. He guides us in prayer, and thus he helps our infirmity.

But the blessed Spirit does more than this, he will often *direct the mind to the special subject of prayer.* He dwells within us as a counsellor, and points out to us what it is we should seek at the hands of God. We do not know why it is so, but we sometimes find our minds carried as by a strong under-current into a particular line of prayer for some one definite object. It is not merely that our judgment leads us in that direction, though usually the Spirit of God acts upon us by enlightening our judgment, but we often feel an unaccountable and irresistible desire rising again and again within our heart, and this so presses upon us, that we not only utter the desire before God at our ordinary times for prayer, but we feel it crying in our hearts all the day long, almost to the supplanting of all other considerations. At such times we should thank God for direction and give our desire a clear road: the Holy Spirit is granting us inward direction as to how we should order our petitions before the throne of grace, and we may now reckon upon good success in our pleadings. Such guidance will the Spirit give to each of you if you will ask him to illuminate you. He will guide you both negatively and positively. Negatively, he will forbid you to pray for such and such a thing, even as Paul assayed to go into Bithynia, but the Spirit suffered him not: and, on the other hand, he will cause you to hear a cry within your soul which shall guide your petitions, even as he made Paul hear the cry from Macedonia, saying, "Come over and help us." The Spirit teaches wisely, as no other teacher can do. Those who obey his promptings shall not walk in darkness. He leads the spiritual eye to take good and steady aim at the very centre of the target, and thus we hit the mark in our pleadings.

Nor is this all, for the Spirit of God is not sent merely to guide and help our devotion, but *he himself "maketh intercession for us"* according to the will of God. By this expression it cannot be meant that the Holy Spirit ever groans or personally prays; but that *he excites intense desire and creates unutterable groanings in us,* and these are ascribed to him. Even as Solomon built the temple because he superintended and ordained all, and yet I know not that he ever fashioned a timber or prepared a stone, so doth the Holy Spirit pray and plead within us by leading us to pray and plead. This he does by arousing our desires. The Holy Spirit has a wonderful power over renewed hearts, as much power as the skillful minstrel hath over the strings among which he lays his accustomed hand. The influences of the Holy Ghost at times pass through the soul like winds through an Eolian harp, creating and inspiring sweet notes of gratitude and tones of desire, to which we should have been strangers if it had not been for his divine visitation. He knows how to create in our spirit hunger and thirst for good things. He can arouse us from our spiritual lethargy, he can warm us out of our lukewarmness, he can enable us when we are on our knees to rise above the ordinary routine of prayer into that victorious importunity against which nothing can stand. He can lay certain desires so pressingly upon our hearts that we can never rest till they are fulfilled. He can make the zeal for God's house to eat us up, and the passion for God's glory to be like a fire within our bones; and this is one part of that process by which in inspiring our prayers he helps our infirmity. True Advocate is he, and Comforter most effectual. Blessed be his name.

The Holy Spirit also divinely operates in the *strengthening of the faith of believers.* That faith is at first of his creating, and afterwards it is of his sustaining and increasing: and oh, brothers and sisters, have you not often felt your faith rise in proportion to your trials? Have you not, like Noah's ark, mounted towards heaven as the flood deepened around you? You have felt as sure about the promise as you felt about the trial. The affliction was, as it were, in your very bones, but the promise was also in your very heart. You could not doubt the affliction, for you smarted under it, but you might almost as soon have doubted that you were afflicted as have doubted the divine help, for your confidence was firm and unmoved. The greatest faith is only what God has a right to expect from us, yet do we never exhibit it except as the Holy Ghost strengthens our confidence, and opens up before us the covenant with all its seals and securities. He it is that leads our soul to cry, "Though my house be not so with God, yet hath he made with me an everlasting covenant ordered in all things and sure." Blessed be the Divine Spirit then, that since faith is essential to prevailing prayer, he helps us in supplication by increasing our faith. Without faith prayer cannot speed, for he that wavereth is like a wave of the sea driven with the wind and tossed, and such an one may not expect anything of the Lord; happy are we when the Holy Spirit removes our wavering, and enables us like Abraham to believe without staggering, knowing full well that he who has promised is able also to perform.

By three figures I will endeavour to describe the work of the Spirit of God in this matter, though they all fall short, and indeed all that I can say must fall infinitely short of the glory of his work. The actual mode of his working upon the mind we may not attempt to explain; it remains a mystery, and it would be an unholy intrusion to attempt to remove the veil. There is no difficulty in our believing that as one human mind operates upon another mind, so does the Holy Spirit influence our spirits. We are forced to use words if we would influence our fellow-men, but the Spirit of God can operate upon the human mind more directly, and communicate with it in silence. Into that matter, however, we will not dive lest we intrude where our knowledge would be drowned by our presumption.

My illustrations do not touch the mystery, but set forth the grace. The Holy Spirit acts to his people somewhat as a *prompter to a reciter.* A man has to deliver a piece which he has learned; but his memory is treacherous, and therefore somewhere out of sight there is a prompter, so that when the speaker is at a loss and might use a wrong word, a whisper is heard, which suggests the right one. When the speaker has almost lost the thread of his discourse he turns his ear, and the prompter gives him the catch-word and aids his memory. If I may be allowed the simile, I would say that this represents in part the work of the Spirit of God in us,— suggesting to us the right desire, and bringing all things to our remembrance whatsoever Christ has told us. In prayer we should often come to a dead stand, but he incites, suggests, and inspires, and so we go onward. In prayer we might grow weary, but the Comforter encourages and refreshes us with cheering thoughts. When, indeed, we are in our bewilderment almost driven to give up prayer, the whisper of his love drops a live coal from off the altar into our soul, and our hearts glow with greater ardour than before. Regard the Holy Spirit as your prompter, and let your ear be opened to his voice.

But he is much more than this. Let me attempt a second simile: he is *as an advocate to one in peril at law.* Suppose that a poor man had a great law-suit, touching his whole estate, and he was forced personally to go into court and plead his own cause, and speak up for his rights. If he were an uneducated man he would be in a poor plight. An adversary in the court might plead against him, and overthrow him, for he could not answer him. This poor man knows very little about the law, and is quite unable to meet his cunning opponent. Suppose one who was perfect in the law should take up his cause warmly, and come and live with him, and use all his knowledge so as to prepare his case for him, draw up his petitions for him, and fill his mouth with arguments,—would not that be a grand relief? This counsellor would suggest the line of pleading, arrange the arguments, and put them into right courtly language. When the poor man was baffled by a question asked in court, he would run home and ask his adviser, and he would tell him exactly how to meet the objector. Suppose, too, that when he had to plead with the judge himself, this advocate at home should teach him how to behave and what to urge, and encourage him to hope that he would prevail,—would not this be a great boon? Who would be the pleader in such a case? The poor client would plead, but still, when he won the suit, he would trace it all to the advocate who lived at home, and gave him counsel: indeed, it would be the advocate pleading for him, even while he pleaded himself. This is an instructive emblem of a great fact. Within this narrow house of my body, this tenement of clay, if I be a true believer, there dwells the Holy Ghost, and when I desire to pray I may ask him what I should pray for as I ought, and he will help me. He will write the prayers which I ought to offer upon the tablets of my heart, and I shall see them there, and so I shall be taught how to plead. It will be the Spirit's own self pleading in me, and by me, and through me, before the throne of grace. What a happy man in his law-suit would such a poor man be, and how happy are you and I that we have the Holy Ghost to be our Counsellor!

Yet one more illustration: it is that of *a father aiding his boy.* Suppose it to be a time of war centuries back. Old English warfare was then conducted by bowmen to a great extent. Here is a youth who is to be initiated in the art of archery, and therefore he carries a bow. It is a strong bow, and therefore very hard to draw; indeed, it requires more strength than the urchin can summon to bend it. See how his father teaches him. "Put your right hand here, my boy, and place your left hand so. Now pull"; and as the youth pulls, his father's hands are on his hands, and the bow is drawn. The lad draws the bow: ay, but it is quite as much his father, too. We cannot draw the bow of prayer alone. Sometimes a bow of steel is not broken by our hands, for we cannot even bend it; and then the Holy Ghost puts his mighty hand over ours, and covers our weakness so that we draw; and lo, what splendid drawing of the bow it is then! The bow bends so easily we wonder how it is; away flies the arrow, and it pierces the very centre of the target, for he who giveth the strength directeth the aim. We rejoice to think that we have won the day, but it was his secret might that made us strong, and to him be the glory of it.

Thus have I tried to set forth the cheering fact that the Spirit helps the people of God.

II. Our second subject is THE PRAYER WHICH THE HOLY

SPIRIT INSPIRES, or that part of prayer which is especially and peculiarly the work of the Spirit of God. The text says, "The Spirit itself maketh intercession for us with groanings which cannot be uttered." It is not the Spirit that groans, but we that groan; but as I have shown you, the Spirit excites the emotion which causes us to groan.

It is clear then the prayers which are indited in us by the Spirit of God are *those which arise from our inmost soul.* A man's *heart* is moved when he groans. A groan is a matter about which there is no hypocrisy. A groan cometh not from the lips, but from the heart. A groan then is a part of prayer which we owe to the Holy Ghost, and the same is true of all the prayer which wells up from the deep fountains of our inner life. The prophet cried, "My bowels, my bowels, I am pained at my very heart: my heart maketh a noise in me." This deep ground-swell of desire, this tidal motion of the life-floods is caused by the Holy Spirit. His work is never superficial, but always deep and inward.

Such prayers will rise within us when the mind is far too troubled to let us speak. We know not what we should pray for as we ought, and then it is that we groan, or utter some other inarticulate sound. Hezekiah said, "Like a crane or a swallow did I chatter." The psalmist said, "I am so troubled that I cannot speak." In another place he said, "I am feeble and sore broken: I have roared by reason of the disquietness of my heart"; but he added, "Lord, all my desire is before thee; and my groaning is not hid from thee." The sighing of the prisoner surely cometh up into the ears of the Lord. There is real prayer in these "groanings that cannot be uttered." It is the power of the Holy Ghost in us which creates all real prayer, even that which takes the form of a groan because the mind is incapable, by reason of its bewilderment and grief, of clothing its emotion in words. I pray you never think lightly of the supplications of your anguish. Rather judge that such prayers are like Jabez, of whom it is written, that "he was more honourable than his brethren, because his mother bare him with sorrow." That which is thrown up from the depth of the soul, when it is stirred with a terrible tempest, is more precious than pearl or coral, for it is the intercession of the Holy Spirit.

These prayers are sometimes "groanings that cannot be

uttered," because *they concern such great things that they cannot be spoken.* I want, my Lord! I want, I want; I cannot tell thee what I want; but I seem to want all things. If it were some little thing, my narrow capacity could comprehend and describe it, but I need all covenant blessings. Thou knowest what I have need of before I ask thee, and though I cannot go into each item of my need, I know it to be very great, and such as I myself can never estimate. I groan, for I can do no more. Prayers which are the offspring of great desires, sublime aspirations, and elevated designs are surely the work of the Holy Spirit, and their power within a man is frequently so great that he cannot find expression for them. Words fail, and even the sighs which try to embody them cannot be uttered.

But it may be, beloved, that *we groan because we are conscious of the littleness of our desire, and the narrowness of our faith.* The trial, too, may seem too mean to pray about. I have known what it is to feel as if I could not pray about a certain matter, and yet I have been obliged to groan about it. A thorn in the flesh may be as painful a thing as a sword in the bones, and yet we may go and beseech the Lord thrice about it, and getting no answer we may feel that we know not what to pray for as we ought; and yet it makes us groan. Yes, and with that natural groan there may go up an unutterable groaning of the Holy Spirit. Beloved, what a different view of prayer God has from that which men think to be the correct one. You may have seen very beautiful prayers in print, and you may have heard very charming compositions from the pulpit, but I trust you have not fallen in love with them. Judge these things rightly. I pray you never think well of *fine* prayers, for before the thrice holy God it ill becomes a sinful suppliant to play the orator. We heard of a certain clergyman who was said to have given forth "the finest prayer ever offered to a Boston audience." Just so! The Boston audience received the prayer, and there it ended. We want the mind of the Spirit in prayer, and not the mind of the flesh. The tail feathers of pride should be pulled out of our prayers, for they need only the wing feathers of faith; the peacock feathers of poetical expression are out of place before the throne of God. "Dear me, what remarkably beautiful language he used in prayer!" "What an

intellectual treat his prayer was!" Yes, yes; but God looks at
the heart. To him fine language is as sounding brass or a
tinkling cymbal, but a groan has music in it. We do not like
groans: our ears are much too delicate to tolerate such
dreary sounds; but not so the great Father of spirits. A
Methodist brother cries, "Amen," and you say, "I cannot bear
such Methodistic noise"; no, but if it comes from the man's
heart God can bear it. When you get upstairs into your
chamber this evening to pray, and find you cannot pray, but
have to moan out, "Lord, I am too full of anguish and too
perplexed to pray, hear thou the voice of my roaring,"
though you reach to nothing else you will be really praying.
When like David we can say, "I opened my mouth and
panted," we are by no means in an ill state of mind. All fine
language in prayer, and especially all intoning or performing
of prayers, must be abhorrent to God; it is little short of
profanity to offer solemn supplication to God after the
manner called "intoning." The sighing of a true heart is
infinitely more acceptable, for it is the work of the Spirit of
God.

We may say of the prayers which the Holy Spirit works in
us that they are *prayers of knowledge*. Notice, our difficulty
is that we know not what we should pray for; but the Holy
Spirit does know, and therefore he helps us by enabling us to
pray intelligently, knowing what we are asking for, so far as
this knowledge is needful to valid prayer. The text speaks of
the "mind of the Spirit." What a mind that must be!—the
mind of that Spirit who arranged all the order which now
pervades this earth! There was once chaos and confusion,
but the Holy Spirit brooded over all, and his mind is the
originator of that beautiful arrangement which we so admire
in the visible creation. What a mind his must be! The Holy
Spirit's mind is seen in our intercessions when under his
sacred influence we order our case before the Lord, and
plead with holy wisdom for things convenient and necessary.
What wise and admirable desires must those be which the
Spirit of Wisdom himself works in us!

Moreover, the Holy Spirit's intercession creates *prayers
offered in a proper manner*. I showed you that the difficulty
is that we know not what we should pray for "as we ought,"
and the Spirit meets that difficulty by making intercession

for us in a right manner. The Holy Spirit works in us humility, earnestness, intensity, importunity, faith, and resignation, and all else that is acceptable to God in our supplications. We know not how to mingle these sacred spices in the incense of prayer. We, if left to ourselves at our very best, get too much of one ingredient or another, and spoil the sacred compound, but the Holy Spirit's intercessions have in them such a blessed blending of all that is good that they come up as a sweet perfume before the Lord. Spirit-taught prayers are offered as they ought to be. They are his own intercession in some respects, for we read that the Holy Spirit not only helps us to intercede but "maketh intercession." It is twice over declared in our text that he maketh intercession for us; and the meaning of this I tried to show when I described a father as putting his hands upon his child's hands. This is something more than helping us to pray, something more than encouraging us or directing us,—but I venture no further, except to say that he puts such force of his own mind into our poor weak thoughts and desires and hopes, that he himself maketh intercession for us, working in us to will and to pray according to his good pleasure.

I want you to notice, however, that *these intercessions of the Holy Spirit are only in the saints.* "He maketh intercession *for us,*" and "He maketh intercession *for the saints.*" Does he do nothing for sinners, then? Yes, he quickens sinners into spiritual life, and he strives with them to overcome their sinfulness and turn them into the right way; but in the saints he works with us and enables us to pray after his mind and according to the will of God. His intercession is not in or for the unregenerate. O, unbelievers you must first be made saints or you cannot feel the Spirit's intercession within you. What need we have to go to Christ for the blessing of the Holy Ghost, which is peculiar to the children of God, and can only be ours by faith in Christ Jesus! "To as many as received him to them gave he power to become the sons of God"; and to the sons of God alone cometh the Spirit of adoption, and all his helping grace. Unless we are the sons of God the Holy Spirit's indwelling shall not be ours: we are shut out from the intercession of the Holy Ghost, aye, and from the intercession of Jesus too, for he hath said, "I pray not for the world, but for them which thou hast given me."

Thus I have tried to show you the kind of prayer which the Spirit inspires.

III. Our third and last point is THE SURE SUCCESS OF ALL SUCH PRAYERS.

All the prayers which the Spirit of God inspires in us must succeed, because, first, *there is a meaning in them which God reads and approves.* When the Spirit of God writes a prayer upon a man's heart, the man himself may be in such a state of mind that he does not altogether know what it is. His interpretation of it is a groan, and that is all. Perhaps he does not even get so far as that in expressing the mind of the Spirit, but he feels groanings which he cannot utter, he cannot find a door of utterance for his inward grief. Yet our heavenly Father, who looks immediately upon the heart, reads what the Spirit of God has indited there, and does not need even our groans to explain the meaning. He reads the heart itself: "He knoweth," says the text, "what is the mind of the Spirit." The Spirit is one with the Father, and the Father knows what the Spirit means. The desires which the Spirit prompts may be too spiritual for such babes in grace as we are actually to describe or to express, and yet they are within us. We feel desires for things that we should never have thought of if he had not made us long for them; aspirations for blessings which as to the understanding of them are still above us, yet the Spirit writes the desire on the renewed mind, and the Father sees it. Now that which God reads in the heart and approves of, for the word to "know" in this case includes approval as well as the mere act of omniscience—what God sees and approves of in the heart must succeed. Did not Jesus say, "Your heavenly Father knoweth that you have need of these things before you ask them"? Did he not tell us this as an encouragement to believe that we shall receive all needful blessings? So it is with those prayers which are all broken up, wet with tears, and discordant with sighs and inarticulate expressions and heavings of the bosom, and sobbings of the heart and anguish and bitterness of spirit, our gracious Lord reads them as a man reads a book, and they are written in a character which he fully understands. To give a simple figure: if I were to come into your house I might find there a little child that cannot yet speak plainly. It cries for something, and it makes very odd and objectionable noises, combined with signs and movements, which are almost meaningless to a stranger, but his mother understands him, and attends to his little pleadings. A mother can translate baby-talk: she comprehends incomprehensible noises. Even so doth our Father in heaven know all about our poor baby talk, for our prayer is not much better. He knows and comprehends the cryings, and moanings, and sighings, and chatterings of his bewildered children. Yea, a tender mother knows her child's needs before the child knows what it wants. Perhaps the little one stutters, stammers, and cannot get its words out, but the mother sees what he would say, and takes the meaning. Even so we know concerning our great Father:—

> "He knows the thoughts we mean to speak,
> Ere from our opening lips they break."

Do therefore rejoice in this, that because the prayers of the Spirit are known and understood of God, therefore they will be sure to speed.

The next argument for making us sure that they will speed is this—that *they are "the mind of the Spirit."* God the ever blessed is one, and there can be no division between the Father, the Son, and the Holy Ghost. These divine persons always work together, and there is a common desire for the glory of each blessed Person of the Divine Unity, and therefore it cannot be conceived without profanity, that anything could be the mind of the Holy Spirit and not be the mind of the Father and the mind of the Son. The mind of God is one and harmonious; if, therefore, the Holy Spirit dwell in you, and he move you to any desire, then his mind is in your prayer, and it is not possible that the eternal Father should reject your petitions. That prayer which came from heaven will certainly go back to heaven. If the Holy Ghost prompts it, the Father must and will accept it, for it is not possible that he should put a slight upon the ever blessed and adorable Spirit.

But one more word, and that closes the argument, namely, that *the work of the Spirit in the heart is not only the mind of the Spirit which God knows, but it is also according to the will or mind of God,* for he never maketh intercession in us other than is consistent with the divine will. Now, the divine will or mind may be viewed two ways. First, there is the will declared in the proclamations of holiness by the Ten Commandments. The Spirit of God never prompts us to ask for anything that is unholy or inconsistent with the precepts of the Lord. Then secondly, there is the secret mind of God, the will of his eternal predestination and decree, of which we know nothing; but we do know this, that the Spirit of God never prompts us to ask anything which is contrary to the eternal purpose of God. Reflect for a moment: the Holy Spirit knows all the purposes of God, and when they are about to be fulfilled, he moves the children of God to pray about them, and so their prayers keep touch and tally with the divine decrees. Oh would you not pray confidently if you knew that your prayer corresponded with the sealed book of destiny? We may safely entreat the Lord to do what he has himself ordained to do. A carnal man draws the inference that if God has ordained an event we need not pray about it, but faith obediently draws the inference that the God who secretly ordained to give the blessing has openly command-ed that we should pray for it, and therefore faith obediently prays. Coming events cast their shadows before them, and when God is about to bless his people his coming favour casts the shadow of prayer over the church. When he is about to favour an individual he casts the shadow of hopeful expectation over his soul. Our prayers, let men laugh at them as they will, and say there is no power in them, are the indicators of the movement of the wheels of Providence. Believing supplications are forecasts of the future. He who prayeth in faith is like the seer of old, he sees that which is yet to be: his holy expectancy, like a telescope, brings distant objects near to him, and things not seen as yet are visible to him. He is bold to declare that he has the petition which he has asked of God, and he therefore begins to rejoice and to praise God, even before the blessing has actually arrived. So it is: prayer prompted by the Holy Spirit is the footfall of the divine decree.

I conclude by saying, see, my dear hearers, the absolute necessity of the Holy Spirit, for if the saints know not what they should pray for as they ought; if consecrated men and women, with Christ suffering in them, still feel their need of the instruction of the Holy Spirit, how much more do you who are not saints, and have never given yourselves up to God, require divine teaching! Oh, that you would know and feel your dependence upon the Holy Ghost that he may prompt you this day to look to Jesus Christ for salvation. It is through the once crucified but now ascended Redeemer that this gift of the Spirit, this promise of the Father, is shed abroad upon men. May he who comes from Jesus lead you to Jesus.

And, then, O ye people of God, let this last thought abide with you,—what condescension is this that this Divine Person should dwell in you for ever, and that he should be with you to help your prayers. Listen to me for a moment. If I read in the Scriptures that in the most heroic acts of faith God the Holy Ghost helpeth his people, I can understand it; if I read that in the sweetest music of their songs when they worship best, and chant their loftiest strains before the Most High God, the Spirit helpeth them, I can understand it; and even if I hear that in their wrestling prayers and prevalent intercessions God the Holy Spirit helpeth them, I can understand it: but I bow with reverent amazement, my heart sinking into the dust with adoration, when I reflect that God the Holy Ghost helps us when we cannot speak, but only groan. Yea, and when we cannot even utter our groanings, he doth not only help us but he claims as his own particular creation the "groanings that cannot be uttered." This is condescension indeed! In deigning to help us in the grief that cannot even vent itself in groaning, he proves himself to be a true Comforter. O God, my God, thou hast not forsaken me: thou art not far from me, nor from the voice of my roaring. Thou didst for awhile leave thy Firstborn when he was made a curse for us, so that he cried in agony, "Why hast thou forsaken me?" but thou wilt not leave one of the "many brethren" for whom he died: thy Spirit shall be with them, and when they cannot so much as groan he will make intercession for them with groanings that cannot be uttered. God bless you, my beloved brethren, and may you feel the Spirit of the Lord thus working in you and with you. Amen and amen.

21

The Paraclete

"And I will pray the Father, and he shall give you another Comforter, that he may abide with you for ever." John 14:16

The unspeakable gift of the Son of God was followed up by the equally priceless gift of the Holy Ghost. Must it not be confessed by us that we think far less of the Holy Spirit than we should? I am sure we do not exalt the Saviour too much, nor is he too often the subject of our meditations; but at the same time, we give to the Holy Spirit a very disproportionate place, even as compared with the Redeemer. I fear that we even grieve the Spirit by our neglect of him.

Let me invite your devout contemplations to the special work of the Holy Spirit. Such an invitation is necessary. The subject has not grown stale, for it too seldom occupies our thoughts. We have not been unduly engrossed with honouring the Spirit of God; for this is a fault seldom or never committed. We have met with uninstructed persons who have glorified the love of Jesus beyond that of the Father, and there are others so occupied with the decrees of the Father as to cast the work of the Son into the background; but very few and far between must be those believers who have dwelt upon the doctrine of the Holy Spirit beyond its proper measure and degree. The mistake has almost invariably been made in the opposite direction.

The personal name of the Third Person of the Blessed Trinity is "the Spirit," or the "Holy Spirit," which words describe his nature as being a pure, spiritual, immaterial

existence, and his character as being in himself and in his
workings pre-eminently holy. We commonly also speak of
him as the "Holy Ghost," but the name is now an erroneous
one. The word "ghost" was the same as "spirit" in years gone
by, when the present translation of the Bible was made, but
it does not popularly signify "spirit" now; superstition has
degraded the word from its elevated meaning, and it might
be as well perhaps if the word were dropped altogether and
we confined ourselves to the more accurate word, "Holy
Spirit." The term "Holy Spirit" is his personal title and we
have in this verse his official title: he is in the English
version called the "Comforter," but the word used in the
original, upon which we will meditate this morning, has a
much wider range of meaning. The word is παρακλητον; we
used it just now in our hymn, Englishing it into "Paraclete":

> "Cheer our desponding hearts,
> Thou heavenly Paraclete;
> Give us to lie, with humble hope,
> At our Redeemer's feet."

Now, it is true that the name "Comforter" is a fair translation from some points of view, but it rather translates a
corner of the word than the whole of it. It is a light which
really streams from the text, but it is one of the seven
prismatic colors rather than the combined light of the very
instructive and wonderful word Paraclete. Understand,
then, that we have now to consider this morning the official
title of the Holy Spirit; may we be filled with loving reverence while we study his gracious work and his official name.

I. First, this morning, I shall try to EXPLAIN HOW THE
SPIRIT OF GOD IS THE PARACLETE. The word Paraclete is so
full, that it is extremely difficult to convey to you all its
meaning. It is like those Hebrew words which contain so
much in a small compass. It is sternly and even primitively
sublime in its simplicity, yet it comprehends great things.
Literally, it signifies *"called to"* or *"called beside"* another to
aid him. It is synonymous verbally, though not in sense,
with the Latin word *advocatus,* a person called in to speak
for us by pleading our cause. Yet, as we have come to use the
word "advocate" in a different sense, that word, although it
would, like that of "comforter," convey a part of the meaning,

would not contain it all. Paraclete is wider than "advocate" and wider than "comforter." I think the meaning of the word "Paraclete" might be put under the two headings of one "called to," and one "calling to." One called to, that is, to come to our aid, to help our infirmities, to suggest, to advocate, to guide, and so on; and one who in consequence thereof, for our benefit, calls to us; for some see in it the idea of monitor, and certainly the blessed Paraclete is our teacher, remembrancer, incentive, and comforter. His work as one called in to help us consists very largely in his strengthening us by admonition, by instruction, by encouragement, and by those works which would come under the head of a teacher, or a comforter. Paraclete is a word too extensive in meaning to be exchanged for any one word in any language. It is most comprehensive, and we shall hope not so much to interpret as to paraphrase it in the first head of our sermon this morning.

Let us take all the passages in John xiv. xv. and xvi. which refer to this title, and study them with care. From the first, which is our text, we learn that the Holy Spirit, as the Paraclete, is to be to us all that Jesus was to his disciples. Read the text, "I will pray the Father, and he will give you *another* Comforter;" plainly teaching that the Lord Jesus Christ is the first Paraclete, and that the Holy Spirit is a second Paraclete, occupying the same position as the living Jesus did. It would not be easy to describe all that Jesus was to his disciples when he dwelt among them. If we called him their "guide, and counsellor, and friend," we should but have begun to catalogue his kindnesses. What a valiant leader is to an army, when his very presence inspires them with valour, when his wisdom and tact conduct them to certain victory, and when his influence over them nerves and strengthens them in the day of battle;—all that, and more, was Jesus Christ to his disciples. What the shepherd is to the sheep, the sheep being foolish, and the shepherd alone wise; the sheep being defenseless, and the shepherd strong to protect them; the sheep being without power to provide for themselves in any degree, and the shepherd able to give them all they require;—all that was Jesus Christ to his people. You see Socrates in the midst of his pupils, and you observe at once that the great philosopher is the factotum of his school; but still some follower of Socrates may improve upon what he teaches. Now, when you see Jesus, you observe at once that all his disciples are but as little children compared with their Master, and that the school would cease at once if the great Teacher were gone. He is not only the Founder but the Finisher of our system. Jesus is to them not only the doctor but the doctrine; "He is the way, and the truth, and the life." The disciple of Christ feels Jesus to be inexpressibly precious. He does not know how many uses Christ can be put to, but this he knows—Christ is all in all to him. As the Orientals say of the palm tree, that every fragment of it is of use, and there is scarcely any domestic arrangement into which the palm tree in some form or other does not enter, even so Jesus Christ is good for everything to his people, and there is nothing that they have to do or feel or know, that is good or excellent, but Jesus Christ enters into it. What would that little company of disciples have been as they went through the streets of Jerusalem without their Lord? Conceive him absent and no other Paraclete to fill his place, and you see no longer a powerful band of teachers equipped to revolutionize the world, but a company of fishermen, without intelligence and without influence, a band which in a short time will melt under the influence of unbelief and cowardice. Christ was all in all to his people while he was here. Now, all that Jesus was, the Spirit of God is now to the church. He is "another Paraclete to abide with us for ever." If there be this day any power in the church of God, it is because the Holy Spirit is in the midst of her. If she be able to work any spiritual miracles, it is through the might of his indwelling. If there be any light in her instruction, if there be any life in her ministry, if there be any glory gotten to God, if there be any good wrought among the sons of men, it is entirely because the Holy Spirit is still with her. The entire weight of influence of the church as a whole, and every Christian in particular, cometh from the abiding presence of the sacred Paraclete. And brethren, we shall do well to treat the Holy Spirit as we would have treated Christ had he been yet among us. Our Lord's disciples told him their troubles; we must trust the Comforter with ours. Whenever they felt that they were baffled by the adversary, they fell back upon their Leader's power;

so must we call in the aid of the Holy Spirit. When they needed guidance they sought direction from Jesus; we also must seek and abide by the Spirit's leadings. When, knowing what to do, they felt themselves weak for the accomplishment of it, they waited upon their Master for strength, and so must we upon the Spirit of all grace. Treat the Holy Spirit with the love and tender respect which are due to the Saviour, and the Spirit of God will deal with you as the Son of God did with his disciples.

Now, beloved, we must pass on in our review of the passages of Scripture which relate to the Paraclete, and remember they are only five. We know that the Holy Spirit comforts the people of God by the mere fact of his presence and indwelling. "I will pray the Father, and he shall give you another Paraclete that he may abide with you for ever." "For," says the seventeenth verse, "he dwelleth with you, and shall be in you." Beloved, I have said that the mere fact of the presence of the Holy Spirit is comfort to the saints, and is it not? Jesus has not left you orphans, oh ye his chosen friends; he has gone, but he has left an equally divine substitute, the Holy Spirit; and if at this moment you do not feel his power, if you are even crying out under a sense of your own natural deadness, yet is it not a comfort to you that there is a Holy Spirit, and that the Holy Spirit dwells in you at this present time? Ye are not required to bring down the Holy Spirit from heaven by praying—

"Come Holy Spirit, heavenly Dove,
With all thy quickening powers."

He has come down from heaven, and has never gone back again; he dwells in his church perpetually, and is not to be brought from on high. He is lawfully to be called upon to work in us, but he is always here. "Oh," say you, "then I must have hope, for if the Spirit of God be in me, I know that he will expel my sin. If I were alone, and had to fight my spiritual battles unhelped, I might despair; but if it be true that the eternal God himself, in the majesty of his omnipotence, dwells within my bosom, then, my heart, be of good comfort and be encouraged! The Lord who is in thee is mightier than all they that are against thee." Satan may roar, the lusts of the flesh may rebel, and the temptations of the world may assail, but if the Holy Spirit be really resident within the believer's heart, then perfection will one day be attained, and the last enemy will be trodden down. It is consolation to us to know that the Holy Spirit dwelleth in us, and he deserves his name of Comforter from the mere fact of his presence and indwelling.

But we pass on to notice that according to the twenty-sixth verse the Spirit of God exercises his office as a Paraclete, and comforts us by his teaching: "The Comforter, who is the Holy Ghost, whom the Father will send in my name, he shall teach you all things, and bring all things to your remembrance, whatsoever I have said unto you." It is a part of the Spirit's work to make us understand what Jesus taught. If he were merely to bring to remembrance the words of Jesus it would do us little good; even as when a child learns his catechism and does not understand it, it is not of much service to him to bring to remembrance the words of the questions and answers; but if you first teach him their meaning, and then bring the words to remembrance, you have conferred upon him a double and an inestimable boon. Now, we can, so far as the letter goes, learn from the Scriptures the words of Jesus for ourselves; but to understand these teachings is the gift of the Spirit of God, and of none else. After he takes the key and lets us into the inner meaning of the Lord's words, after he makes us experimentally and inwardly to know the force and the power of the truth which Christ revealed, then it is very profitable to us to have brought up before our minds the very words of Jesus, and they come to us full of power and sweetness. Now, beloved, you perceive that while the word "Comforter" does not take in all the meaning of the word Paraclete, yet every work of his assists our consolation, and the Holy Spirit as a teacher teaches us truth which comforts us. What comfort is there in the world equal to the words of Jesus, when they are really understood? Is not Jesus Christ himself "the consolation of Israel?" and, therefore, everything that is of him is full of consolation to Israel. If the Spirit of God makes us understand the doctrines of Christ, as for instance, his teaching concerning the pardon of sin by faith, and the love of God towards the contrite, his teaching in his own person of the need of a substitute, and of the provision of a substitute,—if those things be really taught to our souls, the Paraclete becomes indeed a Comforter to us. I can, as God may help me, teach you the letter of God's word, but there is One who teacheth you to profit effectually and savingly. May he exercise his office upon each one of you.

Furthermore, we note that in this manner, through the Holy Spirit we obtain peace. Observe the verse which follows: "Peace I leave with you, my peace I give unto you: not as the world giveth, give I unto you." He who is taught of God naturally enjoys peace, for if I be taught that my sins were laid on Jesus, and the chastisement of my peace was upon him, how can I help having peace? If I am taught that Jesus intercedes for me before the eternal throne, and has taken his blood as my atonement into the holy place, how can I help having peace? And if I am taught the promises of God, and made to know that they are "yea and amen in Christ Jesus," how can I be prevented from enjoying peace? Can I not sing—

> "The gospel bears my spirit up,
> A faithful and unchanging God,
> Lays the foundation for my hope,
> In oaths, and promises, and blood"?

Let the Spirit of God reveal God to you as the everlasting God, who loved you before the world was, as the unchanging God who never can turn away his heart from you; and can you do otherwise than rejoice with exceeding great joy? Let the Spirit of God reveal to you the pierced hands and feet of Jesus, let him enable you to put your finger into the prints of the nails, and touch the wounds of his feet, and lay your heart to his heart,—why, if you have not peace you would be a melancholy miracle of perverse despondency. But you must have rest when you have Jesus Christ, yea, and such a rest that Jesus calls it "my peace," the very peace that is in the heart of Christ, the unruffled serenity of the conquering Saviour, who has finished for ever the work which God gave him to do. What rich comfort is this which the Paraclete brings to us!

But we have not brought out all the meanings yet, for, as we have already said, the word Paraclete signifies *advocate*. You remember in John's first Epistle he uses this expression, "If any man sin, we have an advocate with the Father,

Jesus Christ the righteous." Now in the Greek the passage
stands, "If any man sin, we have a *Paraclete* with the
Father,"—it is the same word which is here rendered
Comforter, and you see clearly that it would not do to render
it Comforter in that place, else it would read, "If any man
sin, we have a Comforter with the Father," which would be
absurd. The word means "advocate" there, and so it must be
here. The Spirit of God exercises for us the office of an
advocate; but he is not an advocate or intercessor in
heaven—our Lord Jesus Christ fills that office. The Holy
Spirit does not intercede *for* the saints, but he "maketh
intercession *in* the saints according to the will of God." God
the Son makes intercession *for* the saints. God the Holy
Spirit makes intercession *in* the saints. Let me show you
how that is, by bringing you back to the chapters which we
are studying. In the fifteenth chapter we find the Saviour
describing his saints in the world as hated and persecuted
for his sake, and he bids them expect this, but he consoles
them in the twenty-sixth and twenty-seventh verses: "When
the Comforter is come, whom I will send unto you from the
Father, even the Spirit of truth, which proceedeth from the
Father, he shall testify of me: and ye also shall bear witness,
because ye have been with me from the beginning." Now the
passage means just this, while Jesus Christ was here, if any
one had anything to say against him or his disciples, forward
to the front came the Master, and he soon baffled his foes, so
that they confessed, "Never man spake like this man." At
this present time our Master and Head is gone from us; how
are we to answer the attacks of the world? Why, we have
another Paraclete to come to the front and speak for us, and
if we had but confidence in him, beloved, he would have
spoken for us much more loudly than sometimes he has
done. But whenever we learn to leave the business in his
hands he will do two things for us: first, he will speak for us
himself; and next, he will enable us also to bear witness. At
this present time many questions of doctrine are mooted,
many objections to the truth are started, and there are many
who would lay the axe at the very root of Christianity, and
cut it down as a rotten tree. What is our answer? I will tell
you. Nearly all the books that have been written to answer
modern philosophies are waste time and waste paper. The

only way in which the church can hold her own and answer
her calumniators is by real power from God. Has she done
anything for the world? Can she produce results? For by her
fruits shall she be proved to be a tree of life to the nations.
Now the Spirit of God, if we would but trust him and give up
all this idolatry of human learning, cleverness, genius,
eloquence, and rhetoric, and I know not what beside, would
soon answer our adversaries. He would silence some of them
by converting them, as he answered Saul of Tarsus by turning him from a persecutor to an apostle. He would silence
others by confounding them, by making them see their own
children and relations brought to know the truth. If there be
not a miraculous spiritual power in the church of God at this
day, she is an impostor. At this moment the only vindication
of our existence is the presence and work of the Paraclete
among us. Is he still working and witnessing for Christ? I
fear he is not in some churches, but *here* we behold him.
Look at his workings in this place. Nearly twenty years ago
our ministry commenced in this city, under much opposition
and hostile criticism, the preacher being condemned on all
hands as vulgar, unlearned, and, in fact, a nine days' wonder. Jesus Christ was preached by us in simpler language
than men had been accustomed to hear, and every one of our
sermons was full of the old-fashioned gospel. Many other
pulpits were intellectual, but we were Puritanical. Rhetorical essays were the wares retailed by most of the preachers,
but we gave the people the gospel, we brought out before the
world the old Reformers' doctrines, Calvinistic truth,
Augustinian teaching, and Pauline dogma. We were not
ashamed to be the "echo of an exploded evangelism," as some
wiseacre called us. We preached Christ and him crucified,
and by the space of these twenty years have we ever lacked
a congregation? When has not this vast hall been thronged?
Have we ever lacked conversions? Has a Sabbath passed
over us without them? Has not the history of this church
from its littleness in Park Street until now been a march of
triumph, with the hearts and souls of men as the spoil of the
war, of which the standard has been Christ crucified? And it
is so everywhere. Only let men come back to the gospel and
preach it ardently, not with comeliness of words and
affectation of polished speech, but as a burning heart

compels them, and as the Spirit of God teaches them to speak it; then will great signs and wonders be seen. We must have signs following, we cannot answer the world else. Let them sneer, let them rave, let them curse, let them lie, God will answer them. It is ours in the power of the Spirit of God to keep on preaching Christ and glorifying the Saviour. Just as Jesus always met the adversary in a moment, and the disciples had no need of any other defender, so we have another Paraclete, who in answer to prayer will vindicate his own cause and gloriously avenge his own elect.

And, then, brethren, we are promised that this same Spirit will make us witness too. It shall be given us in the same hour what we shall speak. The Christians who were brought before the Roman tribunals often nonplussed their enemies, not by excellency of words and human wisdom, but by their holy simplicity and zeal. Christ by his Spirit was manifest in the midst of the primitive saints, and they were victorious through this other Paraclete who was with them.

Moreover, brethren, the advocacy of the Holy Spirit does not merely relate to the ungodly, but it has to do with ourselves. The Spirit of God is an advocate with us, or within us; he leads us into comfort, and advocates our cause before the judgment-seat of our conscience. This work he does in a manner strange to flesh and blood. Beloved, if the Holy Spirit be an advocate within thee, speaking peace within thee by Jesus Christ, I will tell thee how he will plead with thee. First, he will convince thee of sin. He will show thee to be altogether lost, and ruined, and undone; for till thy self-righteousness be swept out of thee there will be no solid consolation. He will convince thee of the master sin of having been an unbeliever in Christ, and he will lay thee low at the foot of the cross as well as at the foot of Sinai, to make thee feel that thou art a sinner against love as well as law, a rebel against the five wounds of Jesus as well as against the ten commands of God: and when he has done this he will convince thee of righteousness, (John xvi. 10) that is to say, he will show thee that the righteousness of Christ renders thee perfectly acceptable with God. He will show thee, in fact, that Jesus is "made of God unto thee righteousness." Then the Spirit of God will comfort thee again by bringing home to thee a sense of judgment. He will show thee that

thou and thy sins were both judged and condemned on
Calvary. He will show thee that the evil which now seeks to
get the mastery over thee, was there and then judged and
condemned to die, so that thou art fighting with a convicted
adversary, who only lingers for a little while and then shall
be entirely dead, even as he now is crucified with Christ.
When the Spirit of God has brought these three things home
to thee, what an advocate he will be with thee! He will say,
"Heart, canst thou now despair? What wilt thou despair
about? Thy sin was laid on Jesus. What dost thou fear? Oh
heart, dost thou lament thy lack of righteousness? Thou hast
it all in Jesus. Wherefore dost thou tremble? Dost thou fear
the coming judgment? Thou hast been judged and condemned in Christ; therefore the sin that is in thee shall die,
and thine inner life shall live eternally." It is blessed when
the Spirit of God argues in our conscience thus. Memory will
say, "Thou didst so and so, that will condemn thee." But the
Spirit of God replies, "That has been already acknowledged.
I have already condemned this sin, but it was laid upon the
great Scape-goat's head and carried away." Then will come
up fear and say, "The Lord will visit this man's sin upon
him." The Spirit of God will plead again, and ask, "Who shall
lay anything to the charge of God's elect? Is God unrighteous
to forget the work and labour of his dear Son?" So with
blessed debating power, the Holy Comforter within our soul
will plead and intercede in us, and we shall obtain
consolation.

Once again, the Holy Spirit is a Paraclete according to the
sixteenth chapter, at the thirteenth verse, by his guiding us
into all truth, which is, I think, more than was meant by his
teaching us all truth. There are a number of caverns, full of
sparkling stalactites, in some parts of the world. Now, it is a
good thing when you are travelling, to be taught where each
of these caverns is—that is teaching you truth; but it is a
better thing when the guide comes forward with his flaming
torch, and conducts you down through the winding passages
into the great subterranean chambers, and holds his
flambeau aloft, while ten thousand crystals, like stars, vying
in colour with the rainbow, flash their beams upon you. So
the Spirit of God will convince you that such and such a
teaching is truth, and that is very much to know; but when

he leads you into it, so that you experimentally know it, taste it, and feel it, oh, then you are admitted to the innermost cave of jewels, where "the diamond lights up the secret mine." It is a blessed thing when the Spirit of God guides us into all truth. A great many Christians never get *into* the truth. They sit on the outside of it, but do not enter in. It is like a great nut to them, they polish the shell and prize it, but if they could once pierce the kernel and taste the interior flavour of the nut, how greatly would they be comforted. John Bunyan used to say he never knew a truth until it was burned into him as with a hot iron. I sympathize deeply in that expression. There are some truths in the Bible which nobody could make me doubt at all, because they are interwoven with my vitality; and others are so profitable to my inmost soul that I could not give them up; they are the very life and joy of my being. There is an old story of a bishop with £10,000 a year, who held an argument with a young man upon the correctness of Episcopacy, and at the end replied to his antagonist,—"Does this young man imagine that he can reason me out of £10,000 a year?" Self-interest in the bishop's case sustained his reasoning; the same is true with me, only in an infinitely higher degree, and in a far more spiritual sense. If the doctrines I preach to you be not true, I am a lost man, my life becomes an agonizing disappointment and my death a horrible calamity. I know the gospel is true, because I have tried and proved its power. I know its inside as well as its outside. I do not merely believe its creed, but its truth is to me real and practical. Hence I say, "Does the fool think he can argue me out of my peace of heart, my joy in the Lord, my hope of heaven?" It cannot be: the experienced believer is invulnerable from head to foot against anything and everything that can be hurled against him by scepticism. We are as sure of the truth of the gospel as we are of our own existence. The old philosopher heard a man assert that we do not exist, and his only reply was to get up and walk: so when we hear arguments against our holy faith, all we have to do is just to live on in the power of the Spirit, and silence gainsayers. May the Holy Spirit thus lead you into all truth —into the secret of the Lord may he conduct you, and there feast you upon fat things, full of marrow, and upon wines on the lees well refined.

Once more, in the sixteenth chapter and fourteenth verse, we are told that the Paraclete glorifies Christ by "taking of the things of Christ and showing them to us." Could infinite wisdom select a sweeter topic for a disconsolate heart than "the things of Christ?" Ah! man, when you speak of the things of Christ to a broken heart you have laid your fingers on the right string. You may bring me the things of Moses and of David, of Solomon and of Daniel, but what are they to me compared with the things of Christ? Bring me the things of Christ. These are the balm of Gilead, these are the plaisters which heal the sore. These are the true medicines of souls diseased. Therefore the Holy Spirit in his infinite wisdom lifts Jesus up before us, makes him great in our esteem, glorifies him in our hearts, and straightway our souls are full of consolation. How could it be otherwise?

I am sorry that my subject is much too long for my time this morning, and therefore I must pass away from this first head to glance at the second point, which I had hoped to have dwelt upon at length.

II. We shall now, secondly, REMARK UPON THE NATURE OF THE HOLY SPIRIT'S COMFORT, and will speak very briefly.

It is evident from the passages we have read to you this morning, that the Spirit of God never dissociates his comfort from his character. John xiv. 15: "If ye love me, keep my commandments. And I will pray the Father, and he shall give you another Comforter." The Spirit of God never comforts a man *in* his sin. Disobedient Christians must not expect consolation; the Holy Spirit sanctifies, and then consoles. Search and look, ye who hang your heads like bulrushes! See what sin it is that makes you sorrow—obey, and ye shall be comforted.

Next, the Spirit of God does not aim at working mere comfort by itself and alone; but he produces peace in the heart as the result of other divinely useful processes. He does not comfort us as a fond mother may please her wayward child by yielding to its foolish wishes. The mother does not teach the child anything, nor does she cleanse its body or purify its heart in order to comfort it; perhaps she even neglects these to please the little one; but the Holy Spirit never acts so unwisely. He blesses by purity and then by peace. When a man is feeling pain he is very desirous that the surgeon should administer some drug which will stop the unpleasant sensation immediately; yet the surgeon refuses to do anything of the kind, but endeavours to remove the cause of the evil, which lies far lower than the pain. Is not the doctor right? So the Spirit of God comforts us by taking away our ignorance and giving us knowledge, by removing our misapprehensions and giving us clear understanding, and by taking away our insensibility and convincing us of sin, of righteousness, and of judgment. Do not expect to get comfort by merely running to sweet texts, or listening to pleasing preachers who give you nothing but cups of sugared doctrine, but expect to find comfort through the holy, reproving, humbling, strengthening, sanctifying processes which are the operation of the Divine Paraclete.

Note next, the comfort of the Holy Spirit is not a comfort founded upon concealment. Some have obtained consolation by conveniently forgetting troublesome truth; now the Holy Spirit lays the whole truth open before us, he brings all truth to our recollection and hides nothing from us; therefore, the comfort we obtain from him is worth having: the consolation, not of fools but of wise men; peace, not for blind bats but for bright-eyed eagles; peace, which age and experience will not invalidate, but which both these will deepen, causing it to grow with our growth and strengthen with our strength. Such is the consolation which the Holy Spirit gives.

And mark, and be glad of it, it is a comfort always in connection with Jesus. If you get near to Jesus in your contemplations, you feel you are approaching those comforts which the Spirit intends you to enjoy. Oh, beloved, do not run for consolation to mere prophecies of the future, or soft reflections about the past. Hard by the cross is the deep well of consolation undefiled, from which the Eternal Spirit draws full buckets for his thirsty people. Be afraid of that comfort which is not based upon truth. Hate the comfort which does not come from Christ. Water from the well of Bethlehem is what you want.

It is comfort, too, which is always available. The comforts of the Holy Spirit do not depend upon health, strength, wealth, position, or friendship; the Holy Spirit comforts us through the truth, and the truth does not change. He comforts us through Jesus, and he is "yea and amen"; therefore, our comforts may be quite as lively when we are dying as when we are in vigorous health, and our consolations may be even more abounding when the purse is empty, and the cruse of oil low, than when all worldly store and cheer abound to us. This is the comfort, beloved, which in all ages has been the mainstay of believers. It was the comfort of the Spirit which brought the martyrs to stand before their accusers and to face death with unblanching cheek; it was the comfort of the Holy Spirit which led the Waldenses to count not their lives dear to them; it made Luther so brave in face of death, and Latimer so merry even upon the blazing stake. Many a man hath died in ecstacy under the power of this consolation, and many a woman has pined away slowly, rejoicing so to do, because, when heart and flesh have failed her, this consolation has been the strength of her soul. If you can know the Holy Ghost as your Paraclete you need not desire any other consolation.

III. And now, finally, let us utter SOME OBSERVATIONS UPON THE WHOLE SUBJECT.

First, to the believer: Dear brother, honour the Spirit of God as you would honour Jesus Christ if he were present. If Jesus Christ were dwelling in your house you would not ignore him, you would not go about your business as if he were not there. Do not ignore the presence of the Holy Ghost in your soul. I beseech you, do not live as if you had not heard whether there were any Holy Spirit. To him pay your constant adorations. Reverence the august guest who has been pleased to make your body his sacred abode. Love him, obey him, worship him.

Take care never to impute the vain imaginings of your fancy to him. I have seen the Spirit of God shamefully dishonored by persons—I hope they were insane—who have said that they have had this and that revealed to them. There has not for some years passed over my head a single week in which I have not been pestered with the revelations of hypocrites or maniacs. Semi-lunatics are very fond of coming with messages from the Lord to me, and it may save them some trouble if I tell them once for all that I will have none of their stupid messages. When my Lord and Master has any message to me he knows where I am, and he will send it to me direct, and not by madcaps. Never dream that events are revealed to you by heaven, or you may come to be like those idiots who dare impute their blatant follies to the Holy Ghost. If you feel your tongue itch to talk nonsense, trace it to the devil, not to the Spirit of God. Whatever is to be revealed by the Spirit to any of us is in the word of God already—he adds nothing to the Bible, and never will. Let persons who have revelations of this, that, and the other, *go to bed and wake up in their senses.* I only wish they would follow the advice, and no longer insult the Holy Ghost by laying their nonsense at his door.

At the same time, since the Holy Spirit is with you, beloved, in all your learning ask him to teach you, in all your suffering ask him to sustain you, in all your teaching ask him to give you the right words; in all your witness-bearing ask him to give you constant wisdom, and in all service depend upon him for his help. Believingly reckon upon the Holy Spirit. We do not continually take him into our calculations as we should. We reckon up so many missionaries, so much money, and so many schools, and so conclude the list of our forces. The Holy Spirit is our great need, not learning or culture. Little knowledge, or great knowledge, shall answer almost as well if the Spirit of God be there; but all your knowledge shall be worthless without him. Let but the Spirit of God come, and all shall be right. I would we took the power of the Spirit into our calculations always. You have a class at school, and do not feel fit to teach it; ask him to help you, and you do not know how well you will teach. You are called to preach, but you feel you cannot; you are dull, and your talk will be flat, stale, unprofitable; bring the Holy Spirit into it, and if he fire you, you shall find even the slender materials you have collected will set the people on a blaze. We ought to reckon upon the Spirit, he is our main force, what if we say he is our sole force, and we grieve him exceedingly when we do not reckon upon him. Love the Spirit, worship the Spirit, trust the Spirit, obey the Spirit, and, as a church, cry mightily to the Spirit. Beseech him to let his mighty power be known and felt among you. The Lord fire your hearts with this sacred flame, for as this made Pentecost stand out from all other days, may it make the close of this year stand out in our history from all other years. Come, Holy Spirit now! Thou art with us, but come with power and let us feel thy sacred might!

To the unconverted, these few words: Dear friend, if thou art ever to be saved, the Holy Spirit is essential to thee. Except thou be born again from above, thou canst never see the kingdom of God, much less enter it. Without the Holy Ghost thou art dead; thou wilt never come to any life unless he quicken thee; and even the Saviour himself upon the cross will never be a Saviour to thee, till the Holy Spirit come and give thee eyes with which to look upon him, and a heart with which to receive him. Remember that. Therefore I charge thee take care that thou honour that Spirit, and say never a word against him, lest thou be found guilty of that sin against the Holy Ghost which shall never be forgiven, neither in this world nor in that which is to come. And let me ask thee, has he ever convinced thee of thy sin in not believing in Jesus? Has he convinced thee, that there is no righteousness but in Christ? Has he convinced thee that God will judge thee and all the rest of mankind according to our gospel by Christ Jesus? If so, since he has done thus much for thee, beseech him now to take of the things of Christ and show them to thee. There is hope for thee there. All the salvation of a sinner lies in Jesus, and when the Spirit of God brings Jesus to the heart he brings salvation. Oh, poor heart, thou wilt never get out of Doubting Castle, never cease to be a captive, till the Spirit bring the things of Jesus to thee; and I pray that he may, and that he may do so at once. Submit thyself now to all that he teaches thee. Believe the truth as he reveals it. Above all, listen thou, and be obedient to that great command, "Believe on the Lord Jesus Christ, and thou shalt be saved." "Incline your ear, and come unto me: hear, and your soul shall live, and I will make an everlasting covenant with you, even the sure mercies of David." "Let the wicked forsake his way, and the unrighteous man his thoughts: and let him return unto the Lord, and he will have mercy upon him; and to our God, for he will abundantly pardon." May the Spirit of God lead you in the way of humble confession of sin, of repentance of sin and of believing in Jesus, and then we will meet in heaven to bless the Eternal Paraclete, with the Father and Son for ever.

22

"Come From The Four Winds, O Breath!"

"Then said he unto me, Prophesy unto the wind, prophesy, son of man, and say to the wind, Thus saith the Lord God; Come from the four winds, O breath, and breathe upon these slain, that they may live."
Ezekiel 37:9

According to some commentators, this vision in the valley of dry bones may refer to three forms of resurrection. Holy Scripture is so marvellously full of meaning, that one interpretation seldom exhausts its message to us. The chapter before us is an excellent example of this fact; and supplies an illustration of several Scriptural truths.

Some think they see here a parable of the resurrection of the dead. Assuredly, Ezekiel's vision pictures what will happen in the day when "the trumpet shall sound, and the dead shall be raised." No matter how dry the bones may be, the bodies of those who sleep in the dust of the earth shall rise again. That which was sown shall spring up from the grave; and, in the case of the children of God, it shall wear a new glory. At the word of Christ it shall come to pass: "For the hour is coming, in the which all that are in the graves shall hear his voice, and shall come forth; they that have done good, unto the resurrection of life; and they that have done evil, unto the resurrection of damnation."

Others see here the resurrection of the almost destroyed host of Israel, which had been divided into two companies, and carried away captive into Babylon. Plague and pestilence and the sword of the Chaldean had gone far to cut off the chosen nation; but God promised to restore his people, thus mingling mercy with judgment, and again setting in the cloud the bow of his everlasting covenant. A partial fulfilment of this promise was given when, for a while, the Lord set up again the tribes of Israel at Jerusalem, and they had a happy rest before the coming of Christ. But Israel's full restoration is yet to be accomplished. The people shall be gathered out of the graves in which, as a nation, they have so long lain buried, and shall be placed in their own land, and then will come to pass the word of Jehovah: "Then shall ye know that I the Lord have spoken it, and performed it, saith the Lord."

There are others who, looking beyond the literal for the spiritual teaching, see, and I think, rightly see, that here is a picture of the recovery of ungodly men from their spiritual death and corruption—a parable of the way in which sinners are brought up from their hopeless, spiritually dead condition, and made to live by the power of the Holy Ghost. I shall, at any rate, use the text in this sense, for I am not now aiming at the interpretation of prophecy, nor concerned greatly with what is to happen in the future. Neither do I wish to conduct you into the deep things of God; but I am just now thinking of practical uses to which I can put this incident, in order to stir up God's people to deal with the Holy Spirit as he should be dealt with, and to urge the unconverted to seek the Lord, in the hope that some of them, as dead and dry as the bones in the valley of vision, may be made to live by his divine power.

Nothing gave me greater comfort, this week, than when I received a note from one saying that, last Thursday night, while I was preaching from the text "Let your soul delight itself in fatness," she was enabled to lay hold on Christ. I had rather have such tidings than to hear the gladdest news of a worldly kind that could be brought to me. Oh, that now also some poor heart may find rest in Christ while we are talking of that divine Spirit who becomes a Comforter to all those to whom he has been first a Quickener! May he come and cause men to live, and then afterwards make them full of gladness! It is his blessed office first to bestow life, and then to give light. Living unto God is the earliest experience of the redeemed, afterwards comes joy in God by the Holy Ghost.

I. Now, first, in using this text, as I have said, for practical purposes, I am going to make this remark upon it: WE ARE NOTHING WITHOUT THE HOLY SPIRIT. I speak, my brethren, now, to you who love the souls of men. I know that there are some among you here who preach and teach with all earnestness, with broken-hearted love; and for the glory of Christ you try to bring men to believe in Jesus. In thus endeavouring to save the souls of the lost and ruined men, you are engaged in a noble work. But I dare say that you have often felt, what I also fully realize, that you have not gone far in your holy service before you are brought face to face with the fact that, in itself, the work you propose to do is an utter impossibility. We begin our labour according to the Word of the Lord, and we prophesy. God helping us, we can do that; and, though the burden of the Lord be heavy, yet if we are told to prophesy again, we can, by his grace, do that also. We can prophesy to dry bones, or prophesy to the wind, according to God's commandment. We are not afraid of seeming to be foolish, since we know that, when "the world by wisdom knew not God, it pleased God, by the foolishness of preaching to save them that believe." But when we preach the Word, and as the result of our preaching expect men to be saved, and so saved that we may know it, we come all of a sudden upon an iron-bound coast, and can get no further. We find that men are dead; what is wanted is that they shall be quickened; and *we* cannot quicken them. There are a great many things we can do—and God forbid that we should leave one of them undone!—but when we come to the creation of life, we have reached a mysterious region into which we cannot penetrate; we have entered the realm of miracles, where Jehovah reigns supreme. The prerogative to give life or to take it away must remain with the Most High; the wit and wisdom of man are altogether powerless to bestow life upon even the tiniest insect. We know of a surety, doctrinally, and we know it with equal certainty by experience, that we can do nothing towards the quickening of men apart from the Spirit of God. If he does not come, and give life, we may preach till we have not another breath left, but we shall not raise from the tomb of sin even the soul of a little child, or bring a single sinner to the feet of Christ.

How, then, should this fact affect us? Because of our

powerlessness, shall we sit still, doing nothing, and caring nothing? Shall we say, "The Spirit of God must do the work, therefore I may fold my arms, and take things easily"? Beloved, we cannot do that. Our heart's desire and prayer for our fellow-men is that they might be saved; and we have sometimes felt that, for their sakes, we could almost be willing to be accursed, if we might bring eternal life to them. We cannot sit still: we do not believe that it was God's intent that any truth should ever lead us into sloth: at any rate, it has not so led us; it has carried us in quite the opposite direction. Let us try to be as practical in this matter as we are in material things. We cannot rule the winds, nor create them. A whole parliament of philosophers could not cause a capful of wind to blow. The sailor knows that he can neither stop the tempest nor raise it. What then? Does he sit still? By no means. He has all kinds of sails of different cuts and forms to enable him to use every ounce of wind that comes; and he knows how to reef or furl them in case the tempest becomes too strong for his barque. Though he cannot control the movement of the wind, he can use what it pleases God to send. The miller cannot divert that great stream of water out of its channel, but he knows how to utilize it; he makes it turn his mill-wheel. Though he cannot resist the law of gravitation, for there seems to be an almost omnipotent force in it, yet he uses that law, and yokes it to his chariot. Thus, though we cannot command that mighty influence which streams from the omnipotent Spirit of God; though we cannot turn it which way we will, for "the wind bloweth where it listeth," yet we can make use of it; and in our inability to save men, we turn to God, and lay hold of his power.

What, then, are we to do? Face to face with spiritual death, conscious of the fact that we cannot remove it, and fully aware that only the Holy Spirit can quicken dead souls, what shall we do? There are certain ways and means by which we can act properly towards this divine Person; certain attitudes of heart which it would be will for us to take up; and certain results which will follow from a clear apprehension of the true state of the case.

First, by this fact, *we must feel deeply humbled, emptied, and cut adrift from self.* Look you, sir, you may study your sermon; you may examine the original of your text; you may critically follow it out in all its bearings; you may go and preach it with great correctness of expression; but you cannot quicken a soul by that sermon. You may go up into your pulpit; you may illustrate, explain, and enforce the truth; with mighty rhetoric you may charm your hearers; you may hold them spellbound; but no eloquence of yours can raise the dead. Demosthenes might stand for a century between the jaws of death; but the monster would not be moved by anything he or all human orators might say. Another voice than ours must be heard; other power than that of thought or suasion must be brought into the work, or it will not be done. You may organize your societies, you may have excellent methods, you may diligently pursue this course and that; but when you have done all, nothing comes of it if the effort stands by itself. Only as the Spirit of God shall bless men by you, shall they receive a blessing through you. Whatever your ability or experience, it is the Spirit of God, who must bless your labour. Therefore, never go to this service with a boast upon you lip of what you can do, or with the slightest trace of self-confidence; else will you go in a spirit which will prevent the Holy Ghost from working with or through you.

O brethren, think nothing of us who preach to you! If ever you do, our power will be gone. If you begin to suppose that such and such a minister, having been blessed of God to so many thousands, will necessarily be the means of the conversion of your friend, your are imputing to a son of man what belongs only to the Son of God; and you will assuredly do that pastor or that minister a serious mischief by tolerating in your heart so idolatrous a thought. We are nothing; you are nothing. "Not by might, nor by power, but by my Spirit, saith the Lord of hosts," is a message that should make us lie in the dust, and utterly despair of doing anything in and of ourselves, seeing that all the power is of God alone. It will do us good to be very empty, to be very weak, to be very distrustful of self, and so to go about our Master's work.

Next, because of our absolute need of the Holy Spirit, *we must give ourselves to prayer before our work, in our work, and after our work.* A man who believes that, do what he may, no soul will be quickened apart from the work of the Spirit of God, and he who has a longing desire that he may save souls, will not venture to his pulpit without prayer. He will not deliver his message without a thousand groans and cries to God for help in every sentence that he utters; and when the sermon is done, his work will not be done; it will have scarcely begun. His sermons will be but a text for long-continued prayer. He will be crying to God continually, to anoint him with the heavenly oil. His prayer will be "Let the Spirit of God be upon me, that I may preach deliverance to the captives; else men will still remain in the prisonhouse in spite of all my toil." And you, beloved, as you believe that doctrine, will not allow the preacher to go to his work without your prayers. You will bear him up in your supplications, feeling that your attendances at the house of God will all be vanity, and the coming together of the people will be as nothing, unless God the Holy Ghost is pleased to bless the Word. This thought will drive you to besiege the throne of grace with strong crying and tears that God would quicken the dead sons of men. If any of you are working without prayer, I will not advise you to cease your work; but I will urge you to begin to pray, not merely as a matter of form, but as the very life of your labours. Let the habit of prayer be constant with you, so that you neither begin any service for God, nor carry it on, nor conclude it, without crying to the Lord for his Holy Spirit to make the work effectual by his almighty power.

We have already gathered much instruction from this truth, if we have learnt to lie low before the Lord, and before the mercy seat.

But we must go a little further. Since everything depends upon the Spirit of God, *we must be very careful to be such men as the Spirit of God can use.* We may not judge others; but have you not met with men whom you could not think the Spirit of God would be likely to bless? If a man is self-sufficient, can the Spirit of God to any large degree bless him? If a man is inconsistent in his daily life, if there is no earnestness about him, if you cannot tell when he is in character or creed, if he contradicts one day what he said the day before, if he is vain-glorious and boastful, is it likely that the Spirit of God will bless him? If any of us should become lazy, indolent, or self-indulgent, we cannot expect the Spirit, whose one end is to glorify Christ, to work with us. If we should become proud, domineering, hectoring how could the gentle Dove abide with us? If we should become despondent, having little or no faith in what we preach, and not expecting the power of the Holy Spirit to be with us, is it likely that God will bless us? Believe me, dear friends, that a vessel fit for the Master's use must be very clean. It need not be of silver or of gold; it may be but a common earthen vessel; but it must be very clean, for our God is a jealous God. He can spy a finger-mark where our eyes could not see it, even with a microscope; and he will not drink out of a vessel which a moment before was at the lips of Satan. He will not use us if we have been used by self, or if we have allowed ourselves to be used by the world. Oh, how clean should we be who expect the Holy Spirit to make use of us. How careful should we be in our private life as well as in our ordinary walk and conversation! This is no small thing. See to it, my brethren and sisters, for much of the promised blessing may depend upon your carefulness.

Next, since we depend wholly upon the Spirit, *we must be most anxious to use the Word, and to keep close to the truth,* in all our work for Christ among men. The Word of God is the Holy Spirit's sword; he will not wield our wooden weapon. He will only use this true Jerusalem blade of God's own fashioning. Let us, then, set high value on the inspired Word; we shall defeat our adversaries by that sword-thrust, "It is written." So spake the Christ; and so he conquered Satan. So also the Holy Spirit speaketh. Be wise, therefore, and let your reliance be not on your own wisdom, but on the word to which you can add, "Thus saith the Lord." If our preaching is of that kind, the Holy Ghost will always set his seal to it. But if you have thought it out, and it is your own production, go, good sir, to Her Majesty's offices, and get letters patent for your invention; but the Holy Ghost will have nothing to do with it. He cares nothing about your "original mind." Our Lord Jesus laid aside all originality, and spake only the words of his Father, the words which the Holy Ghost brought to him. He said to his disciples, in that memorable discourse, before he went out to Gethsemane, "The word which ye hear is not mine, but the Father's which sent me." Let us try to imitate him, being willing not to think our own thoughts, or to speak our own words, but those which God shall give to us. I would rather speak five words out of this Book than fifty thousand words of the philosophers. I had rather be a fool with God than be a wise man with the sagest scientist, for "the foolishness of God is wiser than men; and the weakness of God is stronger than men." You cannot work for Christ except by the Spirit of Christ, and you cannot teach for Christ except you teach Christ; your word will have no blessing upon it, unless it be God's Word spoken through your lips to the sons of men. If we want revivals, we must revive our reverence for the Word of God. If we want conversions, we must put more of God's Word into our sermons; even if we paraphrase it into our own words, it must still be his Word upon which we place our reliance, for the only power which will bless men lies in that. It is God's Word that saves souls, not our comment upon it, however correct that comment may be. Let us, then, be scrupulously careful to honour the Holy Spirit by taking the weapon which he has prepared for us, believing in the full inspiration of the sacred Scriptures, and expecting that God will prove their inspiration by their effect upon the minds and hearts of men.

Again, since we are nothing without the Holy Spirit, *we must avoid in our work anything that us not of him.* We want these dead people raised, and we cannot raise them; only the Spirit of God can do that. Now, in our part of the work, for which God condescendingly uses us, let us take care that there is nothing which would grieve the Spirit, or cause him to go away from us. I believe that, in places where the work of conversion goes on largely, God is much more jealous than he is anywhere else. He watches his church; and if he sees, in the officers of the church, or in the workers, something unholy; if he beholds practices tolerated that are not according to his pure mind; and if, when they are noticed, these evils are winked at, and still further indulged, he will withdraw his blessing until we cease to have a controversy with him. Possibly he might give his blessing to a church which was worse than this in many respects, while he might withdraw it from this church, which has already been so highly favourod, if it countenanced anything contrary to his Word. An ordinary subject of her Majesty might say certain things about her for which he would never be brought to book; but a favourite at court must mind how he behaves. So must we be very sensitive in this divine employment in which we come nearest to Christ; we must be careful to co-operate with him in our work of seeking to pluck brands from the burning. We must mind how we do it, for we may, perhaps, be led to adopt ways and methods which may grieve him; and if we persevere in those ways and methods, after we have learned that they are not according to his will, the Spirit of God will leave us, lest he should seem to be setting his seal upon that of which he does not approve. A headlong zeal even for Christ may leap into a ditch. What we think to be very wise may be very unwise; and where we deem that at least a little "policy" may come in, that little policy may taint the whole, and make a nauseous stench which God will not endure. You must have the Spirit of God; you can do nothing without him; therefore do nothing that would cause him to depart from you.

Moreover, *we must be ever ready to obey the Holy Spirit's gentlest monitions*; by which I mean, the monitions which are in God's Word, and also—but putting this in the second place —such inward whispers as he accords to those who dwell near to him. I believe that the Holy Spirit does still speak to his chosen in a very remarkable way. Men of the world might ridicule this truth, and therefore we speak little of it; but the child of God knows that there are at times distinct movements of the Holy Spirit upon his mind leading him in such and such ways. Be very tender of these touches of God. Some people do not feel these movements; but perhaps if they, with a more perfect heart, feared the Lord, his secret might be revealed to them. That great ship at sea will not be moved by a ripple; even an ordinary wave will not stir it; it is big and heavy. But that cork, out yonder, goes up and down with every ripple of the water. Should a great wave come, it will be raised to the crest of it, and carried wherever the current compels. Let your spirit be little before God, and easily moved, so that you may recognize every impulse of the Spirit, and obey it at once, whatever it may be. When the Holy Ghost moves thee to give up such and such a thing, yield it instantly, lest you lose his presence;

when he impels thee to fulfil such and such a duty, be not
disobedient to the heavenly vision; or if he suggests to thee
to praise God for such and such a favour, give thyself to
thanksgiving. Yield thyself wholly to his guidance. You who
are workers, do ask for the wisdom of the Spirit carefully
and believingly. I do not understand a man going into the
pulpit, and praying the Spirit of God to guide him in what he
shall say, and then pulling it out of his pocket in manuscript.
It looks to me as if he shut the Spirit of God out of any
special operation; at least, all the help he can expect to have
from the Spirit at that particular time must be in the
manner of his reading, though, of course, he may have been
guided in that he has written. Still, there is but scant room
for the Spirit to manifest his power. In the same way, if you
make up your mind how you will deal with people, and what
you will say, it may often happen that, in the process, if you
forget all you meant to say, it would be the best thing that
could happen to you; and if you said exactly what you did not
think it would be prudent to say, the unaccustomed method
might be the thing the Spirit of God would bless. Keep yourself, therefore, before that valley of dry bones free to do just
what the Spirit of God would have you do, that he, through
you, may raise the dead.

Once more: since, apart from the Spirit, we are powerless,
we must value greatly every movement of his power. Notice,
in this account of the vision in the valley, how the prophet
draws attention to the fact of the shaking and the noise, and
the coming of the sinews and the flesh, even before there
was any sign of life. I think that, if we want the Spirit of God
to bless us, we must be on the watch to notice everything he
does. Look out for the first desire, the first fear! Be glad of
anything happening to your people that looks as if it were
the work of the Holy Spirit; and, if you value him in his
earlier works, he is likely to go on and to do more and more,
till at last he will give the breath, and the slain host shall
arise, and become an army for God. Only you cannot expect
the Spirit of God to come and work by you if you are half
asleep. You cannot expect the Spirit of God to put forth his
power if you are in such a condition that, if he saved half
your congregation, you would not know it, and if he saved
nobody, you would not fret about it. God will not bless you

when you are not all awake. The Spirit of God does not work by sleepy men. He loves to have us alive ourselves, and then he will make others alive by us. See to this, dear friends. If we had more time at our disposal, I would speak longer on this part of the subject; but I have said enough now, if God the Holy Spirit blesses it, upon this first great truth that we are nothing without the Holy Spirit.

II. Now, secondly, we may learn, from the action of Ezekiel on this occasion, that WE MAY SO ACT AS TO HAVE THE HOLY SPIRIT. When he first saw the dry bones, there was no wind nor breath; yet, obeying the voice of the Lord in the vision, the breath came, and life followed. How, then, shall we act? I will only give you in brief a few of the conditions to be observed by us.

If we want the Holy Spirit to be surely with us, to give us a blessing, *we must, in the power of the Spirit, realize the scene in which we are to labour.* In this case, the Holy Spirit took the prophet, and carried him out, and set him down in the midst of the valley which was full of bones. This is just a type of what will happen to every man whom the Spirit means to use. Do you want to save people in the slums? Then, you must go into the slums. Do you want to have sinners broken down under a sense of sin? You must be broken down yourself; at least, you must get near to them in their brokenness of heart; and be able to sympathize with them. I believe that no man will command power over a people whom he does not understand. If you have never been to a certain place, you do not know the road; but if you have been there yourself, and you come upon a person who has lost his way, you are the man to direct him. When you have been through the same perplexities that trouble others, you can say to them, "I have been there myself: I know all about it. By God's blessing I can conduct you out of this maze." Dear friends, we must have greater sympathy with sinners. You cannot pluck the brand out of the burning if you are afraid of being singed yourself; you must be willing to smut your fingers on the bars of the grate if you would do it. If there is a diamond dropped into a ditch, you must thrust your arm up to your elbow in the mud, or else you cannot expect to pick the jewel out of the mire. The Holy Spirit, when he blesses a man, sets him down in the midst of the valley full of bones, and causes him to pass by them round about until he fully comprehends the greatness and the difficulty of the work to be accomplished, even as the prophet said, "Behold, there were very many in the open valley; and, lo, they were very dry."

Next, if the Holy Spirit is to be with us, *we must speak in the power of faith.* If Ezekiel had not had faith, he certainly would not have preached to dry bones; they make a wretched congregation; and he certainly would not have preached to the wind, for it must have been a fickle listener. Who but a fool would behave in this manner unless faith entered into the action? If preaching is not a supernatural exercise, it is a useless procedure. God the Holy Ghost must be with us, or else we might as well go and stand on the tops of the hills of Scotland, and shout to the east wind. There is nothing in all our eloquence unless we believe in the Holy Spirit making use of the truth which we preach for the quickening of the souls of men. Our prophesying must be an act of faith. We must preach by faith as much as Noah built the ark by faith; and just as the walls of Jericho were brought down by faith, men's hearts are to be broken by faithful preaching, that is, preaching full of faith.

In addition to this, if we desire to have the Spirit of God with us, *we must prophesy according to God's command.* By prophesying, I do not mean foretelling future events; but simply uttering the message which we have received from the Lord, proclaiming it aloud so that all may hear. You will notice how it is twice said, in almost the same words, "So I prophesied as he commanded me." God will bless the prophesying that he commands, and not any other; so we must keep clear of that which is contrary to his Word, and speak the truth that he gives to us to declare. As Jonah, the second time he was told to go to Nineveh, was bidden by the Lord to "preach unto it the preaching that I bid thee," so must we do if we would have our word believed even as his was. Our message is received when it is the Word of God through us. When the Lord describes the blessing that comes upon the earth by the rain and snow from heaven, he saith, "So shall my Word be that goeth forth out of my mouth." Let us see to it that, before the word goes forth out of our mouth, we have received it from the mouth of God. Then we may hope and expect that the people will receive it also from us. The Spirit of God, that is, the breath of God, goes with the Word of God, and with that alone.

Notice, next, that if we would have the Spirit of God with us, *we must break out in vehemency of desire.* The prophet is to prophesy to the bones; but he does not begin in a formal manner by saying, "Only the winds coming can bring breath to these slain persons." No, he breaks out with an interjection, and with his whole soul heaving with a ground-swell of great desire, he cries, "Come from the four winds, O breath, and breathe upon these slain, that they may live!" He has the people before him in his eye, and in his heart; and he appeals, with mighty desire, to the Spirit of God, that he would come and make them live. You will generally find, in our service to-day, that the men who yearn over the souls of their fellow-men are those whom the Spirit of God uses. A man of no desire gets what he longs for; and that is nothing at all.

Then, if we would have more of the power of the Spirit of God with us, *we must see only the divine purpose, the divine power, and the divine working.* God will have his Spirit to go forth with those who see his hand. "When I have opened your graves, O my people, and brought you up out of your graves, and shall put my spirit in you, and ye shall live, and I shall place you in your own land: then shall ye know that I the Lord have spoken it, and performed it, saith the Lord." It is not my plan that God is going to work out; it is his own. It is not my purpose that the Holy Spirit is going to carry out; it is the purpose of the eternal Jehovah. It is not my power, or my experience, or my mode of thought, which will bring men from death to life; it is the Holy Spirit who will do it, and he only. We must apprehend this fact, and get to work in this spirit, and then God the Holy Spirit will be with us.

III. Bear with me, if I fill up all my time, or if I should even stray beyond it. I want now to address unconverted persons, or those who are afraid that they are still unsaved; and with the text before us, WE WOULD SPEAK HOPEFULLY TO OUR HEARERS.

You who are not yet quickened by the divine life, or are afraid you are not, *we would exhort you to hear the Word of the Lord.* Though you feel that you are as dead as these dry bones, yet if you want to be saved, be frequent in hearing the Word. "Faith cometh by hearing, and hearing by the Word of God." If you wish to find the divine life, thank God that you have that wish, and frequent those houses where Christ is much spoken of, and where the way of eternal life is very plainly set forth. When you mingle with the worshippers, listen with both your ears; try to remember what you hear; and pray all the while that God will bless it to you. "O ye dry bones, hear the Word of the Lord!"

Next, *we could remind you of your absolute need of life from the Spirit of God.* Put it in what shape you like, you cannot be saved except you are born again; and the new birth is not a matter within your own power. "Ye must be born again,"—"from above," as the margin reads, in the third chapter of John's gospel. All the religion of which you are capable will not save you, do what you will; strive as you may with outward ceremonies, or religious observances, there is no hope for you but in the Holy Ghost. There is something to be done for you which you cannot do for yourself. We will not water down that truth, but give it to you just as it stands in the Scriptures; we want you to feel its power.

But *we would have you note what the Holy Spirit has done for others.* There are some of your friends who have been born again. They were as helpless and hopeless as you are; but they are now saved. You know they are, for you have seen their lives. Take note of them, for what the Holy Spirit can work in one he can work in another. Let the grace of God in others comfort you concerning yourself, especially when you hear of great drunkards, or great swearers, or very vicious persons, who have been transformed into saints. Say to yourself, "If the Holy Spirit could make a saint out of such a sinner as that, surely he can make a saint out of me." As you see the flesh and sinews on others who were once as dry as bare bones, be encouraged to hope that it may be even so with you ere long.

May I go a little further, and say that, *we would have you observe carefully what is done in yourself?* I think I am speaking to some here who have already undergone a remarkable change. You cannot say that you have spiritual life; you are afraid that you have not. Still, you are not what you used to be. You have put away many things from you that were once a pleasure to you, and now you take delight in many things which you once despised. There is some hope in that, though it may be nothing more than the sinews coming on the bones, and the flesh upon the sinews. Yet I notice that, where the Holy Ghost begins, he does not leave off till he has finished his work. God takes such a delight in his work, that, having begun it, he completes it. Well did Job say, "Thou wilt have a desire to the work of thine hands." Now, what he has done for you already, encourages me, and should encourage you, to hope that he will yet do much more, continuing his gracious work until life eternal is bestowed upon you.

Furthermore, *we would remind you that faith in Jesus is a sign of life.* If in your heart you can trust yourself to Christ, and believe in him that he can save you, you have eternal life already. "He that believeth on the Son hath everlasting life." If thou canst now, though it be for the first time, trust thyself alone on Christ, faith is the surest evidence of the work of the Holy Ghost. Thou "hast passed from death unto life" already. Thou canst not see the Spirit any more than thou canst see the wind; but, if thou hast faith, that is a blessed vane that turns in the way the Spirit of God blows. "Whosoever believeth that Jesus is the Christ, is born of God." If thou believest, this is true of thee, and if thou dost cast thyself wholly upon Christ, remember that it is written, "He that believeth on him is not condemned;" wherefore be of good cheer.

We beg you not to be led aside to the discussion of difficulties. There are a great many difficulties. To tell dry bones to live, is a very unreasonable sort of thing when tried by rules of logic; and for me to tell you, a dead sinner, to believe in Christ, may seem perfectly unjustifiable by the same rule. But I do not need to justify it. If I find it in God's Word, that is quite enough for me; and if the preacher does not feel any difficulty in the matter, why should you? There is a difficulty, but you have nothing to do with it. There are difficulties everywhere. There is a difficulty in explaining how it is that bread sustains your body; and how that bread, sustaining your body, can be the means of prolonging your life. We cannot understand how the material can impinge upon the spiritual; and there are difficulties in almost everything connected with life. If a man will not do anything till he has solved every difficulty, we had better dig his grave. And you will be in hell if you will not go to heaven without having every difficulty solved for you. Leave the difficulties; there will be time enough to settle them when we get to heaven; meanwhile, if life comes through Jesus Christ, let us have it, and have done with nursing our doubts.

Further, *we would have you long for the visitation of God, the Holy Spirit.* Join with us in the prayer, "Come Holy Spirit, come with all thy power; come from the four winds, O breath!" One wind will not do it, it must come from all quarters. Your heart, filled with all sorts of evil, wants breaking; it wants throwing down like the house of Job's son when Job's children were in it, and "there came a great wind from the wilderness, and smote the four corners of the house, and it fell." Oh, for a wind from the four quarters of heaven, to smite the four corners of the house of your sin, and lay it low! "Come from the four winds, O breath!" As the poet sings—

"Lifeless in the valley,
Come, O breath, and breathe!
New-create and rally!
Come, O breath, and breathe!
Blowing where thou listest,
Thou the word assistest,
Thou death's power resistest,
Come, O breath, and breathe!"

Be willing to have the Holy Spirit as he wills to come. Let him come as a north wind, cold and cutting, or as a south wind, sweet and melting. Say, "Come, from any of the four winds, O breath! Only come." He can come unexpectedly upon you in the pew during these five minutes that remain. You are perhaps thinking about whether you can catch an early train, and get home. May the Holy Spirit lay hold of you before you leave the building, and get you home in real earnest to your God and to your Father! He can come very mightily. There is a great deal about you that would shut him out. But it is hard to keep the wind out when it blows in the fulness of its strength. You may fill up the crevices of the door as you please, but still the wind gets in. Thus, too, is it with the Spirit of God: he comes in might; and he can also come very sweetly. Be not afraid of the Holy Spirit. He can charm you to Christ, as well as drive you to Christ. May he enter your heart even now!

We yearn to see all of you thus made to live. I am praying in my very soul that he would come to every one of you. I do not read that Ezekiel saw part of the valley of dry bones live, and the rest remain dry bones; but that they all lived, and stood upon their feet an exceeding great army. I long to see you all blessed at this service. Why should it not be so? Oh, that the Spirit of God would come and touch everyone of us! Many of you are alive already, blessed be his name! Well, you can have more life, for Christ has come not only that you might have life, but that you "might have it more abundantly." Let the blessed Spirit enter in greater fulness, I beseech you. But pray mightily, that every soul here that is dead may now feel the sacred breath, and begin to live. Then I shall not only hear of one, as last Thursday, but news shall be brought of many upon whom the divine Spirit has sweetly come and led them to Jesus, to be saved now, and to be saved for ever. God grant it! Amen.

23

The Power Of The Holy Ghost

"...the power of the Holy Ghost."   Romans 15:13

Power is the special and peculiar prerogative of God, and God alone. "Twice have I have heard this: that power belongeth unto God." God is God: and power belongeth to him. If he delegates a portion of it to his creatures, yet still it is *his* power. The sun, although he is "like a bridegroom coming out of his chamber, and rejoiceth as a strong man to run his race," yet has no power to perform his motions except as God directs him. The stars, although they travel in their orbits and none could stay them, yet have neither might nor force except that which God daily infuses into them. The tall archangel, near his throne, who outshines a comet in its blaze, though he is one of those who excel in strength and hearken to the voice of the commands of God, yet has no might except that which his Maker gives to him. As for Leviathan, who so maketh the sea to boil like a pot that one would think the deep were hoary: as for Behemoth, who drinketh up Jordan at a draught, and boasteth that he can snuff up rivers; as for those majestic creatures that are found on earth, they owe their strength to him who fashioned their bones of steel and made their sinews of brass. And when we think of man, if he has might or power, it is so small and insignificant, that we can scarcely call it such; yea, when it is at its greatest—when he sways his sceptre, when he commands hosts, when he rules nations—still the power belongeth unto God; and it is true, "Twice have I heard this, that power belongeth unto God." This exclusive prerogative of God is to be found in each of the three persons of the glorious Trinity. The Father hath power: for by his word were the heavens made, and all the host of them; by his strength all things stand, and through him they fulfil their destiny. The Son hath power: for like his Father, he is the Creator of all things; "Without him was not anything made that was made," and "by him all things consist." And the Holy Spirit hath power. It is concerning the power of the Holy Ghost that I shall speak this morning; and may you have a practical exemplification of that attribute in your own hearts, when you shall feel that the influence of the Holy Ghost is being poured out upon me, so that I am speaking the words of the living God to your souls, and bestowed upon you when you are feeling the effects of it in your own spirits.

We shall look at the power of the Holy Ghost in three ways this morning. First, *the outward and visible displays of it;* second, *the inward and spiritual manifestations of it;* and third, *the future and expected works thereof.* The power of the Spirit will thus, I trust, be made clearly present to your souls.

I. First, then, we are to view the power of the Spirit in the OUTWARD AND VISIBLE DISPLAYS OF IT. The power of the Spirit has not been dormant; it has exerted itself. Much has been done by the Spirit of God already; more than could have been accomplished by any being except the Infinite, Eternal, Almighty Jehovah, of whom the Holy Spirit is one person. There are four works which are the outward and manifest signs of the power of the Spirit: creation works; resurrection works; works of attestation, or of witness; and works of grace. Of each of the works I shall speak very briefly.

1. First, the Spirit has manifested the omnipotence of his power in *creation works*; for though not very frequently in Scripture, yet sometimes creation is ascribed to the Holy Ghost, as well as to the Father and the Son. The creation of the heavens above us is said to be the work of God's Spirit. This you will see at once by referring to the sacred Scrip-

tures, Job xxvi. 13th verse, "By his Spirit he hath garnished the heavens; his hand hath formed the crooked serpent." All the stars of heaven are said to have been placed aloft by the Spirit, and one particular constellation called the "crooked serpent" is specially pointed out as his handiwork. He looseth the bands of Orion; he bindeth the sweet influences of the Pleiades, and guides Arcturus with his sons. He made all those stars that shine in heaven. The heavens were garnished by his hands, and he formed the crooked serpent by his might. So also in those continued acts of creation which are still performed in the world; as the bring ing forth of man and animals, their birth and generation. These are ascribed also to the Holy Ghost. If you look at the 104th Psalm, at the 29th verse, you will read, "Thou hidest thy face, they are troubled: thou takest away their breath, they die, and return to their dust. Thou sendest forth thy Spirit, they are created: and thou renewest the face of the earth." So that the creation of every man is the work of the Spirit: and the creation of all life and all flesh-existence in this world is as much to be ascribed to the power of the Spirit as the first garnishing of the heavens, or the fashioning of the crooked serpent. But if you will look in the 1st chapter of Genesis, you will there see more particularly set forth that peculiar operation of power upon the universe which was put forth by the Holy Spirit; you will then discover what was his special work. In the 2nd verse of the 1st chapter of Genesis, we read, "And the earth was without form, and void; and darkness was upon the face of the deep. And the Spirit of God moved upon the face of the waters." We know not how remote the period of the creation of this globe may be— certainly many millions of years before the time of Adam. Our planet has passed through various stages of existence, and different kinds of creatures have lived on its surface, all of which have been fashioned by God. But before that era came, wherein man should be its principal tenant and monarch, the Creator gave up the world to confusion. He allowed the inward fires to burst up from beneath and melt all the solid matter, so that all kinds of substances were commingled in one vast mass of disorder; the only name you could give to the world then was, that it was a chaotic mass of matter; what it should be, you could not guess or define. It was entirely without form, and void; and darkness was upon the face of the deep. The Spirit came, and stretching his broad wings, bade the darkness disperse, and as he moved over it, all the different portions of matter came into their places, and it was no longer "without form, and void;" but became round like its sister planets, and moved, singing the high praises of God—not discordantly as it had done before, but as one great note in the vast scale of creation. Milton very beautifully describes this work of the Spirit in thus bringing order out of confusion, when the King of Glory, in his powerful Word and Spirit, came to create new worlds:—

> "On heavenly ground they stood; and from the shore
> They view'd the vast immeasurable abyss
> Outrageous as a sea, dark, wasteful, wild,
> Up from the bottom turn'd by furious winds
> And surging waves, as mountains, to assault
> Heaven's height, and with the centre mix the pole."

> "Silence ye troubled waves, and thou deep, peace,
> Said then the Omnific Word; your discord end.
> Then on the watery calm
> His brooding wings the Spirit of God outspread
> And vital virtue infused, and vital warmth
> Throughout the fluid mass."

This you see then is the power of the Spirit. Could we have seen that earth all in confusion, we should have said, "Who can make a world out of this?" The answer would have been, "The power of the Spirit can do it. By the simple spreading of his dove-like wings he can make all the things come together. Upon that there shall be order where there was nought but confusion." Nor is this all the power of the Spirit. We have seen some of his works in creation. But there was one particular instance of creation in which the Holy Spirit was more especially concerned; viz., the formation of the body of our Lord Jesus Christ. Though our Lord Jesus Christ was born of a woman and made in the likeness of sinful flesh, yet the power that begat him was entirely in God the Holy Spirit—as the Scriptures express it, "The power of the Highest shall overshadow thee." He was begotten as the Apostles' Creed says, begotten of the Holy Ghost. "That holy thing which is born of thee shall be called the Son of the Highest." The corporeal frame of the Lord Jesus Christ was

a masterpiece of the Holy Spirit. I suppose his body to have
excelled all others in beauty; to have been like that of the
first man, the very pattern of what the body is to be in
heaven, when it shall shine forth in all its glory. That fabric,
in all its beauty and perfection, was modelled by the Spirit.
In his book were all the members written when as yet there
were none of them. He fashioned and formed him; and here
again we have another instance of the creative energy of the
Spirit.

2. A second manifestation of the Holy Spirit's power is to
be found in the *resurrection of the Lord Jesus Christ.* If ye
have ever studied this subject, ye have perhaps been rather
perplexed to find that sometimes the resurrection of Christ
is ascribed to himself. By his own power and Godhead he
could not be held by the bond of death, but as he willingly
gave up his life he had power to take it again. In another
portion of Scripture you find it ascribed to God the Father:
"He raised him up from the dead:" "Him hath God the Father
exalted." And many other passages of similar import. But,
again, it is said in Scripture that Jesus Christ was raised by
the Holy Spirit. Now all these things were true. He was
raised by the Father because the Father said, "loose the
prisoner—let him go. Justice is satisfied. My law requires no
more satisfaction—vengeance has had its due—let him go."
Here he gave an official message which delivered Jesus from
the grave. He was raised by his own majesty and power
because he had a right to come out; and he felt he had, and
therefore "burst the bonds of death: he could be no longer
holden of them." But, he was raised by the Spirit as to that
energy which his mortal frame received, by the which it rose
again from the grave after having lain there for three days
and nights. If you want proofs of this you must open your
Bibles again, 1 Peter, iii. 18. "For Christ also hath once
suffered for sins, the just for the unjust, that he might bring
us to God, being put to death in the flesh but quickened by
the Spirit." And a further proof you may find in Romans, viii.
11—(I love sometimes to be textual, for I believe the great
fault of Christians is that they do not search the Scriptures
enough, and I will make them search them when they are
here if they do not do so anywhere else.)—"But if the Spirit
of him that raised up Jesus from the dead dwell in you, he

that raised up Christ from the dead shall also quicken your
mortal bodies by his Spirit that dwelleth in you."

The resurrection of Christ, then, was effected by the agency of the Spirit; and here we have a noble illustration of his
omnipotence. Could you have stepped, as angels did, into the
grave of Jesus, and seen his sleeping body, you would have
found it cold as any other corpse. Lift up the hand; it falls by
the side. Look at the eye: it is glazed. And there is a death-
thrust which must have annihilated life. See his hands; the
blood distils not from them, they are cold and motionless.
Can that body live? Can it start up? Yes; and be an illustration of the might of the Spirit. For when the power of the
Spirit came on him, as it was when it fell upon the dry bones
of the valley: "He arose in the majesty of his divinity, and
bright and shining, astonished the watchmen so that they
fled away; yea, he arose no more to die, but to live for ever,
King of kings and Prince of the kings of the earth."

3. The third of the works of the Holy Spirit which have so
wonderfully demonstrated his power, are *attestation works*.
I mean by this,—works of witnessing. When Jesus Christ
went into the stream of baptism in the river Jordan, the
Holy Spirit descended upon him like a dove, and proclaimed
him God's beloved son. That was what I style an attestation
work. And when afterwards Jesus Christ raised the dead,
when he healed the leper, when he spoke to diseases and
they fled apace, when demons rushed in thousands from
those who were possessed of them, it was done by the power
of the Spirit. The Spirit dwelt in Jesus without measure, and
by that power all those miracles were worked. These were
attestation works. And when Jesus Christ was gone, you will
remember that master attestation of the Spirit when he
came like a rushing mighty wind upon the assembled apostles, and cloven tongues sat upon them; and you will
remember how he attested their ministry by giving them to
speak with tongues as he gave them utterance; and how,
also, miraculous deeds were wrought by them, how they
taught, how Peter raised Dorcas, how he breathed life into
Eutychus, how great deeds were wrought by the apostles as
well as their Master—so that "mighty signs and wonders
were done by the Holy Ghost, and many believed thereby."
Who will doubt the power of the Holy Spirit after that? Ah!

those Socinians who deny the existence of the Holy Ghost and his absolute personality, what will they do when we get them on creation, resurrection, and attestation? They must rush in the very teeth of Scripture. But mark! it is a stone upon which if any man fall he shall be bruised; but if it fall upon him, as it will do if he resists it, it shall grind him to powder. The Holy Spirit has power omnipotent, even the power of God.

4. Once more, if we want another outward and visible sign of the power of the Spirit, we may look at the *works of grace.* Behold a city where a soothsayer hath the power—who has given out himself to be some great one, a Philip enters it and preaches the Word of God, straightway a Simon Magus loses his power and himself seeks for the power of the Spirit to be given to him, fancying it might be purchased with money. See, in modern times, a country where the inhabitants live in miserable wigwams, feeding on reptiles and the meanest creatures; observe them bowing down before their idols and worshipping their false gods, and so plunged in superstition, so degraded and debased, that it became a question whether they had souls or not; behold a Moffat going with the Word of God in his hand, hear him preach as the Spirit gives him utterance, and accompanies that Word with power. They cast aside their idols—they hate and abhor their former lusts; they build houses, wherein they dwell; they become clothed, and in their right mind. They break the bow, and cut the spear in sunder; the uncivilized become civilized; the savage becomes polite; he who knew nothing begins to read the Scriptures; thus out of the mouths of Hottentots God attests the power of his mighty Spirit. Take a household in this city—and we could guide you to many such—the father is a drunkard; he has been the most desperate of characters; see him in his madness, and you might just as well meet an unchained tiger as meet such a man. He seems as if he could rend a man to pieces who should offend him. Mark his wife. She, too, has a spirit in her, and when he treats her ill she can resist him; many broils have been seen in that house, and often has the neighbourhood been disturbed by the noise created there. As for the poor little children—see them in their rags and nakedness, poor untaught things. Untaught, did I say? They are taught and well taught in the devil's

school, and are growing up to be the heirs of damnation. But some one whom God has blessed by his Spirit is guided to the house. He may be but a humble city missionary perhaps, but he speaks to such a one: O, says he, come and listen to the voice of God. Whether it is by his own agency, or a minister's preaching, the Word, which is quick and powerful, cuts to the sinner's heart. The tears run down his cheeks— such as had never been seen before. He shakes and quivers. The strong man bows down—the mighty man trembles—and those knees that never shook begin to knock together. That heart, which never quailed before, now begins to shake before the power of the Spirit. He sits down on a humble bench by the penitent; he lets his knees bend, whilst his lips utter a child's prayer, but, whilst a child's prayer, a prayer of a child of God. He becomes a changed character. Mark the reformation in his house! That wife of his becomes the decent matron. Those children are the credit of the house, and in due time they grow up like olive branches round his table, adorning his house like polished stones. Pass by the house— no noise or broils, but songs of Zion. See him—no drunken revelry; he has drained his last cup; and, now forswearing it, he comes to God and is his servant. Now, you will not hear at midnight the bacchanalian shout; but should there be a noise, it will be the sound of the solemn hymn of praise to God. And, now, is there not such a thing as the power of the Spirit? Yes! and these must have witnessed it and seen it. I know a village, once, perhaps, the most profane in England —a village inundated by drunkenness and debauchery of the worst kind, where it was impossible almost for an honest traveller to stop in the public house without being annoyed by blasphemy; a place noted for incendiaries and robbers. One man, the ringleader of all, listened to the voice of God. That man's heart was broken. The whole gang came to hear the gospel preached, and they sat and seemed to reverence the preacher as if he were a God, and not a man. These men became changed and reformed; and every one who knows the place affirms that such a change had never been wrought but by the power of the Holy Ghost. Let the gospel be preached and the Spirit poured out, and you will see that it has such power to change the conscience, to ameliorate the conduct, to raise the debased, to chastise and to curb the wickedness of the race, that you must glory in it. I say, there is nought like the power of the Spirit. Only let that come, and, indeed, everything can be accomplished.

II. Now, for the second point, THE INWARD AND SPIRITUAL POWER OF THE HOLY SPIRIT. What I have already spoken of may be seen; what I am about to speak of must be felt, and no man will apprehend what I say with truth unless he has felt it. The other, even the infidel must confess; the other, the greatest blasphemer cannot deny it if he speaks the truth; but this is what the one will laugh at as enthusiasm and what the other will say is but the invention of our fevered fancies. However, we have a more sure word of testimony than all that they may say. We have a witness within. We know it is the truth, and we are not afraid to speak of the inward spiritual power of the Holy Ghost. Let us notice two or three things wherein the inward and spiritual power of the Holy Ghost is very greatly to be seen and extolled.

1. First, in that the Holy Ghost has *a power over men's hearts*. Now, men's hearts are very hard to affect. If you want to get at them for any worldly object you can do it. A cheating world can win man's heart; a little gold can win man's heart; a trump of fame and a little clamour of applause can win man's heart. But there is not a minister breathing that can win man's heart himself. He can win his ears and make them listen; he can win his eyes, and fix those eyes upon him; he can win the attention, but the heart is very slippery. Yes, the heart is a fish that troubles all gospel fishermen to hold. You may sometimes pull it almost all out of the water; but slimy as an eel, it slippeth between your fingers, and you have not captured it after all. Many a man has fancied that he has caught the heart but has been disappointed. It would need a strong hunter to overtake the hart on the mountains. It is too fleet for human foot to approach. The Spirit alone has power over man's heart. Do you ever try your power on a heart? If any man thinks that a minister can convert the soul, I wish he would try. Let him go and be a Sabbath-school teacher. He shall take his class, he shall have the best books that can be obtained, he shall have the best rules, he shall draw his lines of circum-vallation about his spiritual Sebastopol, he shall take the

best boy in his class, and if he is not tired in a week I shall
be very much mistaken. Let him spend four or five Sabbaths
in trying, but he will say, "The young fellow is incorrigible."
Let him try another. And he will have to try another, and
another, and another, before he will manage to convert one.
He will soon find "It is not by might nor by power, but by my
Spirit, saith the Lord." Can a minister convert? Can he touch
the heart? David said, "Your hearts are as fat as grease." Ay,
that is quite true; and we cannot get through so much grease
at all. Our sword cannot get at the heart, it is encased in so
much fatness, it is harder than a nether millstone. Many a
good old Jerusalem blade has been blunted against the hard
heart. Man, a piece of the true steel that God has put into
the hands of his servants has had the edge turned by being
set up against the sinner's heart. We cannot reach the soul;
but the Holy Spirit can. "My beloved can put in his hand by
the hole in the door and my bowels will move for him." He
can give a sense of blood-bought pardon that shall dissolve a
heart of stone. He can

> "Speak with that voice which wakes the dead,
>   And bids the sinner rise:
> And makes the guilty conscience dread
>   The death that never dies."

He can make Sinai's thunders audible; yea, and he can make
the sweet whisperings of Calvary enter into the soul. He has
power over the heart of man. And here is a glorious proof of
the omnipotence of the Spirit that he has rule over the heart.

2. But if there is one thing more stubborn than the heart it
is *the will.* "My lord; Will-be-will," as Bunyan calls him in his
"Holy War," is a fellow who will not easily be bent. The will,
especially in some men, is a very stubborn thing, and in all
men, if the will is once stirred up to opposition, there is
nothing can be done with them. *Freewill* somebody believes
in. *Freewill* many dream of. Freewill! wherever is that to be
found? Once there was free will in Paradise, and a terrible
mess free will made there, for it spoiled all Paradise and
turned Adam out of the garden. Free will was once in
heaven; but it turned the glorious archangel out, and a third
part of the stars of heaven fell into the abyss. I want nothing
to do with free will, but I will try to see whether I have got a

free will within. And I find I have. Very free will to evil, but very poor will to that which is good. Free will enough when I sin, but when I would do good evil is present with me, and how to do that which I would I find not. Yet some boast of free will. I wonder whether those who believe in it have any more power over persons' wills than I have. I know I have not any. I find the old proverb very true, "One man can bring a horse to the water, but a hundred cannot make him drink." I find that I can bring you all to the water, and a great many more than can get into this chapel; but I cannot make you drink; and I don't think a hundred ministers could make you drink. I have read old Rowland Hill, and Whitfield, and several others to see what they did; but I cannot discover a plan of turning your wills. I cannot coax you; and you will not yield by any manner of means. I do not think any man has power over his fellow-creature's will, but the Spirit of God has. "I will make them willing in the day of my power." He maketh the unwilling sinner so willing that he is impetuous after the gospel; he who was obstinate, now hurries to the cross. He who laughed at Jesus, now hangs on his mercy; and he who would not believe, is now made by the Holy Spirit to do it, not only willingly, but eagerly; he is happy, is glad to do it, rejoices in the sound of Jesus' name, and delights to run in the way of God's commandments. The Holy Spirit has power over the will.

3. And yet there is one thing more which I think is rather worse than the will. You will guess what I mean. The will is somewhat worse than the heart to bend, but there is one thing that excels the will in its naughtiness, and that is the *imagination*. I hope that my will is managed by Divine Grace. But I am afraid my imagination is not at times. Those who have a fair share of imagination know what a difficult thing it is to control. You cannot restrain it. It will break the reins. You will never be able to manage it. The imagination will sometimes fly up to God with such a power that eagles' wings cannot match it. It sometimes has such might that it can almost see the King in his beauty, and the land which is very far off. With regard to myself, my imagination will sometimes take me over the gates of iron, across that infinite unknown, to the very gates of pearl, and discovers the blessed glorified. But if it is potent one way it is another; for

my imagination has taken me down to the vilest kennels and
sewers of earth. It has given me thoughts so dreadful, that
while I could not avoid them, yet I was thoroughly horrified
at them. These thoughts will come; and when I feel in the
holiest frame, the most devoted to God, and the most earnest in prayer, it often happens that that is the very time
when the plagues break out the worst. But I rejoice and
think of one thing, that I can cry out when this imagination
comes upon me. I know it is said in the Book of Leviticus,
when an act of evil was committed, if the maiden cried out
against it, then her life was to be spared. So it is with the
Christian. If he cries out, there is hope. Can you chain your
imagination? No; but the power of the Holy Ghost can. Ah, it
shall do it, and it does do it at last; it does it even on earth.

III. But the last thing was, THE FUTURE AND DESIRED
EFFECTS; for after all, though the Holy Spirit has done so
much, he cannot say, "It is finished." Jesus Christ could
exclaim concerning his own labour—"It is finished." But the
Holy Spirit cannot say that. He has more to do yet: and until
the consummation of all things, when the Son himself becomes subject to the Father, it shall not be said by the Holy
Spirit, "It is finished." What, then, has the Holy Spirit to do?

1. First, he has to *perfect us in holiness*. There are two
kinds of perfection which a Christian needs—one is the
perfection of justification in the person of Jesus; and the
other is, the perfection of sanctification worked in him by the
Holy Spirit. At present corruption still rests even in the
breasts of the regenerate. At present the heart is partially
impure. At present there are still lusts and evil imaginations. But, Oh! my soul rejoices to know that the day is
coming when God shall finish the work which he has begun;
and he shall present my soul, not only perfect in Christ, but,
perfect in the Spirit, without spot or blemish, or any such
thing. And is it true that this poor depraved heart is to
become as holy as that of God? And is it true that this poor
spirit, which often cries, "O wretched man that I am, who
shall deliver me from the body of this sin and death!" shall
get rid of sin and death—I shall have no evil things to vex
my ears, and no unholy thoughts to disturb my peace? Oh!
happy hour! may it be hastened! Just before I die, sanctification will be finished; but not till that moment shall I ever

claim perfection in myself. But at that moment when I depart, my spirit shall have its last baptism in the Holy Spirit's fire. It shall be put in the crucible for its last trying in the furnace; and then, free from all dross, and fine like a wedge of pure gold, it shall be presented at the feet of God without the least degree of dross or mixture. O glorious hour! O blessed moment! Methinks I long to die if there were no heaven, if I might but have that last purification, and come up from Jordan's stream most white from the washing. Oh! to be washed white, clean, pure, perfect! Not an angel more pure than I shall be—yea, not God himself more holy! And I shall be able to say, in a double sense, "Great God, I am clean—through Jesus blood I am clean, through the Spirit's work I am clean too!" Must we not extol the power of the Holy Ghost in thus making us fit to stand before our Father in heaven?

2. Another great work of the Holy Spirit which is not accomplished is *the bringing on of the latter-day glory*. In a few more years—I know not when, I know not how—the Holy Spirit will be poured out in a far different style from the present. There are diversities of operations; and during the last few years it has been the case that the diversified operations have consisted in very little pouring out of the Spirit. Ministers have gone on in dull routine, continually preaching—preaching—preaching, and little good has been done. I do hope that perhaps a fresh era has dawned upon us, and that there is a better pouring out of the Spirit even now. For the hour is coming, and it may be even now is, when the Holy Ghost shall be poured out again in such a wonderful manner that many shall run to and fro, and knowledge shall be increased—the knowledge of the Lord shall cover the earth as the waters cover the surface of the great deep; when his kingdom shall come, and his will shall be done on earth even as it is in heaven. We are not going to be dragging on for ever like Pharoah with the wheels off his chariot. My heart exults and my eyes flash with the thought that very likely I shall live to see the out-pouring of the Spirit; when "the sons and the daughters of God again shall prophecy, and the young men shall see visions, and the old men shall dream dreams." Perhaps there shall be no miraculous gifts—for they will not be required; but yet there shall

be such a miraculous amount of holiness, such an extraordinary fervour of prayer, such a real communion with God
and so much vital religion, and such a spread of the
doctrines of the cross, that every one will see that verily the
Spirit is poured out like water, and the rains are descending
from above. For that let us pray: let us continually labour for
it, and seek it of God.

3. One more work of the Spirit which will especially
manifest his power—*the general resurrection.* We have
reason to believe from Scripture that the resurrection of the
dead, whilst it will be effected by the voice of God and of his
Word, (the Son) shall also be brought about by the Spirit.
That same power which raised Jesus Christ from the dead
shall also quicken your mortal bodies. The power of the
resurrection is perhaps one of the finest proofs of the works
of the Spirit. Ah! my friends, if this earth could but have its
mantle torn away for a little while, if the green sod could be
cut from it, and we could look about six feet deep into its
bowels, what a world it would seem! What should we see?
Bones, carcasses, rottenness, worms corruption. And you
would say, "Can these dry bones live? Can they start up?"
"Yes! in a moment! in the twinkling of an eye, at the last
trump, the dead shall be raised." He speaks: they are alive!
See them scattered: bone comes to his bone! See them
naked: flesh comes upon them! See them still lifeless: "Come
from the four winds, O breath, and breathe upon these
slain!" When the wind of the Holy Spirit comes, they live,
and they stand upon their feet an exceeding great army.

I have thus attempted to speak of the power of the Spirit,
and I trust I have shown it to you. We must now have a
moment or two for practical inference. The Spirit is very
powerful, Christian! What do you infer from that fact? Why,
that you never need distrust the power of God to carry you to
heaven. O how that sweet verse was laid to my soul
yesterday!

> "His tried Almighty arm,
> Is raised for your defence;
> Where is the power can reach you there?
> Or what can pluck you thence?"

The power of the Holy Spirit is your bulwark, and all his

omnipotence defends you. Can your enemies overcome omnipotence? then they can conquer you. Can they wrestle with
Deity, and hurl him to the ground? then they might conquer
you. For the power of the Spirit is our power; the power of
the Spirit is our might.

Once again, Christians, if this is the power of the Spirit,
why should you doubt anything? There is your son. There is
that wife of yours for whom you have supplicated so frequently: do not doubt the Spirit's power. "Though he tarry,
wait for him." There is thy husband, O holy woman! and
thou hast wrestled for his soul. And though he is ever so
hardened and desperate a wretch, and treats thee ill, there
is power in the Spirit. And, O ye who have come from barren
churches with scarcely a leaf upon the tree. Do not doubt the
power of the Spirit to raise you up. For it shall be a "pasture
for flocks, a den of wild asses," open, but deserted, until the
Spirit is poured out from on high. And then the parched
ground shall be made a pool, and the thirsty land springs of
water, and in the habitations of dragons, where each lay
shall be grass with reeds and rushes. And, O ye members of
Park Street! ye who remember what your God has done for
you especially, never distrust the power of the Spirit. Ye
have seen the wilderness blossom like Carmel, ye have seen
the desert blossom like the rose; trust him for the future.
Then go out and labour with this conviction, that the power
of the Holy Ghost is able to do anything. Go to your Sunday-
school; go to your tract distribution; go to your missionary
enterprise! go to your preaching in your rooms, with the
conviction that the power of the Spirit is our great help.

And now, lastly, to you sinners:—What is there to be said
to you about this power of the Spirit? Why, to me, there is
some hope for some of you. I cannot save you: I cannot get at
you. I make you cry sometimes—you wipe your eyes, and it
is all over. But I know my Master can. That is my consolation. Chief of sinners, there is hope for thee! This power
can save you as well as anybody else. It is able to break your
heart, though it is an iron one; to make your eyes run with
tears though they have been like rocks before. His power is
able this morning, if he will, to change your heart, to turn
the current of all your ideas; to make you at once a child of
God, to justify you in Christ. There is power enough in the

Holy Spirit. Ye are not straightened in him, but in your own
bowels. He is able to bring sinners to Jesus: he is able to
make you willing in the day of his power. Are you willing
this morning? Has he gone so far as to make you desire his
name, to make you wish for Jesus? Then, O sinner! whilst he
draws you, say, "Draw me, I am wretched without thee."
Follow him, follow him, and, while he leads, tread you in his
footsteps, and rejoice that he has begun a good work in you,
for there is an evidence that he will continue it even unto the
end. And, O desponding one! put thy trust in the power of
the Spirit. Rest on the blood of Jesus, and thy soul is safe,
not only now, but throughout eternity. God bless you, my
hearers. Amen.

24

True Unity Promoted

"Endeavouring to keep the unity of the Spirit in the bond of peace." Ephesians 4:3

You will remember that for several years I have received my morning's text for the first Sabbath in the year from an esteemed brother, a clergyman of the Church of England. This year he very kindly sends me this verse, which I hope will be useful to us all, reminding us of our former faults, and of our present duty in the matter of "endeavouring to keep the unity of the Spirit in the bond of peace."

The Pope has lately been most lustily cursing us all. According to his nature, of course, must be his utterances. We could not expect a blessing where no blessing abides; and, if we get a curse, we only receive a polluted stream from a polluted fountain. It is an old saying, that England never prospers so well, as when the Pope curses her. I hope to see a year of great prosperity this year. Let the poor deluded priest curse as long as he will, our God shall turn it into a blessing. In former days, when some of the Churches of Christ began to shake off the yoke of Popedom from their necks, the plea urged against reformation was the necessity of maintaining unity. "Ye must bear with this ceremony and that dogma; no matter how antichristian and unholy, you must bear with it, 'endeavouring to keep the unity of the Spirit in the bond of peace.'" So spake the old serpent in those early days. "The Church is one; woe unto those who

shall create schism! It may be true that Mary is set up in the
place of Christ, that images are worshipped, cast clouts and
rotten rags adored, and pardons bought and sold for crimes
of every kind; it may be that the so-called Church has
become an abomination and a nuisance upon the face of the
earth; but still, 'endeavouring to keep the unity of the Spirit
in the bond of peace,' you must lie down, restrain the
testimony of the Spirit of God within you, keep his truth
under a bushel, and let the lie prevail." This was the grand
sophistry of the Church of Rome. When, however, she could
not seduce men by talking of love and union, she took upon
herself to use her natural tone of voice, and cursed right and
left right heartily: and let her curse till she expires!
Brethren, there was no force in the argument of the Papist,
if you will look at the text for a moment: the text bids us
endeavor to keep the unity of the *Spirit,* but it does not tell
us to endeavour to maintain the unity of evil, the unity of
superstition, or the unity of spiritual tyranny. The unity of
error, of false doctrine, of priestcraft, may have in it the
spirit of Satan; we do not doubt that; but that it is the unity
of the Spirit of God we do utterly deny. The unity of evil we
are to break down by every weapon which our hand can
grasp: the unity of the Spirit which we are to maintain and
foster is quite another thing. Remember that we are
forbidden to do evil that good may come. But it is to do evil
to restrain the witness of the Spirit of God within us; to
conceal any truth which we have learned by revelation of
God; to hold back from testifying for God's truth and Word,
against the sin and folly of man's inventions, would be sin of
the blackest hue. We dare not commit the sin of quenching
the Holy Spirit, even though it were with the view of
promoting unity. But the unity of the Spirit never requires
any sinful support; that is maintained not by suppressing
truth, but by publishing it abroad. The unity of the Spirit
has for its pillars, among other things, the witnessing of
spiritually enlightened saints to the one faith which God has
revealed in his Word. That is quite another unity which
would gag our mouths and turn us all into dumb driven
cattle, to be fed or slaughtered at the will of priestly
masters. Dr. McNeil has, very properly, said that a man can
scarcely be an earnest Christian in the present day without

being a controversialist. We are sent forth to-day as sheep in
the midst of wolves: can there be agreement? We are kindled
as lamps in the midst of darkness: can there be concord?
Hath not Christ himself said, "Think not that I am come to
send peace on earth: I came not to send peace, but a sword?"
You understand how all this is the truest method of endeavouring to keep the unity of the Spirit; for Christ the man of
war, is Jesus the Peacemaker; but in order to the creation of
lasting, spiritual peace, the phalanx of evil must be broken,
and the unity of darkness dashed to shivers. I pray God
evermore to preserve us from a unity in which truth shall be
considered valueless, in which principle gives place to policy,
in which the noble and masculine virtues which adorn the
Christian hero are to be supplemented by an effeminate
affectation of charity. May the Lord deliver us from indifference to his word and will; for this creates the cold unity
of masses of ice frozen into an iceberg, chilling the air for
miles around: the unity of the dead as they sleep in their
graves, contending for nothing, because they have neither
part nor lot in all that belongs to living men. There is a unity
which is seldom broken, the unity of devils, who, under the
service of their great liege master, never disagree and
quarrel: from this terrible unity keep us, O God of heaven!
The unity of locusts who have one common object, the
glutting of themselves to the ruin of all around, the unity of
the waves of Tophet's fire, sweeping myriads into deeper
misery: from this also, O King of heaven, save us evermore!
May God perpetually send some prophet who shall cry aloud
to the world "Your covenant with death shall be disannulled,
and your agreement with hell shall not stand." May there
ever be found some men, though they be rough as Amos, or
stern as Haggai, who shall denounce again and again all
league with error and all compromise with sin, and declare
that these are the abhorrence of God. Never dream that holy
contention is at all a violation of my text. The destruction of
every sort of union which is not based on truth, is a
preliminary to the edification of the unity of the Spirit. We
must first sweep away these walls of untempered mortar—
these tottering fences of man's building—before there can be
room to lay the goodly stones of Jerusalem's walls one upon
the other for lasting and enduring prosperity. In this spirit

have I spoken to clear a way to reach my text.

It is clear from the text, *that there is a unity of the Spirit to be kept;* secondly, that *it needs keeping;* and, thirdly, that *a bond is to be used.* When we have enlarged upon these points, we shall use the text in its practical application, first to Christians in their connexion with other Churches, and then to members of the same Church in their connexion with each other.

I. First, THERE IS A UNITY OF THE SPIRIT OF WHICH THE TEXT SPEAKS, WHICH IS WORTHY TO BE KEPT.

You will observe it is not an *ecclesiastical unity,* it is not endeavouring to keep the unity of the denomination, the community, the diocese, the parish—no, it is "endeavouring to keep the unity of the Spirit." Men speak of the Episcopal Church, the Wesleyan Church, or the Presbyterian Church. Now I hesitate not to say that there is nothing whatever in Scripture at all parallel to such language; for there I read of the seven Churches in Asia, the Church in Corinth, Philippi, Antioch, etc. In England, if I speak according to the Word of God, there are some thousands of Churches holding the episcopal form of government; in Scotland, some thousands of godly Churches ordered according to Presbyterian rule; among the Wesleyans, Churches adhering to the form of government first carried out by Mr. Wesley; but it is not according to the method of Scripture but only according to human invention to speak of a whole cluster of Churches as one Church. Although myself much inclined to a Presbyterian union among our Churches, I cannot but perceive in Holy Scripture that each Church is separate and distinct from every other Church; the whole being connected by those divers bonds and ligaments which keep all the separate members together, but not so connected as to run into one another to lose their separateness and individuality. There is nothing in Scripture which says, "Endeavouring to keep up your ecclesiastical arrangements for centralization;" but the exhortation runs thus: "Endeavouring to keep the unity of the Spirit."

Again, you will observe it does not say, "Endeavouring to keep the *uniformity* of the Spirit." The Spirit does not recognize *uniformity.* The analogy of his work in nature is against it. The flowers are not all tinted with the same hue, nor do they exhale the same odours. There is variety everywhere in the work of God. If I glance at providence, I do not perceive that any two events happen after the same form—the page of history is varied. If, therefore, I look into the Church of God, I do not expect to find that all Christians pronounce the same shibboleth, or see with the same eyes. The same, "one Lord one faith, one baptism, one God and Father of all, we rejoice to recognize; but as to uniformity of dress, liturgical verbiage, or form of worship, I find nothing of it in Scripture. Men may pray acceptably standing, sitting, kneeling, or lying with their faces upon the earth; they may meet with Jesus by the river's side, in the temple porch, in a prison, or in a private house; and they may be one in the same Spirit although the one regardeth a day, and the other regardeth it not.

But what is this unity of the Spirit? I trust, dear brethren, that we know it by having it in possession; for it is most certain that we cannot *keep* the unity of the Spirit, if we have it not already. Let us ask ourselves the question, "Have we the unity of the Spirit?" None can have it but those who have the Spirit, and the Spirit dwells only in new-born believing souls. By virtue of his having the Spirit, the believer is in union with every other spiritual man, and this is the unity which he is to endeavour to keep. This unity of the Spirit is manifested in *love*. A husband and wife may be, through providence, cast hundreds of miles from one another, but there is a unity of spirit in them because their hearts are one. We, brethren, are divided many thousands of miles from the saints in Australia, America, and the South Sea, but loving as brethren, we feel the unity of the Spirit. I was never a member of a Church meeting in the backwoods of America; I never worshipped God with the Samoans, or with my brethren in New Zealand; but notwithstanding all this, I feel the unity of the Spirit in my soul with them, and everything which concerns their spiritual welfare is interesting to me.

This unity of the Spirit is caused by a *similarity of nature*. Find a drop of water glittering in the rainbow, leaping in the cataract, rippling in the rivulet, lying silent in the stagnant pool, or dashing in spray against the vessel's side, that water claims kinship with every drop of water the wide world over, because it is the same in its elements; and even so there is a unity of the Spirit which we cannot imitate, which consists in our being "begotten again unto a lively hope by the resurrection of Jesus Christ from the dead," bearing in us the Holy Ghost as our daily quickener, and walking in the path of faith in the living God. Here is the unity of spirit, a unity of life, nature working itself out in love. This is sustained daily by the Spirit of God. He who makes us one, keeps us one. Every member of my body must have a communion with every other member of my body. I say *must*. The question never arises, that I know of, between the members of my body whether they will do so or not. As long as there is life in my frame, every separate portion of my body must have communion with every other portion of it. Here is my finger—I may discolour it with some noxious drug; my head may not approve of the staining of my finger; my head may suggest a thousand ways by which that finger ought to be put through a purgation, and this may be all right and proper; but my head never says, "I will cut off that finger from communion." My tongue speaks loudly against the noxious fluid which has done my finger mischief and has blistered it so as to cause pain to the whole body, yet the head cannot say, "I will have that finger cut off," unless the body is willing to be for ever mutilated and incomplete. Now, it is not possible to mutilate the body of Christ. Christ does not lose his members or cast off parts of his mystical body. And therefore it never ought to enter the head of any Christian man whether or not he shall have communion in spirit with any other Christian, for he cannot do without it: as long as he lives he must have it. This does not check him in boldly denouncing the error into which his brother may have fallen, or in avoiding his intimate acquaintance while he continues to sin; but it does forbid the thought that we can ever really sever any true believer from Christ, or even from us, if we be in Christ Jesus.

The unity of the Spirit is preserved, then, by the Holy Ghost infusing daily life-floods into the one mystical body; and in proportion as the life-floods become more strong, that union becomes more manifest. Let a spirit of prayer be poured out on all our Churches, conventionalities will be dashed down, divisions will be forgotten, and, locked in each

others arms, the people of God will show to the world that
they are one in Christ Jesus.

There are some points in which this unity of the Spirit is
certain to discover itself. In *prayer,* how truly does Mont-
gomery put it:—

> "The saints in prayer appear as one,
>   In word, and deed, and mind,
> While with the Father and the Son,
>   Sweet fellowship they find."

There is a unity of *praise* too. Our hymn books differ after all
very little; we still sing the same song, the praise of the same
Saviour. This unity will soon discover itself in *co-working:*
they have a union in their conflict with the common foe, and
in their contention for the common truth. This will lead to
communion—I do not mean sitting down to the same table to
eat bread and drink wine—that is only the outward union—
but I mean that communion which consists in heart beating
true to heart, and in the feeling, that they are one in Christ
Jesus. It was a motto with Bucer, "To love all in whom he
could see anything of Christ Jesus." Be this your motto,
brother in Christ. Make not your love an excuse for not
offering stern rebuke, but rebuke because you love. Some
persons think that unless you smooth your tongue and cover
your words with sugar, no matter though it may be sugar of
lead—unless you cringe, and compliment, and conceal, there
is no love in your heart; but I trust it will be our privilege to
show in our own persons, some of us, how sternly we can
dissent and yet love; how truly be Nonconformists to our
brethren's error, and yet in our very nonconformity prove
our affection to them, and to our common Master. It is said
of some men that they appear to have been born upon the
mountains of Bether, for they do nothing but cause division;
and baptized in the waters of Meribah, for they delight in
causing strife. This is not the case with the genuine
Christian; he cares only for the truth, for his Master, for the
love of souls; and when these things are not imperilled, his
own private likes or dislikes never affect him. He loves as
much to see another Church prosper as his own: so long as
he can know that Christ is glorified it is a matter of
comparative indifference to him by what minister God's arm

is made bare, in what place souls are converted, or to what
particular form of worship men addict themselves: yet ever
does he hold to this, that there is no unity of the Spirit
where there is a lie in the case; that where the souls of men
are concerned he would be a traitor to God if he did not bear
witness against the error which damns, and testify to the
truth which saves; and where the crown jewels of his
Master's kingdom are concerned he dares not traitorously
hold his tongue; but though his fellow-subjects cast his name
out as evil, he counts it all joy so long as he is faithful to his
Master and discharges his conscience as before the Judge of
quick and dead.

II. Secondly, THIS UNITY NEEDS KEEPING.

It is a very difficult thing to maintain, and that for several
reasons. Our sins would, very naturally, break it. If we were
all angels, we should keep the unity of the Spirit, and not
need even the exhortation to do so; but, alas! we are proud,
and *pride* is the mother of division. Diotrephes, who loves to
have the pre-eminence, is very sure to head a faction. *Envy,*
too, how that separates very friends! When I cannot be
satisfied with anything which is not hammered on my anvil
or run in my mould; when another man's candle grieves me
because it gives more light than mine; and when another
man troubles me because he has more grace than I have—
oh! there is no unity in this case. *Anger*—what a deadly foe
is that to unity! when we cannot brook the smallest
disrespect; when the slightest thing brings the blood into our
face; when we speak unadvisedly with our lips: but surely I
need not read the long list of sins which spoil this unity of
the Spirit, for they are legion. O, may God cast them out
from us, for only so can we keep the unity of the Spirit. But,
beloved, our very *virtues* may make it difficult for us to keep
this unity. Luther is brave and bold, hot and impetuous; he
is just the man to lead the van and clear the way for the
Reformation. Calvin is logical, clear, cool, precise; he seldom
speaks rashly. It is not in the order of things that Luther
and Calvin should always agree. Their very virtues cause
them to fall out, and, consequently, Luther, in a bad temper,
calls Calvin a pig, and a devil; and, albeit, Calvin once
replied, "Luther may call me what he will, but I will always
call him a dear servant of Christ," yet John Calvin knew how

to pierce Luther under the fifth rib when he was in the
humour. In those days the courtesies of Christians to one
another were generally of the iron-gauntlet order, rather
than the naked hand; for all were so much called to war for
the sake of the truth; that even their fellow soldiers were
treated with suspicion; and it may be with us that the very
watchfulness of truth, which is so valuable, may make us
suspect where there is no need for suspicion, and our
courage may take us as sometimes a fiery horse has carried
a young warrior beyond where he intended to have ridden,
where he may be taken prisoner to his own damage. We
must watch, the best of us must watch, lest we fight the
Lord's battles with Satan's weapons, and so even from love
to God and his truth, violate the unity of the Spirit.

The unity of the Spirit ought to be kept, dear friends,
because Satan is so busy to mar it. He knows that the
greatest glory of Christ will spring from the unity of his
Church. "That they all may be one; as thou, Father, art in
me, and I in thee, that they also may be one in us: that the
world may believe that thou hast sent me." There is no
Church happiness where there is not Church unity. Let a
Church be disaffected and divided, the schism in the body is
death to all hallowed fellowship. We cannot enjoy communion with each other unless our hearts be one. Our work
for God, how feebly is it done when we are not agreed! The
enemy cannot desire a better ally than *strife* in the midst of
our camp. "Can ye not agree," said a warrior of old "when
your enemy is in sight!" Christians, can you not agree to
keep the unity of the Spirit when a destroying Satan is ever
on the watch seeking to drag immortal souls down to
perdition? We must be more diligent in this matter; we must
seek to purge out from ourselves everything which would
divide, and to have in our hearts every holy thought which
would tend to unite us with our brethren. I am not, when I
join a Christian Church, to say, "I am quite certain I shall
never break its unity." I am to suspect myself of a liability to
that evil, and I am to watch with all diligence that I keep the
unity of the Spirit.

III. In the third place, in order to the keeping of this,
THERE IS A BOND PROVIDED, THE BOND OF PEACE.

Beloved, there should be much peace, perfect peace,

unbounded peace between the people of God. We are not aliens; we are *"fellow-citizens* with the saints, and of the household of God." Realize your fellow-citizenship; treat not Christian people as foreigners, and this bond of fellow-citizenship will be one bond of peace. You are not enemies. Men may be fellow-citizens and yet hate one another, but you are *friends,* you are all friends to Christ, and in him you are all friends to one another; let that be another bond. But you go farther; you are not mere friends, you are *brethren,* born of the same parent, filled with the same life; and shall not this be a bond? See that ye fall not out by the way; strive not one with another, for ye are brethren. This is not all; you are nearer than this; you are *members of the same body.* Shall this mysterious union fail to be a bond of peace to you? Wilt thou, being the foot, contend with the eye? or wilt thou, being the eye, contend with the hand, and say, "I have no need of thee"? If it be indeed the truth, and not a fiction, that we are members of his body, of his flesh, and of his bones— since the joints and bones in other men's bodies do not disagree, let it never be said of the mystical body of our blessed Lord, that there was such a monstrous thing in it, that the various parts would not co-work, but, fell to battling one with another.

I believe I have brought out the meaning of the text. There is a unity of the Spirit which is worthy to be kept—we ought to keep it—we must try to keep it in the bond of peace.

To come to the practical conclusion of the subject. First, *in the connexion of one Church with another;* and, secondly, *in the connexion of one Church member with another.*

It is not a desirable thing that all Churches should melt into one another and become one; for the complete fusion of all Churches into one ecclesiastical corporation would inevitably produce another form of Popery, since history teaches us that large ecclesiastical bodies grow more or less corrupt as a matter of course. Huge spiritual corporations are, as a whole, the strongholds of tyranny and the refuges of abuse; and it is only a matter of time when they shall break to pieces. Disruption and secession must occur, and will occur, where a unity is attempted which is not meant in God's Word; but it will be a blessed thing when all the Churches walk together in the unity of the Spirit; when this

Church, although it has been baptized into the Lord Jesus Christ, and laments the neglect of that ordinance by others, yet feels that the unity of the Spirit is not to be broken, and holds out its right hand to all who love our Lord Jesus Christ in sincerity; when yonder Church, governed by its elders, feels a unity with another Church which is presided over by its bishop; when a certain Church, which holds with mutual edification and no ministry, is yet not quarrelsome towards those who love the ministry of the Word; when, in fact, we have agreed in this one thing, that we will search the Word independently and act out according to our light what we find to be true; but having so done we will keep the unity of Spirit in the bond of peace. I say this is most desirable and this it is that we are to seek after; not the fusion of all into one denomination, but the keeping of each Church in its own distinct independent testimony in love with every other Church that is doing the same.

Now, in order to do this, I have a few suggestions to offer. It is quite certain we shall never keep the unity of the Spirit if this Church shall declare that it is superior to every other. If there be a Church which says, "We are *the* Church, and all others are mere sects; we are established, and others are only tolerated;" then it is a troubler in Israel, and must hide its head when the unity of the Spirit is so much as hinted at. Any Church which lifts up its head on high and boasts over other Churches has violated the unity of the Spirit. If other Churches reply, "One is our Master and all we are brethren," they do not violate the unity of the Spirit, for they simply claim their rights and speak the truth. That other Church which forgets its true position as one in the family, and begins to set itself up as mistress, and claim pre-eminence over its fellow-servants, has put it out of its own power to keep the unity of the Spirit, for it has violated it once for all.

A Church that would keep the unity of the Spirit, again, must not consider itself to be so infallible, that not to belong to its membership is sin. What right has any one Church to set itself up as the standard, so that those who join it not are necessarily Dissenters? It is true my Episcopal brother is a Dissenter, he dissents from me; it is true he is a Nonconformist, for he does not conform to me: I would not, however, call him by such names, lest I should arrogate to

my own Church to be *the one* Church, and so should break
the unity of the Spirit. If I turn to history, I may believe that
my Church can claim a long line of ancestors descending
from the apostles, without ever running through the Church
of Rome, but shall I therefore call a brother who does not
quite see this succession, a schismatic, and denominate his
assembly a conventicle? If he is a schismatic because he does
not come to my place, why am I not a schismatic because I
do not go to his? Well, but, he divides the Church! He ought
to come and worship with me. Ought I not to go and worship
with him? Ah! but we are the larger number! Are divine
things to be ruled by the majority? Where would the Church
of God be any day if it came to polling? I am afraid the devil
would always be at the head of the poll. We wish to keep the
unity of the Spirit, and if we have a little sister, we will treat
her all the more kindly, owing to the fewness of her members. If I want to "keep the unity of the Spirit in the bond of
peace," I must never call in the magistrate to force my
brother to pay for washing my surplice, ringing my bell, and
winding up my clock. I must not tell my brother that he is
bound to pay for the support of my worship. "Oh!" he says,
"my dear friend, I pay for the maintenance of the worship
which I believe to be correct, and I am quite willing that you
should do the same for yours; I would voluntarily assist you
if you were poor; but you tell me you will put me in prison if
I do not pay, and yet tell me to keep the unity of the Spirit;
but, my dear friend, it is not keeping the unity of the Spirit
to take away my stool, and my table and my candlestick, and
say you will put me in 'limbo,' or hail me before an ecclesiastical court. You send the constable after me; and then if
I say a word about it, you say, 'Charity hopeth all things.'"
Yes, among the rest, it hopes that you will give up your sin
in this matter.

If we should stand possessed of a piece of ground where we
bury our dead, and if there should happen to come a member
of another Christian Church who would wish to lay his poor
dead baby in our ground, there being no other convenient
spot anywhere, and he asks the favour, I think we can
hardly be thought to keep the unity of the Spirit if we tell
him, "No, nothing of the kind; you had your child sprinkled,
therefore it cannot be buried with us Christians; we will not

have your sprinkled baby lying alongside of our baptized dead." I do not think that is keeping the unity of the Spirit. And I do not think when some Churches have turned from their grave-yard gate the mourners who have brought an unbaptized infant, and when the mourners have gone back weeping to their homes—I do not think such Churches have been endeavouring to keep the unity of the Spirit in the bond of peace. Again, if Churches are to agree one with another, they must not make rules that ministers who are not of their own denomination shall not occupy their pulpits. I should be ashamed of you, if you passed a resolution that no one dissenting from us should stand in my pulpit. But we know a Church which says, "No matter how good a man may be; he may be a man as venerated as John Angell James; or he may have all the excellencies of a William Jay—we would not, perhaps, mind hearing him in a Town Hall, but into the sacredness of our particular rostrum these interlopers must not intrude; for, says this Church, "Ours *are* ministers, yours are only lay-teachers; ours *are* sacraments: the cup of blessing which we bless is the blood of Christ, and the bread which we break is the body of Christ; you have no sacramental efficacy with you; you are not a Church in fact, but only a body of schismatics, meeting together to carry out what you think to be right. We tolerate you; that is all we can do." Where is the unity of the Spirit there? My dear friends, I received this text from one of the most holy men in the Church of England: if I expound it slightly for her benefit, he will, I trust, excuse me, for I do so in all honesty, desiring to aid him and many others in revision and reform. If *this* Church were in the same condition as the Church of England, I would pray to be as plain in my remarks. I say it is an anachronism; it is a thing out of date for the nineteenth century, for any one Church in this land, and that Church the only one which defiles her hand by taking State-pay, to stand up and say, "We are the Church; our ministers are *the* ministers; our people are *the* people; and now, dear brethren, shake hands, and endeavour to keep the unity of the Spirit of God." Why, it is preposterous. Let us meet on equal ground; let us lay aside all pretences to superiority; let us really aid and not oppress each other; let us mingle in prayer; let us unite in confession of sin; let us join heartily in reforming our errors, and a true Evangelical Alliance will cover our land. If any Church will take the Bible as its standard, and in the power of the Spirit of God preach the name of Jesus, there are thousands of us who will rejoice to give the right hand of fellowship with a hearty greeting to all such, and we are every day striving to get other Churches and ourselves more and more into that condition in which, while holding our own, we can yet keep the unity of the Spirit in the bond of peace.

Now, a few words to you *in regard to your relationship to one another as members of the same Church.* If we are to endeavour to keep the unity of the Spirit in the bond of peace in the same Church, then we must avoid everything that would mar it. *Gossip*—gossip is a very ready means of separating friends from one another. Let us endeavour to talk of something better than each other's characters. Dionysius went down to the Academy to Plato. Plato asked what he came for. "Why," said Dionysius, "I thought that you, Plato, would be talking against me to your students." Plato made this answer: "Dost thou think, Dionysius, we are so destitute of matter to converse upon that we talk of thee?" Truly we must be very short of subjects when we begin to talk of one another. It is better far that we magnify Christ than detract from the honour of his members. We must lay aside all envy. Multitudes of good people liked the Reformation, but they said they did not like the idea of its being done by a poor miserable monk, like Martin Luther; and so there are many who like to see good things done, and good works carried on, but do not care to see it done by that upstart young brother, or that poor man, or that woman who has no particular rank or state. As a Church let us shake off envyings; let us all rejoice in God's light; and as for pride—if any of you have grown vainglorious of late, shake it off. I hope to exercise a ministry in this place which will drive out those of you who will not acknowledge your brethren when they are poorer or of less education than yourselves. What if the man does mar the Queen's English when he talks— what does that matter, so long as his heart is right? As long as you can feel he loves the Master, surely you can put up with his faults of language, if he can put up with your faults of action. Then let us cultivate everything that would tend to unity. Are any sick? Let us care for them. Are any suffering? Let us weep with them. Do we know one who has less love than others? Then let us have more, so as to make up the deficiency. Do we perceive faults in a brother? Let us admonish him in love and affection. I pray you be peacemakers, everyone. Let the Church go on as it has done for the last eleven years, in holy concord and blessed unity. Let us remember that we cannot keep the unity of the Spirit unless we all believe the truth of God. Let us search our Bibles, therefore, and conform our views and sentiments to the teaching of God's Word. I have already told you that unity in error is unity in ruin. We want unity in the truth of God through the Spirit of God. This let us seek after; let us live near to Christ, for this is the best way of promoting unity. Divisions in Churches never begin with those full of love to the Saviour. Cold hearts, unholy lives, inconsistent actions, neglected closets; these are the seeds which sow schisms in the body; but he who lives near to Jesus, wears his likeness and copies his example, will be, wherever he goes, a sacred bond, a holy link to bind the Church more closely than ever together. May God give us this, and henceforth let us endeavour to keep the unity of the Spirit in the bond of peace. I commend the text to all believers, to be practiced through the coming year. And to those who are not believers, what can I say but that I trust their unity and their peace may be broken for ever, and that they may be led to Christ Jesus to find peace in his death? May faith be given, and then love and every grace will follow, so that they may be one with us in Christ Jesus our Lord. Amen.

25

The Holy Ghost The Need Of The Age

"O thou that art named the house of Jacob, is the spirit of the Lord straitened? are these his doings? do not my words do good to him that walketh uprightly?"   Micah 2:7

Brethren, what a stern rebuke to the people of Israel is contained in the title with which the prophet addressed them—"O thou that art named the house of Jacob"! It is as much as to say to them—"You wear the name, but you do not bear the character of Jacob." It is the Old Testament version of the New Testament saying, "Thou hast a name to live, and art dead." They gloried that they were the seed of Israel, they vaunted the peculiar privileges which came to them as the descendants of God's honoured and chosen servant Jacob; but they did not act in the same way as Jacob would have acted: they were devoid of Jacob's faith in Jehovah, they knew nothing of Jacob's power of prayer, and nothing of his reliance upon the covenant. The words of Micah imply that the descendants of Jacob in his day were proud of the name of "house of Jacob," but that they were not worthy of it. Nothing is more mischievous than to cling to a name when the thing for which it stands has disappeared. May we never come to such a stage of declension, that even the Spirit of God will be compelled, in speaking to us, to say, "O thou that art called the church of God!" To be named Christians, and not to be Christians, is to be deceivers or deceived. The name brings with it great responsibility, and if it be a name only, it brings with it terrible condemnation. It is a crime against

the truth of God if we dare to take the name of his people
when we are not his people. It is a robbery of honour from
those to whom it is due; it is a practical lie against the Holy
Ghost; it is a defamation of the character of the bride of
Christ to take the name of Christian when the Spirit of
Christ is not among us. This is to honour Christ with our lips
and disgrace him by our lives. What is this but to repeat the
crime of Judas, and betray the Son of man with a kiss?
Brothers and sisters, I say again, may we never come to this!
Truths, not names; facts, not professions, are to be the first
consideration. Better to be true to God, and bear the names
of reproach which the adversary is so apt to coin, than to be
false to our Lord, and yet to be decorated with the names of
saints, and regarded as the most orthodox of believers.
Whether named "the house of Jacob" or not, let us be
wrestlers like Jacob, and like him may we come off as prevailing princes—the true Israel of God!

When the Lord found his chosen people to be in such a
state that they had rather the name than the character of
his people, he spoke to them of the spirit of the Lord. Was
not this because their restoration must come from that
direction? Was not their evil spirit to be removed by the
Lord's good Spirit? "O thou that art named the house of
Jacob, is the spirit of the Lord straitened?" I believe,
brethren, that whenever the church of God declines, one of
the most effectual ways of reviving her is to preach much
truth concerning the Holy Spirit. After all, he is the very
breath of the church. Where the Spirit of God is, there is
power. If the Spirit be withdrawn, then the vitality of
godliness begins to decline, and the energy thereof is near to
dying out. If we ourselves feel that we are backsliding, let us
turn to the Spirit of God, crying, "Quicken thou me in thy
way." If we sorrowfully perceive that any church is growing
lukewarm, be it our prayer that the Holy Spirit may work
graciously for its revival. Let us direct the attention of our
fellow Christians under declension to the Spirit of God. They
are not straitened in him, but in themselves; let them turn
to him for enlargement. It is he alone who can quicken us
and strengthen the things which remain which are ready to
die. I admire the wisdom of God here, that when speaking by
the prophet he rebukes the backsliding of the people, he

immediately directs their minds to the Holy Spirit who can bring them back from their wanderings, and cause them to walk worthy of the vocation wherewith they were called. Let us learn from this divine wisdom, and in lowly reverence and earnest faith let us look to the Spirit of the Lord.

In speaking to Israel upon the Spirit of God, the prophet Micah uses the remarkable language in our text, upon which I would now speak to you. "O thou that art named the house of Jacob, is the spirit of the Lord straitened? are these his doings? do not my words do good to him that walketh uprightly?" May the Holy Ghost help me to speak, and you to hear!

I. And, first, I think we may consider these words to have been spoken TO DENOUNCE THOSE WHO WOULD CONTROL THE SPIRIT OF GOD. "Is the spirit of the Lord straitened?" Can you hold him a captive, and make him speak at your dictation?

On turning to the connection you will find that there were certain prophets sent of God to Israel who were unpopular. The message which they brought was not acceptable: the people could not endure it, and so we read in the sixth verse; "Prophesy ye not, say they to them that prophesy: they shall not prophesy to them, that they shall not take shame." The words of these prophets came so home to their consciences and made them so ashamed of themselves, that they said, "Do not prophesy: we wish not to hear you." To these Micah replies, "Is the Spirit of the Lord to be straitened by you?"

There were some in those days who would altogether have silenced the Spirit. They would banish all spiritual teaching from the earth, that the voice of human wisdom might be uncontradicted. But can they silence the Spirit of God? Has he not continually spoken according to his own will, and will he not continue to do so? Is he not the free Spirit who, like the wind, bloweth where he listeth? If the adversaries could have slain with the sword all the messengers of God, would he not have found others? and if these also had been killed, could he not out of stones have raised up heralds of his truth? While the Scriptures remain, the Holy Spirit will never be without a voice to the sons of men; and while he remains, those Scriptures will not be left without honest hearts and tongues to expound and enforce them. Is it possible for men anywhere to silence the Spirit of God? They may be guilty of the crime because they desire to commit it, and attempt to do so; but yet its accomplishment is beyond their reach. They may "quench the Spirit" in this and that man; but not in those in whom he effectually worketh. The Almighty Spirit may be resisted, but he will not be defeated. As well might men attempt to stop the shining of the sun, or seal up the winds, or still the pulsing of the tides, as effectually to straiten the Spirit of the Lord.

"When God makes bare his arm,
What can his work withstand?"

Jehovah speaks, and it is done; who shall resist his word? When his Spirit attends that word, shall it fall to the ground? "My word," saith he, "shall not return unto me void"; and all the sinners on earth and all the devils in hell cannot alter that grand decree. Every now and then there seems to be a lull in the history of holy work, a silence as of God, as if he were wearying of men, and would speak no longer to them. But ere long, in some unexpected quarter, the voice of the Lord is heard once more; some earnest spirit breaks the awful silence of spiritual death, and again the adversary is defeated. Outbursts of the great spirit of life, and light, and truth come at the divine will, when men least look for them or desire them. When Jesus has been crucified, even then the Holy Ghost descends, and the victories of the cross begin. No, my brethren, the Spirit of the Lord is not silenced: the voice of the Lord is heard above the tumults of the people.

The apostate Israelites also tried to straiten the Spirit of God *by only allowing certain persons to speak in his name.* They would have a choice of their prophets, and a bad choice too. See in the eleventh verse: "If a man walking in the spirit and falsehood do lie, saying, I will prophesy unto thee of wine and of strong drink; he shall even be the prophet of this people." They had a liking for preachers who would indulge their lusts, pander to their passions, and swell their pride with windy flatteries. This age also inclines greatly to those who have cast off the restraints of God's revelation, and utter the flattering inventions of their own boasted "thought." Your liberal spirits, your large-hearted men, your despisers of the old and hunters after the new—these are the idols of many. As for those who would urge upon men separation from the world and holiness to the Lord, they are Puritanic, and out of date. In Micah's days Israel would only hear false prophets; the rest they would not listen to. "What!" says Micah, "is the spirit of the Lord then to be shut up to speak to you by such men as you would choose? Is he not to speak by whomsoever he pleases?"

It is the tendency of churches in all ages to fetter the free Spirit. Now they are afraid that we shall have too many preachers, and they would restrain their number by a sort of trades-unionism. In certain churches none must speak in God's name unless they have gone through a certain human-ly-prescribed preparation, and have been ordained after a regulation manner: the Spirit of God may speak by the ordained, but he must not speak by others. In my inmost soul I treasure the liberty of prophesying. Not the right of every man to speak in the name of the Spirit, but the right of the Spirit to speak by whomsoever he pleases. He will rest on some rather than on others, and God forbid that we should straiten his sovereignty! Lord, send by whomsoever thou wilt send; choose whom thou wilt to the sacred office of ministers of God. Amongst the poor and illiterate the Spirit of God has had voices as clear and bold as among the educated and refined, and he will have them still; for he is not straitened, and it is the way of him to use instruments which pour contempt upon all the vain-glory of men. He anoints his own to bear witness for his truth by life and lip; these the professing church may criticize, and even reject, saying, "The Lord has not spoken by these;" but the word of the Lord will stand, notwithstanding the judgment of men. God's true ministers shall be owned of him: wisdom is justified of her children. The Lord's Spirit will not be straitened or shut up by all the rules, and modes, and methods which even good men may devise. The wind bloweth where it listeth, and the power of the Spirit waiteth not for man, neither tarrieth for the sons of men.

Further, this people tried to straiten the Spirit of God *by changing his testimony.* They did not wish the prophets to speak upon subjects which caused shame to them. They bade them prophesy smooth things. Tell us that we may sin with safety; tell us that the punishment of sin is not so over-

whelming as we have feared. Stand up and be advocates for
the devil by flattering us with "a larger hope." Hint to us
that, after all, man is a poor, inoffensive creature, who does
wrong because he cannot help it, and that God will wink at
his sins; and if he does punish him for a while, will soon set
it all right. That was the style of teaching which Israel
desired, and no doubt they found prophets to speak in that
manner, for the demand soon creates the supply. But Micah
boldly asks, "Is the spirit of the Lord straitened?" Do you
think that he will have his utterances toned down, and his
revelation shaped to suit your tastes?

Brethren, let me ask you, do you imagine that the gospel is
a nose of wax which can be shaped to suit the face of each
succeeding age? Is the revelation once given by the Spirit of
God to be interpreted according to the fashion of the period?
Is "advanced thought" to be the cord with which the spirit of
the Lord is to be straitened? Is the old truth that saved men
hundreds of years ago to be banished because something
fresh has been hatched in the nests of the wise? Think ye
that the witness of the Holy Ghost can be shaped and
moulded at our will? Is the divine Spirit to be rather the
pupil than the teacher of the ages? "Is the spirit of the Lord
straitened?" My very soul boils within me when I think of
the impudent arrogance of certain wilful spirits from whom
all reverence for revelation has departed. They would teach
Jehovah wisdom; they criticize his word and amend his
truth. Certain Scriptural doctrines are, forsooth, discarded
as dogmas of the medieval period; others are denounced as
gloomy because they cannot be called untrue. Paul is
questioned and quibbled out of court, and the Lord Jesus is
first belauded and then explained away. We are told that the
teaching of God's ministers must be conformed to the spirit
of the age. We shall have nothing to do with such treason to
truth. "Is the spirit of the Lord straitened?" Shall his
ministers speak as if he were? Verily, that same treasure of
truth which the Lord has committed unto us we will keep
inviolate so long as we live, God helping us. We are not so
unmindful of the words of the apostle, "Hold fast the form of
sound words," as to change a syllable of what we believe to
be the word of the Lord.

Certain of these backsliding Israelites went so far as *to*

oppose the testimony of God. Note in the eighth verse—"Even of late my people is risen up as an enemy." It is sad when God's own people become the enemies of God's own Spirit; yet those who professed to be of the house of Jacob, instead of listening to the voice of the living God, began to sit in judgment upon his word, and even to contradict the same. The worst foes of the truth are not infidels, but false professors. These men called themselves God's people, and yet fought against his Spirit. "What then," saith Micah, "is the spirit of the Lord straitened?" Will the Spirit of God fail? Will his operations on the hearts of men come to nothing? Will the truth of God be put to shame, and have no influence over human minds? Shall the gospel be driven out of the world? Will there be none to believe it? none to proclaim it? none to live for it? none to die for it? We ask, with scorn, "Is the spirit of the Lord straitened?" Brethren, my confidence in the success of the old faith is not lessened because so many forsake it. "For all flesh is as grass, and all the glory of man as the flower of grass. The grass withereth, and the flower thereof falleth away: but the word of the Lord endureth for ever. And this is the word which by the gospel is preached unto you." If all the confessors of the faith could be martyred, even from their ashes, like a heavenly phoenix, the truth would rise again. The Spirit of the Lord lives, and therefore the truth of God must live also. Is not all truth immortal? How much more that which is the shrine of God! The Spirit's witness concerning the sin of man, the grace of God, the mission of Jesus, the power of his blood, the glory of his resurrection, reign, and advent—this witness, I say, cannot cease or fail. It is to be greatly lamented that so many have turned aside unto vanities, and are now the enemies of the cross; but fear ye not, for the victory is in sure hands. O ye that would control the Spirit of God, remember who he is, and bite your lips in despair; what can ye do against him? Go bit the tempest, and bridle the north wind, and then dream that the Spirit of the Lord is to be straitened by you! He will speak when he pleases, by whom he pleases, and as he pleases, and his word shall be with power. None can stay his hand, nor say unto him, "What doest thou?" Thus much upon the first use of our text.

II. The second use of it is this, TO SILENCE THOSE WHO

WOULD CENSURE THE SPIRIT. Some even dare to bring
accusations against the Holy Spirit of God. Read the text
again: "O thou that art named the house of Jacob, is the
spirit of the Lord straitened? *are these his doings?*" If aught
be amiss, is he to be blamed for it?

The low estate of the Church, is that to be laid at God's
door? It is true that the Church is not so full of life and
energy and power and spirituality and holiness as she was
in her first days, and therefore some insinuate that the
gospel is an antique and an effete thing: in other words, that
the Spirit of God is not so mighty as in past ages. To which
the answer is, "Is the Spirit of the Lord straitened? are these
his doings?" If we are lukewarm, is that the fault of the
Spirit of fire? If we are feeble in our testimony, is that the
fault of the Spirit of power? If we are weak in prayer, is that
the fault of the Spirit who helpeth our infirmities? Are these
his doings? Instead of blaming the Holy Ghost, would it not
be better for us to smite upon our breasts and chasten our
hearts? What if the church is not "fair as the moon, clear as
the sun, and terrible as an army with banners," as once she
was; is not this because the gospel has not been fully and
faithfully preached, and because those who believe it have
not lived up to it with the earnestness and holiness which
they ought to have exhibited? Is not that the reason? In any
case, are these his doings? Can you lay the blame of
defection and backsliding, of want of strength, of want of
faith, at the door of the Holy Ghost? God forbid! we cannot
blame the Holy One of Israel.

Then it is said, "Look at *the condition of the world*. After
the gospel has been in it nearly two thousand years, see how
small a part of it is enlightened, how many cling to their
idols, how much of vice, and error, and poverty, and misery,
are to be found in the world!" We know all these sad facts;
but are these his doings? Tell me, when has the Holy Spirit
created darkness or sin? Where has he been the author of
vice or oppression? Whence come wars and fightings? Come
they from him? Come they not from our own lusts? What if
the world be still an Augean stable, greatly needing cleansing; has the Spirit of God in any degree or sense rendered it
so? Where the gospel has been fully preached, have not the
words of the Lord done good to them that walk uprightly?

Have not cannibals, even during the last few years, been reclaimed and civilized? Has not the slave trade, and other villainies, been ended by the power of Christian influence? How, then, can the Spirit of Christ, the spirit of the gospel, be blamed? Will you attribute the darkness to the sun? Will you charge the filthiness of swine to the account of the crystal stream? Will you charge the pest upon the fresh breeze from the sea? It were quite as just, and quite as sensible. No, we admit the darkness and the sin and the misery of men. Oh, that our head were waters and our eyes a fountain of tears, that we might weep day and night concerning these things! But these are not the work of the Spirit of God. These come of the spirit from beneath. He that is from above would heal them. He is not straitened. These are not his doings. Where his gospel has been preached, and men have believed it and lived according to it, they have been enlightened, and sanctified, and blessed. Life and love, light and liberty, and all other good things, come of the Spirit of the Lord.

> "Blessings abound where'er he reigns;
> The prisoner leaps to lose his chains,
> The weary find eternal rest,
> And all the sons of want are bless'd."

But some have said, "Yes, but then see *how few the conversions are nowadays!* We have many places of worship badly attended, we have others where there are scarcely any conversions from the beginning of the year to the end of it." This is all granted, and granted with great regret; but "is the spirit of the Lord straitened: are these his doings?" Cannot we find some other reason far more near the truth? O sirs, if there are no conversions we cannot fall back upon the Spirit of God, and blame him. Has Christ been preached? Has faith been exercised? The preacher must take his share of blame; the church with which he is connected must also inquire whether there has been that measure of prayer for a blessing on the word that there ought to have been. Christians must begin to look into their own hearts to find the reason for defeat. If the work of God be hindered in our midst, may there not be some secret sin with us which hinders the operation of the Spirit of God? May he not be compelled by the very holiness of his character to refuse to work with an unholy or an unbelieving people? Have ye never read, "He did not many mighty works there because of their unbelief"? May not unbelief be turning a fruitful land into barrenness? The Spirit himself is not straitened in his power; but our sin has made him hide himself from us. The want of conversions is not his doing: we have not gone forth in his strength. We shake off with detestation the least trace of a thought that should lay any blame to the Spirit of the Most High. Unto us be shame and confusion of face as at this day.

But it is also said that there is *a want of power largely manifested by individual saints.* Where are now the men who can go up to the top of Carmel and cover the heavens with clouds? Where are the apostolic men who convert nations? Where are the heroes and martyr spirits of the better days? Have we not fallen upon an age of little men, who little dare and little do? It may be so; but this is no fault of the great Spirit. Our degeneracy is not his doing. We have destroyed ourselves, and only in him is our help found. Instead of crying to-day, "Awake, awake, O arm of the Lord," we ought to listen to the cry from heaven which saith, "Awake, awake, O Zion; Shake thyself from the dust, and put on thy beautiful garments." Many of us might have done great exploits if we had but given our hearts thereto. The weakest of us might have rivalled David, and the strongest among us might have been as angels of God. We are straitened in ourselves; we have not reached out to the possibilities of strength which lie within grasp. Let us not wickedly insinuate a charge against the good Spirit of our God; but let us in truthful humility blame ourselves. If we have not lived in the light, can we marvel that we are in great part dark? If we have not fed upon the bread of heaven, can we wonder that we are faint? Let us return unto the Lord. Let us seek again to be baptized into the Holy Ghost and into fire, and we shall yet again behold the wonderful works of the Lord. He sets before us an open door, and if we enter not, we are ourselves to blame. He giveth liberally and upbraideth not, and if we be still impoverished, we have not because we ask not, or because we ask amiss. Thus much, then, have I spoken, using the text to silence those who would censure the Spirit of God.

III. In the third place, our subject enters a more pleasing phase, while I use it TO ENCOURAGE THOSE WHO TRUST IN THE SPIRIT OF THE LORD. My brethren, let us this morning with joy remember that the Spirit of the Lord is not straitened.

Let this meet our trouble about *our own straitness.* What narrow and shallow vessels we are! How soon we are empty! We wake up on the Sabbath morning and wonder where we shall find strength for the day. Do you not sigh, "Alas!" I cannot take my Sunday-school class to-day with any hope of teaching with power; I am so dreadfully dull and heavy; I feel stupid and devoid of thought and feeling"? In such a case say to yourself, "Is the spirit of the Lord straitened?" He will help you. You purpose to speak to some one about his soul, and you fear that the right words will not come. You forget that he has promised to give you what you shall speak. "Is the spirit of the Lord straitened?" Cannot he prepare your heart and tongue? As a minister of Christ I have constantly to feel my own straitness. Perhaps more than any other man I am faced by my own inefficiency and inability to address such an audience so often, and to print all that is spoken. Who is sufficient for these things? I do not feel half as capable of addressing you now as I did twenty years ago. I sink as to conscious personal power, though I have a firmer faith than ever in the all-sufficiency of God. No, the Spirit of the Lord is not straitened. Still is that promise our delight: "My grace is sufficient for thee." It is a joy to become weak that we may say with the apostle, "When I am weak then am I strong." Behold, the strength of the Lord is gloriously revealed, revealed to perfection in our weakness. Come, ye feeble workers, ye fainting labourers, come and rejoice in the unstraitened Spirit. Come, you that seem to plough the rock and till the sand, come and lay hold of this fact, that the Spirit of the Lord is omnipotent. No rock will remain unbroken when he wields the hammer, no metal will be unmelted when he is the fire. Still will our Lord put his Spirit within us and gird us with his power, according to his promise, "As thy days, so shall thy strength be."

This also meets another matter, namely, *the lack of honoured leaders.* We cry at this time, "where are the eminent teachers of years gone by?" The Lord has made a man more precious than the gold of Ophir. Good and great men were the pillars of the church in former times, but where are they now? Renowned ministers have died, and where are their successors? It is not an unfrequent thing with the older brethren for them to say one to the other, "Do you see the young men springing up who will equal those whom we have lost?" I am not among those who despair for the good old cause; but certainly I would be glad to see the Elishas who are to succeed the Elijahs who have gone up. Oh, for another Calvin or Luther! Oh, for a Knox or a Latimer, a Whitefield or a Wesley! Our fathers told us of Romaine and Newton, Toplady and Rowland Hill: where are the like of these? When we have said "where?" echo has answered "where?" But herein is our hope: the Spirit of the Lord is not straitened. He can raise up standard-bearers for his hosts. He can give to his church stars in her firmament as bright as any that ever gladdened our fathers' eyes. He that walketh among the golden candlesticks can so trim the lamps that those which are dim shall burn with sevenfold splendour. He who found a Moses to face Pharaoh, and Elijah to face Jezebel, can find a man to confront the adversaries to-day. To equip an army of apostolic men would be a small matter to the Creator of heaven and earth. Let us have no fear about this. He that ascended on high, leading captivity captive, gave such large gifts unto men, that unto the end of the dispensation they will not be exhausted. Still doth he give evangelists, pastors, and teachers, according as the need of the church may be. Let us cast away all fear as to a break in the succession of witnesses; for the word of the Lord endureth for ever, and it shall never lack a man to declare it.

Brethren, the great truth now before us may prevent our being dismayed by *the peculiar character of the age in which we live.* It is full of a terrible unrest. The earthquake in the Riviera is only typical of a far greater disturbance which is going on everywhere. The foundations of society are quivering; the corner-stones are starting. No man can foretell what the close of this century may see. The age is growing more and more irreverent, unbelieving, indifferent. The men of this generation are even more greedy of gain, more in haste after their ambitions, than those that preceded them. They are fickle, exacting, hungering after excitement and sensation. Here comes in the truth—"The Spirit of the Lord is not straitened." Was not the gospel intended for every age, and for every condition of human society? Will it not meet the case of London and Ireland as well as the case of the old Roman empire, in the midst of which it first began its course? It is even so, O Lord! Our fathers trusted in thee; they trusted in thee, and thou didst deliver them; and we with joyful confidence fall back upon the same delivering power, saying in our hearts, "The Spirit of the Lord is not straitened," he will bear us through.

But, then, sometimes we are troubled because of *the hardness of men's hearts*. You that work for the Lord know most about this. If anybody thinks that he can change a heart by his own power, let him try with any one he pleases, and he will soon be at a nonplus. Old Adam is too strong for young Melancthon: our trembling arm cannot roll away the stone of natural depravity. Well, what then? The Spirit of the Lord is not straitened! Did I hear you cry, "Alas! I have tried to reclaim a drunkard, and he has gone back to his degradation"? Yes, he has beaten *you*, but is the Spirit of the Lord straitened? Do you cry, "But he signed the pledge, and yet he broke it"? Very likely *your* bonds are broken; but is the Spirit of the Lord straitened? Cannot he renew the heart, and cast out the love of sin? When the Spirit of God works with your persuasions, your convert will keep his pledge. "Alas!" cries another, "I hoped I had rescued a fallen woman, but she has returned to her iniquity." No unusual thing this with those who exercise themselves in that form of service; but is the Spirit of the Lord straitened? Cannot he save the woman that was a sinner? Cannot he create a surpassing love to Jesus in her forgiven spirit? *We* are baffled, but the Spirit is not. "But it is my own boy," cries a mother. "Alas! I brought him up tenderly from his youth, but he has gone astray. I cannot persuade him to hear the word: I cannot do anything with him." Dear mother, register that confession of inability, and then by faith write at the bottom of it, "But the Spirit of the Lord is not straitened." Have faith in God, and never let your discovery of your own weakness shake your firm conviction that with God all things are possible. It seems to me to be a fountain of comfort, a storehouse of strength. Do not limit the Holy One of Israel, nor conceive of the Holy Ghost as bounded and checked by the difficulties which crop up in fallen human nature. No case which you bring to him with affectionate tears and with an earnest faith in Jesus shall ever be dismissed as incurable. Despair of no man, since the Lord of hosts is with us.

Ah well! says one, but I am oppressed with *the great problem which lies before the Church*. London is to be rescued, the world is to be enlightened. Think of India, China, and the vast multitudes of Africa. Is the gospel to be preached to all these? Are the kingdoms of this world to become the kingdoms of our Lord? How can these things be! Why, sirs, when I think of London alone, a world of poverty and misery, I see the sheer impossibility of delivering this world from the power of darkness. Do you prefer a theory which holds out no hope of a converted world? I do not wonder! Judge after the sight of the eyes and the hearing of the ears, and the thing is quite beyond all hope. But is the Spirit of the Lord straitened? Surely the good Lord means to convince the Church of her own powerlessness, that she may cast herself upon the divine might. Looking around she can see no help for her in her great enterprise: let her look up and watch for his coming who will bring her deliverance. Amid apparent helplessness the Church is rich in secret succours. If the Spirit of God shall anoint our eyes we shall see the mountain full of horses of fire and chariots of fire round about the servants of the Lord. Behold, the stars in their courses fight against our adversaries; the earth shall yet help the woman, and the abundance of the seas shall yield their strength unto God. When the time cometh for the Lord to make bare his arm, we shall see greater things than these, and then we shall wrap our faces in a veil of blushing confusion to think that we ever doubted the Most High. Behold, the Son of Man cometh; shall he find faith among us? Shall he find it anywhere on the earth? The Lord help us to feel in our darkest hour that his arm is not shortened!

IV. I must close by remarking that this text may be used TO DIRECT THOSE WHO ARE SEEKING AFTER BETTER THINGS. I hope that in this audience there are many who are desiring to be at peace with God through Jesus Christ. You are already convinced of sin, but you are by that conviction driven to despondency and almost to despair. Now notice this: whatever grace you need in order to have salvation the Holy Spirit can work it in you. You want a more tender sense of sin. Is the Spirit of the Lord straitened? Can he not give it to you? You want to be able to perceive the way of salvation; can he not instruct you? You want to be able to take the first step to Christ; you want, in fact, to trust him wholly and alone, and so find peace in him. Is the Spirit of the Lord straitened? Can he not give you faith? Do you cry, "I would believe, but I cannot tell how"? The Spirit will help you to believe. He can shed such light into your mind, that faith in Christ shall become an easy and a simple thing with you. The Spirit of God is not straitened: he can bring you out of darkness into his marvellous light. If you are quite driven from all reliance on your own natural power, then cry unto him, "Lord, help me!" The Holy Spirit has come on purpose to work all our works in us. It is his office to take of the things of Christ and to show them unto us. Yield yourself to his gracious direction. Be willing and obedient, and he will lead you into all truth.

Notice again: although you are under deep depression of spirit, and you feel shut up, so that you cannot come forth; yet the Spirit of the Lord is not straitened. He is not weighed down nor discouraged. His name is the Comforter, and he can comfort to purpose. What though you be to-day ready to lay violent hands upon yourself by reason of the trouble of your restless thoughts, yet is the Spirit of the Lord straitened? Look you to the strong for strength, even to your God. Doth not the Lord cry to you, "Look unto me, and be ye saved, all ye ends of the earth; for I am God, and there is none else"? Your strength as well as your salvation lies in him. When we were yet without strength, in due time Christ died for the ungodly. Trust ye in the Lord for ever; for in the Lord Jehovah there is everlasting strength. Trust, implicitly trust, for the Spirit of God is not straitened. Your despondency and unbelief are not his doings, they are your own. He has not driven you into this misery. He invites you to come forth of it, and trust the Son of God, and rest in the finished righteousness of Christ, and you shall come at once into light and peace.

May I invite you to remember how many persons have

already found joy, peace, and salvation by believing the teaching of the Spirit of God. In the text the question is asked, "Do not my words do good to him that walketh uprightly?" Many of us can bear testimony to-day that the word of the Lord is not word only, but power. It has done good to us. The gospel has not only been much to us, it has been everything to us. Personally, I do not believe and preach the gospel because I have made a choice, and have preferred it to any other theory of religion out of many others which might have been accepted. No. There is no other truth to me. I believe it because I am a saved man by the power of it. The truth revealed by the Spirit has new-created me. I am born again by this living and incorruptible seed. My only hope of holiness in this life, and of happiness in the life to come, is found in the life and death, the person and merit, of the Lord Jesus Christ, the Son of God. Give up the gospel! I may when it gives me up; but not while it grasps my very soul. I am not perplexed with doubt, because the truth which I believe has wrought a miracle on me. By its means I have received and still retain a new life, to which I was once a stranger. I am like the good man and his wife who had kept a lighthouse for years. A visitor who came to see the lighthouse, looking out from the window over the waste of waters, asked the good woman, "Are you not afraid of a night when the storm is out and the big waves dash right over the lantern? Do you not fear that the lighthouse and all that is in it will be carried away?" The woman remarked that the idea never occurred to her. She had lived there so long that she felt as safe on the lone rock as ever she did when she lived on the mainland. As for her husband, when asked if he did not feel anxious when the wind blew a hurricane, he answered, "Yes, I feel anxious to keep the lamps well trimmed, and the light burning, lest any vessel should be wrecked." As to anxiety about the safety of the lighthouse, or his own personal security in it, he had outlived all that. Even so it is with me: "I know whom I have believed, and am persuaded that he is able to keep that which I have committed to him against that day." From henceforth let no man trouble me with doubts and question-ings, I bear in my soul the proofs of the Spirit's truth and power, and I will have none of your artful reasonings. The gospel to me is truth: I am content to perish if it be not true. I risk my soul's eternal fate upon the truth of the gospel, and I know no risk in it. My one concern is to keep the lamps burning, that I may thereby enlighten others. Only let the Lord give me oil enough to feed my lamp, so that I may cast a ray across the dark and treacherous sea of life, and I am well content. Now, troubled seeker, if it be so, that your minister and many others in whom you confide have found perfect peace and rest in the gospel, why should not you? Is the Spirit of the Lord straitened? Do not his words do good to them that walk uprightly? Will not you also try their saving virtue?

In conclusion, just a hint to you. The words of God do good to those who walk uprightly. If they do no good to you, may it not be that you are walking crookedly? Have you given up all secret sin? How can you hope to get peace with God if you live according to your own lusts? Give up the hopeless hope. You must come right out from the love of sin if you would be delivered from the guilt of sin. You cannot have your sin and go to heaven: you must either give up sin or give up hope. "Repent" is a constant exhortation of the Word of God. Quit the sin which you confess. Flee the evil which crucified your Lord. Sin forsaken is through the blood of Jesus turned into sin forgiven. If you cannot find freedom in the Lord, the straitness is not with the Spirit of God, but your sin lieth at the door blocking up the gangway of grace. Is the Spirit of God straitened? No, his words "do good to them that walk uprightly," and if you in sincerity of heart will quit your sin, and believe in Christ, you also shall find peace, and hope, and rest. Try it, and see if it be not so. Amen.

	INDEX OF SERMONS	Text	Volume	Sermon
1	A Fatal Deficiency	Romans 8:9	MTP-19	1133
2	Grieve Not The Holy Spirit	Ephesians 4:30	MTP-13	738
3	The Private Tutor	John 14:24-26	MTP-31	1842
4	The First Fruit Of The Spirit	Galatians 5:22	MTP-30	1782
5	The Heavenly Wind	John 3:8	MTP-23	1356
6	Intimate Knowledge Of The Holy Spirit	John 14:17	MTP-35	2074
7	Filled With The Spirit/Drunkenness With Wine	Ephesians 5:18	MTP-35	2111
8	Covenant Blessings	Ezekiel 36:26-27	MTP-18	1046
9	The Leading Of The Spirit	Romans 8:14	MTP-21	1220
10	The Sword Of The Spirit	Ephesians 6:17	MTP-37	2201
11	The Holy Ghost-The Great Teacher	John 16:13	NPSP-1	50
12	The Oil Of Gladness	Psalm 45:7	MTP-22	1273
13	Praying In The Holy Ghost	Jude 20	MTP-12	719
14	Adoption-The Spirit And The Cry	Galatians 4:6	MTP-24	1435
15	The Holy Spirit Glorifying Christ	John 16:14	MTP-8	465
16	The Personality Of The Holy Ghost	John 14:16-17	NPSP-1	4
17	The Fruit Of The Spirit: Joy	Galatians 5:22	MTP-27	1582
18	The Pentecostal Wind And Fire	Acts 2:2-4	MTP-27	1619
19	The Great Teacher And Remembrancer	John 14:26	MTP-59	3353
20	The Holy Spirit's Intercession	Romans 8:26-27	MTP-26	1532
21	The Paraclete	John 14:16	MTP-18	1074
22	"Come From The Four Winds, O Breath!"	Ezekiel 37:9	MTP-38	2246
23	The Power Of The Holy Ghost	Romans 15:13	NPSP-1	30
24	True Unity Promoted	Ephesians 4:3	MTP-11	607
25	The Holy Ghost The Need Of The Age	Micah 2:7	MTP-33	1952

NPSP New Park Street Pulpit 1855-1860
MTP Metropolitan Tabernacle Pulpit 1861-1917